Other books of interest from
Haynes Publishing:

WORLD DIRECTORY OF AIRLINER CRASHES
An all-time record of more than 10,000 passenger
aircraft accidents
by Terry Denham

DISASTERS AT SEA
Every ocean-going passenger ship
catastrophe since 1900
by Milton H. Watson
Updated & expanded by William H. Miller

RAILWAY DISASTERS OF THE WORLD
Principal passenger train accidents of the
20th century
by Peter Semmens

SIR JAMES MARTIN
The authorised biography of the Martin-Baker
ejection seat pioneer
by Sarah Sharman
Foreword by HRH The Duke of Edinburgh

INTERNATIONAL AIR BAND RADIO HANDBOOK
The guide to world-wide air traffic control
by David J. Smith

AIR BAND RADIO HANDBOOK
by David J. Smith

WORLD ENCYCLOPAEDIA OF AIRCRAFT
MANUFACTURERS
From the pioneers to the present day
by Bill Gunston

BRITAIN'S AVIATION MEMORIALS & MEMENTOES
by David J. Smith

MODERN FIGHTER AIRCRAFT TECHNOLOGY
AND TACTICS
Into combat with today's fighter pilots
by Anthony Thornborough

Jacket illustrations
Front: Trailing fire from a wing, Pacific Southwest
Airlines Boeing 727 plunges to earth over San Diego,
California, following collision with light aircraft, 25
September 1978 (New Images, Gamma Liason/FSP).
Back: Rescue personnel swarm around the shattered
fuselage of an AVIANCA Boeing 707 that crashed on
Long Island, New York, after running out of fuel, 25
January 1990 (Stephen Spak, Gamma Liason/FSP).

AVIATION DISASTERS

As part of our ongoing market research, we are always pleased to receive comments about our books, suggestions for new titles, or requests for catalogues. Please write to: The Editorial Director, Patrick Stephens Limited, Sparkford, Nr Yeovil, Somerset BA22 7JJ.

AVIATION DISASTERS

The world's major civil airliner crashes since 1950

second edition

David Gero

Patrick Stephens Limited

First published in 1993
Reprinted 1993 (twice)
Reprinted 1994
Second edition 1996

British Library Cataloguing in Publication Data:
A catalogue record for this book is available from the British Library

ISBN 1 85260 526 X

Library of Congress catalog card no. 95-79127

Patrick Stephens Limited is an imprint of Haynes Publishing, Sparkford, Nr Yeovil, Somerset, BA22 7JJ.

Printed in Britain by Butler & Tanner Ltd., London and Frome

Contents

Introduction

Wandering through a local library some years ago, I came across what might be described as the 'disaster shelf'. On it was an assortment of books chronicling various calamities that have afflicted civilisation throughout its history.

Most of the publications on the shelf were dedicated to marine catastrophes. The lure of the sea and the adventure associated with one of the oldest forms of public transport can probably account for the number. There was also a volume on the subject of train crashes for the benefit of railway enthusiasts, and a few others detailing earthquakes, hurricanes and other natural disasters over which we have little or no control.

Absent was a single book on a subject that has interested me most of my life, and is probably of considerable interest to many readers, namely aviation. For this and other reasons I elected to embark on this project, and here is the final product, the first commercial reference publication on the subject of aviation disasters.

Generally the major airlines of the world suffer between two and three dozen mishaps resulting in fatalities every calendar year. Since the task of presenting all the disasters occurring over a period of four decades would be beyond the scope of any single book, I have concentrated on only the most significant ones.

The primary criterion for entry into this volume is severity. I have included accounts on every mishap on a passenger flight with at least 60 fatalities involving an air carrier of the Industrialised World that has taken place since 1950. And I have details on every calamity causing at least 80 deaths that is known to have occurred.

Whenever possible I have endeavoured to obtain information from 'official' sources. Generally, civil air mishaps are investigated by Government bodies, such as the National Transportation Safety Board (NTSB) in the US and the Air Accidents Investigation Branch (AIB) in the UK, which publish accident reports or summary briefs. Recommendations coming therefrom are then implemented by Government regulatory bodies, perhaps the best known of which are the US Federal Aviation Administration (FAA) and the British Civil Aviation Authority (CAA). I have also relied heavily on the aviation media, speciality publications whose writers are more knowledgeable on the subject than most journalists, which will normally guarantee greater accuracy. I must also give praise to the many international airlines that offered assistance.

Readers may observe that *Aviation Disasters* is biased, both in number of accounts and details, toward operators in Western Europe, North America, Oceania and Japan. This should not be construed as meaning that these nations have inferior safety records (just the opposite, in fact, they are the safest), but rather can be explained by their greater volume of air traffic coupled with their willingness to share accident information (which probably accounts largely for their superior records).

In writing this book I have gone to great lengths to provide specific details of individual mishaps, even to the point of listing the specific model of a certain type of aircraft and its serial number, and the approximate or in some cases exact local time of occurrence. It was a very challenging project!

Although my name appears on its cover, this book was the result of the work of many people in many different countries, and they must share in the credit. I hope you find it both interesting and enlightening.

David Gero
San Gabriel, California

Acknowledgements

The author would like to thank the following organisations and individuals for their help in the preparation of this book:

Airbus Industrie; Air Accidents Investigation Branch (UK); Air Canada (J. A. Mitchell, Flight Safety Division); Airclaims Ltd. Contact: Paul Hayes; Airclaims CIS. Contact: Elena Kuznetsova; Aircraft Accident Investigation Board (Denmark), (Niels Jaksobsen); Aircraft Accident Investigation Board (Norway), (T. B. Kirkvaag, Ragnar Rygnestad); Air France (Gail Muntner, Office of Public Affairs); Mete Akkaya, Turkish Representative to the ICAO; Alitalia; All Nippon Airways Safety Promotion Committee (Yoshi Funatsu); Argentine Air Force (Guillermo Raul Barreira, Mario Santamaria); Belgian World Airlines (SABENA) (J. Deschutter); Arif Boediman, Indonesian Representative to the ICAO; Boeing Canada de Havilland (Colin Fisher); British Airways Air Safety Branch (Roy Lomas, C. N. Hall); Bureau of Air Safety Investigation (Australia) (W. G. Duffy, F. St G. Hornblower, D. J. Nicholas, R. J. Sibbison); Canadian Airlines International Ltd. Contact: P. G. Howe; Canadian Aviation Safety Board. Contacts: Nicole Brind'Amour, Manon Ouimet van Riel, Joyce Pedley; Centro de Investigacao e Prevencao de Acidentes Aeronauticos (Brazil). Contacts: Osmar Nascimento Amorim, Renato Tristao de Menezes, Paulo Fernando Peralta, Carlos Machado Vallim, Paulo C. F. Viana; Civil Aviation Authority (UK); Civil Aviation Department (Hong Kong). Contact: Y. S. Fong; Departamento Administrativo de Aeronautica Civil (Colombia). Contacts: Carlos German Barrero Fandino, William Mejia Restrepo; Department of Civil Aviation (Malta). Contact: C. D. Caruana; Department of Civil Aviation (Pakistan). Contact: Patrick Callaghan; Department of Transport (South Africa). Contact: Barend P. K. Jordaan; Department of Transport and Power (Ireland). Contacts: G. Guihen, J. McStay; Direccion General de Aeronautica Civil (Mexico). Contact: Carlos Moran Moguel; Direccao-Geral Da Aviacao Civil (Portugal). Contact: Jose Camilo Pastor; Direction des Journaux Officiels (France). Contacts: Jeannine Valin, Monique Masson; Director General Of Civil Aviation (India). Contact: B. R. Chopra; Directorate Of Civil Aviation (Iceland); Embassy of South Africa to the US. Contact: Neville C. Parkins; Embassy of the US to Peru. Contact: David Stebbing; Embassy of the US to Venezuela. Contact: Hans Mueller; Federal Aircraft Accident Investigation Bureau (Switzerland). Contacts: Erich Keller, A. D. Salzmann; Federal Ministry of Transport (Germany). Contact: I. A. Kramer; Hellenic Republic Ministry of Communications, Civil Aviation Authority (Greece). Contacts: G. Fotiades, K. Mavrogenis, G. Tzouvalis; Inspection Generale de l'Aviation Civile et de la Meteorologie (France). Contacts: Robert Davidson, M. Dulac; International Civil Aviation Organisation (ICAO). Contacts: Tracey Martineau, Germaine Zaloum; Japan Aeronautical Engineers' Association; Japan Airlines. Contacts: M. Osaki, Geoffrey Tudor; Japan Air System. Contact: H. Kanai; KLM Royal Dutch Airlines. Contact: Peter Offerman; Nick Komons, Historian, Federal Aviation Administration (US); Library of Congress (US); Lockheed; Lufthansa German Airlines. Contact: Norbert Wagner; Ministere des Communications Administration de l'Aeronautique (Belgium). Contact: J. Van Laer; Ministerio de Transportes, Turismo y Comunicaciones (Spain). Contact: Jose Bellido Grela: Ministerio de Transportes y Comunicaciones (Peru). Contact: Luis Bouroncle Loayza: Ministry of Defence (UK). Contacts: Les Howard, Eric Munday; Ministry of Transport (Israel). Contact: Giora Chalamish; Ministry of Transport (Japan); Ministry of Transport and Public Works (The Netherlands). Contact: F. A. van Reijsen, Ministry of Transportation and

Communications Bureau (Philippines). Contact: M. S. Talento, Jr; National Archives (US). Contacts: Vernon Brooks, Janet Kennelly, Jane Lange, A'Donna Thomas, Jessie White; National Board of Aviation (Finland). Contacts: Seppo Hamalainen, Jorma Kivinen; National Transportation Safety Board (US). Contact Susan Stevenson; Nordic Delegation to the ICAO. Contact O. Mydland; Office of Air Accidents Investigation (New Zealand). Contacts. L. J. Banfield, L. F. Blewett, Ron Chippindale; Philippine Airlines. Contact: Enrique Santos; Public Archives of Canada. Contact: Glenn Wright; Qantas Airways. Contact: John J. White; Scandinavian Airlines System (SAS). Contact: Gunnel Thorne; Swedish Civil Aviation Administration. Contacts: Klas Bask, Roland Nilsson; Swissair FAH Historical Society; US Air Force Historial Research Center. Contact: Lt Col Alan Clair; US Air Force Inspection and Safety Center. Contacts: John J. Clark Jr, Vincent Murone; US Department of Defense; Venezolana Internacional de Aviacion SA (VIASA). Contact: Capt Eduardo Nieto Willett.

Special thanks to: Monique Bouscarle, Inspection Generale de l'Aviation Civile et de la Meteorologie (France); Loyita Worley, Civil Aviation Authority (UK); and the entire staff at the Los Angeles Regional Office of the National Transportation Safety Board (US).

Research services were provided by: ARIOMA Editorial Services (Moira and Patrick Smith); Jacques Clairoux; Alan Cooper; Diane Hamilton; Historial Newspaper Service (John Frost); Sarah Molumhy; Kathryn Powers; Graham K. Salt; A. Spanier; Task Force Pro Libra Ltd (Susan Hill, Anne Williams); and Hilary Thomas.

Translation services were provided by: Raymundo Aguirre; Agnes Allard; Lupe Anaya; Victoria Aranda; Ramona Barranco; Robert Beck; Berlitz Translation Services; Else Bokkers; Alice Bonnefoi; Martin Bredboell; Richard Brome; Jim Buendia; Dale Carter; Luca Cortelezzi; Vivian Curtis; Francisco Fan; Iris Fiorito, Fliteline Language Services; Mitsuko Fujiwara; Guillaume Gavillet; Patrick Germain; Francoise Gerardin; David Green; Boris Hasselblatt; Inge Hochner; Vanna Hungerford; Kayo Ide; Milena Kaylin; Noriyuki Kawabata; Yan Kuhn; Giancarlo Losi; Marci Moody; Masako Ohnuki, Delores Pedro; Poly-Languages Institute; Julio Puchalt; Liselotte Runde; Millicent Sharma; Monique Swadowski; Delfina Vadi; Natalie Vetchinne; Ruth Quirk Von Woo; Marie-Antoinette Zrimc.

Publications consulted included the following: *Aeroplane and Commercial Aviation News* magazine; *Aircraft Accident Digest* (International Civil Aviation Organisation-ICAO); *Air Disasters* by Stanley Stewart (Ian Allan Ltd, 1986); *Airliner Production Lists* by Tony Eastwood and John Roach (The Aviation Hobby Shop); *Anvil of the Gods* by Fred McClement (J. B. Lippincott Co, 1964); *Aviation/Space Dictionary* by Ernest J. Gentle and Lawrence W. Reithmaier (Aero Publishers Inc, 1980); *Aviation Week and Space Technology* magazine; *Crash* by Rob and Sarah Elder (Atheneum Publishers, 1977); *Daily Express* newspaper; *Daily Mirror* newspaper; *Destination Disaster* by Paul Eddy, Bruce Page and Elaine Potter (Times Newspapers, 1976); *Flight International* magazine; *Hostile Actions Against Civil Aviation* (Air Incident Research); *It Doesn't Matter Where You Sit* by Fred McClement (Holt, Rinehart and Winston, 1969); *Jane's Aerospace Dictionary* by Bill Gunston (Jane's Publishing Co Ltd, 1986); *Jane's All The World's Aircraft* (Jane's Information Group); *Jet Airliner Checklist* by Paul Rainford (Executive Aircraft Historians, 1988); *KE 007: A Conspiracy of Circumstance* by Murray Sayle (in the New York Times Review of Books, 25 April 1985); *La Opinion* newspaper; *Lloyd's List* newspaper; *Los Angeles Times* newspaper; *Loud and Clear* by Robert J. Serling (Dell Publishing Co, 1970); *Newsweek* magazine; *New York Times* newspaper; *Paris Match* magazine; *Proceedings* magazine, September 1989 (US Naval Institute); *Prop Airliner Checklist* by Tony Hyatt (Executive Aircraft Historians, 1988); *Reader's Digest* magazine, February 1973: article entitled 'Nightmare in the Jungle'; *Recovered Mail* by Henri L. Nierinck (R-Editions, 1980); *Shootdown* by Richard W. Johnson (Viking Penguin Inc, 1986); *Skin Diver* magazine, May 1975: article entitled 'Wings of Death', excerpted from Dr Joseph B. MacInnis' book *The Underwater Man*; *Soviet Airliners* by Peter Hillman (Executive Aircraft Historians, 1989); *Time* magazine; *The Times Atlas of the World*; *The Times* (of London) newspaper; *The World Book Encyclopaedia* (Field Enterprises Corp); *World Airline Accident Summary* (Civil Aviation Authority-CAA); and *World Commercial Aircraft Accidents* by Chris Kimura.

Other sources of information included the following: *Tracking the Pan Am Bombers*, an edition of the *Frontline* television series, produced by the Public Broadcasting System (PBS).

The following accident accounts are copyrighted by Airclaims CIS, Moscow, Russian Federation: Aeroflot Tu-104 (15 August 1958); Tu-104 (17 October 1958); Tu-104 (30 June 1962); An-10 (28 July 1962); Tu-104 (2 September 1962); Il-18 (2 September 1964); Il-18 (16 November 1967); Il-18 (29 February 1968); Il-18 (6 February 1970); Tu-104 (25 July 1971); An-10 (18 May 1972); Il-18 (31 August 1972); Il-18 (1 October 1972); Il-62 (13

October 1972); Tu-104 (30 September 1973); Tu-104 (13 October 1973); Il-18 (27 April 1974); Il-18 (6 March 1976); An-24/Yak-40 collision (9 September 1976); Tu-104 (13 January 1977); Tu-134 collision (11 August 1979); Tu-154 (8 July 1980); Tu-154 (16 November 1981); Yak-42 (28 June 1982); Il-62 (6 July 1982); Tu-134 (30 August 1983); Tu-154 (11 October 1984); Tu-154 (23 December 1984); Tu-134/An-26 collision (3 May 1985); Tu-154 (10 July 1985); Tu-134 (27 August 1992); Yak-40 (28 August 1993); Tu-154 (3 January 1994); A310 (22 March 1994); and Aviaimpex Yak-42D (20 November 1993).

PICTURE SOURCES
Aeroflot; Air Britain Historians Ltd (Glyn Ramsden); Airbus Industrie (Sean Lee); Aircraft Photographic; All Nippon Airways Public Relations Section; American Airlines; Aviation Photo News; The Bettmann Archive; Black Star (Cheryl Himmelstein, Judith Wolf); Boeing Commercial Airplane Group (Danielle Gerrard); British Aerospace. Contacts: Mike Brown, P. N. P. Smith; Eastern Airlines; Fokker BV. Contact: Leo J. N. Steijn; Gamma Liaison. Contacts: Jennifer Coley, Grace How; General Dynamics; General Microfilm; Lux Photographic Services; McDonnell Douglas. Contact: Harry Gann; Adrian Meredith Photography; Pan American World Airways; Popperfoto/Uniphoto Press International (Toyoo Ohta); Programmed Communications Ltd. Contact: Sheila Hamilton; Sikorsky Aircraft; Sygma. Contact: Claire Gouldstone; Trans World Airlines, United Airlines; Wide World Photos (Holly Jones); Aviation Photo News; and Avions de Transport Regional.

The
1950s

Commercial aviation truly came of age in the 1950s. The air travel boom that had begun shortly after the Second World War, introducing to the average person that which previously had been available only to those wealthy and daring enough to step on to an aeroplane, was in full swing. More flights were available to more destinations, with airliners carrying more passengers at greater speeds and higher levels of safety and comfort than ever before.

A number of larger and higher-performance aircraft saw their first passenger service in the 1950s. These included the Douglas DC-7 and Lockheed Super Constellation, which represented the peak in piston engine transport development. In 1952 the de Havilland Comet introduced the first jet passenger service. The aircraft had to be withdrawn from use only two years later due to a serious structural deficiency, but the new refined Comet would return in 1958, providing the first jet airliner service across the Atlantic. It was joined by such jets as the French Caravelle and US Boeing 707; the latter would serve for many years as the backbone of long-haul air transport. Also introduced during this period were several models of propeller/turbine aircraft, or turboprops, including the Vickers Viscount, Bristol Britannia and Lockheed Electra.

One of the most notable safety advances coming into operation in the 1950s was airborne weather radar. But of course the increased passenger-carrying capability of an aircraft would mean more casualties in the event of a crash, and, indeed, in 1956 commercial aviation suffered its first disaster to claim more than 100 lives when two transports collided over the Grand Canyon. Concern over air traffic control would cloud the industry throughout the latter half of the decade and into the 1960s.

Date: 12 March 1950 (c 14:50)
Location: Near Sigginstone, South Glamorgan, Wales

Operator: Fairflight Ltd (UK)
Aircraft type: Avro Tudor V (*G-AKBY*)

The airliner was on a charter service, carrying Welsh rugby fans home from Dublin, Ireland, where they had watched their team defeat the Irish in an international match. During its approach to land on Runway 28 at Llandow Airport, located some 15 miles (25 km) west-south-west of Cardiff, the four-engine transport assumed a glide path that gave eyewitnesses the impression that it would touch the ground prematurely.

While at an approximate height of 100 to 150 ft (30–50 m), a small increase in power was noted, which slightly reduced the aircraft's descent rate. This was followed by the sudden application of full power and, concurrently, by its nose pitching up. Climbing to about 300 ft (100 m), the Tudor stalled, then plunged into a field some 2,500 ft (750 m) from the threshold of the runway at a steep angle and on its right side, and with its undercarriage and flaps extended. There was evidence that the ignition had been switched off before impact, which may have accounted for the absence of a post-crash fire. All but three passengers among the 83 persons aboard were killed, including the entire crew of five; the survivors suffered injuries. The weather on this Sunday afternoon was good, with a visibility of 15 miles (c 25 km) and westerly winds blowing at 10 to 15 knots.

An investigative court found that due to an inadequate amount of baggage placed forward in relationship to the passenger load, the aircraft's centre-of-gravity was at least 9 ft (2.7 m) aft of the specified limit. This probably resulted in insufficient elevator control remaining to counteract the rise of the nose upon the application of full power at a velocity that, while well above the stalling speed, was low enough to create a condition of acute instability. The court also regarded as unsatisfactory the loading instructions pertaining to

The crash of the Fairflight Tudor V in Wales nearly tripled the death toll of the worst previous British commercial aviation disaster.
(Popperfoto/Uniphoto Press)

the Tudor V, which did not contain adequate directions in determining how passengers and their luggage should be distributed. It said that the system then in use placed an unduly heavy burden of responsibility on the pilot.

For the trip to and from Dublin, there had been an alteration in the seating arrangement of the aircraft to allow for six more passengers than the maximum permissible, and this had required amending its certificate of airworthiness. However, the loading of the transport was not in compliance with the provisions of this amendment.

The court recommended that whenever an aircraft's seating arrangements were to be changed, a new 'daily certificate' and 'technical log' should be prepared, and that it should be the function of the maintenance engineer responsible for the alterations to record in these documents the relevant information for reference by the pilot, with a provision for cross-checks.

Date: 24 June 1950 (c 01:25)
Location: Lake Michigan, US
Operator: Northwest Airlines (US)
Aircraft type: Douglas DC-4 (*N95425*)

Operating as Flight 2501, the aircraft crashed into Lake Michigan some 20 miles (30 km) north-north-west of Benton Harbor, Michigan, while en route from New York, New York, to Minneapolis, Minnesota, the first segment of a domestic transcontinental service destined for Seattle, Washington. All 58 persons aboard (55 passengers and three crew members) perished.

The DC-4 was last reported cruising in the early morning darkness at 3,500 ft (c 1,050 m) after a request for descent to 2,500 ft (c 750 m), which the crew made for no reason, had been

denied due to conflicting air traffic in the area.

Subsequently recovered from the surface of the water were such light debris as cabin furnishings and personal effects. The bottom of the lake was 150 ft (c 50 m) below the surface and covered by a layer of silt and mud estimated to be 30 to 40 ft (c 10–12 m) thick, and despite a search using divers and sonar equipment, the main wreckage could not be located.

It was known that the disaster occurred shortly after the aircraft entered an area of severe turbulence associated with thunderstorm activity, which probably resulted in either structural failure or a loss of control, but there was insufficient evidence to determine which one of these possibilities actually caused the crash.

The forecast of a squall line in the area had been issued 1 hr 40 min before the accident, but this information was not made available to the flight.

Date: 31 August 1950 (c 02:00)
Location: Near Wadi Natrun, Egypt
Operator: Trans World Airlines (TWA) (US)
Aircraft type: Lockheed 749A Constellation (*N6004C*)

Flight 903 took off from Farouk Airport, serving Cairo, bound for Rome, Italy, one segment of a service originating at Bombay, India, with an ultimate destination of New York City. About 20 min later ground witnesses observed the aircraft to be afire. Subsequently it crashed and burned some 65 miles (105 km) north-west of the capital city, and all 55 persons aboard (48 passengers and a crew of seven) were killed.

The accident was attributed to the failure of the rear master rod bearing in the Constellation's No 3 power plant, which caused the rear crank-pin to

Trans World Airlines Lockheed 749A Constellation, identical to the aircraft that crashed in the Egyptian desert. (Trans World Airlines)

overheat and collapse. This condition allowed the piston strokes to increase until the pistons began to strike the valves and cylinder heads. All the rear articulated and rear master rods then failed and sliced through the walls of the rear row of cylinders, tearing away a section of the crankcase. In turn, the fire seal was distorted and displaced. The general breakage was so widespread that oil lines were severed, and the release of the inflammable fluid and its fumes led to the fire.

Intensifying after the aircraft had turned back toward Cairo, the blaze ultimately melted the adjoining dural structure rearward of the firewall, causing the involved engine (whose propeller had been feathered) to fall free. Numerous other parts also separated as the fire burned through the top skin of the starboard wing.

Unable to reach the airport, the crew apparently attempted a forced landing on a desert plain in the early morning darkness, and while still under control the Constellation struck the ground in a slight nose-and-right-wing-low attitude, with its undercarriage and flaps retracted.

There was a distinct possibility that sludge that had built up within the crank pins had broken away and obstructed the flow of oil, resulting in the master rod bearing failure. Because of this accident and other master rod bearing failures in the same model of Wright engine, several corrective measures were taken. These included more frequent oil changes, improved oil screens and the development of a crank-pin plug to reduce sludge accumulation.

Date: 13 November 1950 (c 18:00)
Location: French Alps
Operator: Curtiss-Reid Flying Services Ltd (Canada)
Aircraft type: Douglas DC-4 (*CF-EDN*)

The airliner was on a charter service from Rome, Italy, to Montreal, Canada, with a stop planned at Paris, France, its passengers being Catholics returning home from a pilgrimage to the Vatican.

Drifting some 50 miles (100 km) to the east of the prescribed route, the DC-4 struck Mt de l'Obiou, in the Devoluy range, about 30 miles (50 km) south of Grenoble. All 58 persons aboard, including seven crew members, perished. The crash occurred in darkness and, reportedly, cloudy weather conditions.

The pilot had probably realised the deviation and tried to take corrective action, but did not see the mountain in time.

Date: 30 June 1951 (c 02:00)
Location: Near Fort Collins, Colorado, US
Operator: United Air Lines (US)
Aircraft type: Douglas DC-6 (*N37543*)

All 50 persons aboard (45 passengers and a crew of five) perished when the aircraft, designated as Flight 610, crashed some 50 miles (80 km) north-north-west of Denver, where it was to have landed during a domestic transcontinental service from San Francisco, California, to Chicago, Illinois, its last scheduled stop having been at Salt Lake City, Utah.

Following passage of the Cheyenne radio range station, the DC-6 was to have turned right and headed south toward Denver. Instead, the turn was well in excess of 90 degrees, which placed it on a south-south-westerly heading. Flying in darkness, the cleanly-configured aircraft continued in this direction until it struck cloud-obscured Crystal Mountain, at an approximate elevation of 8,500 ft (2,600 m), disintegrating on impact. Despite some localised fires, there was no major post-crash blaze.

It could not be determined why the flight had not followed the prescribed airway. One plausible theory was that the captain had depressed the wrong toggle switches on the aircraft's audio selector control panel (this could have happened in the darkened cockpit, especially considering that the switches were not obvious and were usually activated by feel). As a result, he may have silenced the signals of the Denver low-frequency radio range, whose beam demarcated the proper track, but allowed receipt of the Denver visual aural range (VAR) signals. This radio range, which would only have been used by the crew to determine at what point the turn should be initiated, ran roughly parallel to the low-frequency range, and its signals were such that they would be difficult to differentiate.

It was also considered possible that the pilot had tuned his automatic direction finder (ADF) in such a way that it had been affected by the radio range station at Fort Bridger, Wyoming.

The US Civil Aeronautics Administration (CAA) later took action to eliminate confusion between the Denver and VAR ranges. Meanwhile, the carrier modified its audio selector panels to prevent a possible mistake in switch selection, and also implemented a programme with a particular emphasis on route training and equipment qualification for its crews.

Date: 24 August 1951 (c 05:30)
Location: Near Union City, California, US
Operator: United Air Lines (US)
Aircraft type: Douglas DC-6B (*N37550*)

Flight 615 had been cleared for a straight-in landing approach to Oakland Municipal Airport, a scheduled stop during a domestic transcontinental service destined for nearby San Francisco, which originated at Boston, Massachusetts. Descending in twilight through a broken layer of stratus clouds, with a base of about 1,500 ft (500 m), and in patches of fog that obscured the terrain, the aircraft crashed some 15 miles (25 km) south-east of the airport. All 50 persons aboard (44 passengers and six crew members) perished in the disaster.

Although the DC-6B was to have proceeded along the Oakland radio range course, neither of its two low-frequency receivers were tuned to the station. Instead, the captain had deviated from the prescribed instrument procedures, and may have

The shattered remains of the United Air Lines DC-6 lie in the Rocky Mountains of Colorado following the accident that took 50 lives. (Wide World Photos)

attempted to fly by visual reference, using the first officer's automatic direction finder (ADF) to maintain the proper course. As a result the flight was approximately 3 miles (5 km) to the right of the on-course beam and well below the minimum prescribed altitude of 3,500 ft (c 1,050 m).

Its main undercarriage down and flaps either retracted or partially extended, the aircraft struck a hill at an elevation of about 1,000 ft (300 m), or less than 30 ft (10 m) below its crest, while on a north-westerly heading and at a ground speed of between 225 and 240 mph (c 360–385 kmh), then disintegrated in a fiery explosion.

Subsequently the carrier enacted a requirement that crews operate under instrument flight rules (IFR) when above an overcast, to assure adherence to minimum altitudes.

Date: 16 December 1951 (c 15:10)
Location: Elizabeth, New Jersey, US
Operator: Miami Airline Inc (US)
Aircraft type: Curtiss Wright C-46F (*N1678M*)

The twin-engine transport had just taken off from Newark Airport on a non-scheduled domestic service to Tampa, Florida, when control tower personnel noticed smoke emanating from its right side. Although the tower controller cleared the crew for an immediate landing, the message was not acknowledged. At about the same time another ground witness, a Miami Airline captain, also observed *N1678M* trailing smoke. Believing that the source of the smoke was an overheated right

Above A United Air Lines DC-6B, the type that crashed during a landing attempt at Oakland airport. (McDonnell Douglas)

Below Trailing smoke from its right engine, the Miami Airline C-46F is photographed shortly before it crashed in Elizabeth, New Jersey, US. (UPI/Bettmann)

brake, he telephoned the control tower, suggesting that the crew be instructed to extend the gear. The pilots, unfortunately, followed his advice.

Minutes later, the C-46 began a gradual descending left turn, its starboard propeller still windmilling. Suddenly its port wing dropped, and the airliner struck the roof of a house and a building, then crashed in the Elizabeth River. The wreckage, which had come to rest largely inverted in the shallow water, then erupted into flames. All 56 persons aboard were killed, including a regular crew of three and an off-duty airline employee riding as a passenger, who was not on the manifest. Additionally, one person on the ground was seriously injured.

The accident was ascribed to faulty maintenance procedures by the airline. Examination of the right power plant revealed that the 15 hold-down studs on the No 10 cylinder had failed from fatigue due to improper installation of their securing nuts. This caused the cylinder to separate completely from the crankcase during or shortly after take-off.

The fire that erupted in the base of the failed cylinder could have resulted from several sources of ignition, including a continuous egress of both liquid and atomised lubricating oil, a connecting rod that had broken and was flailing, or from opened exhaust or inlet ducts. Activation of the fire-extinguishing system failed to check the blaze, and it ultimately burned through lines carrying fuel, oil and hydraulic fluid, and through the closed doors of the right wheel well. And when the undercarriage was lowered, the flames were allowed freer entry into this compartment, causing even more damage. The gear extension would also have increased drag, and this, coupled with the power loss, the inability

of the crew to feather the right propeller (probably because the fire destroyed an electrical or oil line) and the fact that the transport was loaded by nearly 120 lb (c 55 kg) above its maximum allowable gross weight, caused a stall at a height of about 200 ft (60 m), which led to the crash.

Numerous violations by the carrier over a period of 3½ years, most involving the overloading of aircraft, were noted in the investigative report of the US Civil Aeronautics Board (CAB). Additionally, inadequacies were identified in the method by which the airline trained its pilots in the area of emergency procedures, and this could have had a bearing on what appeared to be a delay in such action being taken by the crew of *N1678M*.

Date: 11 April 1952 (c 12:20)
Location: North of San Juan, Puerto Rico
Operator: Pan American World Airways (US)
Aircraft type: Douglas DC-4 (*N88899*)

Operating as Flight 526A, the airliner took off from Isle Grande Airport, serving San Juan, bound for New York City. Shortly afterwards, the crew noticed a loss of pressure and an increase in temperature in the oil of the No 3 power plant; they turned back, subsequently feathering the corresponding propeller. The No 4 engine then began to run rough when power was increased. Minutes later the DC-4 crash-landed in the Atlantic Ocean, some 5 miles (10 km) off the northern coast of the island, its undercarriage and flaps having been extended beforehand. The ditching took place in turbulent seas, and the transport, its empennage having broken off in the impact, remained afloat for

Pan American World Airways DC-4 identical to the aircraft that ditched off northern Puerto Rico, with a loss of 52 lives. (Pan American World Airways)

only about 3 minutes. Among the 69 persons aboard, 52 passengers lost their lives; the five crew members were among the 17 survivors rescued. Only 13 bodies were found, and the aircraft sank in water approximately 2,000 ft (600 m) deep and could not be recovered.

Maintenance personnel reported finding aluminium shavings in the oil sump and screen and the nose section housing of the No 3 engine the previous day. Though mechanics changed the nose section, this alone was not in accordance with prescribed procedures under the circumstances. This led the US Civil Aeronautics Board (CAB) to conclude that *N88899* was not airworthy upon its departure from San Juan. The accident was therefore attributed to inadequate maintenance by the airline, and to the actions of the pilot.

It was ruled that the captain's persistence in attempting to re-establish a climb without using all available power after a critical loss of power in the No 4 engine resulted in a nose-high attitude, a progressive loss of air speed and a settling of the aircraft at too low an altitude to effect recovery.

An additional factor that might have reduced the survivability of the disaster was the failure of the flight crew to warn the cabin attendants of the situation, which prevented them from preparing the passengers for the water landing. Furthermore, the life rafts were all stowed in a single compartment, and only one could be launched after the ditching.

Today's routine procedure of briefing passengers before extended over-water flights as to the location and use of flotation equipment and emergency exits was an outcome of this tragedy.

The wreckage of the Pan American World Airways Boeing 377 Stratocruiser rests in the Brazilian jungle after an in-flight break-up. (UPI/Bettmann)

Date: 29 April 1952 (c 03:40)
Location: Central Brazil
Operator: Pan American World Airways (US)
Aircraft type: Boeing 377 Stratocruiser (*N1039V*)

In the last message received from Flight 202, the airliner was reportedly at an altitude of 14,500 ft (c 4,400 m) in visual flight rules (VFR) conditions, with an estimation that it would be abeam of the Carolina check point in 90 min. But there was no further communication with *N1039V*.

Two days later the burned wreckage of the Stratocruiser was found scattered for nearly 1 mile (1.5 km) and lying inverted in a tropical forest area in the south-eastern corner of Para state, some 1,000 miles (1,600 km) north-north-west of Rio de Janeiro, where it had last stopped before proceeding on to Port-of-Spain, Trinidad, one segment of a service originating at Buenos Aires, Argentina, with an ultimate destination of New York City. All 50 persons aboard (41 passengers and a crew of nine) perished in the crash.

It was apparent that the aircraft had disintegrated in flight, while cruising in pre-dawn darkness on an approximate heading of 340 degrees, and that the sequence of events began with the separation of its No 2 engine/propeller assembly due to highly unbalanced forces. Then, possibly because of severe buffeting, there was a partial failure of the left horizontal stabiliser. Examination of the debris indicated that the outer portion of the stabiliser continued to hang on, oscillating in such a manner as to cause the elevators to snap upward, placing a very high down-load on the tail surfaces. This would in turn have caused a considerable increase in lift on the wings, a sufficient force to break the left one in an upward direction, just beyond the missing inboard power plant. The resulting nose-down pitching motion attributed to the loss of the wing coupled with the existing down-load on the horizontal tail surfaces would likely have caused the empennage to break off in a downward direction, which must have been almost simultaneous with the wing failure. Both the left wing and the tail assembly were found a distance from the main wreckage, confirming that these components had separated before the impact with the ground.

Since it could not be located, there was no way of knowing exactly what happened to the No 2 engine. However, in other accidents involving the same type of aircraft, such separations were precipitated by the failure of a propeller blade, with the resulting imbalance generating destructive forces. As noted in the investigative report, the type of propeller with which the Boeing 377 was equipped had been known to experience fatigue failure after suffering comparatively minor damage.

Three years later, and following the loss of another Stratocruiser and four lives under similar circumstances, the US Civil Aeronautics Administration (CAA) issued an advisory that operators of the type replace the hollow steel propeller blades then in use with solid metal ones. Another preventative measure was the development of propeller blade imbalance detectors, the use of which became a CAA requirement, also in 1955.

Date: 2 May 1953 (c 16:35)
Location: Near Jagalogori, West Bengal, India
Operator: British Overseas Airways Corporation (BOAC)
Aircraft type: de Havilland Comet 1 (*G-ALYV*)

Exactly one year after the inauguration of the Comet in regular service, this particular one became the first jet airliner to crash fatally during a scheduled passenger operation.

Flight 783/057 had taken off from Dum-Dum Airport, serving Calcutta, bound for Delhi, one segment of a service originating at Singapore, with an ultimate destination of London. Only 6 min later it plunged to earth in flames some 30 miles (50 km) north-west of Calcutta. All 43 persons aboard (37 passengers and six crew members) perished.

The accident occurred during a violent thunderstorm, with heavy rain and high winds. Wreckage was scattered over flat terrain for a distance of about 5 miles (10 km), indicating that the Comet had come apart in the air. The structural failure was believed to have resulted from stresses that exceeded its designed limits, due either to an encounter with severe gusts, or to over-controlling or a loss of control by the crew. However, both the carrier and the manufacturer doubted this latter theory.

A study of the wreckage strongly suggested the failure of both elevator spars caused by a heavy down-load that may have been associated with a pull-up manoeuvre after the aircraft had encountered a sudden down-draught. This was followed by the failure of both wings, which could have then struck the tailplane, shearing off the vertical stabiliser. Fire erupted after the wings snapped.

The BOAC disaster in India occurred one year to the day after the de Havilland Comet 1 inaugurated the world's first commercial jet passenger service. (British Airways)

The Comet was upset at an estimated height of 7,000 ft (c 2,000 m), while climbing to its cruising altitude.

Date: 12 July 1953 (c 20:40)
Location: Pacific Ocean
Operator: Transocean Air Lines (US)
Aircraft type: Douglas DC-6A (*N90806*)

The transport crashed in darkness approximately 350 miles (550 km) east of Wake Island, from where it had taken off less than 2 hours earlier, bound for Honolulu, Hawaii, one segment of a non-scheduled service from Guam to Oakland, California, US. Searchers later found a small amount of debris and 14 bodies, but there were no survivors among the 58 persons aboard (50 passengers and a crew of eight).

According to its last message, the aircraft was cruising between cloud layers at 15,000 ft (c 5,000 m). There were indications of thunderstorm activity in the area along the route taken, which contained moderate to heavy turbulence.

Due to insufficient evidence, the cause of the disaster could not be determined. Had there been a mechanical or structural failure, the occurrence must have been sudden. As concluded from the examination of the recovered victims and wreckage, the impact with the water was at a high velocity, which would point to a loss of control by the pilots.

There was no evidence of either sabotage or in-flight fire.

Date: 27 July 1955 (c 07:40)
Location: Near Petrich, Bulgaria
Operator: El Al Israel Airlines
Aircraft type: Lockheed 049 Constellation (*4X-AKC*)

Designated as Flight 402/26, the aircraft was en route from London to Tel Aviv, Israel, with a scheduled stop at Vienna, Austria. However, during the second segment of the flight, following its passage of Belgrade, Yugoslavia, the Constellation began to stray to the left of the prescribed airway. Its track eventually took the transport over the extreme south-western portion of Bulgaria, shortly after which it was attacked, in three phases, by two Bulgarian jet fighters.

The first attack probably took place at its cruising altitude of 18,000 ft (c 5,500 m), and the second at about 8,000 ft (2,500 m), after it had been hit, was afire and descending apparently in search of a place to land. In the final attack, which was at an approximate height of 2,000 ft (600 m), an explosion occurred in its right wing, and the airliner then broke up and plummeted to earth. All 58 persons aboard (51 passengers and seven crew members) perished.

An Israeli investigative commission concluded that the navigational error probably originated with an incorrect radio compass indication due to the effects of thunderstorm activity in the area. This must have led the crew to believe falsely that it had reached the reporting point at Skopje, Yugoslavia, when in fact it was still 7 minutes from that position. Presumably the course of the flight was then altered to a heading of 142 degrees, which would have been required for it to remain within the airway.

At a point some 40 miles (65 km) east of the proper track, it entered Bulgarian airspace. The only message received from the Constellation after that time was a brief 'SOS DE 4X-AKC'. However, accounts from ground witnesses in Yugoslavia and Greece were used in reconstructing the attack, and numerous bullet holes found in its wreckage confirmed how the aircraft had been destroyed.

The commission rejected the contention of the Bulgarian government that the El Al crew was notified within the established regulations but refused to land before the fighters opened fire. Bulgaria, which also maintained that the transport had strayed much farther into its airspace, did, however, admit that its defence forces exhibited 'a certain haste' in shooting down the aircraft, and expressed regret over the incident.

Under the prevailing meteorological conditions, with cumulo-nimbus clouds and westerly winds of 70 knots (which were 50 knots above those forecast), and considering the absence of navigational aids between Belgrade and Skopje, the crew could not have been aware of the aircraft's drift.

The commission recommended more very-high-frequency omni-directional range (VOR) stations along the airway used by Flight 402/26 (Amber 10), which at the time had only one such precision navigational aid.

Date: 6 October 1955 (c 07:25)
Location: Near Centennial, Wyoming, US
Operator: United Air Lines (US)
Aircraft type: Douglas DC-4 (*N30062*)

All 66 persons aboard (63 passengers and a crew of three) perished when the aircraft crashed into Medicine Bow Peak, some 30 miles (50 km) west of Laramie.

Designated as Flight 409, the DC-4 had taken off earlier from Denver, Colorado, bound for Salt Lake City, Utah, one segment of a domestic transcontinental service originating at New York, New York, with an ultimate destination of San Francisco, California. It was some 20 miles (30 km) to the west of the prescribed course and on a north-westerly heading when it struck a sheer rock wall at an approximate elevation of 11,500 ft (3,500 m), or only about 60 ft (20 m) below its crest. The transport disintegrated on impact, and most of the wreckage and bodies tumbled down the mountain, coming to rest at the bottom of the cliff.

The meteorological conditions in the area at the time consisted of a broken overcast, with the clouds covering the tops of the mountains, and isolated snow showers.

In its investigation, the US Civil Aeronautics Board (CAB) could find no evidence of mechanical failure in the aircraft, and considered it doubtful, due to the captain's familiarity with the route and the facilities available and comparatively good visibility along it, that the disaster could have resulted from a navigational error. Not completely

The black streak in the centre of the picture marks the crash site of the United Air Lines DC-4 on Medicine Bow Peak. (Wide World Photos)

ruled out was that the two pilots had been physically incapacitated, possibly by poisonous gases emitted by a malfunctioning cockpit heater. However, there were other indications, including witness accounts, that the DC-4 had been under control prior to the crash.

The CAB found it difficult to accept that the captain had attempted a short-cut over the high terrain, especially considering the weather, the lack of cabin pressurisation in the aircraft, and the fact that the time saved by such action would have been inconsequential. It therefore had to conclude that the deviation was intentional on the part of the pilot, for reasons unknown.

Date: 18 February 1956 (c 13:20)
Location: Near Żurrieq, Malta
Operator: Scottish Airlines (UK)
Aircraft type: Avro York (*G-ANSY*)

Operating under contract to the (British) Air Ministry and carrying 45 service personnel as passengers and five civilian crew members, the four-engine transport took off from Luqa Airport, Malta, bound for England. Its undercarriage retracted normally, but around this time smoke was seen emanating from its left outboard power plant. Instead of turning right as instructed, the York appeared to drift to the left. Shortly afterwards it banked steeply to port, then plummeted almost vertically into the cliffs along the southern coast of the Mediterranean island, exploding on impact. All 50 persons aboard were killed.

Evidence indicated that the No 1 engine had malfunctioned, stemming from the failure of its boost enrichment capsule, which was found to have two cracks in the second convolution from the top, associated with corrosion and normal stresses. The resulting weak fuel mixture caused the flame traps to become incandescent, and this condition was responsible for a series of backfires. Ultimately the heat generated by the continuous burning in the induction system resulted in the disintegration of the supercharger rotor, leading to the complete failure of the power plant.

The initiating factor, the loss of power, should alone not have caused the accident. Instead, the crash was attributed to the mechanical malfunction in combination with a judgement error on the part of the pilot, who did not stop the leftward swing of the aircraft using the rudder, did not correct its nose-high attitude, and failed to feather the No 1 propeller in order to reduce drag. Also, the full retraction of the aircraft's flaps increased the stalling speed of the York. These omissions led to a loss of air speed and consequent loss of directional control.

Better pilot training for emergency conditions and an improved boost enrichment capsule, with a

An Avro York, shown in the livery of another airline, but the type operated by Scottish Airlines that crashed on Malta. (British Airways)

spring-balance safety device, were among the recommendations made by the court of inquiry in the wake of the disaster.

Date: 20 June 1956 (c 01:30)
Location: Off New Jersey, US
Operator: Linea Aeropostal Venezolana (Venezuela)
Aircraft type: Lockheed 1049E Super Constellation (*YV-C-AMS*)

Trouble was first reported about 1 hr 20 min after the airliner had taken off from New York International Airport on a scheduled service to Caracas, Venezuela. The pilot radioed that its No 2 propeller was overspeeding and could not be feathered. Turning back toward its point of departure, the Super Constellation was soon joined by a US Coast Guard aircraft to provide an escort.

Shortly after the flight reported sighting New York City in the early morning darkness, the dumping of fuel was begun in preparation for landing. Moments later, however, the transport caught fire and made a sharp turn to the right. Upon completion of this turn, a quivering, incandescent mass separated from its port side. The aircraft then started to climb while veering left, during which time three more incandescent masses were seen to break away. At the top of its climb, and while in a vertical attitude at an approximate height of 9,000 ft (2,700 m), the Super Constellation broke apart, then plunged into the Atlantic Ocean in flames some 30 miles (50 km) east of Asbury Park. All 74 persons aboard (64 passengers and a crew of 10) were killed. Searchers recovered little wreckage and only a few bodies from the water, which was about 100 ft (30 m) deep at the crash site.

Although the reason for the disaster could not be determined with absolute certainty, it was assumed that the vibration resulting from the uncontrollable propeller caused one of the inside wing attachments to loosen or break somewhere between the fuel tank and the dump chute, at the symmetrical point of the oscillation.

Three years later a requirement went into effect mandating propeller pitch locks on piston-engine transport aircraft, devices designed to prevent the type of overspeeding that proved disastrous to *YV-C-AMS*.

Date: 30 June 1956 (c 11:30)
Location: Northern Arizona, US
First aircraft
Operator: Trans World Airlines
  (TWA) (US)
Type: Lockheed 1049 Super Constellation
  (*N6902C*)
Second aircraft
Operator: United Air Lines (US)
Type: Douglas DC-7 (*N6324C*)

The inadequacies of the US air traffic control (ATC) system were brought to full realisation by this horrifying collision, the first commercial aviation disaster to claim more than 100 lives.

Both four-engine transports had departed on this Saturday morning from Los Angeles International Airport, California, on domestic services. The first

to take off was TWA Flight 2, scheduled to stop at Kansas City, Missouri, before continuing on towards its final destination of Washington, DC, with 64 passengers and six crew members aboard. It was followed by United Flight 718, en route to Chicago, Illinois, with an ultimate destination of Newark, New Jersey, and carrying 53 passengers and a crew of five. The two aircraft were operating in accordance with instrument flight rules (IFR), cruising at assigned altitudes along prescribed airways. The proposed true air speed of the Super Constellation was about 310 mph (500 kmh), and that of the DC-7 approximately 330 mph (530 kmh).

At one point, while over the Mojave Desert of Southern California, Flight 2 asked whether it could ascend to 21,000 ft (6,400 m). Since this height had already been allocated to United 718, the request

An artist's impression of the mid-air crash over the Grand Canyon, based on Civil Aeronautics Board findings, showing how the left wing of the DC-7 sliced into the rear fuselage of the Super Constellation. (Mel Hunter, Life magazine)

Following the collision the TWA aircraft fell in canyon near the Colorado River (lower arrow), and the United transport crashed atop Chuar Butte about 1 mile (1.5 km) away. (Popperfoto/Uniphoto Press International)

was denied by the Los Angeles ATC centre. It was, however, cleared to fly 1,000 ft (c 300 m) 'on top of' the general cloud layer. Ironically, this turned out to be 21,000 ft, as later confirmed by the crew. Subsequently, both aircraft would leave the designated airways and proceed north-eastwards (with *N6902C* flying to the north of *N6342C*), taking more direct courses towards their intended destinations. (This was common practice at the time in high-altitude operations, enabling crews to take advantage of the most favourable wind and weather conditions as well as taking the shortest routes possible.) Their paths would cross high over Grand Canyon National Park, some 70 miles (110 km) north of Flagstaff.

In their last regular position reports, both flights estimated they would reach the Painted Desert reference point, an imaginary line demarcated by two navigational aids that stretched north-westwards from Winslow, Arizona, into southern Utah, at the same time, 11:31. There would be no

further communication with either aircraft until a frantic message was transmitted from the DC-7 about half an hour later. Sent by the first officer, it was later deciphered to be 'Salt Lake . . . seven eighteen . . . we are going in!'

The fragmented, burned wreckage of the two transports was found the following day on the west side of the canyon, near the confluence of the Colorado and Little Colorado Rivers. All 128 persons aboard both aircraft perished in the tragedy. Investigation by the US Civil Aeronautics Board (CAB), which included a detailed examination of the debris, confirmed that a mid-air crash had taken place.

The collision was believed to have occurred at or near 21,000 ft, probably in a clear area, despite the presence of nearby thunderhead build-ups. At the time of impact, the angle of the two aircraft relative to each other was approximately 25 degrees. Initial contact appeared to have been between the DC-7's left aileron tip and the centre vertical tail fin of the Super Constellation. Instantly thereafter, the lower surface of the former's left wing struck the upper aft fuselage section of the latter. During this time the No 1 propeller of the DC-7 inflicted a series of cuts in the aft baggage compartment of the other aircraft. This entire sequence must have taken place in less than half a second.

At the moment they collided, the DC-7 was rolled about 20 degrees right wing-down in relation to the Super Constellation, with its wing above the latter's fuselage and its nose lower than that of the other. This attitude might indicate the initiation of evasive action by one or both, but this could not be proven.

Following the collision, the TWA transport, its empennage having been severed (which would have caused an explosive cabin decompression), pitched down and plummeted, in an inverted attitude, into a draw on the north-east slope of Temple Butte. The United aircraft, meanwhile, which was missing about 20 ft (6 m) of its left outer wing, fell less steeply, probably on a turning path, and crashed near the top of Chuar Butte, approximately 1 mile (1.5 km) north-east of the TWA impact site, scattering wreckage and victims down the precipitous, inaccessible terrain.

It could not be determined with certainty why the pilots failed to see each other's aircraft in time to prevent the accident. Evidence suggested that it was due to intervening clouds restricting visibility before they reached the clear area; cockpit visibility limitations; preoccupation with normal duties or with unrelated activities, such as trying to give the passengers a more scenic view of the canyon; physiological limits to human vision; or to a combination of these factors. Also significant was the lack of traffic advisory information provided to either crew due to inadequate facilities and an insufficient workforce.

During a CAB public hearing, air traffic control personnel were questioned as to whether such advisories should have been given to the flights, especially considering that both were known to have been at the same altitude and estimating that they would reach the Painted Desert position at the same time. The controller directly involved explained that he had no way of knowing exactly where the aircraft would cross the line, which was nearly 175 miles (280 km) long. He further stated that since both were then in uncontrolled airspace, their crews would have been operating under the 'see-and-be-seen' guidelines associated with visual flight rules (VFR) procedures.

One of the mysteries of the disaster was that both flights had estimated that they would reach the Painted Desert at almost the same moment the collision took place, which was some 3 minutes flying time from that point.

A number of improvements came out of this tragedy, with increased funding by the government for air navigational facilities and a modernisation of the nation's air traffic control system. Procedural changes included greater adherence in air carrier operations to prescribed routes and assigned flight levels. Nevertheless, the collision menace would continue to plague US aviation for the next half-decade, culminating in a catastrophe over New York City involving, ironically, United Air Lines and TWA (see separate entry, 16 December 1960).

Date: 9 December 1956 (c 19:15)
Location: Near Hope, British Columbia, Canada
Operator: Trans-Canada Air Lines
Aircraft type: Canadair DC-4M-2 North Star (*CF-TFD*)

Flight 810-9 departed from Vancouver, en route to Calgary, Alberta, the first segment of a domestic service with an ultimate destination of Montreal, Quebec. Some 50 min later, the pilot reported a fire in its No 2 power plant, which had been shut down, and that he was turning back. In the last radio transmission from the aircraft, clearance for descent to 8,000 ft (c 2,500 m) was acknowledged.

Despite an intensive search, no trace of the North Star was found until May 1957, when a small group of mountaineers came upon it, quite by accident, on Mt Sleese, some 50 miles (80 km) east of Vancouver. The transport had slammed into a sheer granite wall at an approximate elevation of 7,500 ft (2,300 m) and disintegrated. It was apparent that all 62 persons aboard (59 passengers and three crew members) had perished in the crash. Debris was scattered across, and more than 2,000 ft (600 m) down, the mountain. Due to the poor accessibility of the terrain, the wreckage and remains of the victims could not be recovered.

The disaster occurred in darkness and the weather in the area at the time was bad, with broken cloud layers at various altitudes, rain showers, severe turbulence, icing conditions and winds ranging from 65 to 85 knots.

According to the board of inquiry report, there was a high probability that while flying under the power of three engines, the aircraft had encountered severe icing, turbulence or some other difficulty, or a combination of adverse factors, whose sudden or dire nature was such that the crew was unable to maintain control or even send a distress message. It could not be determined why the North Star was approximately 12 miles (20 km) south of the assigned airway at the time of impact.

One of the recommendations made by the board was to encourage pilots to dump fuel in order to regain or maintain the performance of an aircraft after the loss of engine power.

Trans-Canada Air Lines Canadair North Star, the type that crashed in British Columbia with a loss of 62 lives. (Programmed Communications Ltd)

Date: 14 March 1957 (13:46)
Location: Wythenshawe, Cheshire, England
Operator: British European Airways (BEA)
Aircraft type: Vickers Viscount 701 (*G-ALWE*)

The first fatal crash of a turboprop airliner engaged in a regular passenger operation involved Flight 411, which was about to complete a service from Amsterdam, Netherlands. During the final, visual phase of an attempted landing at Manchester's Ringway Airport, after a ground-controlled approach (GCA) radar-monitored let-down through a broken layer of clouds, the Viscount suddenly commenced a steep right turn and plunged into a residential area, killing all 20 persons aboard (15 passengers and a crew of five) and two others on the ground (a woman and her infant son). Initial contact was with its starboard wing-tip approximately half a mile (0.8 km) from the threshold of the runway and some 500 ft (150 m) to the right of its extended centreline, and the

aircraft then struck the houses and burst into flames. Two residences were destroyed.

Investigation revealed that an improperly machined and seated lug in a starboard wing flap unit had broken prior to the accident, and the corresponding bolt, which was fatigued, then failed under the normal aerodynamic stresses. This caused the two inboard sections of the flap, which had been extended in preparation for landing, to move away from and then rise above the trailing edge of the wing. The wing then dropped, resulting in the sharp bank to the right. Evidence also suggested that the gust lock control wire had been displaced, which would have jammed the aileron and kept the crew from regaining control.

Subsequently, Vickers initiated a modification programme to prevent a recurrence of what happened to *G-ALWE*. Reinforcing gussets and angle plates were added to the lower part of the flap units on the Viscount, and a fishplate added to

The first turboprop airliner to provide a regular service suffered its first fatal crash on a passenger flight when a British European Airways Viscount 701 plunged into a residential area near Manchester airport. (British Aerospace)

the outside of the wing surface. As a further safeguard should a unit become detached, the clearance in the locking lever was increased. The manufacturer also introduced a method of examining the bolts in an aircraft that took tension loads or those that fitted into holes reamed out on assembly.

Date: 16 July 1957 (03:36)
Location: Off Biak Island, Netherlands New Guinea
Operator: KLM Royal Dutch Airlines
Aircraft type: Lockheed 1049E Super Constellation (*PH-LKT*)

No reason was given by the pilot for his request to make a low pass over the Mokmer airport, from where the aircraft, operating as Flight 844, had taken off a few minutes earlier. He did, however, announce over the public address system his intention to give everyone a final glimpse of the island before proceeding on to Manila, Philippines, the first en route stop of a service with an ultimate destination of Amsterdam.

Granted permission, the Super Constellation began its approach from the east, gradually descending over the sea. At a point approximately half a mile (0.8 km) from the shore it crashed, burst into flames, broke apart and sank. Only 10 passengers survived, rescued by native boats. The other 58 persons aboard, including all nine crew members, were killed. Efforts to recover

the wreckage from the water, which was some 800 ft (250 m) deep, were unsuccessful.

An investigative board was only able to conclude that the disaster resulted from either pilot error or technical failure. There was, of course, the possibility that both factors had come into play. As noted in the accident report, in the dark, moonlit conditions, the pilot might have misjudged his height over the sea, especially considering that he would have lost sight of the runway lights once the aircraft was below an altitude of about 200 ft (60 m), owing to trees and other obstacles. Reports of an in-flight fire by some ground witnesses could not be confirmed.

The board recommended against low runs in commercial air carrier services.

Date: 11 August 1957 (c 14:15)
Location: Near Issoudun, Quebec, Canada
Operator: Maritime Central Airways (Canada)
Aircraft type: Douglas DC-4 (*CF-MCF*)

The transport was on a transatlantic charter service from London to Toronto, Ontario, its passengers British veterans from the Second World War who were returning home as passengers after visiting their native land with their families. Two en route refuelling stops were planned at Keflavik, Iceland, where it landed, and at Goose Bay, Newfoundland, which the pilot elected to fly past.

Flying at an altitude of 6,000 ft (c 1,800 m), the

aircraft entered a thunderstorm in which heavy rain and strong, gusty winds were reported. Subsequently it plunged to earth almost vertically at a speed calculated to be in excess of 230 mph (370 kmh), bursting into flames on impact. All 79 persons aboard, including a crew of six, perished. A crater marked the crash site, some 15 miles (25 km) south-south-west of the city of Quebec.

Although there was no way of knowing exactly what events had taken place, an investigative board ascribed the disaster to an encounter with severe turbulence that ultimately led to a loss of control. One possibility was that the aircraft had assumed a nose-high attitude due to the turbulent conditions, which, coupled with the fact that the fuel tanks were only partially filled, allowed air to be drawn into the engines, causing a loss of power in one or more of them. Advancing the throttles, a pilot's natural reaction to such a situation, could have caused the propellers to overspeed once power was restored and, in turn, for the crew to lose control.

It was also plausible that the same extreme attitude had led to a stall. The pilots might have countered by altering engine power settings to maintain air speed and altitude. A violent nose-down pitch of the transport at the time of recovery from the stall, with a resultant increase in air speed, and a sudden application of power could also cause the propellers to overspeed to the point where they could not be controlled by their governors. Recovery from this condition, especially in heavy turbulence, would have been unlikely.

The fact that the aircraft's centre-of-gravity was believed to have been at or slightly beyond the aft limit would have aggravated the situation in either case.

No weather bulletin had been issued regarding the storm activity west of Quebec, and the crew could have unwittingly flown into the cumulo-nimbus. On the other hand, being low on fuel due to his earlier decision not to land at Goose Bay, the pilot could have elected to penetrate rather than circumnavigate what might have appeared as a minor build-up of clouds. The pilots had been on duty for nearly 20 hours, and the resulting fatigue would have adversely affected their ability to cope with such a situation.

One of the safety recommendations made in the investigative report was to establish a Canadian national standard of on-duty time limitations for flight crews. This policy would later be adopted, as it had already been in some other countries, in order to reduce the risk of fatigue.

Date: 8 November 1957 (c 16:30)
Location: Pacific Ocean
Operator: Pan American World Airways (US)
Aircraft type: Boeing 377 Stratocruiser (*N90944*)

Searchers sift through the shattered remains of the Maritime Central Airways DC-4 that crashed in Quebec. (National Archives of Canada)

Designated as Flight 7 and carrying 44 persons (36 passengers and a crew of eight), the airliner had taken off from San Francisco, California, US, bound for Honolulu, Hawaii, its first scheduled stop during an around-the-world service. In its last position report, sent when it was slightly beyond the midway point between the two cities and cruising at an altitude of 10,000 ft (c 3,000 m), there were no indications of any abnormalities; but nothing further was heard from the Stratocruiser.

About a week later, searchers recovered a small amount of debris, including cabin furnishings and packets of mail, and 19 bodies floating some 940 miles (1,510 km) north-east of Honolulu and approximately 90 miles (145 km) north of the flight's intended track. There were no survivors from the disaster, which was never explained due to a lack of tangible evidence.

Among the victims, about half probably died from drowning; most were wearing life preservers, indicating that preparations for a ditching had been made. A forced landing in the ocean may actually have been attempted, but with the aircraft breaking up on impact. It was determined that a post-crash fire on the surface of the water had taken place.

There was no evidence of an explosion or major in-flight fire. However, a localised blaze in the fuselage or in a power plant may have occurred. With regard to the latter, the fire may have been in conjunction with the break-up or separation of the engine, as had been noted in previous Boeing 377

A Pan American World Airways Boeing 377 Stratocruiser, the type that crashed under mysterious circumstances in the Pacific Ocean. (Pan American World Airways)

accidents. This would also be expected to cause difficulty in maintaining directional control, which could explain why the aircraft was so far off the normal course. But there was no absolute proof of such a mechanical failure. The weather was not considered a factor.

Date: 21 April 1958 (c 08:30)
Location: Near Sloan, Nevada, US
First aircraft
Operator: United Air Lines (US)
Type: Douglas DC-7 (*N6328C*)
Second aircraft
Operator: US Air Force
Type: North American F-100F Super Sabre
(*56-3755A*)

This disaster occurred suddenly in the clear morning sky when the airliner and jet fighter collided at a height of 21,000 ft (6,400 m), approximately 10 miles (15 km) south-west of Las Vegas, and both then plummeted into the desert below and exploded. All 47 persons aboard the DC-7 (42 passengers and five crew members) and both pilots of the F-100 (a trainee and his instructor) perished.

Operating as Flight 736, the commercial transport was en route from Los Angeles, California, to Denver, Colorado, the first segment of a domestic transcontinental service with an ultimate destination of New York City, and had been cruising along a designated airway in a north-north-easterly direction under instrument flight rules (IFR) procedures. The military aircraft was on an instrument training mission being conducted under visual flight rules (VFR), and descending from 28,000 ft (c 8,500 m) while on a south-easterly heading.

The fighter had initiated an evasive manoeuvre and the airliner probably began one just before the collision, and the former was banking to the left at the time of impact. Its right wing slashed into the right outer wing of the DC–7, shearing off these sections from both aircraft. Both crews were able to transmit 'Mayday' distress messages during their fall to earth, and the instructor pilot in the front seat of the F-100 ejected at a low altitude before the jet crashed.

Despite a visibility of more than 35 miles (55 km) in the area, the high rate of the nearly head-on closure, calculated to have been about 765 mph (1,230 kmh), together with human and cockpit limitations, precluded the ability of either crew to avoid the accident through visual separation. An additional factor was the failure of both the US Civil Aeronautics Administration (CAA) and the US Air Force to reduce the collision danger, especially considering that training operations out of Nellis Air Force Base were being conducted largely within the confines of several airways, and that numerous close encounters with military jets had been reported by airline crews for more than a year prior to the tragedy.

Subsequent procedural changes by civilian and military authorities would help lessen the chance of a similar disaster, at least in this particular region.

Date: 18 May 1958 (c 04:30)
Location: Near Casablanca, Morocco
Operator: Belgian World Airlines (SABENA)
Aircraft type: Douglas DC-7C (*OO-SFA*)

Trouble developed in the aircraft's No 1 engine as the DC-7C was en route from Lisbon, Portugal, to Leopoldville, in the Belgian Congo (Zaire), the second segment of a scheduled service originating at Brussels, Belgium. Due to a reported vibration, the power plant was shut down and the flight diverted for a precautionary landing at Cazes Airport.

An approach was begun to Runway 21 in pre-dawn darkness, but at a point some 1,500 ft (500 m) beyond its threshold and with the transport less than 15 ft (5 m) above the ground, the pilot initiated an overshoot. This action, which probably resulted from an encounter with conditions of reduced visibility on account of patchy fog, reflected an error in judgement on his part, since the aircraft was neither properly configured nor flying at a sufficient speed to carry out such a manoeuvre. Safe operating procedures would have dictated that power be applied gradually, air speed be increased to assure that control be maintained, and flaps be retracted to the take-off position in the event of a balked landing.

Following the application of full power on the three remaining engines, the DC-7C stalled at an approximate height of 80 ft (25 m), clipped a small building, then struck a hangar while in a steep nose-down and sharp left-banking attitude. The aircraft immediately burst into flames, its undercarriage retracted but flaps fully extended at impact. The accident claimed the lives of 65 persons aboard, including the entire crew of nine. Four passengers survived.

Examination revealed pre-crash damage to a cylinder in the power plant that was feathered, probably caused by a loosening of the exhaust valve regulating screw leading to overheating around the valve and its seat, to the point that the metal actually melted. Though this technical fault necessitated the

Above *The wreckage of the United Air Lines DC-7 is confined to a relatively small area in the desert, indicating a steep descent to the ground after the collision with the jet fighter.* (Wide World Photos)

Below *This crash of a SABENA DC-7C into an airport hangar near Casablanca claimed the lives of 65 persons aboard the airliner.* (Wide World Photos)

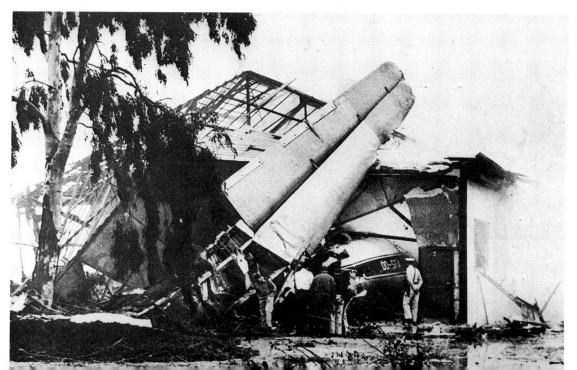

forced landing, it was not blamed for the subsequent disaster.

Date: 14 August 1958 (c 03:45)
Location: North Atlantic Ocean
Operator: KLM Royal Dutch Airlines
Aircraft type: Lockheed 1049H Super
  Constellation (*PH-LKM*)

Designated as Flight 607E, the aircraft had taken off from Shannon Airport, Ireland, bound for Gander, Newfoundland, Canada, its next scheduled stop during a transatlantic service from Amsterdam to New York City. Not more than 10 min after its last radio transmission, which was normal, the Super Constellation plunged into the sea some 100 miles (150 km) off the Irish coast and approximately due west of Galway Bay. All 99 persons aboard (91 passengers and eight crew members) perished.

The transport had been climbing to its cruising altitude and was presumed to have reached a height of about 13,000 ft (4,000 m) just before the catastrophe took place, in pre-dawn darkness. A small amount of debris was later recovered, including parts from the cabin and cockpit and the undercarriage wheels, as were the remains of 34 victims. The depth of the ocean in the area and the fact that its exact location was not known precluded any attempt to salvage the main wreckage.

On the available evidence, an investigative board was unable to establish with certainty the cause of the disaster. However, it regarded with 'a high degree of probability' that the crash resulted from overspeeding of an outer propeller.

According to this hypothesis, the sequence of events would have begun with a fracture in one of the driving gears of a power plant blower, occurring when the supercharger was accelerated; the engines with which *PH-LKM* was equipped were known to be susceptible to such failures. A fracture would release metal particles into the oil system, which would in turn clog a valve in the propeller governor and prevent its proper operation. Under the circumstances, it would not be possible to shut off the oil supply to the pitch mechanisms of the individual blades. The crew would thus be unable to feather the propeller, even by stopping the flow of fuel. This condition might provoke a flight disturbance that could only be corrected by the prompt and powerful handling of the aileron and rudder controls, and ultimately result in an uncontrolled descent.

In the short period of time in which the malfunction probably occurred, the pilots might not have been able to recognise the situation soon enough to restore control. For that reason, the board had no cause to suspect incorrect action by the crew in response to the emergency nor any neglect on the part of maintenance personnel. It also expressed satisfaction that the propeller governors of the type used by KLM had been fitted with a device designed to improve the reliability of the feathering mechanism subsequent to the crash of *PH-LKM*.

The weather in the area at the time of the accident was good and was not considered a contributing factor.

Date: 15 August 1958 (time unknown)
Location: Near Chita, Russian Federated Soviet
  Socialist Republic, USSR
Operator: Aeroflot (USSR)
Aircraft type: Tupolev Tu-104A (*SSSR-42349*)

All 64 persons aboard (54 passengers and a crew of 10) perished when the jet airliner crashed during a scheduled domestic service from Moscow to Khabarovsk.

The accident occurred at night and in instrument meteorological conditions shortly after the aircraft had been cleared by the flight manager on the ground to fly over an area of thunderstorm activity. Climbing to about 40,000 ft (12,000 m) above the ground, which was in excess of its operational ceiling when considering its weight, the Tu-104 then encountered a vertical air flow associated with the storm, causing it to assume an extreme nose-high altitude, with the result that it lost longitudinal stability. The aircraft stalled and plummeted to earth, the pilots unable to effect recovery due to a lack of bank angle and pitch indication in the cockpit, this because the artificial horizon did not function at high angles of attack.

Date: 17 October 1958 (time unknown)
Location: Near Kanash, Russian Soviet Federated
  Socialist Republic, USSR
Operator: Aeroflot (USSR)
Aircraft type: Tupolev Tu-104A (*SSSR-42362*)

The jet airliner had been en route from Omsk to Moscow, the domestic segment of a service originating at Peking, China, before it crashed some 400 miles (650 km) east of the Soviet capital, and all 80 persons aboard (71 passengers and a crew of nine) perished.

Flying at night and in instrument meteorological conditions at about 36,000 ft (11,000 m), the flight had been instructed by the ground manager to proceed to an alternative airport due to deteriorating weather at its original destination. During a climbing turn, the jet encountered severe turbulence associated with a thunderstorm, assuming an extreme nose-high attitude to the point of a longitudinal upset. It then stalled, plunged to the ground and caught fire. As in the above mentioned incident, recovery was not possible due to a lack of bank and pitch indications in the

An Aeroflot Tupolev Tu-104A jet airliner, two of which were involved in remarkably similar accidents during a two-month period in 1958. (Aviation Photo News)

cockpit, the artificial horizon not functioning when at high angles of attack.

One remarkable aspect of this disaster was the action of the captain, who described everything as it happened as he attempted to recover from the uncontrolled descent, ending the radio transmission with words of farewell. The information he provided proved useful in identifying the cause of this and the Tu-104 crash two months earlier, leading to design changes. The aircraft was found to have a very slow and limited response when in manual control, and its autopilot did not function efficiently in controlling bank at high altitude. Besides structural modification of the stabiliser, additional attitude instruments were installed to supplement the single artificial horizon then in use.

Date: 3 February 1959 (23:55)
Location: New York, New York, US
Operator: American Airlines (US)
Aircraft type: Lockheed 188A Electra (*N6101A*)

Flight 320 had been cleared for a back course instrument landing system (ILS) approach to Runway 22 at La Guardia Airport at the end of a domestic service from Chicago, Illinois. However, during the attempt to land, in darkness and adverse meteorological conditions, the four-engine turboprop descended below the minimum altitude and ultimately crashed in the East River off Rikers Island, approximately 1 mile (1.5 km) from the runway threshold and some 600 ft (180 m) to the right of its extended centreline. The accident killed 65 of the persons aboard, including the captain and a stewardess. Five passengers, the first and second officers and the other stewardess survived with various injuries.

This was a disaster in which the combined effects of several interrelated factors came into play. Primarily the crash was believed to have resulted from the failure of the crew to monitor properly essential instruments for determining attitude and height due to preoccupation with particular aspects of the aircraft and its environment. The contributing elements were cumulative.

Though highly experienced, none of the three flight crewmen had served much time in the Electra, whose instrumentation differed from that found in the piston-engined transports with which they were familiar. Specifically, its altimeters had a window through which 1,000 ft levels were given in single digits, with a triangular-shaped index on each side. Conceivably, the index on the left could have been mistaken for the 1,000 ft pointer used on earlier altimeters, giving the impression that it was indicating a height of 2,500 ft. Similarly, the index on the right could have been mistaken for the 100 ft pointer. Additionally, its vertical speed indicator (VSI) was more sensitive, giving a reading that more closely represented the actual performance of the aircraft. An indication that should alarm a pilot probably would not have evoked the same response with an earlier design of VSI. In this case, the difference could have led to an excessive descent rate during the approach.

A post-crash examination of the instruments also revealed that the captain's altimeter had been incorrectly set. The resulting indication could have been as much as 125 ft (c 40 m) too high, which would have been significant during a landing.

The captain was also criticised for a faulty approach technique, which utilised the heading mode of the autopilot until the final seconds of the flight, contrary to the operating manual. Records in fact showed that despite more than 28,000 hours of flying time, the pilot had never before executed a back course ILS approach at La Guardia Airport in instrument conditions.

The weather was regarded as an additional contributing factor, with a ceiling of only 300–400 ft

The American Airlines Electra crash in New York City came less than a month after this type of aircraft entered regular service. (American Airlines)

(c 100–120 m), a visibility of 2 miles (c 3 km) in light rain and fog, and a 6-knot wind from a south-south-westerly direction. Under the circumstances, and especially considering the sparsity of lights in the approach area, it was quite possible that the crew had been deceived by a sensory illusion that created a false impression regarding the height and attitude of the aircraft.

But while the captain may have erred, the first officer could still have prevented the accident, according to the US Civil Aeronautics Board (CAB) report, by following the prescribed procedures and being fully alert and attentive to all his cockpit duties. It was likely that he was paying close attention to the apparent difficulties of the pilot in maintaining the localiser path, to the point that he failed to call out altitude and air speed indications below 600 ft, as required. Just before impact, the co-pilot was probably anticipating breaking out of the overcast and, having seen lights on the ground or water, concentrating on making visual identification of the airport, and thus not monitoring the instruments.

The Electra struck the water while in a shallow descent at a ground speed of about 150 mph (250 kmh); with its undercarriage and flaps extended, it then broke apart and sank in water some 30 ft (10 m) deep. More than 90 per cent of its wreckage was

The empennage and rear fuselage section of the Electra is raised from the East River following the accident that claimed 65 lives. (UPI/Bettmann)

A Trans World Airlines Lockheed 1649A Starliner, the type that crashed in Italy after a mid-air explosion. (Trans World Airlines)

subsequently recovered, as were the bodies of all but two of the victims; death was attributed to both trauma and drowning. The eight survivors owe their lives to a tugboat that happened to be in the area at the time and rescued them from the river.

Two recommendations made by the CAB, pertaining to the use of flight simulators to train crews on aircraft featuring novel systems or operating characteristics, and the installation on turboprop commercial transports (as on pure jets) of flight data recorders, would later become standard throughout the airline industry.

Date: 26 June 1959 (c 17:35)
Location: Near Varese, Lombardia, Italy
Operator: Trans World Airlines (TWA) (US)
Aircraft type: Lockheed 1649A Starliner
　(*N7313C*)

Operating as Flight 891 and on a service originating at Athens, Greece, with an ultimate destination of Chicago, Illinois, US, the aircraft was at an approximate height of 11,000 ft (3,400 m) and climbing when an explosion shattered its right wing. The Starliner then plummeted into a field some 20 miles (30 km) north-west of Milan and burst into flames, the crash occurring about 15 min after it had taken off from that city's Malpensa Airport, bound for Paris, France. All 68 persons aboard (59 passengers and nine crew members) perished.

The late afternoon disaster occurred during light rain and low overcast, with a ceiling of around 2,000 ft (600 m), and a visibility of approximately 2 miles (3 km). There was also thunderstorm activity in the area.

An investigative board examined several possible reasons for the tragedy, but discarded most of them, including metal fatigue, structural failure due to turbulence, and sabotage. Not completely ruled out, however, was that the maximum speed of the aircraft had been exceeded during an uncontrolled descent.

In the absence of concrete evidence, the theory considered most plausible was the ignition of gasoline vapours emanating from one or both of the No 7 fuel tank vent pipes as a consequence of static electricity discharges, or streamer corona, which developed in these outlets. This would have led to the explosion of the vapours in that tank, followed by an excess of pressure or another explosion in an adjacent fuel tank, No 6.

Tests proved such a scenario to be within the realm of possibility under certain atmospheric conditions, and only when the aircraft was ascending; in addition, the weather at the time of the accident was conducive to this phenomenon, with frequent electrical discharges. Static discharges could have occurred had the Starliner been struck anywhere by lightning, or had it flown through clouds that were electrically charged.

Following the explosion in the wing of *N7313C*, which took place near its No 3 nacelle, aerodynamic forces caused the separation of its tail assembly.

Research begun in the wake of this disaster on the potential threat to aircraft posed by electrical discharges was under way when lightning destroyed a commercial jet in 1963 (see separate entry, 8 December 1963).

The
1960s

The term 'jet set' became part of our vernacular during the 1960s, and no wonder, considering the tremendous affect on business and pleasure travel brought about by jet aircraft, the popularity of which contributed to a soar in passenger traffic.

Half-way through the decade a new generation of short-haul aircraft, such as the Boeing 727, Douglas DC-9 and Hawker Siddeley Trident, would for the first time bring jet passenger service to smaller communities and airports. This was also the era of the VC-10, which would be the pride of the British commercial aviation industry until the coming of supersonic air travel in the 1970s. By the late 1960s many major airlines had retired their last propeller-driven transports, and were boasting of 'all-jet' fleets.

The reliability and durability of jet aircraft were credited with continued improvement in the industry's safety record during this period. But while the number of accidents in relation to the number of flights decreased, greater passenger capacity increased the potential for a major disaster. Prior to 1960 there had been but one airline crash to claim more than 100 lives; by the beginning of 1970 that figure had risen to 18.

However, despite the potential for even more serious disasters with the advent in the late 1960s of aircraft capable of carrying more than 200 passengers, the record death toll of 134 set in the collision over New York City would not be exceeded until the last year of the decade.

Date: 18 January 1960 (c 22:20)
Location: Near Charles City, Virginia, US
Operator: Capital Airlines (US)
Aircraft type: Vickers Viscount 745D (*N7462*)

The four-engine turboprop crashed and burned in a wooded area some 30 miles (50 km) south-east of Richmond, Virginia, killing all 50 persons aboard (46 passengers and a crew of four). It was dark at the time, and the local weather consisted of light, scattered showers and patchy fog.

Designated as Flight 20, the aircraft had stopped at Washington, DC, during a domestic service from Chicago, Illinois, to Norfolk, Virginia. Cruising at 8,000 ft (c 2,500 m), it would have encountered conditions conducive to icing, ie sub-zero temperatures, clouds and rain. It was believed that the crew delayed arming the power plant ice-protection systems, leading to the failure of at least two engines. The others must have flamed out after a descent to a lower altitude was initiated, either from the ingestion of melted ice or because the anti-icing system had been left on in the warmer air. Under the circumstances, all four propellers would have autofeathered.

The Viscount was apparently put into a dive in an attempt to drive the propellers out of their feathered positions while, simultaneously, the crew tried to restart the engines. Successful re-lights were either interrupted by autofeathering action due to the premature advancing of the power levers prior to complete restart, or prevented by insufficient battery electrical energy associated with the loss of engine rotation.

In the final seconds of the flight, the crew managed to restart No 4 engine, but the application of full power created an asymmetrical control difficulty, causing the aircraft to make two left-hand circles, as confirmed by witnesses. No 3 must also have been relit just prior to impact. It was possible that the pilots saw the ground and initiated a pull-up before the turboprop slammed to earth in a nearly level attitude, with no forward velocity.

The reason for the delay in activating the ice-protection systems may have been due to the captain's lack of knowledge that they must be switched on below a specified temperature; late anticipation of ice accretion; variations in

temperature instrument indications; or to a combination of these factors.

As a result of this accident, the airline dropped the phrase 'descend to a warmer climate for relight' from its emergency check-list and instructed its Viscount pilots that engine restart could be accomplished at any height providing that the correct drill was followed.

Above *Tree trunks piercing the wings and fuselage indicate an impact with no forward velocity in the crash of this Capital Airlines Viscount.* (Wide World Photos)

Below *A crater marks the crash site of the Northwest Airlines Electra that lost a wing over Indiana.* (Wide World Photos)

Date: 17 March 1960 (15:25)
Location: Near Cannelton, Indiana, US
Operator: Northwest Airlines (US)
Aircraft type: Lockheed 188C Electra (*N121US*)

Following a scheduled stop at Chicago, Illinois, Flight 710 took off for Miami, Florida, on the second leg of a domestic service originating at Minneapolis, Minnesota. Less than an hour later, while cruising at an altitude of 18,000 ft (c 5,500 m), the Electra suffered catastrophic structural failure. Its entire right wing and a large portion of its left having separated, the fuselage of the aircraft plummeted almost vertically into a field at a speed in excess of 600 mph (965 kmh). All 63 persons aboard (57 passengers and six crew members) perished. A crater measuring 40 ft (12 m) across at its widest point and approximately 10 ft (3 m) deep marked the crash site, some 10 miles (15 km) southeast of Tell City and just north of the Ohio River. Most of the wreckage and the remains of the victims lay buried and were recovered during the subsequent excavation of the crater. The right wing was found more than 2 miles (3 km) from the main wreckage, confirming that a break-up in the air had taken place.

An intensive investigation prompted by this and a similar Electra accident six months earlier, which included both flight and ground testing, revealed

that the two tragedies had apparently resulted from uncontrolled propeller oscillation, also known as 'whirl mode'. In the case of *N121US*, the propeller wobble was transferred to the outboard nacelles, whose oscillations induced flutter in the wings to the point of overstress. The initial failure was in the right wing, which folded rearward.

Prior damage was, however, considered a prerequisite for undampened 'whirl mode' to reach a destructive level, and the source of the damage to this particular aircraft may have been a hard landing at Chicago's Midway Airport, occurring about 90 min before the crash, which was reported by some of the passengers who disembarked there. An encounter with severe clear air turbulence, which had been noted by other pilots flying in the area around the time of the disaster, probably contributed to the start of the flutter.

As a result of the findings into this and the first crash, every Electra in service was modified. Nacelle-wing improvements included the installation of additional support features and the replacement of existing structures with heavier materials.

Date: 27 July 1960 (22:38)
Location: Forest Park, Illinois, US
Operator: Chicago Helicopter Airways (US)
Aircraft type: Sikorsky S-58C (*N879*)

The first fatal crash of a commercial helicopter engaged in a regular passenger operation occurred during a commuter service between Chicago's two air carrier airports, from Midway to O'Hare International.

Flight 698 was cruising at its assigned height of 1,500 ft (c 500 m) when one of its four main rotor blades snapped. After it had descended to a lower altitude, its tail rotor and cone separated from vibrations generated by the imbalance of the main rotor assembly, attributed to the loss of the blade, and the aircraft then crashed in a cemetery and burst into flames, killing all 13 persons aboard (11 passengers and two pilots). The accident took place in darkness and clear weather conditions on the outskirts of Chicago, approximately half-way between the two airports.

The failure of the main blade was initiated by a fatigue fracture, which had apparently developed in the 68 hours of flying since its last inspection.

The first fatal crash of a commercial helicopter on a regular passenger service involved a Chicago Helicopter Airways Sikorsky S-58 on an intra-urban flight. (Sikorsky)

Date: 29 August 1960 (c 06:50)
Location: Off Dakar, Senegal
Operator: Air France
Aircraft type: Lockheed 1049G Super
Constellation (*F-BHBC*)

Operating as Flight 343, the airliner was to have landed at Yoff Airport, serving Dakar, a scheduled stop during a service originating at Paris, France, with an ultimate destination of Abidjan, in the Ivory Coast. Following an unsuccessful landing, it began a second attempt, flying over the airport towards the west. A few minutes later, and after reporting 'down-wind' while at a height of 1,000 ft (c 300 m), the Super Constellation crashed in the Atlantic Ocean approximately 1 mile (1.5 km) from the shore, in the midst of a rain squall. All 63 persons aboard (55 passengers and a crew of eight) perished.

The disaster occurred shortly before sunrise and in meteorological conditions that also consisted of a low overcast, with 7/8 cloud coverage at 2,000–3,000 ft (c 600–1,000 m), and a visibility that varied from one minute to the next. There was also thunderstorm activity in the area.

Its undercarriage and flaps extended, the aircraft was believed to have struck the surface of the sea at a relatively steep angle, and while probably banked to the right. Most of the victims' bodies were recovered, but salvage operations yielded only about 20 per cent of the wreckage from the water, which was some 130 ft (40 m) deep.

Although the cause could not be determined, it was considered possible that the crash resulted from structural failure or a loss of control due to turbulence; sensory illusion; distraction of the flight crew, which could have been associated with a lightning strike; inaccuracy of an air speed indicator or altimeter; or faulty reading of the latter instrument.

Date: 19 September 1960 (c 06:00)
Location: Guam, Mariana Islands
Operator: World Airways (US)
Aircraft type: Douglas DC-6AB (*N90779*)

The airliner, which was being flown under contract to the US Military Air Transport Service (MATS) and was carrying as passengers American service personnel and some dependents, had landed at Agana Naval Air Station during a flight from the Philippines to Travis Air Force Base, California, US. It departed before dawn, bound for Wake Island, its next en route stop.

Less than a minute after its take-off from Runway 06L, the transport crashed on Mt Barrigada, about 2 miles (3 km) east of the air base and some 5 miles (10 km) east-north-east of the island's capital city, bursting into flames on impact. Killed in the accident were 80 of the 94 persons aboard,

including seven crew members; the navigator was among the injured survivors. The casualties were more attributable to the effects of the fire than the crash itself.

Its undercarriage and flaps having been retracted, the aircraft was in a slight right bank but practically level longitudinally when it initially struck trees at an approximate elevation of 600 ft (180 m), or slightly less than 100 ft (30 m) below the summit of the peak.

The pilot had failed to comply with the published departure procedures applicable to the runway used by initiating a right turn before attaining an altitude of 1,000 ft (c 300 m). Despite the visual flight rules (VFR) conditions existing at the time, with scattered clouds at 1,400 ft (c 430 m), a high overcast and a visibility of about 15 miles (25 km), it was doubtful whether in the darkness and haze the crew could have seen the single flashing red beacon atop the mountain, the only visual warning of the obstacle.

As a safety measure, the minimum height requirement was later included in the air traffic control departure information.

Date: 4 October 1960 (17:40)
Location: Boston, Massachusetts, US
Operator: Eastern Air Lines (US)
Aircraft type: Lockheed 188A Electra (*N5533*)

Designated as Flight 375, the turboprop crashed in Winthrop Bay about a minute after taking off from Runway 05 at Boston's Logan International Airport, killing 62 persons aboard (59 passengers and the three members of the flight crew). The 10 injured survivors included both stewardesses.

Bound for Philadelphia, Pennsylvania, the aircraft's first scheduled stop during a domestic service with an ultimate destination of Atlanta, Georgia, it had just become airborne when it struck a flock of starlings, and a large number of the birds were ingested into three of its four engines. The No 1 was shut down when its propeller autofeathered, No 2 flamed out completely and No 4 experienced a partial loss of power. This asymmetrical power condition, which was aggravated by the recovery of full power to the No 4 engine before the No 2 relit, resulted in a yaw to the left. Meanwhile, the overall power loss caused the transport to decelerate. The Electra then stalled during a skidding left turn while continuing to yaw, and after its port wing dropped and nose pitched up, it rolled left into a spin and plummeted almost vertically into the shallow water of the Boston Harbour inlet, some 500 ft (150 m) from the shore, its undercarriage retracted and flaps extended at impact. The meteorological conditions at the time, consisting of scattered clouds and a visibility of 15 miles (c 25 km), were not considered a factor in the crash.

The only means of regaining control and air

speed prior to the spin would have been to intentionally reduce power and lower the nose, but the low altitude of the aircraft, which at that point was less than 150 ft (50 m), precluded any such recovery action by the pilots.

As a result of this accident, the US Federal Aviation Agency (FAA) initiated a research programme aimed at improving the tolerance of turbine engines to bird ingestion.

Date: 16 December 1960 (c 10:30)
Location: New York, New York, US
First aircraft
Operator: United Air Lines (US)
Type: Douglas DC-8 Series 11 (*N8013U*)
Second aircraft
Operator: Trans World Airlines (TWA) (US)
Type: Lockheed 1049 Super Constellation (*N6907C*)

The same two carriers involved in the 1956 Grand Canyon disaster (see separate entry, 30 June 1956) were the principals in this mid-air crash, which exhibited some other amazing similarities. One of the aircraft was of the identical make and model in both cases, while the other was produced by the same manufacturer and only one generation apart. In addition, the combined death toll of those aboard the two transports was the same in each accident.

There were also some significant differences, most notably that this time both aircraft were operating in accordance with instrument flight rules (IFR) and, presumably, under the watchful eye of ground radar. This collision was tragic proof that, despite procedural changes and technological advances since the first accident, serious inadequacies still existed in the US air traffic control (ATC) system.

United Flight 826 had originated at Chicago, Illinois, bound for New York International Airport, with the DC-8 jet carrying 77 passengers and seven crew members. TWA Flight 266 was also on a domestic service, from Dayton and Columbus, Ohio, and was scheduled to land at New York's other major airport, La Guardia. Aboard the piston-engine Super Constellation were 39 passengers plus a crew of five. The weather over the city on this Friday morning was overcast, with a ceiling of about 5,000 ft (1,500 m), accompanied by fog and snow or sleet, conditions that were not conducive to visual flight rules (VFR) operations.

Following its passage of Allentown, Pennsylvania, and just before beginning its descent from 25,000 ft (c 7,500 m), the DC-8 was assigned a shortened route. This new clearance, which would in fact be regarded as a contributing factor in the subsequent collision, reduced its distance by some 12 miles (20 km) to the Preston Intersection, a position defined by two radials from two different very-high-frequency omni-directional range (VOR) stations, where the aircraft should have entered a 'racetrack' holding pattern to await landing instructions.

Unbeknown to the New York centre, one of the DC-8's two VOR receivers was inoperative. As a result, the crew would have to establish a holding fix by tuning the single receiver from one station to the other, a time-consuming process; and with the shortened clearance, the pilots would have less time to accomplish this task. In the final seconds before the accident, the centre advised the crew that radar service was terminated, and that it should contact Idlewild Approach Control. There was, however, no actual 'hand-off' from one control facility to the other. The last message from the jet, directed to approach control, was 'Approaching Preston at five thousand'.

Simultaneous with these events, the Super Constellation was descending in preparation for its own landing. The transport was receiving radar vectors from La Guardia Approach Control, and had last been instructed to make a left turn and assume a heading of 130 degrees. After noticing an unidentified

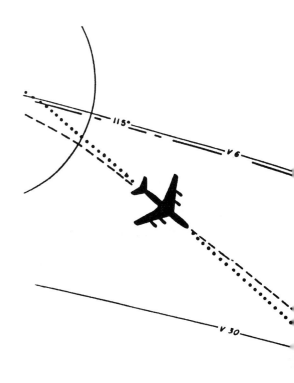

A United Air Lines DC-8, the type that collided with a Trans World Airlines Super Constellation over New York City, became the first US commercial jet to crash fatally during passenger service. (United Air Lines)

The courses of the United and TWA flights leading up to the collision over Staten Island. (Civil Aeronautics Board)

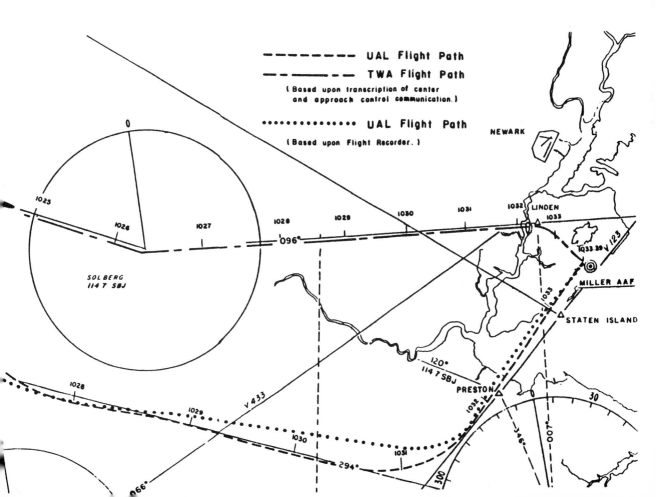

blip on his radarscope, the controller advised the TWA flight that it appeared to be jet traffic '. . . off your right, now three o'clock at one mile, north-eastbound'. The two targets then merged.

The aircraft collided at 10:33 while in the clouds at an approximate altitude of 5,000 ft (1,500 m), almost directly over Miller Army Air Field, located in New Dorp, on Staten Island. Flying along Airway V123 at a ground speed of about 380 mph (610 kmh), an excessive velocity that also contributed to the accident, the DC-8 overtook the Super Constellation from behind and to the latter's right side, striking the top of its fuselage at an angle of about 110 degrees. Cabin insulation and human remains were later found in the DC-8's right out-board engine, a grim reminder of how it must have sliced into the passenger compartment. At the time of impact, the jet was in a nearly straight and level attitude, the propeller transport banking to the left.

The Super Constellation broke into three main sections and plummeted to earth in flames, crashing at the airfield. Scattered among its debris were pieces of the DC-8, including the No 4 power plant and starboard wing outboard of the engine. Following the collision, the jet continued in a north-

A scene of devastation is left by the crash of the United Air Lines jet in Brooklyn, where six persons lost their lives in addition to the 128 aboard the two aircraft. (UPI/Bettmann)

easterly direction for another 8.5 miles (c 13.5 km) before it plunged into the Park Slope section of Brooklyn and exploded in flames, its empennage coming to rest at the intersection of Sterling Place and Seventh Avenue.

Three occupants were removed alive from the wreckage of the Super Constellation, but died shortly afterwards. One passenger on the jet, an 11-year-old boy riding in the aft part of its cabin, was thrown into a snowbank and miraculously lived through the crash with severe burns and other injuries, only to succumb in hospital the following day, leaving no survivors from either aircraft. The final toll was 134 persons killed, including six on the ground in Brooklyn, where several others were injured. There was considerable damage in the area where the DC-8 crashed; the impact and resulting fires destroyed 10 tenements, some shops and a church.

Due to an apparent navigational error by its crew, the jet had proceeded beyond its clearance limit and the confines of the airspace allocated to the flight. It was probably more than coincidental that the distance it had travelled beyond its intended holding position and the point of the collision equalled the length of the short-cut. In its investigative report, the US Civil Aeronautics Board (CAB) concluded that the pilots did not take note of the change in time and distance associated with the new clearance.

There were indications that, in lieu of a second VOR unit, the crew had used its automatic direction finding (ADF) equipment to take cross-bearings. This would have required rapid mental calculation, and the display could easily have been misinterpreted. Had the No 1 ADF receiver been tuned to the Scotland low-frequency radio beacon, the captain, when transitioning to it, may have confused this instrument with the VOR. (The pictorial display of the ADF at the location of the collision would under the circumstances resemble the VOR when it was tuned to the appropriate station.) Thus, when the flight reported that it was approaching Preston, it was already well beyond that point.

But the United crew was not alone in its culpability, because the CAB further determined that the New York control centre did not adequately monitor the aircraft, and the controller failed to observe it proceed through the Preston intersection. When he reported radar service as being terminated, the jet was nearly 10 miles (15 km) beyond its clearance limit.

This accident brought about a major revitalisation of the nation's ATC system. Most significant was the development of the system of 'positive control'. Under this principle, radar control would be exerted over all aircraft flying above 24,000 ft (c 7,300 m), and positive control would extend down to 8,000 ft (c 2,500 m) on high-density airways, and to most airline operations (all that employed jets). A new speed limit below 10,000 ft (c 3,000 m) and within 30 nautical miles (55 km) of the destination airport was also imposed, as were strict guidelines in the transferral of flights from one control facility to another.

Additionally, the installation of two devices would be required on all aircraft weighing more than 12,500 lb (5,670 kg) that operated in US airspace. The first of these was the transponder, which would help identify the aircraft's target on radar. The second was distance-measuring equipment (DME), designed to assist pilots in determining their exact position by calculating the mileage between navigational facilities. Later refinements included three-dimensional radar and alphanumeric displays for easy identification of the radar blip.

The system is far from foolproof, however, and lapses still occur periodically. But one of the primary objectives of the positive control system, ie to provide separation of air carrier flights, has worked exceedingly well. In fact, not since 1960 has a catastrophic mid-air collision between two large commercial aircraft occurred anywhere over the United States.

Date: 15 February 1961 (10:05)
Location: Near Brussels, Belgium
Operator: Belgian World Airlines (SABENA)
Aircraft type: Boeing 707-329 (*OO-SJB*)

Among the passengers who boarded Flight 548 at New York International Airport were the 18 members of the US figure skating team, including the coach, on their way to a world meet in Prague, Czechoslovakia. Following the 8½ hr transatlantic trip, the 707 began its approach to land at Brussels National Airport.

Everything seemed normal, but as the aircraft was about to touch down on Runway 20, engine power increased and its undercarriage and flaps were then retracted in what appeared to be an overshoot manoeuvre. Climbing to an estimated height of 1,500 ft (c 500 m), the Boeing completed three left-hand circles while ascending and descending as thrust was both increased and decreased. During this period of time its attitude became generally steeper until finally, while in a near-vertical left bank, the jetliner nosed down and crashed in a field approximately 1 mile (1.5 km) from the runway threshold, near Berg, a village located in the province of Brabant some 20 miles (30 km) north-east of the capital city, bursting into flames on impact. All 72 persons aboard, including 11 crew members, perished. A farmer on the ground was also killed and a second seriously injured.

The airport weather at the time, which was not considered a factor, consisted of a high overcast and a visibility of about 2 miles (3 km).

The wreckage of the SABENA Boeing 707 continues to smoulder following the crash in the Belgian countryside. (Wide World Photos)

A Belgian investigative commission concluded that the accident was probably related to the material failure of the aircraft's flying controls. Two hypotheses were considered possible: either the jamming of the outboard ailerons near the neutral position, or the unwanted extension of the spoilers; although it could not be corroborated, available evidence pointed to the latter.

Examination of the wreckage revealed that the sheer rivets in the follow-up mechanism between all four spoilers and their hydraulic valves were broken. Had these rivets been sheared in flight, the spoilers could have either gone into a fully extended position or retracted with only a minimal amount of aileron movement. Ultimately this could lead to the asymmetrical deployment of the spoilers, causing severe lateral instability. In this case, the right inboard spoiler was extended at the time of the crash, and the left inboard one probably retracted. The position of either outboard spoiler could not be determined.

There were indications that the crew had tried to by-pass the spoilers. However, the left outboard by-pass valve was not functioning properly and remained jammed in the open position, which would have prevented such action. In such an event the only recourse would have been to suppress the hydraulic pressure pumps, but there would have been little time to accomplish this. Moreover, the pilots would have difficulty identifying the problem, especially considering that the spoilers were not visible from the cockpit.

Representing the nation of manufacture, the US Federal Aviation Agency (FAA) doubted the Belgian theory, maintaining that the 707 should have been controllable even with an outboard spoiler fully extended. It suspected that a malfunction in the stabiliser adjusting mechanism had caused the accident.

The recommended modifications to the 707 included in service bulletins sent out by Boeing and SABENA involved the spoiler follow-up crank shear joint and the outboard spoiler shut-off valve, replacement of the control wheel stabiliser switch, and the installation of a supplementary brake for the stabiliser trim actuator. The commission also suggested the introduction of a spoiler position indicator.

Date: 10 May 1961 (c 02:30)
Location: Eastern Algeria
Operator: Air France
Aircraft type: Lockheed 1649A Starliner
  (*F-BHBM*)

Operating as Flight 406, the airliner crashed and burned in the Sahara Desert while en route from Fort Lamy (Ndjamena), Chad, to Marseilles, France, one segment of a service originating at Brazzaville, Congo, with an ultimate destination of Paris. All 78 persons aboard (69 passengers and a crew of nine) perished.

Cruising in early morning darkness and clear weather conditions, the Starliner broke up at an approximate altitude of 20,000 ft (6,000 m) before it plunged to earth some 30 miles (50 km) south-west of Ghadamis, Libya. Its empennage and other components were reportedly found about 1 mile (1.5 km) from the main wreckage site.

The most probable cause of the catastrophe was sabotage with nitrocellulose explosive.

Date: 30 May 1961 (c 01:20)
Location: Near Lisbon, Portugal
Operator: KLM Royal Dutch Airlines
Aircraft type: Douglas DC-8 Series 53 (*PH-DCL*)

Designated as Flight 897, the jetliner was being operated by the Dutch carrier for the Venezuelan airline VIASA on a service from Rome, Italy, to Caracas, Venezuela, with three en route stops. Only about 5 minutes after it had taken off from Lisbon airport, the DC-8 plunged into the Atlantic Ocean south of the Tagus River estuary, and all 61 persons aboard (47 passengers and 14 crew members) perished.

The crash took place in darkness, and the meteorological conditions in the area probably consisted of light rain, light to moderate turbulence, a 20-knot wind out of the west, a visibility of around 5 miles (10 km) and a low overcast, with 4/8 strato-cumulus clouds at about 2,000 ft (600 m) and solid altostratus.

Located on the ocean floor some 2 miles (3 km) off shore and at a depth of approximately 100 ft (30 m), about 75 per cent of the wreckage was subsequently recovered. Evidence indicated that the aircraft, which was last reported climbing through 6,000 ft (c 1,800 m), struck the surface of the water at a speed in excess of 500 mph (800 kmh), and while in a slight descent and banked to the right.

There was no evidence of any pre-impact defects or malfunctions, though they could not be definitely excluded. Nor could the possibility, though remote, of sabotage or some other malicious act. There were indications that the jetliner went into a spiral dive from a steep left-banking attitude, possibly due to crew inattentiveness or because one or both pilots were misled by the failure of an artificial horizon or some other vital flight instrument, in either case resulting in a loss of control. The attitude of the DC-8 at the moment of impact pointed to over-correction during the attempt to level off, but the loss of altitude must have been too rapid for the crew to effect recovery.

The investigative board recommended the installation in commercial aircraft of a third, independent horizon that could be referred to in the event of a malfunction in either or both of the captain's and first officer's instruments, a safety

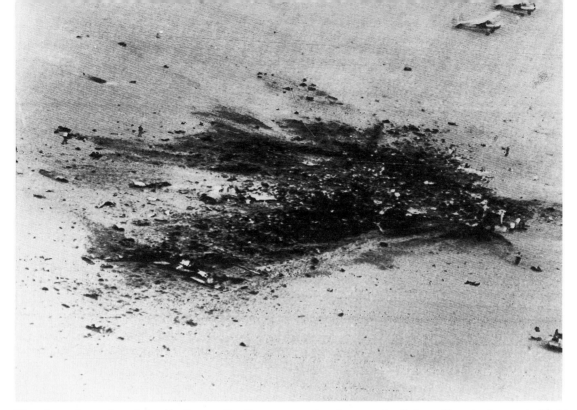

The charred remains of the Air France Starliner are scattered across the Sahara Desert after an in-flight break-up believed to have been caused by a bomb. (Wide World Photos)

feature that would come into use some years later.

Date: 1 September 1961 (c 02:05)
Location: Near Hinsdale, Illinois, US
Operator: Trans World Airlines (TWA) (US)
Aircraft type: Lockheed 049 Constellation (*N86511*)

Operating as Flight 529, the transport crashed and disintegrated in a fiery explosion some 10 miles (15 km) west of Chicago's Midway Airport, from where it had taken off only 5 minutes earlier, bound for Las Vegas, Nevada, one segment of a domestic transcontinental service originating at Boston, Massachusetts, with an ultimate destination of San Francisco, California. All 78 persons aboard (73 passengers and a crew of five) perished.

The Constellation had been flying on a westerly course in early morning darkness and good weather conditions, which at the airport consisted of a high overcast and a visibility of 3 miles (c 5 km), before it plunged into a cornfield in a nose-down attitude and while banked slightly to the left, its undercarriage and flaps retracted at the moment of impact. A portion of its horizontal stabiliser to which the right vertical fin was attached had separated in flight.

Examination of the wreckage revealed that a ⁵⁄₁₆in nickel steel bolt was missing from the parallelogram linkage of the aircraft's elevator boost system, and the US Civil Aeronautics Board (CAB) concluded that it must have fallen out prior to the crash. This would have caused the elevator to move to its full upward position, creating a stall. In response to the violent pitch-up, one or both pilots could have been expected to apply forward pressure to the control column, but this action would also make it difficult, if not impossible, to move the handle in order to shift the elevator system to manual operation, which would be the only way of overcoming the situation. Under the circumstances, the crew was unable to maintain control. The pre-impact empennage damage was the apparent result of the accelerated stall vibrations.

Though the theory could not be substantiated, the most probable reason for the bolt's loss was that it had not been properly secured during the replacement of the parallelogram assembly, which had taken place some 10 months earlier. Over a period of time the nut had backed off until the bolt finally came out on the fatal flight.

Citing the 'excellent service history' of the Constellation, the US Federal Aviation Agency (FAA) rejected the recommendations of the CAB for modifications in the aircraft's elevator boost system that it made in the light of this accident.

Date: 10 September 1961 (c 03:55)
Location: Near Limerick, Ireland
Operator: President Airlines (US)
Aircraft type: Douglas DC-6B (*N90773*)

The aircraft was on a charter service from Dusseldorf, (West) Germany, to Chicago,

The plunge of this President Airlines DC-6B into the estuary of Ireland's River Shannon occurred moments after the transport had taken off. (UPI/Bettmann)

Illinois, US, with two en route stops. Aboard were European passengers, mostly Germans, plus six crew members, all Americans. Shortly after it had taken off from Runway 24 at Shannon Airport, Ireland, in pre-dawn darkness and during a fog, bound for Gander, Newfoundland, Canada, the DC-6B plunged into the estuary of the River Shannon. Cleared for a right turn, the transport had instead turned to the left, and was in a bank of at least 90 degrees when it crashed in the shallow water approximately 1 mile (1.5 km) from the end of the runway.

The bodies of 84 persons were subsequently recovered, one more than listed on the manifest, and there were no survivors (one passenger was found alive in the wreckage but later died in hospital).

The disaster probably resulted from the failure of the captain to maintain control, either due to a defective artificial horizon or a fault in the aircraft's right-hand aileron tabs. Contributing factors may have been the unfavourable meteorological conditions, which at the time of the take-off were below the minima authorised by the carrier, and possible crew fatigue.

Date: 12 September 1961 (21:09)
Location: Near Rabat, Morocco
Operator: Air France
Aircraft type: Sud-Aviation Caravelle III
(*F-BJTB*)

Designated as Flight 2005, the jet airliner crashed and burned while attempting to land at Sale Airport, which also serves Rabat, a scheduled stop during a service from Paris to Casablanca, Morocco, and all 77 persons aboard (71 passengers and a crew of six) were killed.

Immediately after the pilot had reported his intention to break through a thick, low fog over

the non-directional beacon (NDB), the control tower replied that the navigational facility was not in line with the runway, but the flight did not acknowledge the message. Its undercarriage down and flaps partially extended, the Caravelle struck the ground in a slight nose-down attitude and while probably banked gently to the left. Bouncing twice, it finally slammed into the side of a gorge and broke apart some 5 miles (10 km) from the threshold of Runway 04 and approximately 1 mile (1.5 km) to the left of its extended centre-line. It was dark at the time, and the airport weather consisted of a solid overcast at about 100 ft (30 m) and a horizontal visibility of around 1,500 ft (500 m).

Material failure appeared unlikely, and both altimeters were found to have been correctly set. Therefore the hypothesis considered more probable than any other as causing the accident was an altimeter misreading of 1,000 ft. The error could have been made at the beginning of the descent, then, retaining it, the pilot may have given his full attention to the pointer in order to bring the aircraft to what he believed was the minimum authorised height. As noted in the investigative report, the reading of the Kollsman window altimeter, with which *F-BJTB* was equipped, could be subject to misinterpretation.

Date: 8 November 1961 (c 21:30)
Location: Near Richmond, Virginia, US
Operator: Imperial Airlines (US)
Aircraft type: Lockheed 049E Constellation
(*N2737A*)

The four-engine transport was being flown under a US military contract, carrying 74 army recruits on their way to Fort Jackson, near Columbia, South Carolina, plus five civilian crew members, the latter including a student flight engineer in addition to the regular one. Both pilots were qualified captains. Having boarded passengers at Newark, New Jersey, Wilkes Barre, Pennsylvania, and Baltimore, Maryland, the Constellation proceeded towards its ultimate destination.

As the aircraft took off from Baltimore, a momentary fluctuation was noted in the fuel pressure of its No 3 power plant, probably due to the failure of its fuel boost pump, which may have been fitted with the wrong kind of electrical brush (as, it turns out, was the No 2). In response, the student engineer opened both the No 3 and 4 cross-feed valves; but because of the inoperative boost pump, the higher pressure in the cross-feed manifold supplied by the operating pump held closed a check valve between the manifold and the No 3 fuel tank. Fuelling both starboard engines, the gasoline supply in the No 4 tank was soon exhausted, causing both power plants to fail.

Immediately taking over, the regular flight engineer then committed a procedural error by leaving on the No 4 boost pump, which allowed air to be drawn into the fuel supply lines of both the No 3 and No 4 engines, thus preventing either from being restarted. The corresponding propellers were feathered, and the crew elected to land at Byrd Field, located just outside the Richmond suburb of Sandston.

During the approach to Runway 33, the captain acting as co-pilot inexplicably switched to Runway 02. However, the landing had to be abandoned altogether when the undercarriage would not extend, this because of the crew's failure to activate a cross-over valve that would have permitted the use of hydraulic pressure from the No 1 and 2 engines to assume the function normally borne by the two right-hand ones.

As the transport circled the airport in an anti-clockwise direction, this time to land on Runway 33, its banking angle was steepened to the point where it resulted in a loss of air speed and, in turn, altitude. Responding to the higher sink rate, brought about by the poorly executed go-around manoeuvre, the crew applied full power to the two port engines, but under the strain of the overboosting No 1 quickly failed. Unable to maintain height on only one power plant, the Constellation, which had flown about half a mile (0.8 km) beyond the extended centreline of the runway, finally crashed approximately 1 mile (1.5 km) from its threshold. A sharp pull-up was made just before the aircraft slammed into a wooded area and erupted into flames, its main undercarriage down on impact but nose gear still retracted.

Although the crash itself was totally survivable, the post-impact fire – specifically, the effects of carbon monoxide poisoning – resulted in 77 fatalities. Only the pilot-in-command and the regular flight engineer, both of whom were injured, survived. It was dark at the time of the accident, but

The fiery crash of this Imperial Airlines Constellation killed 77 persons, most of whom were army recruits. (Wide World Photos)

the meteorological conditions were good.

The disaster was attributed to a lack of command co-ordination and decision, as illustrated by the action of the first officer in changing runways; faulty judgement; and insufficient knowledge of the equipment, which created an emergency situation that the crew could not handle.

In addition to the lack of competence in the cockpit, other irregularities were identified in the company's operations. These included the finding of rust in the fuel system of *N2737A* and in the truck that had serviced it. And although the contamination was not considered a causative factor in the multiple engine failure, it did reflect a lack of compliance with civil air regulations by Imperial Airlines. As a result, the US Federal Aviation Agency (FAA) revoked the carrier's operating certificate some six weeks after the crash.

Date: 1 March 1962 (10:08)
Location: New York, New York, US
Operator: American Airlines (US)
Aircraft type: Boeing 707-123B (*N7506A*)

Operating as Flight 1, the jetliner took off from Runway 31L at New York International Airport on a domestic transcontinental service to Los Angeles, California. Following one left turn, the 707 began a second, back towards the south-east, but instead of levelling off it continued rolling to port until it was inverted. Then, from an approximate height of 1,500 ft (500 m) and less than 2 minutes after becoming airborne, the aircraft plunged into Jamaica Bay, disintegrating on impact and bursting into flames. All 95 persons aboard (87 passengers and a crew of eight) perished.

Its undercarriage and flaps fully retracted, the jetliner had crashed in the shallow waters of Pumpkin Patch Channel during low tide and at a speed of about 230 mph (370 kmh), leaving a crater some 10 ft (3 m) deep on the bottom of the bay. Much of the debris was buried and had to be excavated from the mud.

The condition of both the wreckage and bodies of the flight crew somewhat hampered the probe into the tragedy by the US Civil Aeronautics Board (CAB). There was, however, no evidence of in-flight fire or explosion, incapacitation of the pilots or malfunction in the aircraft's aileron control system. The weather at the time was excellent, with high, scattered clouds and a visibility of 15 miles (c 25 km).

Examination did, however, reveal anomalies in the rudder control system of the 707. Wires were found to be frayed or severed in the voltage rate generator of the rudder servo unit, a device designed to convert electrical signals from the automatic flight control system into proportional mechanical forces to adjust the vertical control surface. There were also scratches or gouges on the sleeving enclosing the wires. This apparently did not occur on impact, because similar damage was found in other units still on the production line. It was concluded that the damage resulted from the improper use of tweezers when tying the wire bundles to the motor housing. In its investigative report, the CAB expressed the opinion that the wires were weakened to the point that vibration and other disturbances eventually caused their final separation.

An American Airlines Boeing 707-123B, identical to the aircraft that crashed after take-off from New York International Airport. (American Airlines)

The shattered remains of the 707 continue to burn on the surface of Jamaica Bay following the accident that took 95 lives. (Wide World Photos)

As established by testing, the crossing or otherwise short-circuiting of the wires could cause a 'hard-over' signal by the yaw damper, a mechanism designed to sense the onset of a lateral control abnormality and automatically adjust the rudder, and of which the servo is a component. In the case of *N7506A*, it apparently resulted in an unexpected rudder deflection to the left, producing yaw, sideslip and roll that in turn led to a loss of control. The reason the crew allowed the aircraft to fall into the stall regime may have been due to a combination of factors, including the initial masking of the control problem by turbulence; difficulty in recognising the situation because of less reliance on instrument references in the visual meteorological conditions; an unintentional nose-high attitude occurring as the crew struggled with the controls; the absence of the stick shaker warning indication prior to the initiation of the stall buffet; or the continued operation of the malfunctioning yaw damper. There was also speculation that the pilot's attempt to maintain the specified flight path, which included turns for the purpose of noise abatement and avoiding the traffic pattern of nearby La Guardia Airport, could have been a factor in the accident by preventing a smooth climb-out of the departing aircraft.

There were also indications that, in an attempt to regain control, the crew had throttled back the two port engines, then disengaged the yaw damper and deactivated the rudder boost system.

Differing with the findings of the CAB, the US Federal Aviation Agency (FAA) concluded that the disaster probably resulted from the loss of an improperly installed bolt from the 707's hydraulic boost system. As a consequence, control of the system was lost, causing the rudder to deflect to the full limits of its range, producing a similar yawing action to that which would have been produced by a servo malfunction. The CAB did note in its report that such an occurrence could have been the initiating abnormality that led to the crash.

Despite its own hypothesis as to the cause, the accident prompted the FAA to issue an airworthiness directive requiring the inspection of servo rate generator motors of the type used on *N7506A* to check for damaged wire bundles.

Date: 4 March 1962 (c 19:20)
Location: Near Douala, Cameroun
Operator: Caledonian Airways (UK)
Aircraft type: Douglas DC-7C (*G-ARUD*)

All 111 persons aboard (101 passengers and 10 crew members) perished when the aircraft, which had been leased from the Belgian airline SABENA and was being operated by Caledonian on behalf of Trans-Africa Air Coach Ltd, crashed about a minute after taking off from Runway 12 at Douala Airport, bound for Lisbon, Portugal, its next en route stop during a charter service to Luxembourg from Lourenço Marques (now Maputo), Mozambique.

Following an unusually long take-off ground run, the DC-7C appeared to gain altitude with difficulty. Flying nearly level longitudinally and banked slightly to the left, the transport first struck trees approximately 1.5 miles (2.5 km) beyond the end of the runway, some 1,500 ft (500 m) to the left of its extended centreline and only about 65 ft (20 m) above its elevation, then slammed into a swamp, disintegrated and burned. At the moment of impact its undercarriage was in the up position, and its flaps were also retracted or nearly so, though there were indications that the crew had tried to re-extend them after observing some abnormality. The accident occurred on a dark, moonless night, and the meteorological conditions at the time consisted of a low, broken overcast, with 3/8 fracto-cumulus clouds at approximately 1,300 ft (400 m), 2/8 strato-cumulus at about 2,000 ft (600 m), and a visibility of around 10 miles (15 km). There was also light rain and thunderstorm activity in the area.

The aircraft's starboard elevator spring tab was found to be jammed, and the investigative commission concluded that this could have happened prior to the crash. A spring tab is designed to reduce the efforts of the pilot, especially when operating at higher air speeds. In this case such a jamming could have increased by up to three times the amount of pull force on the control column required to carry out a successful rotation. This would also account for the long take-off ground run and could have led to a negative rate of climb.

Had it occurred, the mechanical malfunction may have been aggravated by a climb technique adopted by the carrier that emphasised gaining speed and could, in turn, result in flight at a low altitude; by the fact that the flap retraction procedure utilised by the airline did not stipulate a minimum height for such other than that needed for obstacle clearance; and by the presence in the first officer's seat of a check pilot, whose attention might have been directed more towards the captain than the indications of his own instruments. A defect in some flight instrument, such as the pilot's flight director or the emergency artificial horizon, was not completely eliminated by the commission as a possible cause of the accident, though this would not have explained the decision of the crew to re-extend the flaps.

Subsequently the manufacturer designed a modification in the spring tab mechanism used on this type aircraft to eliminate the possibility of accidental jamming. Safety improvements were also made at Douala Airport, with the installation of three white lights at an approximate height of 130 ft

(40 m) and about 4 miles (6.5 km) from the runway threshold to provide a visual fix along the centreline.

Date: 16 March 1962 (c 00:30)
Location: Philippine Sea
Operator: The Flying Tiger Line Inc (US)
Aircraft type: Lockheed 1049H Super Constellation (*N6921C*)

The four-engine transport was en route from Guam to the Philippines, one segment of a transpacific service originating at Travis Air Force Base, California, US, with an ultimate destination of Saigon (Ho Chi Minh City) in (then) South Vietnam, being conducted under contract to the US Military Air Transport Service (MATS). It was carrying 93 US and three South Vietnamese service personnel plus a civilian crew of 11 Americans, a total of 107 persons.

Cruising in darkness and, apparently, good weather conditions, with scattered clouds, the aircraft was last reported at an altitude of 18,000 ft (c 5,500 m). There was no indication of any difficulty in its final radio transmission, but when the Super Constellation failed to arrive at Clark Air Force Base, located near Manila, a search was begun that went on for more than a week, involving nearly 50 aircraft and eight vessels and covering 144,000 square miles (c 230,000 sq km) of open sea. But no trace of it was ever found.

Members of a ship's crew had reported seeing an explosion in the sky from which two flaming objects appeared to fall into the ocean, at the approximate time and location where *N6921C* was believed to have been, ie some 800 miles (1,300 km) east of the Philippines and in an area where the depth of the water ranged from 2 to 3 miles (c 3–5 km).

In its investigative report, the US Civil Aeronautics Board (CAB) concluded that they had probably witnessed the catastrophic demise of the airliner. But whether it was a victim of mechanical or structural failure, sabotage, or some other adverse factor, could not be determined due to a lack of tangible evidence.

Date: 22 May 1962 (c 21:15)
Location: Near Unionville, Missouri, US
Operator: Continental Air Lines (US)
Aircraft type: Boeing 707-124 (*N70775*)

Designated as Flight 11, the jetliner was en route from Chicago, Illinois, to Kansas City, Missouri, the first segment of a domestic service scheduled to terminate at Los Angeles, California, when it crashed along the Iowa/Missouri border, killing all 45 persons aboard (37 passengers and a crew of eight). One passenger was found alive in the wreckage but succumbed to injuries about 1½ hours after his rescue.

Flying in darkness and clear meteorological conditions at an approximate height of 37,000 ft (11,300 m), the aircraft had just circumnavigated some thunderstorm activity when it was rocked by an explosion, and shortly afterward disintegrated. The major part of it fell into a field about 5 miles (10 km) north-north-west of Unionville, though pieces were found over a path 40 miles (c 65 km) long in a north-easterly direction, and some light debris was found up to 120 miles (c 190 km) away from the main wreckage area.

Early suspicions of foul play were soon proven when the US Federal Bureau of Investigation (FBI) established that dynamite had been detonated within the fuselage of the 707, apparently in the used towel bin underneath the wash basin in its right rear lavatory. Following the blast, the crew must have initiated an emergency descent, donning smoke masks and lowering the undercarriage, but the aircraft broke up at a high altitude. Losing the aft 38 ft (11.5 m) of its fuselage, the jetliner pitched down, causing most of its left wing, the outer portion of its right wing and all four engines to break off.

The bomb was believed to have been carried aboard by a passenger in a suicide-for-insurance plot, with his wife named as the beneficiary. In the process he committed the first successful sabotage of a commercial jet.

Date: 3 June 1962 (c 12:35)
Location: Villeneuve-le-Roi, Val-de-Marne
　France
Operator: Air France
Aircraft type: Boeing 707-328 (*F-BHSM*)

The jet airliner was on a charter service to the United States, bound for Atlanta, Georgia, via New York City. Except for one Frenchman, its passengers were all Americans returning home from a tour of Europe sponsored by the Atlanta Art Association.

Using Runway 08, the 707 began its take-off from Orly Airport, located just outside Paris. Accelerating normally, it commenced rotation, and its nose remained slightly raised for about 5 seconds until dropping back to the ground when the brakes were applied, the jet reaching a speed of approximately 200 mph (320 kmh) but never becoming airborne. Thick smoke streamed from its wheels as the crew tried to bring the 707 to a halt, and its path then curved to the right, suggesting a desperate attempt to ground-loop. However, the aircraft ran off the end of the runway while still travelling along its centreline. Rolling on to grass, its main undercarriage was torn off, the left gear first, and after hitting the approach lights the jet began to break apart. Striking a house and garage, it finally came to rest some 1,500 ft (500 m) beyond the end of the runway. Fire, which had erupted during the ground slide, soon engulfed the main part of the wreckage. The accident killed 130 persons aboard the 707, including eight crew members. Two stewardesses seated in the rear of its cabin survived with injuries.

The aircraft's horizontal stabiliser was found to be improperly trimmed, specifically at a setting of 1.5 units nose-up; this was slightly more than 2 units towards the nose-down position. Such a condition would have produced resistance on the control column at the time of rotation and

The main portion of the Continental Air Lines Boeing 707 lies in a field after an in-flight break-up attributed to a bomb blast. (UPI/ Bettmann)

The crash of this Air France Boeing 707 near Paris killed 130 persons after an aborted take-off from Orly Airport. (UPI/Bettmann)

lift-off that may have seemed prohibitive to the pilot-in-command, even to the point that he believed the stabiliser to be jammed.

An investigative board concluded that the incorrect setting resulted from the failure of the trim servo motor, which would also have prevented the crew from rectifying the problem. However, the cause of the malfunction could not be determined. The pilot may have tried to identify the source of the trouble before he abandoned the take-off, but by then it was too late to stop or even slow down on the remaining runway.

Tests revealed that the 707 could have taken off safely despite the out-of-trim condition, although the captain lacked the data required to make a decision in such a short period of time.

The weather conditions at the time on this Sunday, consisting of scattered clouds and good visibility, were not considered a factor in the disaster.

Date: 22 June 1962 (04:01)
Location: Basse-Terre, Guadeloupe, West Indies
Operator: Air France
Aircraft type: Boeing 707-328 (*F-BHST*)

Operating as Flight 117, the jet airliner crashed some 15 miles (25 km) west-north-west of Le Raizet Airport, serving Pointe-a-Pitre, on Grande-Terre, where it was to have landed, one of six en route stops during a service from Paris to Santiago, Chile. All 113 persons aboard (103 passengers and a crew of 10) perished.

Shortly before the accident, the 707 reported passing over the Pointe-a-Pitre non-directional beacon (NDB) at 5,000 ft (c 1,500 m). It then executed a turn back towards the east to begin its final approach. The aircraft was about 10 miles (15 km) off the procedural let-down track when it slammed into a tropical forest on a hill at an approximate elevation of 1,500 ft (500 m) near the town of Sainte-Rose, its undercarriage still retracted at the moment of impact. Some of the wreckage did burn, but there was no major post-crash fire. It was dark at the time and the weather conditions consisted of violent thunderstorm activity, with a visibility of around 5 miles (10 km) and a ceiling of about 1,000 ft (300 m) within the squall and 300-500 ft (100–150 m) higher to the east of that area.

The disaster was attributed to the following

sequence of events: 1) break-down of the very-high-frequency omni-directional range (VOR) station at Pointe-a-Pitre (the pilot of the 707 had expressed concern over the fact that the navigational aid was unserviceable in radio communications with the control tower prior to the crash); 2) insufficient meteorological information given the flight; and 3) an incorrect automatic direction finder (ADF) indication due to the effects of the poor atmospheric conditions.

A precision approach would not have been possible because the airport had no instrument landing system (ILS). It does today, providing an extra measure of security to arriving aircraft.

Date: 30 June 1962 (time unknown)
Location: Near Krasnoyarsk, Russian Soviet
Federated Socialist Republic, USSR
Operator: Aeroflot (USSR)
Aircraft type: Tupolev Tu-104A (*SSSR-42340*)

The jetliner crashed and burned on a scheduled domestic service from Irkutsk to Omsk, and all 84 persons aboard (76 passengers and eight crew members) perished.

Cruising at about 29,000 ft (9,000 m) in daylight and instrument meteorological conditions, the aircraft went into an uncontrolled descent; at an approximate height of 2,600 ft (800 m) above the ground, it began to rotate, and subsequently plunged to earth in a clean configuration with both engines operating.

An investigative commission was unable to determine the cause of the crash, though special research could not identify any mechanical failures prior to impact.

Date: 7 July 1962 (c 00:15)
Location: Near Junnar, Maharashtra, India
Operator: Alitalia (Italy)
Aircraft type: Douglas DC-8 Series 43 (*I-DIWD*)

Originating at Sydney, Australia, Flight 771 was to have made six en route stops during a service scheduled to terminate at Rome, Italy. Following its departure from Bangkok, Thailand, the DC-8 proceeded on towards India, with a planned landing at Santa Cruz Airport, serving Bombay. Cleared for descent to 4,000 ft (c 1,200 m), the pilot was granted permission to make a 360-degree turn over the outer marker. There were no further communications with the flight.

The jet airliner crashed into a hill at an approximate elevation of 3,600 ft (1,100 m), only about 5 ft (1.5 m) from the top, some 50 miles (100 km) east-north-east of the airport and at a position that was about 5 miles (10 km) to the left of the proper track. All 94 persons aboard (85 passengers and a crew of nine) were killed. There were localised fires in the wreckage but no major post-impact blaze. The accident occurred in darkness and instrument weather conditions, with light rain reported by witnesses.

An Indian investigative court attributed the disaster to a navigational error that led to the false impression on the part of the pilot that he was closer to his destination than was actually the case, which in turn resulted in a premature descent below the obstructing terrain. This hypothesis was bolstered by his request to circle over the outer marker, which indicated that he believed the flight to be in close proximity to that navigational aid. There were also indications that, despite his stated intention, the captain had elected to execute a straight-in approach to Runway 27. Considered by the court as contributing factors were the failure of the pilot to make use of the available navigational facilities in order to ascertain his position; infringement of the minimum safe altitude; and his unfamiliarity with the terrain along this particular route.

The airline blamed the crash on 'defective, wrong and incomplete' clearance given by the approach controller. It said that there should have been no such clearance while the DC-8 was still outside the control zone. The company further asserted that air traffic control in the Bombay area was 'poorly organised, constituting a hazard to international aircraft'. Indian authorities disputed the accusations, stating that terrain clearance was the responsibility of pilots, not air traffic controllers, and noted that, in descending below 4,000 ft, the Italian pilot had even disregarded the clearance limit.

Date: 28 July 1962 (time unknown)
Location: Near Adler, Russian Soviet Federated
Socialist Republic, USSR
Operator: Aeroflot (USSR)
Aircraft type: Antonov An-10A (*SSSR-11186*)

The four-engine turboprop crashed and burned near the Adler airport, where it was to have landed during a scheduled domestic service from L'vov, Ukraine, killing all 81 persons aboard (74 passengers and seven crew members).

Cleared by the approach controller for descent down to about 5,000 ft (1,500 m), the airliner slammed into a mountainside at an approximate elevation of 2,000 ft (600 m), its undercarriage and flaps still retracted at the moment of impact. The accident occurred in daylight and instrument meteorological conditions, with a cloud base of about 2,000 ft (600 m), and with the flight not visible on ground radar due to the 'shadow' effect of the mountains.

Combining as causative factors in this crash were the introduction by the air traffic control service of changes in the approach pattern at the Adler airport without approval by state aviation authorities and without informing the flight units about these changes, and inadequacies in the areas of flight control and crew training in operations there and on the part of authorities over training for flights in mountainous regions in general.

Date: 2 September 1962 (time unknown)
Location: Near Khabarovsk, Russian Soviet
  Federated Socialist Republic, USSR
Operator: Aeroflot (USSR)
Aircraft type: Tupolev Tu-104A (*SSSR-42366*)

The jetliner crashed and burned about 10 minutes after it had taken off from the Khabarovsk airport, on a scheduled domestic service to Petropavlovsk-Kamchatskiy, located on Kamchatka. All 86 persons aboard (79 passengers and a crew of seven) perished.

As the twin-engine jet was climbing at a height of about 15,000 ft (5,000 m), the crew radioed to the air traffic controller that it had begun shaking, and was experiencing uncontrolled roll and yaw. They also reported a 'grey-green cloud' near the aircraft. The subsequent crash occurred at night and in instrument meteorological conditions.

With the flight data recorder (FDR) having been destroyed in the crash, the investigative commission had no objective data from which it could reconstruct the development of the abnormal situation. The cause was therefore undetermined. Examination of the wreckage did not disclose any pre-impact failures in the aircraft or its systems.

Date: 27 November 1962 (c 03:40)
Location: Surco District, Department of Lima, Peru
Operator: SA Empresa de Viacao Aerea Rio
  Grandense (VARIG) (Brazil)
Aircraft type: Boeing 707-441 (*PP-VJB*)

Designated as Flight 810, on a service that had originated at Porto Alegre, Rio Grande do Sul, Brazil, with an ultimate destination of Los Angeles, California, US, the jet airliner was preparing for a scheduled landing at the Lima-Callao airport when it crashed some 15 miles (25 km) south of the capital city. All 97 persons aboard (80 passengers and 17 crew members) perished.

The aircraft had initiated an overshoot procedure at the suggestion of approach control because it was too high on its first attempt to land. It then passed over the airport while turning to the left and assumed a southerly heading before initiating a 180-degree turn required for interception of the instrument landing system (ILS) back course to Runway 33.

However, the 707 continued on in a north-north-easterly direction for almost 3 minutes, proceeding through the northbound course, and was on a heading of 333 degrees when it struck La Cruz Peak, which rises to about 2,500 ft (750 m), exploding on impact. At the time of the crash, the aircraft was flying nearly straight and level, with its main undercarriage extended (the position of the nose gear could not be determined).

It was dark at the time of the accident, being before dawn, and the weather conditions in the general vicinity consisted of a low overcast, specifically 8/8 stratus clouds at approximately 2,000 ft (600 m), with a visibility of about 10 miles (15 km) and a slight breeze from a direction of 200 degrees.

Although the cause of the deviation that led to the disaster could not be established, one possible theory centred on the instrument presentation of inaccurate navigational information.

Had the aircraft's automatic direction finder (ADF) equipment been tuned to the wrong non-directional beacon (NDB), and the Collins integral instrument incorrectly adjusted so as to confuse the exactly reversed front and back courses of the ILS, the crew would have been given an indication that the correct approach path was forward and to the right. In reality, an immediate left turn was needed to intercept the west side of the ILS back course.

An ADF indication of 90 degrees to the left, which would have occurred as the 707 continued on a heading of 12 degrees, could have convinced the crew that the ILS at the airport was not functioning properly. The aircraft had turned back just before the accident took place, approximately 8 miles (13 km) east of the proper approach track.

Date: 1 February 1963 (c 17:15)
Location: Ankara, Turkey
First aircraft
Operator: Middle East Airlines (Lebanon)
Type: Vickers Viscount 754 (*OD-ADE*)
Second aircraft
Operator: Turkish Air Force
Type: Douglas C-47 (*CBK-28*)

Flight 265 was nearing the end of a service from Nicosia, Cyprus, as it prepared for a scheduled landing at Ankara's Esenboga Airport. It was carrying a relatively light load, with only 11 of its passenger seats filled plus a crew of three. Proceeding under instrument flight rules (IFR), the four-engine turboprop was cleared for a non-directional beacon (NDB) procedure approach, the crew lowering the undercarriage and extending the flaps. Meanwhile, *CBK-28* was returning to Etimesgut Airport under visual flight rules (VFR), its three crew members (and only occupants) having completed a training mission.

The collision of commercial and military transports over Ankara wreaked havoc after both aircraft fell into the city. (Wide World Photos)

The two aircraft collided and fell separately into the city, touching off fires and destroying or damaging numerous buildings, houses and vehicles. I ⸱ ᵗhe carnage, 87 persons on the ground were killed addition to the 17 aboard, and 50 others suffered juries. The collision had occurred at a height of under 7,000 ft (c 2,000 m), shortly before sunset and in what eye-witnesses described as a 'cloudless' sky. Visibility was reportedly in excess of 10 miles (15km).

Overtaking the military transport from behind and at an angle of about 40 degrees, the crew of the airliner apparently did not see the C-47 until the last moment, when a pull-up manoeuvre was made, but to no avail. The nose and right wing of the Viscount first struck the C-47, then the former's right inboard propeller sliced off the latter's left horizontal stabiliser. A portion of the fuselage skin on the starboard side of the airliner was torn off, and some of the passengers tumbled out. At the time of impact, the Viscount had been descending on a heading of about 280 degrees and at an estimated air speed of around 150 mph (250 kmh), and the C-47 descending in a clean configuration on a heading of approximately 240 degrees and at an estimated air speed of 140 mph (225 kmh).

Representing the nation of registry of the airliner, the Lebanese Directorate of Civil Aviation expressed reservations about the accident report, which it said did not take into account 'all the important elements' that could have caused or contributed to the collision. One of these was that the Turkish investigative commission did not consider the presence of a military flight training zone extending into the holding and approach pattern allocated to civil aircraft without any co-ordination or direct contact between the military and civilian air traffic control units.

Also questioned was the meteorological information given in the report, which may not have been accurate. The crew of a US Air Force C-130 transport had in fact reported 6/10 cloud coverage at 5,000 ft (c 1,500 m) and a visibility of only 5 miles (10 km) over the Ankara NDB, as was noted in the Turkish report.

Date: 3 June 1963 (c 10:15)
Location: North Pacific Ocean
Operator: Northwest Airlines (US)
Aircraft type: Douglas DC-7C (*N290*)

The aircraft was being flown under contract to the US Military Air Transport Service (MATS) and was en route from McChord Air Force Base, located near Tacoma, Washington state, to Elmendorf Air Force Base, Anchorage, Alaska. Most of its passengers were service personnel and their dependents.

In its last known message, the crew asked whether the aircraft could ascend from its cruising altitude of 14,000 ft (c 4,300 m) to 18,000 ft (c 5,500 m); no reason was given. The Canadian radio operator replied that the requested height was already occupied by a Pacific Northern Airlines flight. Less than 10 min later, the DC-7C plunged into the sea some 130 miles (210 km) west-south-west of Annette Island, Alaska, and about 50 miles (80 km) off the north-western tip of the (Canadian) Queen Charlotte Islands, and all 101 persons aboard, including a civilian crew of six, perished.

Subsequently, human remains and approximately 1,500 lb (700 kg) of debris, mostly cabin furnishings, personal effects and unused survival equipment, were recovered. But the depth of the ocean in the area, around 8,000 ft (2,500 m), precluded any attempt to recover the main wreckage.

The US Civil Aeronautics Board (CAB) concluded that the aircraft was probably intact when it crashed at a high rate of speed, apparently while in a nearly inverted attitude. There was no evidence of an in-flight explosion or fire, although a post-impact blaze apparently burned on the surface of the water.

According to a pilot flying the same route at about the same time, the weather was characterised by scattered clouds at different altitudes and light turbulence; the conditions were also conducive to icing. In fact, the request by the crew of *N290* to ascend could have been motivated by an encounter with either icing or turbulence. Between its last radio transmission and the crash, during which time it did not respond to any calls, the crew may have been preoccupied by an emergency situation or experienced trouble with the communications equipment, possibly due to static (as was reported by the other pilot). However, due to the lack of evidence the cause of the disaster could not be determined.

Date: 28 July 1963 (c 01:50)
Location: Off Bandra, Maharashtra, India
Operator: United Arab Airlines (Egypt)
Aircraft type: de Havilland Comet 4C (*SU-ALD*)

Operating as Flight 869 and on a service from Tokyo, Japan, to Cairo, Egypt, the jetliner crashed in the Arabian Sea some 10 miles (15 km) off shore while preparing to land at Santa Cruz Airport, serving Bombay, which was a scheduled stop. All 63 persons aboard (55 passengers and eight crew members) perished.

The pilot had been granted permission to make a left-hand, instead of the normal right-hand, procedural turn, then proceeded out over the ocean on the westbound leg of the let-down track, which was contrary to instructions from approach control.

It was dark at the time and meteorological conditions at the airport were adverse with rain, 3/8 cloud coverage at approximately 800 ft (250 m) and 6/8 at about 8,000 ft (2,500 m), and a visibility of around 2 miles (3 km).

Only three bodies and bits of wreckage were recovered, hampering attempts to determine the cause of the tragedy. However, from the facts available it was concluded that the pilot must have lost control of the aircraft while turning in an area of severe turbulence and heavy rain resulting in a high-speed impact with the water.

Date: 4 September 1963 (c 07:20)
Location: Durrenasch, Aargau, Switzerland
Operator: Swissair AG
Aircraft type: Sud-Aviation Caravelle III (*HB-ICV*)

Prior to departure from Zurich-Kloten Airport, the pilot of the aircraft was authorised to taxi half-way down Runway 34, probably using the engines to disperse the fog that hung low over the area at the time. Returning to the beginning of the runway, the Caravelle, which was designated as Flight 306, took off for Geneva, the domestic segment of an international service scheduled to terminate at Rome, Italy.

Less than 10 min later, the jet airliner plunged to earth and exploded some 15 miles (25 km) west-south-west of Zurich and frighteningly close to two farmhouses, leaving a crater approximately 65 ft (20 m) in diameter and about 20 ft (6 m) deep. All 80 persons aboard, including a crew of six, perished in the disaster.

Fragments of the aircraft's No 4 left main gear wheel and tyre were found on and beyond the end of the runway. The wheel flange had apparently split as the jet was being positioned for take-off, causing the corresponding tyre to explode, apparently due to overheating in the brake system. Fire then erupted, probably when fuel lines were damaged in the blast, and the volatile liquid came in contact with the overheated brake components.

It was considered possible that the similarly stressed No 3 wheel had ruptured after the Caravelle had become airborne, causing more damage and, in turn, an in-flight fire. More likely, however, was that the blaze known to have started on the ground in the No 4 wheel continued to burn following gear retraction, then ignited the No 3, causing its failure. Whatever the case, the flames must have spread rearward, resulting in serious damage. The aircraft's electrical system apparently malfunctioned, and its flight control and hydraulic systems as well as its structural integrity could also have been adversely affected by the fire. Additionally there was a loss of power in its left engine, which might have resulted from either deliberate action by the crew or to interruption of its fuel supply.

Reaching a maximum altitude of approximately 9,000 ft (2,700 m), the jet began to descend while on a south-westerly heading, and during this period of time the crew transmitted a 'Mayday' distress message. Before it crashed, the Caravelle shed

The ground impact of the Swissair Caravelle left a crater and damaged adjacent houses. (Swiss Federal Aircraft Accident Investigation Bureau)

numerous parts, including a portion of the left wing and rear fuselage, which ultimately must have led to a loss of control.

The overheating was most probably caused by intentional braking on the part of the pilot as the aircraft taxied down the runway. However, the possibility of unintentional braking action resulting from a mechanical defect or irregularity could not be ruled out, even though there was no evidence of any such condition.

Among the passengers on the flight were 43 inhabitants of Humilkon, a Swiss village with a population of only about 200.

Date: 29 November 1963 (c 18:30)
Location: Near Sainte Therese de Blainville, Quebec, Canada
Operator: Trans-Canada Air Lines
Aircraft type: Douglas DC-8 Series 54F (*CF-TJN*)

The jetliner, which was operating as Flight 831 on a domestic service to Toronto, Ontario, plunged to earth about 5 minutes after taking off from Dorval Airport, serving Montreal, disintegrating and erupting into flames on impact. All 118 persons aboard (111 passengers and seven crew members) perished. A water-filled crater marked the scene of the crash, some 10 miles (15 km) north-west of Montreal and approximately 15 miles (25 km) from the airport. The accident occurred in darkness and during a fog and light rain, with a breeze out of the north-east of 12 mph (c 20 kmh) and a visibility of 4 miles (c 6.5 km).

The DC-8, which had taken off from Runway 06 and then begun a left turn before disappearing from the airport radar screen, was in a clean configuration and on a north-north-westerly heading when it crashed at a steep angle. At the time of impact, its velocity was calculated to have been between 540 and 560 mph (870–900 kmh).

Examination of the wreckage revealed that the horizontal stabiliser was set at an angle of between 1.65 and 2 degrees nose-down trim and had been moved to that position by hydraulic power, factors that proved very significant. It was concluded that this setting, which would be unusual on an aircraft climbing out from take-off, resulted from action, apparently intentional, by the flight crew.

A number of theories were explored by the investigative commission, but the one considered

A water-filled crater marks the scene of the Trans-Canada Air Lines DC-8 disaster that took 118 lives. (National Archives of Canada)

'most probable' as causing the disaster was the unprogrammed extension of the aircraft's pitch trim compensator. This would have had the effect of moving the control column back and the elevators up, resulting in a nose-high attitude. The pilot would likely have counteracted this condition by trimming the stabiliser to or near to the limit of the nose-down setting, inadvertently creating an adverse effect on the stability of the jetliner and placing it in a diving descent. As its velocity increased, the force required to pull back on the control column would have become prohibitive. Recovery could, however, still have been made by re-trimming the horizontal stabiliser, but at a high rate of speed the activating motor might not be able to overcome the high aerodynamic forces.

Under the circumstances, the only possibility for recovery would have been to release pressure on the control column, thereby relieving the forces being applied to the empennage and unstalling the hydraulic motor so the stabiliser could be moved. Such action would, of course, have momentarily worsened the situation by actually steepening the descent and increasing the air speed. The upset in this case was believed to have occurred at an approximate height of 6,000 ft (c 1,800 m), which would not have been sufficient to carry out such a procedure.

Though not severe, existing turbulence could have contributed to the accident by affecting the attitude of the aircraft, minor changes that could have built up into large displacements. An aggravating factor was that the jetliner had been flying at night and in cloud, and its pilots would thus have been without visual reference to either the ground or the horizon.

There were two other possible reasons for the crew to have applied nose-down trim. The first was that icing of the pitot system had caused an erroneously low air speed reading, prompting the pilot to lower the nose of the aircraft to increase velocity. The second possibility was an inaccurate artificial horizon indication due to failure of the associated vertical gyro or a loss of power, leading to the same action. Despite their weaknesses, neither of these two theories could be entirely dismissed.

There was no evidence of structural failure, malfunction of the engines, flight controls or any other major system, collision with another object, in-flight explosion or fire, or incapacitation of the crew.

The recommendation that turbine-powered commercial transports be fitted with flight data recorders, made by the commission in its report on the crash of *CF-TJN*, would later become a requirement for such aircraft registered in Canada.

Date: 8 December 1963 (20:59)
Location: Near Elkton, Maryland, US
Operator: Pan American World Airways (US)
Aircraft type: Boeing 707-121 (*N709PA*)

Originating at San Juan, Puerto Rico, Flight 214 had stopped at Baltimore, Maryland, before proceeding on towards its ultimate destination of Philadelphia, Pennsylvania. The crew advised that it would hold for landing, along with five other aircraft, until high winds had subsided at Philadelphia International Airport. During a routine conversation between the approach controller and a National Airlines DC-8, a distress message was heard from the 707, believed to be 'Mayday . . . Mayday . . . Mayday . . . Clipper two one four out of control. Here we go!'

Trying to contact the Pan American flight, the controller got a reply from the DC-8, its co-pilot stating that 'Clipper two fourteen is going down in flames'.

Spinning uncontrollably, the jet airliner plunged into a cornfield between Elkton and the Delaware border and disintegrated in a fiery explosion. All 81 persons aboard (73 passengers and a crew of eight) perished. The weather in the area of the crash was described as cloudy, with thunderstorm activity and light rain.

Scores of witnesses observed lightning in the night sky, and several reported seeing one bolt hit the 707. Examination of the wreckage revealed an irregularly-shaped hole about 1.5 in (5 mm) in diameter and numerous small lustrous craters in its left wing tip, confirming that the aircraft had indeed been struck.

By eliminating all other conceivable causes, the US Civil Aeronautics Board (CAB) concluded that lightning had precipitated the accident by igniting the fuel/air mixture in the left reserve tank, or possibly in the left surge tank or even at the vent outlet. The resulting explosion blew apart the port outer wing structure as the 707 was in a holding pattern at an altitude of 5,000 ft (c 1,500 m), causing an immediate loss of control. Prior to its impact with the ground, all four engines broke off due to excessive forces imposed during the fall, and large fires were observed on both wings, attributed to secondary explosions in other fuel tanks.

The exact mechanics of ignition remained a mystery, but, as noted in the investigative report, many strange phenomena have been associated with lightning. Among these are 'streamers' induced by the intense electric field within a storm that extend out from the extremities of an aircraft and toward an approaching lightning stroke, which have sufficient energy to ignite fuel vapours. Other potential sources of ignition are plasma, shock waves and sparking.

Within two weeks of this accident, the US Federal Aviation Agency (FAA) made a recommendation for the installation of lightning discharge wicks on all commercial jet transports

registered in the country, and later issued airworthiness directives requiring modification of the fuel tank access door and the thickening of the skin covering the wing tips on Boeing jets. In 1967 the FAA took further action to reduce the lightning threat by ordering the installation on certain models of the 707 and its close relative, the 720, of either a system designed to extinguish automatically any flame propagating through the fuel tank outlets, or auxiliary vents that would prevent the accumulation of fuel vapours in the regular ones. (Research conducted subsequent to the CAB inquiry indicated that in the case of *N709PA* the vapours probably did ignite in a fuel vent.)

Also due to this and other crashes the airline industry began phasing out use of JP-4 jet fuel and switching to the less volatile kerosene.

Date: 25 February 1964 (02:05)
Location: Near New Orleans, Louisiana, US
Operator: Eastern Air Lines (US)
Aircraft type: Douglas DC-8 Series 21 (*N8607*)

Designated as Flight 304, the jetliner took off from New Orleans International (Moisant) Airport, bound for Atlanta, Georgia, its next scheduled stop during a service from Mexico City to New York City. Approximately 5 minutes later, the DC-8 crashed in Lake Pontchartrain, some 20 miles (30 km) north-east of the airport, and all 58

A portion of the fuselage is the only recognisable part of the Pan American World Airways Boeing 707 after its crash in a cornfield. (UPI/Bettmann)

persons aboard (51 passengers and seven crew members) perished. The disaster occurred in early morning darkness and instrument meteorological conditions. At the airport at around this time there was a ceiling of 1,000 ft (c 300 m), a visibility of around 5 miles (10 km), turbulence and a 12-knot wind out of the west.

Subsequently, about 60 per cent of the aircraft's wreckage, located in water some 20 ft (6 m) deep, was recovered from the bottom of the lake. The DC-8 had disintegrated on impact, the largest piece found being a 5 ft (1.5 m) section of the rudder, and this, coupled with the fact that the pertinent portion of the flight data recorder (FDR) tape was not recovered, hampered the investigation of the disaster. However, by using the records of *N8607*, and by studying problems that had afflicted other DC-8s, the US Civil Aeronautics Board (CAB) was able to determine the probable sequence of events leading up to the crash.

Examination of its right and left jack-screws indicated that the aircraft's horizontal stabiliser was set in the full nose-down trim. Whether it had been placed that way intentionally or unintentionally by the crew, or resulted from a malfunction, such a setting following take-off was considered unusual.

The abnormal longitudinal trim component position coupled with moderate to severe wind shear-type turbulence that the flight was believed to have encountered probably caused a reduction in the aircraft's stability characteristics.

A review of its records disclosed a history of trouble with the pitch trim compensator (PTC) installed on *N8607* at the time of the accident. It had been removed from various aircraft 15 times over a four-year period, nearly half of these as a result of unprogrammed extensions. The unit was known to have been inoperative since the outbound flight to Mexico City the previous day. Numerous autopilot difficulties had also been reported on this particular DC-8, which could have resulted from such extensions.

Had the PTC actuator been partially or fully extended, it was likely that the pilots trimmed the stabiliser to the full-down position to counteract the nose-up attitude of the aircraft. This could have placed the DC-8 in a steep descent. Failure of the chain sprocket in the stabiliser drive mechanism must then have occurred, probably as the crew tried to apply nose-up trim. This malfunction could have led to either the introduction of a pilot-induced oscillation, or control input, resulting in a loss of

The flight path of the Eastern Air Lines DC-8 from take-off at New Orleans International Airport until its crash in Lake Pontchartrain. (Civil Aeronautics Board)

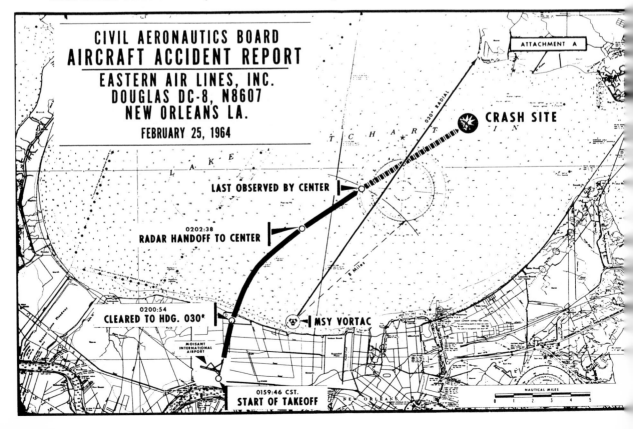

CIVIL AERONAUTICS BOARD
AIRCRAFT ACCIDENT REPORT
EASTERN AIR LINES, INC.
DOUGLAS DC-8, N8607
NEW ORLEANS LA.
FEBRUARY 25, 1964

ATTACHMENT A

CRASH SITE

LAST OBSERVED BY CENTER

0202:38
RADAR HANDOFF TO CENTER

0200:54
CLEARED TO HDG. 030°

MSY VORTAC

0159:46 CST.
START OF TAKEOFF

NAUTICAL MILES

control, or contributed to the failure to recover therefrom.

The upset probably took place at a height below 6,000 ft (c 1,800 m), which would not have allowed the pilots to effect full recovery. Examination of the engines indicated that the crew had employed reverse thrust in an attempt to arrest the descent, and almost succeeded, since the cleanly configured jetliner was believed to have been essentially level at the moment of impact.

Cases of misrigging in the PTC units of other DC-8s were discovered during the investigation into the crash of Flight 304 and it was concluded that maintenance personnel had installed a bushing upside-down in the one used on N8607. This would have caused the actuator to extend even farther.

Besides the mechanical failure and the adverse flying conditions, factors that may have played a role in the disaster were the aircraft's attitude indicator, which was difficult to interpret at night, and the unstable characteristics of the DC-8 itself at certain air speeds. In a related matter, it was determined that the functional tests used by Eastern and other carriers were incapable of detecting certain PTC computer malfunctions.

Several modifications in the Douglas transport were made and new maintenance and operating procedures implemented in the wake of this tragedy. These included a reduction in the nose-down travel of the aircraft's horizontal stabiliser and replacement of the PTC actuator bell-crank arm, the latter designed to improve longitudinal stability. There were also changes in the method of dealing with an inoperative PTC or an unwanted extension, and a warning light was installed to alert crews in the event of the latter condition.

Date: 29 February 1964 (c 15:15)
Location: Near Innsbruck, Austria
Operator: British Eagle International Airlines
Aircraft type: Bristol Britannia 312 (*G-AOVO*)

Flight 802 had originated at London's Heathrow Airport and was scheduled to land at Kranebitten Airport, serving Innsbruck. Upon arrival over its intended destination, clouds covered the area, and the conditions were in fact below the airline's minima for such a landing. But the pilot-in-command, a veteran who had flown into Innsbruck on nine previous occasions, decided against proceeding to an alternate airport.

The four-engine turboprop was first reported in the holding pattern above the Innsbruck very-high-frequency omni-directional range (VOR) station, the pilot stating that he could not break through the overcast. It was last reported at a height of 10,000 ft (c 3,000 m) before the air traffic control centre lost radio contact with the flight. Ground witnesses heard what was believed to have been the Britannia in or above the clouds around this time.

The following day, more than 18 hours later, its wreckage was found on a steep eastern slope of Glungezer Mountain, in the Alps, some 10 miles (15 km) east-south-east of the airport, itself located about 2.5 miles (4 km) west of the city. The aircraft had crashed at an approximate elevation of 8,500 ft (2,600 m), while in a slight nose-up attitude, with undercarriage retracted and flaps set at 15 degrees, and the impact precipitated an avalanche that carried most of the debris and victims' bodies more than 1,300 ft (400 m) down the mountainside. All 83 persons aboard (75 passengers and a crew of eight) were killed. An evasive pull-up manoeuvre may have been initiated an instant before impact; there was no post-crash fire. The mountain at the time was obscured by cloud, with snow flurries in the area.

It was concluded that the pilot had intentionally descended below the minimum safe altitude of 11,000 ft (c 3,300 m) in an apparent attempt to penetrate the overcast. A technical defect in the aircraft, altimeter error or an encounter with severe icing or turbulence were all ruled out. The flight continued to descend whilst making several turns over the mountains. In the final moments before the crash, the crew was flying without visual contact of the ground, in violation of Austrian regulations pertaining to the Innsbruck airport. At the time of the accident, the Britannia was on a westerly heading but neither in the airport circuit nor on landing approach.

Despite the prevailing conditions, other aircraft were operating in and out of the airport, and this may have been a factor in the erroneous decision by the pilot of Flight 802 to continue the descent.

One of the safety recommendations made in the investigative report was that operations conducted under visual flight rules (VFR) should not be allowed under any circumstances in instrument meteorological conditions.

Date: 1 March 1964 (c 11:30)
Location: Near Zephyr Cove, Nevada, US
Operator: Paradise Airlines (US)
Aircraft type: Lockheed 049 Constellation (*N86504*)

All 85 persons aboard (81 passengers and four crew members) were killed when the aircraft, operating as Flight 901A, crashed approximately 10 miles (15 km) north-east of Tahoe Valley Airport, located across the border in California, where it was to have landed at the end of an intra-state service from Salinas and San Jose.

It was snowing at the airport shortly before the Constellation arrived over the Lake Tahoe very-high-frequency omni-directional range (VOR) station, with a visibility of 3 miles (5 km) and a ceiling of 2,000 ft (c 600 m), conditions that were not conducive to visual flight rules (VFR)

The tail assembly of the British Eagle International Airlines Britannia lies in snow on Glungezer Mountain following the crash near Innsbruck. (Wide World Photos)

operations. However, the airport had no approved instrument flight rules (IFR) approach procedure. Nevertheless, the pilot attempted to land, and this deviation from the prescribed VFR procedures led to an unsuccessful approach and, subsequently, to 'geographical disorientation'. The aircraft was last seen proceeding out over Lake Tahoe in a northerly direction before it disappeared into a snowstorm.

The wreckage was located the following day on a snow-covered ridge of Genoa Peak, some 5 miles (10 km) east of the lake. Its undercarriage retracted but flaps extended, the Constellation was heading towards the east and in a nearly level attitude when initially it struck trees at an approximate elevation of 8,675 ft (2,650 m).

Under the circumstances, the captain should have either waited for the weather to improve or diverted to an alternate airport. In trying to land either without, or despite, knowledge of the existing meteorological conditions, he violated company policy. The crew may have attempted to fly through Daggett Pass and levelled off at what they believed to be a safe altitude. Or the aircraft might not have been able to climb any higher due to airframe icing, since *N86504* was not equipped to fly in such conditions.

Other factors that may have contributed to the accident were a discrepancy in the pilot's altimeter, which could have resulted in an erroneous height display of about 280 ft (85 m) too high; a possible error of 15 degrees or more in the aircraft's compass

system, and strong winds over the lake, which could have caused a drift towards the mountains. The procedures used by the general aviation carrier in reporting the weather were also considered unsatisfactory, and in this case the crew had been provided with a falsified meteorological report.

The crash came tragically close to being averted altogether. Had the Constellation been only 300 ft (c 100 m) higher or 1,000 ft (c 300 m) further south, it would have cleared the terrain safely and entered VFR conditions.

Date: 2 September 1964 (time unknown)
Location: Island of Sakhalin, USSR
Operator: Aeroflot (USSR)
Aircraft type: Ilyushin Il-18B (*SSSR-75531*)

The four-engine turboprop crashed near the Yuzhno-Sakhalinsk airport, where it was to have landed during a scheduled domestic service from Krasnoyarsk, RSFSR, and all 87 persons aboard (78 passengers and a crew of nine) lost their lives.

After they had insisted upon one, the crew was granted permission by the air traffic controller to make a direct approach without completing the standard traffic pattern. Subsequently, the airliner initiated a premature descent, then slammed into a wooded hillside at an approximate elevation of 2,000 ft (600 m) and caught fire, the accident occurring at night and in adverse weather conditions.

Blamed for the crash were the combined effects of the error by the controller, who lacked the availability of radar with which to monitor the flight, and of the crew, as well as inadequate knowledge of the approach conditions at this particular airport and poor in-flight planning on the part of the latter.

Date: 2 October 1964 (05:45)
Location: Near Trevelez, Granada, Spain
Operator: Union des Transports Aeriens (UTA) (France)
Aircraft type: Douglas DC 6B (*F-BHMS*)

The airliner was on a scheduled international service originating at Paris, with two en route stops and an ultimate destination of Port-Etienne, Mauritania. About 1½ hr after its departure from Palma de Mallorca, in the (Spanish) Balearic Islands, the transport slammed into a mountain at an approximate elevation of 7,000 ft (2,000 m) in the Sierra Nevada region, some 20 miles (30 km) south-east of the city of Granada. All 80 persons aboard (73 passengers and a crew of seven) perished in the crash, which occurred shortly before sunrise. Around the time of the accident, the weather conditions at Granada were good, with the sky clear and a visibility of between 5 and 10 miles (c 10–15 km).

The aircraft had deviated by about 5 degrees from, but flew at altitudes within the established safety margin for, the planned route. Since the autopilot error could be plus or minus 1 degree, the remaining 4 degrees may have been caused by the wind or some other undiscovered anomaly.

However, since no instruments or other components were found on which a technical investigation could be conducted, the cause of deviation could not be determined.

Date: 6 February 1965 (08:36)
Location: Near San Jose de Maipo, Santiago, Chile
Operator: Linea Aerea Nacional de Chile (LAN-Chile)
Aircraft type: Douglas DC-6B (*CC-CCG*)

Designated as Flight 107, the airliner crashed at an approximate elevation of 11,500 ft (3,500 m) in the Volcan Pass region of the Andes Mountains, some 30 miles (50 km) south-east of the capital city of Santiago, from where it had taken off earlier, bound for Buenos Aires, Argentina, and Montevideo, Uruguay. There was no fire, but the DC-6B disintegrated on impact, and all 87 persons aboard (80 passengers and seven crew members) perished.

An investigative board attributed the accident to a lack of discipline on the part of the pilot-in-command, who followed a route that was neither in accordance with the approved flight plan nor with the carrier's operations manual relating to crossing the mountains. The weather was not considered a factor.

Date: 8 February 1965 (18:26)
Location: Near New York, New York, US
Operator: Eastern Air Lines (US)
Aircraft type: Douglas DC-7B (*N849D*)

Flight 663 had taken off from John F. Kennedy International Airport bound for Richmond, Virginia, its next scheduled stop during a domestic service originating at Boston, Massachusetts, with an ultimate destination of Atlanta, Georgia. Meanwhile, a Pan American World Airways Boeing 707 jetliner was approaching from the south and preparing to land at the airport at the end of an international service from San Juan, Puerto Rico. The two aircraft were operating under instrument flight rules (IFR) and positive control, with air traffic controllers providing radar vectors to both and maintaining separation in accordance with established guidelines. The shortcomings of the separation criteria then in effect would soon be brought to full realisation by what was about to happen.

The last message from the Eastern crew was a 'Good night'. Less than 2 minutes later the Pan American co-pilot reported a near collision with another aircraft; also the radar target representing Flight 663 was no longer visible. The cleanly-configured DC-7B had plunged into the Atlantic Ocean approximately 7.5 miles (12 km) off Jones Beach, and some 15 miles (25 km) south-east of the airport, exploding on impact. All 84 persons aboard (79 passengers and a crew of five) perished. Meanwhile the 707 landed safely without further incident. It was dark at the time of the accident, and the weather consisted of scattered clouds above 10,000 ft (3,000 m) and a visibility of 7 miles (11 km).

Some of the victims' bodies were found, and the aircraft's main wreckage was located on the ocean floor, in about 80 ft (25 m) of water, with more than 60 per cent of it later being recovered. Examination of the debris revealed no evidence of mechanical or structural failure, or pre-impact fire or explosion.

In its inquiry, the US Civil Aeronautics Board (CAB) was able to reconstruct the probable flight paths of both the DC-7B and the 707. Realising a potential conflict with the latter, the departure controller had instructed the eastbound Eastern flight to turn southward, allowing it to continue to climb until it was at least 1,000 ft (300 m) above the descending, northbound jet. In the process, however, he placed the two aircraft on nearly head-on courses. Although the DC-7B was determined to have been indeed higher, the 707 could have appeared to the

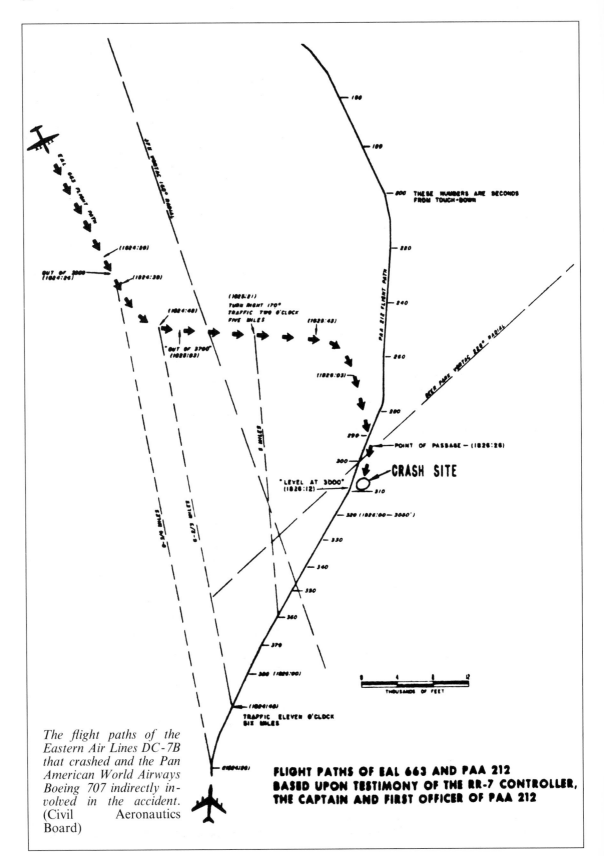

The flight paths of the Eastern Air Lines DC-7B that crashed and the Pan American World Airways Boeing 707 indirectly involved in the accident. (Civil Aeronautics Board)

FLIGHT PATHS OF EAL 663 AND PAA 212 BASED UPON TESTIMONY OF THE RR-7 CONTROLLER, THE CAPTAIN AND FIRST OFFICER OF PAA 212

Eastern pilots as being at the same height and thus a collision threat, when viewed from a distance of 5 miles (c 10 km) against a featureless background, and with the horizon not visible, the single light source not providing sufficient stimulus for depth perception.

It was therefore likely that the crew of *N849D* initiated a descent. Simultaneously, the Pan American crew, fearful of a potential conflict with the piston-engine transport, also began to descend, which probably appeared to negate the action of the Eastern pilot. At that point his only recourse was to make a sharp turn to the right and/or pull up.

The captain and first officer of the 707 confirmed that the DC-7B was in or near a vertical bank when it passed their aircraft left-to-right at about the same altitude, ie around 3,000 ft (1,000 m). As a result of the unusual attitude created by the avoidance manoeuvre, the pilots of *N849D* apparently experienced spatial disorientation and were not able to re-orient themselves by reference to their instruments in time to effect full recovery. Impact occurred with the aircraft in a nearly level but slight nose-up attitude, with its right wing slightly low.

Subsequently the US Federal Aviation Agency (FAA) instituted a new procedure at the New York airport in which a minimum of 2,000 ft (c 600 m) would be provided between inbound and outbound air traffic in areas conducive to optical illusions, twice the amount required at the time of the disaster.

Date: 20 May 1965 (c 01:50)
Location: Near Cairo, Egypt
Operator: Pakistan International Airlines
Aircraft type: Boeing 720B (*AP-AMH*)

Operating as Flight 705 and inaugurating a new route on the carrier's service to London from Karachi, Pakistan, the jetliner was preparing to land when it crashed and burned some 5 miles (10 km) from the Cairo airport, a scheduled stop, killing 121 persons aboard (108 passengers and the entire crew of 13). The six surviving passengers were injured.

Cleared for a non-precision instrument approach to Runway 34, the aircraft was turning left on to the base leg of the airport circuit when its rate of descent began to increase, ultimately reaching about 2,400 ft/min (730 m/min), approximately triple the norm. Its indicated air speed also increased slightly until the 720B struck the ground while in a gentle left bank, with its undercarriage retracted and flaps set at 20 degrees. Wreckage was scattered over the hilly, desert terrain on a north-easterly heading for a distance of nearly 1 mile (1.5 km), with the main portion of the aircraft having come to rest upside down. The accident occurred in early morning darkness, although the sky was cloudless with a visibility of about 5 miles (10 km).

The reason for the abnormal continuation of the descent until impact could not be determined.

Oscillations in the height and speed parameters of the flight data recorder (FDR) read-out indicated the possibility of an attempt to counteract a nose-down condition, although this could not be positively established. It was noted, however, that in the clear weather the bright lights surrounding the airport should have provided the pilot with adequate visual reference in order to detect an abnormal attitude and take immediate corrective action.

This and four other air carrier and military aircraft crashes occurring over a period of less than 10 years prompted the International Federation of Air Line Pilots Associations (IFALPA) to recommend that its members discontinue using Runway 34 at Cairo except in daylight and good meteorological conditions. Among other concerns, IFALPA complained of the absence of an instrument landing system (ILS), poor signal strength and transmission continuity in the locator beacon, inadequate runway lighting and a let-down procedure that did not conform with the practices recommended by the International Civil Aviation Organisation (ICAO), ie by allowing an obstacle clearance of less than 1,000 ft (c 300 m).

Date: 8 July 1965 (c 16:40)
Location: Near 100 Mile House, British Columbia, Canada
Operator: Canadian Pacific Air Lines
Aircraft type: Douglas DC-6B (*CF-CUQ*)

Designated as Flight 21, the aircraft was en route from Vancouver to Prince George, its first scheduled stop during a domestic service with an ultimate destination of Whitehorse, Yukon Territory, when it crashed and burned approximately midway between the two cities. All 52 persons aboard (46 passengers and a crew of six) perished.

The DC-6B was last reported cruising at flight level 160 when its crew transmitted three 'Mayday' distress calls. Witnesses who had seen the transport flying in clear conditions reported a mid-air explosion before it plummeted vertically into a wooded area. Its empennage, including the vertical and horizontal stabiliser assemblies, had separated from the rest of the fuselage as a result of the blast, which was determined to have occurred in the left rear lavatory.

It was believed that a saboteur had ignited a mixture of acid and gunpowder, which may have been poured into the toilet bowl, in a possible suicide-for-insurance scheme.

Date: 8 November 1965 (19:01)
Location: Near Constance, Kentucky, US
Operator: American Airlines (US)
Aircraft type: Boeing 727-23 (*N1996*)

It was dark and the weather was getting worse as Flight 383 prepared for a scheduled landing at

Wreckage of the Pakistan International Airlines Boeing 720B is strewn over the Egyptian desert after the unexplained crash that took 121 lives. (Wide World Photos)

Greater Cincinnati Airport, at the end of a domestic service from New York, New York. Nevertheless, the crew elected to make a visual approach, and were cleared to land on Runway 18.

As the aircraft was turning left on to the final approach course, the first officer radioed '. . . we'll pick up the ILS here'. Seconds later the jetliner slammed into a wooded hillside approximately 2 miles (3 km) from the threshold of the runway and about a quarter of a mile (400 m) to the left of its extended centreline, and some 225 ft (70 m) below the published airport elevation, bursting into flames on impact. The accident killed 58 persons aboard the 727, including five crew members. A stewardess and three passengers, among them an off-duty American Airlines pilot, survived with injuries.

The aircraft was in a slight nose-up attitude with its undercarriage still retracted and flaps set at 25 degrees at the moment of initial impact. There was thunderstorm activity in the area at the time, with a ceiling of 2,500 ft (c 750 m), a broken overcast at 1,500 ft (c 500 m) and scattered clouds at 1,000 ft (c 300 m), and a visibility of 2 miles (c 3 km). The wind was from the west at a velocity of 8 knots.

The accident was believed to have resulted from the failure of the flight crew to monitor properly the aircraft's height during the approach. Following a level-off, the final descent was continued for 1½ min, apparently without sufficient reference to the altimeters. In its investigative report, the US Civil Aeronautics Board (CAB) said that it found the error 'difficult to reconcile' when considering that both pilots were experienced captains, with the one acting as first officer administering a flight check as part of the other's upgrading to 727 captain status.

Several interrelated factors were thought to have contributed to this failure. Perhaps the most significant was the deteriorating visibility conditions when the flight began to encounter rain and clouds while on the base leg of the airport circuit. The terrain features themselves may have created the illusion of having sufficient altitude. This could have happened had the crew associated the lights of residences located along the Ohio River with the elevation of the airport due to the absence of lighting on the rising terrain in between. Furthermore, since the crew had to look left throughout the final turn in order to keep the airport in sight, the only other ground lights visible under the circumstances would have been those in the river valley.

The configuration of the aircraft at the time of the crash indicated that there had been a delay in the completion of the final check-list by the crew. A rush of cockpit activities could have been an additional element of distraction as the pilots tried to maintain visual contact with the approach lights.

The captain and first officer had flown together several times before, and therefore must have established a pattern of relying on each other's abilities. This could actually have been to the detriment of safety in this case had one pilot concentrated on maintaining visual contact, believing the other was monitoring his instruments.

Another indeterminable factor may have been a reduction in visibility due to the initial effect of the windscreen rain repellent and, possibly, to lightning flashes.

It was not known exactly how the pilots had used the airport's instrument landing system (ILS). Under the existing conditions, it would have been wise to execute a full ILS approach, but because of a 20 min delay in the departure of the flight from New York City, they probably decided to carry out a visual procedure in order to expedite the landing.

Date: 11 November 1965 (c 19:50)
Location: Salt Lake City, Utah, US
Operator: United Air Lines (US)
Aircraft type: Boeing 727-22 (*N7030U*)

The second fatal crash of a Boeing 727 in three days involved Flight 227, which was on a domestic transcontinental service from New York, New York, to San Francisco, California, with four en route stops, the last of these at Salt Lake City Municipal Airport.

It was dark at the time, but the meteorological conditions were good, with a ceiling of 14,000 ft (c 4,300 m), a broken overcast at 10,000 ft (c 3,000 m) and scattered clouds at 7,000 ft (c 2,000 m), and a visibility of 25 miles (40 km), so the crew opted for a straight-in-visual approach to Runway 34L, using the instrument landing system (ILS) for vertical guidance. About 1 min before impact, the aircraft was still 1,300 ft (c 400 m) above the proper glide path and its descent rate some three times that recommended. It was around this time that the captain brushed off the first officer's attempt to increase power. Moments later, the pilot realised his predicament and applied take-off thrust. But by then it was too late.

The jetliner slammed to earth some 300 ft (100 m) short of the runway threshold, resulting in the failure of its main undercarriage; the right gear was driven upward and rearward, rupturing both fuel lines and the No 3 generator leads. The 727 slid on the underside of its fuselage and its extended nose gear for more than 2,800 ft (850 m), finally coming to rest about 150 ft (50 m) to the left of the runway. Fire, which must have been ignited by sparks from either the scraping of the fuselage on the pavement or the severed generator leads, then gutted the fuselage. Although there had been no serious cases of trauma in the actual crash, the effects of the post-impact blaze claimed the lives of 43 passengers. Among the 48 survivors, 35 persons were injured, including the entire crew of six.

In its investigative report, the US Civil Aeronautics Board (CAB) refuted the contention of the captain that the aircraft's engines did not respond to the application of power, and blamed the accident on his failure to arrest the excessive descent rate. An examination of the pilot's records disclosed a pattern of inconsistent performance and a tendency to deviate from standard operating procedures since transitioning to jets.

As a result of this and the Cincinnati crash (8 November 1965), as well as two other fatal Boeing 727 accidents that occurred in the approach phase of operation during 1965 and 1966, considerable concern was expressed about the safety of the tri-jet transport. However, the CAB could find no design deficiencies or unsatisfactory flying characteristics in the aircraft. Although its rate of descent while in the landing configuration proved higher than earlier model jets, this was a built-in feature enabling it to fly in and out of smaller airports.

In the crash of Flight 227, one of the stewardesses was unable to reach her assigned duty station for the evacuation, which may have cost some lives. Subsequently, United Air Lines adopted a policy of

An American Airlines Boeing 727-23, identical to the aircraft that crashed during a landing approach to Greater Cincinnati Airport. (Boeing)

The flaming hulk of the United Air Lines Boeing 727 following its crash at Salt Lake City Municipal Airport. (Wide World Photos)

posting flight attendants near emergency exits during take-offs and landings, and this later became standard procedure throughout the industry.

The circumstances of this accident also prompted the US Federal Aviation Agency (FAA) to establish additional training guidelines and qualification requirements for commercial jet pilots.

Date: 24 January 1966 (c 08:00)
Location: French Alps
Operator: Air-India
Aircraft type: Boeing 707-437 (*VT-DMN*)

Operating as Flight 101 and on a service originating at Bombay, India, with an ultimate destination of London, the jet airliner was preparing for a scheduled stop at Geneva, Switzerland, when it was instructed to maintain 1,000 ft 'on top' of the clouds. However, the 707 descended below flight level 190 – the minimum safety altitude – then slammed into a ridge of Mont Blanc, approximately 200 ft (60 m) below its summit, and on a probable heading of 330 degrees. The aircraft disintegrated on impact, and all 117 persons aboard (106 passengers and 11 crew members) perished.

The sequence of events began when the pilot-in-command, who knew one of his two very-high-frequency omni-directional range (VOR) receivers was unserviceable, miscalculated his position relative to the mountain, radioing the message 'I think we are passing abeam Mont Blanc now'. The Geneva centre controller noted the error upon checking the radar screen and attempted to correct it by stating that the aircraft had '5 miles to the Mont Blanc'. But due to the controller's imprecise phraseology, the pilot may have misunderstood the comment as merely an acknowledgement of his previous transmission, and not that the 707 had yet to reach this point.

Complicating matters were a number of other factors. It was around dawn, and with the sun being low on the horizon and behind the aircraft, thus producing no obvious shadows, it would have been difficult to distinguish the snow-covered terrain from the clouds.

The crew could also have been faced with a 'white-out'. This phenomenon can cause an absence of shadows combined with diffused illumination (especially when snow or ice crystals are suspended in the air), as well as a reduction in horizontal visibility and an apparent increase in luminance; the physiological characteristics of illumination of the retina, myopia and other minor vision defects; and also have psychological effects, from a disorientation of one's vertical sense to a loss of both a sense of direction and of distance perception.

There was a cloud layer in the area of Mont Blanc that extended up to about 500 ft (150 m) above the elevation of the crash site and shrouded its summit, with light snowfall, severe turbulence and down-draughts near the terrain. The speed and direction of the wind was estimated as 35 knots from WNW at the level of impact and 60 knots from NNW at the peak.

Because of local variations in atmospheric pressure in the vicinity of the mountain, the aircraft's altimeters may have indicated 800 to 1,000 ft (c 250–300 m) higher than its actual altitude.

All of these factors could have led to an inadvertent descent into the cloud bank with insufficient time for the crew to obtain visual reference before hitting the ridge.

Date: 4 February 1966 (c 19:00)
Location: Tokyo Bay, Japan
Operator: All Nippon Airways (Japan)
Aircraft type: Boeing 727-81 (*JA8302*)

Designated as Flight 60, the jetliner crashed about 7.5 miles (12 km) east-south-east of

Bits of wreckage speckle the snow where the Air-India Boeing 707 hit Mont Blanc in the French Alps. (UPI/Bettmann)

Tokyo International (Haneda) Airport, where it was scheduled to land at the end of a domestic service from Chitose Airport, located on Hokkaido, near Sapporo. All 133 persons aboard (126 passengers and a crew of seven) were killed.

It was dark at the time, but the weather conditions in the moonlight were good, with scattered cumulus clouds reported at an approximate height of 2,000–3,000 ft (600–1,000 m) in the area north of Kisarazu. Visibility was some 5–10 miles (10–15 km).

The captain had initiated a descent while operating under visual flight rules (VFR) procedures, and the aircraft was observed at a height of perhaps 2,000 ft (c 600 m) or lower shortly before the accident. It was on its approach to Runway 33R, as cleared, when the co-pilot of a Japan Air Lines jet reported seeing the flash of an explosion, presumably the crash. However, the cleanly-configured 727 was not properly aligned with the runway at the moment it slammed into the water.

All of the victims' bodies were later recovered from the bay, as was about 90 per cent of the aircraft's wreckage, and examination of the latter revealed no evidence of any pre-impact fire, explosion or mechanical failure. Nor were there any

The empennage of the All Nippon Airways Boeing 727 is raised from Tokyo Bay after the crash that claimed 133 lives. (UPI/Bettmann)

signs of malfunction or error in the altimeters or other vital instruments. There was no indication of any abnormalities in the last radio message from the flight, which was transmitted only seconds before the accident.

The cause of the disaster and the reason why the aircraft had been at an unusually low altitude for night visual flight prior to the crash could not be determined.

Date: 4 March 1966 (c 20:15)
Location: Near Tokyo, Japan
Operator: Canadian Pacific Air Lines
Aircraft type: Douglas DC-8 Series 43 (*CF-CPK*)

Flight 402 circled in a holding pattern for nearly half an hour waiting for the fog to lift at Tokyo International (Haneda) Airport, a scheduled stop during a transpacific service from Hong Kong to Vancouver, British Columbia, Canada, before initiating its descent. When the conditions got worse the landing was abandoned altogether, and the aircraft began to proceed to its alternative airport, at T'ai-pei, Taiwan. Shortly afterwards, however, the flight was advised of an improvement in the visibility at Haneda, with the runway visual range (RVR) increasing to 3,000 ft (c 1,000 m), and the pilot consequently requested clearance to return and then started descending.

In the darkness the DC-8 would be making a ground-controlled approach (GCA) to Runway 33R, with the crew referring to instrument landing system (ILS) indications. During the final seconds of the flight, the controller warned the aircraft: '. . . dropping low, ten to fifteen, twenty feet low . . . level off momentarily . . . precision minimum, level off, twenty feet low', but the crewman handling the radio only responded 'Tower, would you turn your . . . runway lights down?'

The jetliner then made a sharp decline, but was in an approximately level attitude with undercarriage and flaps extended when it hit the approach lights, the initial impact occurring with a main gear wheel some 2,800 ft (850 m) from the runway threshold. It then struck a sea-wall with the bottom of its fuselage, was thrown over that structure and finally crashed near the end of the runway, bursting into flames. The accident killed 64 persons aboard the aircraft, including all 10 crew members, and injured the eight surviving passengers, who were seated in the centre part of the cabin and managed to escape through a torn portion of the fuselage or the forward door.

According to the investigative committee, the principal cause of the crash was the decision by the pilot-in-command to attempt a landing under the circumstances. It was believed that he initiated a steep rate of descent with the intention of executing the final approach at a lower altitude. Poor visibility due to the illusive fog condition probably misled the pilot and affected his judgement.

Date: 5 March 1966 (c 14:15)
Location: Near Gotemba, Shizuoka, Japan
Operator: British Overseas Airways Corporation (BOAC)
Aircraft type: Boeing 707-436 (*G-APFE*)

It must have been a grisly sight for the occupants of Flight 911 as the 707 taxied by the remains of the Canadian Pacific DC-8 which had crashed on landing the previous night (see above), before taking off from Tokyo International (Haneda) Airport, bound for Hong Kong, one segment of an around-the-world service originating at and destined for London. Little could any of them have known that in less than half-an-hour they would meet the same fate.

In an apparent attempt to expedite the departure or, perhaps, to give his passengers a scenic view of the majestic Mt Fuji, Capt Bernard Dobson elected to make a visual climb-out, flying off the designated airway. This deviation would be a significant factor in the subsequent accident, because it would take the flight into an area of severe turbulence. It was an exceptionally clear day, but the winds were blowing at the summit of the peak at a velocity of 60 to 70 knots.

The jet airliner was heading towards the west when it began to descend while shedding parts after flying over Gotemba, located some 50 miles (80 km) south-south-west of Tokyo, at an altitude of approximately 15,000 ft (5,000 m). Its empennage then separated, and, at a height of about 7,000 ft (2,000 m), the forward fuselage section broke away. Other components, including the right outer wing and all four engine/pylon assemblies, were also torn away as the 707 plummeted to earth. Trailing vapour, the main fuselage section and still-attached wings fell into a wooded area at the eastern base of the mountain, and the forward part crashed some 1,000 ft (300 m) away and caught fire. All 124 persons aboard (113 passengers and a crew of 11) were killed. Wreckage was scattered over an area approximately 10 miles (15 km) long and 1 mile (1.5 km) wide.

It was believed that the aircraft broke up in a very short period of time after encountering an abnormally strong gust of wind that generated a load considerably in excess of its design limits. Although it was impossible to forecast, and its existence could not be confirmed, the investigative commission did not deny that turbulence of such severity as to destroy a jet transport could have been produced by a powerful mountain wave present in the lee of Fujiyama. One theory suggested a difference between waves associated with an isolated peak, as was the case here, and those formed in the normal way, ie by extended ridges.

Metallurgical tests revealed fatigue cracks in a bolt hole in the vertical stabiliser rear spar starboard attachment fitting of *G-APFE*. However, it could not be determined clearly how this condition contributed to the structural failure.

Among the passengers on Flight 911 were 75 Americans travelling together, dealers or executives with a Minnesota-based company and their spouses who had taken a trip to the Far East as a reward for outstanding sales.

Above *BOAC Boeing 707 G-APFE is photographed taxiing past the wreckage of the Canadian Pacific DC-8 which had crashed the previous night, before taking off from Tokyo International Airport on its own fatal flight.* (Wide World Photos)

Below *The front fuselage section of the BOAC Boeing 707, with wings still attached, plummets to earth after the in-flight break-up.* (Black Star)

Date: 22 April 1966 (20:30)
Location: Near Ardmore, Oklahoma, US
Operator: American Flyers Airline Corporation (US)
Aircraft type: Lockheed 188C Electra (*N183H*)

The aircraft was being operated under contract to the US Military Airlift Command and on a domestic transcontinental service from Monterey, California, to Columbus, Georgia. Except for an off-duty flight engineer riding in the cockpit jump seat, its passengers were recent recruits on their way to Fort Benning for advanced training.

During an approach to land at Ardmore Municipal Airport, an en route refuelling stop, the four-engine turboprop crashed and burned in the foothills of the Arbuckle Mountains, and 83 persons aboard were killed, including the five members of the regular crew and the sole non-revenue passenger. The 15 survivors suffered various injuries. It was dark at the time of the accident, and the latest given weather consisted of a low ceiling, with broken clouds at 700 ft (c 200 m) and a solid

overcast at about 1,000 ft (300 m), and a visibility of 3 miles (c 5 km) in fog and drizzle.

The crew had originally planned a landing on Runway 08, using automatic direction finder (ADF) instrument procedures, but instead deviated to the north of the proper track, possibly to avoid thunderstorm activity. They then started a visual, circling approach to Runway 30. The Electra was in a right turn with its undercarriage down and flaps extended when it crashed just below the crest of a hill approximately 1.5 miles (2.5 km) north-east of the airport.

Investigation by the US Civil Aeronautics Board (CAB) revealed no evidence of any mechanical failure or defect in the aircraft. However, an autopsy performed on the body of the 59-year-old captain was considerably more revealing, disclosing severe coronary arteriosclerosis. So dire was his condition that two pathologists concluded that he may have died of heart failure prior to the crash. Perhaps even more disturbing was that the pilot, who also served as president of the airline, had falsified his application for a first class medical certificate, required as part of his airline transport rating (ATR). It was learned that he had a history of heart trouble dating back 18 years, and also suffered from diabetes. Both ailments would have been disqualifying factors for issuance of the certificate.

It was believed that the captain was flying the Electra and became incapacitated during the final stages of the approach. He may have slumped across the control wheel or back in his seat, in either case causing the transport to roll to the right. At the time the first officer would probably have been looking outside, trying to keep the airport in sight, and he might not have noticed the pilot's seizure until the change in attitude or, perhaps, when alerted by one or both of the other two men on the flight deck. The late recognition of the situation, coupled with the aircraft's response time, precluded a successful recovery at such a low altitude. In addition, a duty time of 16 hours on the day of the accident probably contributed to the captain's susceptibility to such incapacitation.

Following this disaster, the CAB announced that it would work with the US Federal Aviation Agency (FAA) in exploring ways to improve the quality of medical information received from pilots.

Date: 1 September 1966 (00:47)
Location: Near Ljubljana, Slovenia, Yugoslavia
Operator: Britannia Airways (UK)
Aircraft type: Bristol Britannia 102 (*G-ANBB*)

The turboprop airliner was on a charter service from Luton, England, and crashed while attempting to land at Ljubljana's Brniki Airport, killing 98 of the 117 persons aboard (92 passengers and six crew members). All the survivors, who included a stewardess, were injured.

During the approach to Runway 31, the crew reported seeing the airport, then requested radar assistance, implying that visual contact had been lost. Shortly afterwards, the controller observed the target on the radar screen turn to the right, but no correction was made even after he instructed the crew to turn left 3 degrees. Its undercarriage extended and flaps set at 15 degrees, the Britannia slammed into a forest, broke apart and caught fire approximately 1.5 miles (2.5 km) from the threshold of the runway and some 2,300 ft (700 m) north of its extended centreline. The accident occurred in darkness, but despite the presence of shallow fog in the area, the visibility was good, with scattered strato-cumulus clouds at about 6,000 ft (1,800 m).

The pilot-in-command probably did not set his altimeter to the given airfield pressure (QFE), but the approach was conducted as though it were, and as a result the aircraft went some 1,250 ft (380 m) below the procedural safely height. Nor was the first officer's altimeter set correctly, though it was not the same as the captain's. The discrepancy was not detected due to the apparent failure of the crew to carry out the required altimeter cross-checks.

The disregard of the proper procedures may be explained by the fact that the approach was conducted in moonlight and good weather conditions, which enabled the crew to sight the runway while still at least 7 miles (11 km) away. But whereas the runway lights may have been visible, the pilots would not have been able to discern their low altitude. The visual effect of the upward-sloping runway made the situation worse, giving them a wrong impression of their approach angle. The controller's failure to provide the crew with altitude information was not considered a contributing factor.

One of the recommendations of the commission that investigated the crash was to make instructions related to flight procedures precise and well-defined. Britannia Airways' policy that allowed the setting of an altimeter to the QFE 'at a convenient time' was cited as being imprecise and conducive to pilot error.

Date: 24 November 1966 (c 16:30)
Location: Near Bratislava, Czechoslovakia
Operator: Transportno Aviatsionno
    Bulgaro-Soviet Obshchestvo (TABSO)
    (Bulgaria)
Aircraft type: Ilyushin Il-18B (*LZ-BEN*)

All 82 persons aboard (74 passengers and a crew of eight) were killed when the four-engine turboprop crashed and burned in the 'Little Carpathians' range of mountains about 5 miles (10 km) from the city's international airport, from where it had taken off only 2 minutes earlier.

Operating as Flight 101, a service originating at

This BOAC Bristol Britannia 102, which would also later join the Britannia Airways' fleet, was a sister to the aircraft that crashed in Yugoslavia. (British Aerospace)

Sofiya, Bulgaria, and scheduled to terminate at (East) Berlin, the airliner was diverted to Bratislava due to adverse meteorological conditions. Some 5 hours later the captain elected to proceed on to Prague, where he had originally intended to land.

Following its departure, the Il-18 maintained the assigned altitude but did not turn to starboard as instructed. Cleanly configured, the aircraft was in a slight left bank when it hit a wooded hillside at an approximate elevation of 1,380 ft (420 m), the accident occurring in twilight. The airport was completely overcast at the time, with 6/8 stratus clouds at about 1,200 ft (350 m) and 8/8 nimbostratus at around 3,000 ft (1,000 m), a visibility of approximately 4.5 miles (7 km) and a moderate, continuous rain.

Although not determined with certainty, an investigative commission concluded that the most probable cause of the crash was the insufficient evaluation of both the weather and the relief of the terrain by the pilots, and their failure to adapt the flight to these conditions. The situation became dangerous only when the crew did not comply with the accepted flight clearance, which was either intentional or due to an unexpected occurrence that they did not understand or with which they could not cope.

With regard to the former theory, the immediate replies to messages from the ground raised doubts as to whether sufficient and concentrated attention was being given by the entire flight crew in making decisions. One noteworthy item was that the radio operator was not fully proficient in English, which could have complicated matters for the pilot.

With regard to the second theory, the possibility of an incorrect artificial horizon indication due to a defect in the instrument could not be dismissed. Such a faulty reading would have explained the failure of the crew to maintain the required 15-degree bank, which, probably in conjunction with excessive speed, may have caused the deviation. Turbulence was another possible contributing factor.

Date: 20 April 1967 (02:13)
Location: Near Nicosia, Cyprus
Operator: Globe Air AG (Switzerland)
Aircraft type: Bristol Britannia 313 (*HB-ITB*)

The turboprop airliner, on a non-scheduled service from Bangkok, Thailand, to Basel, Switzerland, crashed and burned while trying to land at the Nicosia airport, killing 126 persons aboard (117 passengers and nine crew members). Three passengers and a stewardess, who were found near the wreckage of the tail section, survived with injuries.

The Britannia had diverted from Cairo, one of three planned en route stops, but it could not be determined why the captain did not proceed to the prescribed alternate airport at Beirut, Lebanon, since the weather there was better than at Nicosia.

Following an overshoot, the pilot made a second landing attempt, but during the visual approach to Runway 32 he apparently misjudged the distance while in the airport circuit and descended too low to clear the rising terrain. The aircraft was in a left bank and on a heading of 68 degrees when it

The body of a victim is carried away from the wreckage of the Swiss Britannia that crashed on Cyprus.
(Wide World Photos)

struck a hillock about 20 ft (6 m) below its crest.

The accident occurred in darkness and during a thunderstorm, with 5/8 cloud coverage at 250 ft (c 75 m) and 5/8 estimated at 2,000 ft (c 600 m), and a visibility of approximately 4.5 miles (7 km). There was also a 7-knot wind from the east.

At the time of the crash, both pilots had exceeded by nearly 3 hours their authorised duty time. It was also noted in the investigative report that the first officer had less than 50 hours flying time in Britannia aircraft.

Date: 3 June 1967 (22:06)
Location: Near Prats-de-Mollo-la-Preste, Roussillon, France
Operator: Air Ferry Ltd (UK)
Aircraft type: Douglas DC-4 (*G-APYK*)

A holiday trip to the Mediterranean ended tragically in this, the first of two major disasters involving British supplemental airlines occurring during a single weekend.

The vintage transport was to have landed at Perpignan, at the end of a charter service from Manston, England. However, while nearing its destination the aircraft started to deviate to the west of the prescribed track, by nearly 10 miles (15 km) at the last reporting point and even further as it began what might have been an approach and landing manoeuvre. In the final moments of the flight, when asked by the approach controller 'Yankee Kilo, you not have my field in sight?', a crewman responded with an 'affirmative', but due to a misunderstanding brought about by the somewhat contradictory question, the controller did not realise that the crew had not in fact made visual contact with the airport.

Just before the accident, the DC-4 initiated a wide left turn, then rolled back into a fast right turn of approximately 90 degrees, which was followed by a steep left turn. During this last turn, and while in a bank of about 60 degrees, the aircraft hit a rock spur at an approximate elevation of 3,800 ft (1,150 m), which sheared off its entire port wing. The transport, which was cleanly configured and on a northerly heading at the time of the initial impact, finally crashed at the bottom of a ravine some 700 ft (200 m) below that point and burst into flames. All 88 persons aboard (83 passengers and a crew of five) perished.

The accident took place about 25 miles (40 km) south-west of Perpignan, in the Mont Canigou massif of the Pyrenees, at night and in good weather, with scattered cumulus and strato-cumulus clouds and a visibility in excess of 5 miles (c 10 km). There was little or no wind.

The accident was believed to have resulted from a series of errors on the part of the flight crew. It appeared that the pilots did not use the Perpignan very-high-frequency omni-directional range (VOR) station for navigational purposes, erred in dead reckoning, and may have confused two towns, Prades for Rivesealtes. Their estimated time of arrival was also incorrect by 10 min behind what normally would be expected, apparently because a fixed amount of time reserved for the landing procedure had been included in the calculations of the company's flight plan. And even though they did not have the runway in sight and were probably not referring to the aircraft's radio-navigational instruments, the crew proceeded to descend below the minimum safety altitude, apparently from a point that had not been properly identified.

It was concluded that the pilot saw the mountain upon turning on the landing lights and endeavoured to turn back on a reciprocal heading by making the tight left bank that preceded the crash.

The irrational conduct of the crew itself had an underlying cause, which was discovered through the medical aspects of the inquiry. Toxicological examinations on the remains of the three flight crewmen (who included a supernumerary pilot) revealed high levels of carbon monoxide. Since the impact was non-survivable, the highly toxic fumes must have been inhaled before the crash and would have been sufficient to cause intoxication to the point of affecting their powers of judgement. Flight at the cruising altitude of 9,000 ft (c 2,700 m), where the air is thinner, would have aggravated the situation, leading to hypoxia. The source of the carbon monoxide could only have been the aircraft's heater; if the joints of its exhaust pipe were cracked or otherwise defective, the fumes could easily seep into the cockpit.

Additional factors were the misunderstandings between the crew and the controller, attributed to language difficulties and, in particular, the lack of standard phraseology used, and the failure of the latter to check the bearing of the DC-4 during radio communications and thus detect the deviation in its track.

Date: 4 June 1967 (c 10:10)
Location: Stockport, Cheshire, England
Operator: British Midland Airways
Aircraft type: Canadair C-4 (*G-ALHG*)

A derivative of the famed Douglas DC-4, the Canadian-built C-4 (dubbed the 'Argonaut' by British operators) had a history of reliability since

The crash of this British Midland Airways Argonaut in an open space in the centre of Stockport avoided a potentially higher death toll. (Wide World Photos)

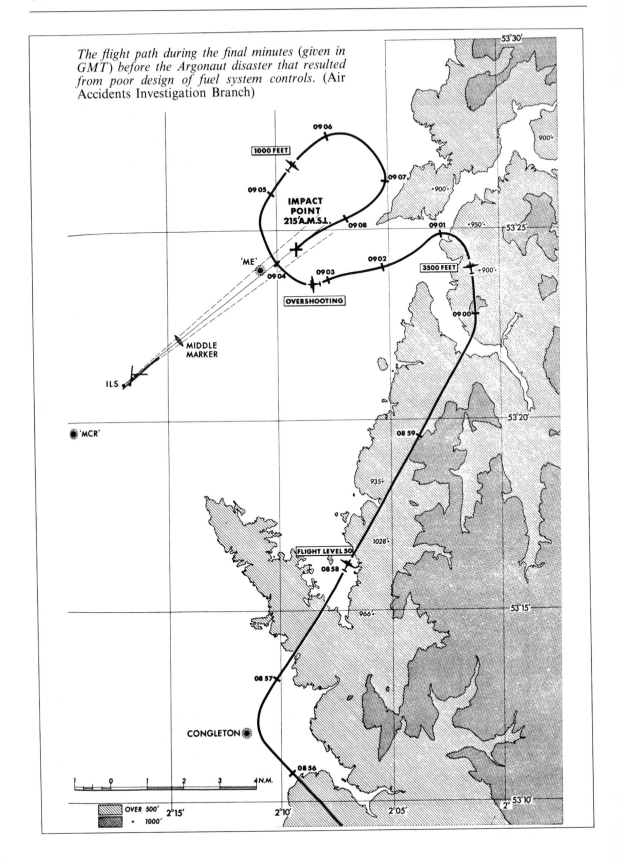

The flight path during the final minutes (given in GMT) before the Argonaut disaster that resulted from poor design of fuel system controls. (Air Accidents Investigation Branch)

its introduction into service in the late 1940s. Strangely, it would take this accident two decades later to reveal a potentially serious flaw in the four-engine transport.

This particular aircraft was to have landed at Ringway Airport, serving Manchester, at the end of a non-scheduled service from Palma de Mallorca in the (Spanish) Balearic Islands. It was carrying a full load of British holidaymakers plus five crew members.

However, during a radar-monitored instrument landing system (ILS) approach to Runway 24, both the aircraft's starboard power plants malfunctioned, and Capt Harry Marlow radioed that he was initiating an overshoot and reported '. . . a little bit of trouble with rpm'. The C4 completed a 360-degree right turn, during which it broke through the low overcast, and was approximately on the ILS localiser when it crashed in the centre of town and some 5 miles (10 km) short of the runway threshold. Its port wing was torn off upon striking a three-storey building, and the airliner hit the ground in a nearly level attitude. At the moment of impact its undercarriage was retracted and flaps were set at 10 degrees.

Initially there were only small, scattered fires, but about 10 min after the crash an explosion occurred in the starboard wing, and the blaze rapidly spread to the fuselage. The flames beat back rescuers after only 10 passengers could be saved, all of whom were injured, as was the stewardess, who had been thrown clear through a tear in the cabin. Also found alive was Capt Marlow, who escaped serious physical harm but suffered from retrograde amnesia and could not remember anything about the flight. The other 72 persons aboard lost their lives, including the first officer, a supernumerary engineer and a steward. The meteorological conditions at the airport shortly before the disaster consisted of rain, 3/8 cloud coverage at 300 ft (c 100 m), 7/8 at 400 ft (c 120 m) and 8/8 at 5,000 ft (c 1,500 m), and a horizontal visibility of approximately 1 mile (1.5 km).

The immediate cause of the accident was the loss of power in both starboard engines, resulting in control difficulties that prevented the crew from maintaining height, especially with one of the propellers windmilling. The source of the problem was not mechanical, however, but rather in the design of the fuel cocks and the location in the cockpit of their actuating levers. So awkward was their placement on the console that a pilot could rather easily put one or more of the levers in the wrong position, and only a slight error in the positioning of a lever could create a situation in which a cross-feed valve would be 'cracked', or improperly closed, allowing for the inadvertent transfer of fuel from one tank to another. This condition could represent a threat to safety after a long flight if fuel were to be transferred from a tank that the crew believed was sufficiently filled.

Other C-4 operators had experienced cases of inadvertent fuel transfer, but these were not communicated to the appropriate British government authorities. Nor had users of the type been adequately informed of the potential hazard by the manufacturer. British Midland Airways' engineers in fact did not even realise that such an inadvertent transfer of fuel was possible. But there was no doubt that such a condition had caused fuel starvation and, in turn, the power loss in the No 4 engine of *G-ALHG*. Its No 3 power plant may have failed for the same reason or, perhaps, because the pilot misidentified the engine for the one that had initially malfunctioned. It was then possible that the pilot had realised his mistake and correctly feathered the No 4 propeller, but did not restore power in time to the No 3 engine to prevent the crash.

Aggravating the woes of the crew were the poor handling characteristics of the C-4 in the event of such a power loss. In its report the investigative board noted that due to that fact, the lack of instruments to indicate engine failure, and the poor design of the fuel system controls, the aircraft would not have been certified under 1967 standards.

Though the outcome proved disastrous, the captain was not faulted for executing a go-around under the circumstances. He did show skill in apparently cutting power and setting the transport down in the only open space available.

Tragically, many of those killed had survived the impact but were trapped and died in the inferno. But it could have been worse. Immediately beyond the crash site were tall blocks of flats, the town hall and police station, and Stockport Infirmary.

Date: 19 July 1967 (12:01)
Location: Near Hendersonville, North Carolina US
First aircraft
Operator: Piedmont Airlines (US)
Type: Boeing 727-22 (*N68650*)
Second aircraft
Operator: Lanseair Inc (US)
Type: Cessna 310 (*N3121S*)

Designated as Flight 22, the 727 took off 2 minutes before noon from Asheville Municipal Airport, bound for Roanoke, Virginia, one segment of a domestic service originating at Atlanta, Georgia, with an ultimate destination of Washington, DC. Meanwhile, the 1955 model twin-engine Cessna was preparing to land at Asheville at the end of an intra-state flight from Charlotte. Both were operating under instrument flight rules (IFR).

Rather than following its clearance, ie to proceed from the Asheville very-high-frequency omni-directional range (VOR) station to the Asheville radio beacon located north-west of the airport, the corporate aircraft strayed about 10 miles (15 km) to the south-west and into airspace allocated to the jetliner. The two collided at an approximate altitude of 6,000 ft (1,800 m) some 15 miles (25 km) south-east of the city of Asheville. All 79 persons aboard the transport (74 passengers and a crew of five) and the three occupants of the general aviation aeroplane (including an experienced commercial pilot and a qualified private pilot) perished.

The cause of the deviation by *N3121S* could not be determined, but the investigation centred on a possible misidentification of or failure to locate the Asheville beacon.

The first significant event in the accident sequence was a remark by the Atlanta centre controller for the Cessna to 'expect ILS approach at Asheville'. This advisory should not have been accepted as a clearance, but if it were, it could have set the stage for disaster. Asheville has four different approaches, and the instrument landing system procedure uses the Broad River radio beacon, located south-east of the airport, as a fix.

Minutes later, the Asheville approach controller transmitted to *N3121S* a message containing an error, radioing 'Three one two one Sugar cleared over the VOR to the Broad River, correction, make that the Asheville radio beacon'.

Though immediately revised, the initial use of Broad River in the transmission could have continued the chain of misunderstanding. Furthermore, the clearance contained no reference to the type of approach. Later the controller did clear the Cessna for an ADF-2 (automatic direction finder) approach, using the Asheville beacon, but by then the aircraft was already well off course and only 76 seconds away from colliding with the 727.

The crews were unaware of one another, as they were communicating with the ground on different radio frequencies. However, the Cessna pilots could have overheard a message to another Piedmont flight that received clearance for an ILS approach, only adding to their confusion.

A portion of a three-year-old approach chart was found in the wreckage of the corporate aircraft, on which the geographical location of the Asheville beacon was not even depicted. In addition, the Cessna's automatic direction finder (ADF) receiver was determined to have been tuned to the Broad River facility.

The final message from *N3121S* was 'We're headed for the . . . Asheville now'. There was a possibility that the pilots had thought the Asheville and Broad River beacons were one and the same. They must have maintained the same south-westerly heading while trying to locate the navigational aid, or abandoned their efforts altogether and continued visually.

Converging at an estimated speed of 350–400 mph (c 550-650 kmh), the aircraft approached through a broken overcast, which would have reduced the time available for detection and avoidance. Also, the preoccupation of the Cessna's crew with its navigational difficulties and that of the 727 with normal departure procedures could have reduced their vigilance.

Witnesses reported that the actual collision took place in an area clear of clouds, with the light aeroplane pulling up sharply just before impact. There was no evidence that the airline crew at any point saw the other aircraft.

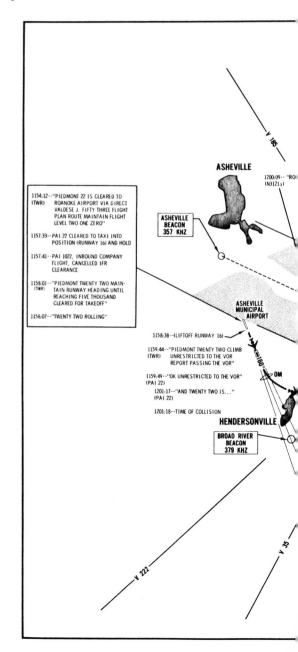

The initial contact was between the left outer wing and nose of the Cessna and the left forward fuselage section of the 727, which at the time was in a gentle left bank and on a heading of 100 degrees. The jetliner then nosed over, plunged into a wooded area in an inverted attitude and a steep angle of descent and exploded. The corporate aeroplane disintegrated in flight and was not observed after the collision.

In summary, the disaster may have resulted from inadequate knowledge of the Asheville area by the Cessna's pilot-in-command and poor flight planning on his part for apparently not reviewing

and becoming familiar with the latest charts, and the failure of the air traffic control (ATC) system to provide timely information that could have placed the aircraft on the correct course or at least alerted the pilot to his misunderstanding. It should be noted, however, that at no point did the Cessna pilot request assistance or clarification of any of the ATC instructions.

An airway map indicating the assigned route of the light aircraft (east to west) and the south-westerly deviation that led to the collision with the jetliner. (National Transportation Safety Board)

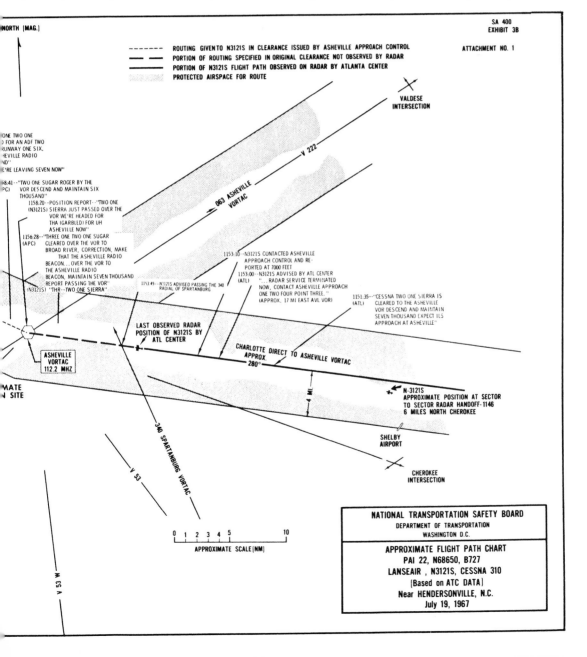

The blazing wreckage of the Piedmont Airlines Boeing 727 that crashed after collision with a twin-engine Cessna 310. (Wide World Photos)

An underlying factor in this accident was the absence of surveillance radar at the airport, which simply lacked the level of traffic at the time to make it eligible for such an installation. Though not an infallible method of separating aircraft, its use in this case would have given the controller the opportunity to detect and thus correct the deviation of the light aeroplane from its prescribed flight path.

As a safety measure, the US Federal Aviation Administration (FAA) would later require that approach/landing charts display all available navigational aids.

Date: 12 October 1967 (c 07:25)
Location: Off south-western Turkey
Operator: British European Airways (BEA)
Aircraft type: de Havilland Comet 4B (*G-ARCO*)

Originating at London, Flight 284 had stopped at Athens, Greece, before taking off for Nicosia, Cyprus. The last segment of the service was being conducted by BEA on behalf of Cyprus Airways, but retained the same flight number.

At around 07:00, and while cruising at flight level 290, the jetliner passed a westbound BEA Comet, whose captain later stated that the meteorological conditions in the area were clear and smooth. There were no further communications with CY 284 after it contacted Nicosia at 07:18.

Three hours later, wreckage from *G-ARCO* was spotted floating in the Mediterranean Sea some 100 miles (150 km) east-south-east of the island of Rhodes, in the general vicinity where it had fallen. For the 66 persons aboard (59 passengers and a crew of seven), there was no chance for survival. Subsequently, a small amount of debris, mostly cabin furnishings and personal effects, was recovered, as were the bodies of 59 victims. Most of the wreckage sank in water that was more than 6,000 ft (1,800 m) deep and could not be salvaged.

It was apparent from the scattering and state of the flotsam and bodies that a mid-air break-up had occurred. But there was no evidence of structural weakness or prior damage in the aircraft.

A significant lead in the subsequent inquiry was uncovered through the examination of one of the many recovered seat cushions. Its condition, under investigation at the Royal Armament Research and Development Establishment (RARDE), was remarkably similar to cushions used to muffle explosions in cases of safe-breaking. In addition to the numerous superficial characteristics, the cushion was found to contain many small particles of metal and fibres as well as about 20 perforations. Laboratory tests confirmed that it had been subjected to the effects of a high explosive, irrefutable proof that the jetliner had been sabotaged.

The bomb had detonated in the cabin, probably on or above the floor and near to the side support of a seat that was believed to have been occupied by a passenger (one of the victims' bodies exhibited indications of exposure to such a blast). The type of explosive used could not be identified.

By analysing the distribution of the debris, it was possible to determine that the Comet did not disintegrate at the cruising altitude of 29,000 ft (c 9,000 m). The blast apparently caused severe damage and created an out-of-control condition, and the aircraft suffered structural failure at an approximate height of 15,000 ft (5,000 m), its fuselage breaking into at least two major sections.

No suspects were ever apprehended or motive established, though the bombing may have been an attempt to kill the leader of the Greek forces in Cyprus after he was incorrectly identified as being among those who boarded the jetliner at Athens. On the other hand, this may have been some kind of insurance swindle. Two of the passengers were found to have been carrying abnormally high coverage, with one of the policies having been taken out shortly before the flight.

It was recommended in the investigative report that flight data recorders be so equipped as to

A British European Airways Comet 4B of the type destroyed by an explosive device over the Mediterranean Sea. (British Aerospace)

facilitate their recovery from deep water, a proposal that would see future application.

Date: 16 November 1967 (time unknown)
Location: Near Sverdlovsk, Russian Soviet
   Federated Socialist Republic, USSR
Operator: Aeroflot (USSR)
Aircraft type: Ilyushin Il-18B (*SSSR-75538*)

All 107 persons aboard (99 passengers and a crew of eight) were killed in the crash of the four-engine turboprop. The accident occurred at night and in instrument meteorological conditions, with a ceiling of around 300 ft (100 m), shortly after the airliner had taken off from the Sverdlovsk airport, on a scheduled domestic service to Krasnoyarsk.

Climbing to an approximate height of 700 ft (200 m) above the ground, and after initiating a left turn whilst in the clouds, the aircraft suddenly turned right, plunged to earth in a bank of about 90 degrees and caught fire.

Although there had been no distress message and the unprotected flight data recorder (FDR) mounted on the Il-18 was destroyed, investigation revealed that the crash apparently resulted from an incorrect indication of the main artificial horizons and of the compass system due to an electrical power failure, with the pilots then unable to determine the correct attitude of the aircraft with their back-up instruments and in conditions that precluded flight by visual reference. Action taken to arrest the descent without recovering from the steep bank proved insufficient to save the flight.

Date: 20 November 1967 (c 21:00)
Location: Near Covington, Kentucky, US
Operator: Trans World Airlines (TWA) (US)
Aircraft type: Convair 880 (*N821TW*)

Flight 128 was scheduled to land at Greater Cincinnati (Ohio) Airport during a domestic transcontinental service from Los Angeles, California, to Boston, Massachusetts, but during the approach to Runway 18 the jetliner crashed and burst into flames, killing 70 persons aboard (65 passengers and five crew members); ten passengers and two cabin attendants survived with various injuries.

The instrument landing system (ILS) localiser was operational at the time, but the glide slope, approach lights and middle marker beacon were inoperative due to runway construction, conditions of which the crew had been informed.

Its undercarriage extended and flaps set at 50 degrees, the aircraft was in a nearly level attitude and on the correct heading of 180 degrees when it began hitting trees at an indicated air speed of about 220 mph (350 kmh). The initial impact took place some 9,350 ft (2,850 m) from the runway threshold and approximately 430 ft (130 m) to the right of its extended centreline, and the jetliner then crashed into a pasture.

The visual approach had been conducted at night and in deteriorating weather conditions without adequate altimeter cross-reference. Additionally, the captain may have been deceived by a sensory illusion with regard to height.

The approach was normal until passage of the outer marker, whereupon there was a breakdown in

A Trans World Airlines Convair 880, identical to the aircraft that crashed during a landing attempt at Greater Cincinnati Airport. (Trans World Airlines)

the application of the prescribed procedures. The first officer did not call out the above-ground altitude of 500 ft, the 100 ft increments below that level or the arrival at the decision height, nor did he announce any deviation from the localiser centreline or in the air speed, altitude or rate of descent of the aircraft. At the time that these call-outs should have been made, as transcribed on the cockpit voice recorder (CVR) tape, the co-pilot and flight engineer were carrying out the final landing checklist, and even though

As is often the case in aviation disasters, the tail assembly is the only recognisable part of the TWA jetliner after the fiery crash. (UPI/Bettmann)

the former may have referred to his instruments, this activity coupled with an atmosphere of complacency due to his confidence in the captain, reinforced perhaps by the fact that the two had flown together before, could have led to the omissions.

Meanwhile, the pilot may have divided his attention between trying to make visual contact with the ground and monitoring his instruments. In the vicinity of the Ohio River the flight encountered a snow shower, which reduced visibility to 1.5–2 miles (2.5–3 km). The airport had an indefinite ceiling of 1,000 ft (c 300 m). Under these circumstances, he may have been faced with trying to re-orient himself with the instruments.

It was believed that the captain had used the lights in the river valley as a visual reference to establish his final approach altitude. In darkness and under lowering visibility conditions, it is possible that these lights could be confused as being at the same elevation of the airport, therefore creating the false impression of having sufficient height for terrain clearance. Furthermore, as studies have shown, lights on upsloping terrain in the area could have produced the sensation of being higher than was actually the case.

The cockpit conversation also indicated that the pilot did not have the minimum altitude clearly in his mind and levelled off at 400 ft (c 120 m) above the river rather than at the prescribed height of about 1,300 ft (400 m), or 400 ft above the elevation of the airport. He may have realised that something was wrong in the final seconds of the flight, as an instant before initial impact he initiated a pull-up and was heard to say 'Come on you'.

A claim by the airline that the crash may have resulted from erroneous instrument readings due to ice or water blocking the static ports was rejected by the US National Transportation Safety Board (NTSB), which investigated the accident.

Date: 29 February 1968 (time unknown)
Location: Near Bratsk, Russian Soviet Federated
  Socialist Republic, USSR
Operator: Aeroflot (USSR)
Aircraft type: Ilyushin Il-18D (*SSSR-74252*)

The airliner was en route from Krasnoyarsk to Petropavlovsk-Kamchatskiy, on Kamchatka, one segment of a scheduled domestic service originating at Moscow, and cruising in darkness at flight level 260 when some sort of emergency developed.

Although the crew did not communicate with air traffic control, an abrupt descent was begun and accelerated until aerodynamic forces broke up the four-engine turboprop at an approximate altitude of 10,000 ft (3,000 m) above the ground, and it then crashed and burned. Killed were all but one of the 82 persons aboard, including nine crew members; the miraculous survival of a single passenger, who suffered only minor injuries, was attributed to the fact that his seat (to which he remained safety belted) separated together with a large section of airframe skin, gliding slowly to earth like a leaf and landing atop a tree.

The cause of the disaster remained unidentified although the descent could have been prompted by a fuel leak and the discovery of direct or indirect signs of an in-flight blaze (traces of fire were observed on the port wing).

Date: 5 March 1968 (20:32)
Location: Basse-Terre, Guadeloupe, West Indies
Operator: Air France
Aircraft type: Boeing 707-328C (*F-BLCJ*)

Operating as Flight 212, the jet airliner had been cleared for a visual approach to land at Le Raizet Airport, serving Pointe-a-Pitre, on Grande-Terre, which was a scheduled stop. It had also landed at Quito, Ecuador, and Caracas, Venezuela, during a service originating at Santiago, Chile, and ultimately bound for Paris.

The pilot-in-command reported 'airfield in sight' before receiving the clearance; less than 2 minutes later the 707 struck a ridge of La Soufriere, a dormant volcano and the highest point on the island, the accident taking place some 15 miles (25 km) south-south-west of the airport. All 63 persons aboard (49 passengers, a regular crew of 11 and three off-duty crew members) perished.

When it crashed, the aircraft was on a heading of 50 to 60 degrees and probably in a very shallow descent. Its undercarriage was retracted, and flaps were set at 25 degrees. The jet exploded on impact with the heavily wooded terrain at an approximate elevation of 4,000 ft (1,200 m), and its wreckage was still burning a week later. Found in the debris was an air speed indicator reading of about 370 mph (595 kmh), and an altimeter recovered showed a height of between 3,500 and 4,300 ft.

All 63 persons aboard perished when the 707 ploughed into the dormant volcano and virtually disintegrated.
(UPI/Bettmann)

It was dark at the time with a quarter moon, and witnesses reported the sky as being clear in the vicinity of the accident. However, a few stratiform clouds covering the eastern slopes of the mountains and a cloud cap at the summit of La Soufriere were observed.

It was believed that the crew had initiated a descent from an incorrectly identified point. Difficulties encountered by the flight in establishing radio contact with the airport control tower probably rendered the captain impatient, and as a consequence he may have lost track of the passage of time and the fact that he was not following the normal route. This in turn could have led to the false impression on his part that the aircraft had been closer to its destination than was actually the case.

Despite the pilot's message (which was interpreted to mean that the city lights were visible and not as positive identification of the airport), the French investigative commission doubted that Pointe-a-Pitre could have been seen from his position or height. He must have mistaken for Pointe-a-Pitre the town of Basse-Terre, located on the island of the same name, since witnesses in this area reported seeing an aircraft at an unusually low altitude. The error, resulting in a descent below the minimum safety level, was then not corrected by cross-checking with existing navigational aids.

Despite a lengthy search, the flight data recorder (FDR) belonging to the 707 was not recovered, and this coupled with the location and state of destruction of the wreckage prevented the investigative commission from bringing to light the factor or factors that caused the error by the crew. Nor could a reason be found to explain the adoption by the pilot-in-command of a flight profile that would have undoubtedly delayed his arrival at Pointe-a-Pitre by 2 to 3 minutes.

There was no evidence of anything of a technical nature being wrong with the aircraft as directly contributing to the disaster.

Date: 24 March 1968 (c 12:10)
Location: Off Wexford Harbour, Ireland
Operator: Aer Lingus – Irish International Airlines
Aircraft type: Vickers Viscount 803 (*EI-AOM*)

This perplexing crash occurred while the four-engine turboprop, designated as Flight 712, was on a service to London from Cork, Ireland, with 61 persons aboard (57 passengers and a crew of four). Before radio contact was lost, it broadcast a message later determined to be 'Twelve thousand feet, descending . . . spinning rapidly'.

The Viscount was believed to have gone into a spin, spiral dive or similar manoeuvre at the cruising altitude of 17,000 ft (c 5,200 m). It appeared that a recovery had been made at less than 12,000 ft (c 3,700 m), but not without inflicting some structural deformation of the airframe, most

probably on the horizontal stabilisers and elevators, causing pitch control difficulties. And it was this condition that sent the airliner plunging into St George's Channel approximately 10 miles (15 km) east of Carnsore Point. Searchers recovered the bodies of 14 victims, but there were no survivors.

Located in water about 230 ft (70 m) deep, some 60 per cent of the wreckage was later salvaged. Additionally, a portion of the spring tab from the inboard end of the port elevator that apparently became detached in flight was found washed up on a beach.

It was concluded that the aircraft had flown in the disabled condition for at least 10 min, and before impact its engines were apparently throttled back intentionally. The Viscount then struck the water in a steep angle of descent and with considerable vertical velocity but a relatively low forward speed, ie less than 150 mph (250 kmh). The weather in the general area consisted of 3/8 stratus clouds between 500 and 1,500 ft (c 15–500 m), 6/8 altostratus between 12,000 and 15,000 ft (c 3,700–5,000 m) and high cirrocumulus.

There was insufficient evidence to determine the cause of the initial descent that led to the structural damage. An in-flight fire or explosion, power plant failure, bird strike, crew incapacitation or encounter with severe turbulence were either ruled out or considered highly improbable. Although there was no substantiating evidence of such an occurrence, the known facts did point to the possibility of a collision with another aircraft, possibly a pilotless drone, a near collision that necessitated an evasive manoeuvre, or an upset of the Viscount by its wake turbulence. This theory gained further support when, more than six years after the disaster, the wing of a target drone was reportedly found in the vicinity where the airliner had gone down. But no such vehicle was known to have been launched anywhere in the area on the day of the crash.

Date: 20 April 1968 (c 18:50)
Location: Near Windhoek, South-West Africa (Namibia)
Operator: South African Airways
Aircraft type: Boeing 707-344C (*ZS-EUW*)

Operating as Flight 228/129, the aircraft had landed at J. G. Strijdom Airport, serving the capital city, before continuing on to Luanda, Angola, its next scheduled stop during a service originating at Johannesburg, South Africa, with an ultimate destination of London. After taking off from Runway 08 the 707 climbed to an approximate altitude of 600 ft (180 m) above airfield elevation, whereupon it levelled off and then began to descend. Only about a minute after becoming airborne, the jetliner crashed some 3 miles (5 km) from the end of the runway, bursting into flames on impact. The accident claimed the lives of 123 persons aboard, including the entire crew of 12 and a passenger who was found alive at the crash site but succumbed days later. Five other passengers, all of whom were seated near the front of the cabin, survived with various injuries.

Since *ZS-EUW* was not equipped with either a flight data recorder (FDR) or cockpit voice recorder (CVR), the exact sequence of events and the actions of the flight crew could not be ascertained. However, through the subsequent investigation it was possible to conclude that the disaster resulted from human error rather than mechanical failure or a defect in the aircraft or any of its systems.

It was evident that the undercarriage had been raised immediately after lift-off, and that soon thereafter the flaps were fully retracted and the engine output reduced from take-off to climb power. Though in accordance with the prescribed procedures, these alterations in flap configuration and thrust would have caused the loss of height unless the pilot checked that tendency and maintained a climbing attitude by appropriate action or until the jetliner attained considerably more speed. Instead, he appeared to have changed the stabiliser trim to maintain the same pitch attitude as though he believed that the aircraft was ascending; at that point, however, the 707 was in fact descending. Additionally, the co-pilot must have insufficiently monitored the flight instruments to appreciate that the aircraft was losing altitude.

Despite the clear, windless weather conditions, it was a dark, moonless night and there were few lights on the ground in the area, if any. This absence of external visual references, along with spatial disorientation and the crew's preoccupation with the normal checks that are made after take-off, probably contributed to the accident.

Factors that might have contributed were temporary confusion in the mind of the pilot on the position of the inertial-lead vertical speed indicator, arising from the difference in the instrument panel layout in the 'C' version of the Boeing 707-344 as compared with the 'A' and 'B' models with which the captain and first officer were familiar; the pilot's misreading, by 1,000 ft, of the drum-type altimeter, which is susceptible to ambiguous interpretation on the thousands scale; and distraction on the flight deck caused by a bird or bat strike or some other minor occurrence such as smoke from overheating electrical equipment or a startling noise caused by something falling in the galley.

Although crew incapacitation had been ruled out, the investigative report did note that the captain's blood pressure was slightly above normal, and that his vision had deteriorated somewhat.

The impact with the ground took place at a speed in excess of 300 mph (480 kmh), with the 707 banked slightly to the left. Wreckage was strewn over an area nearly 1 mile (1.5 km) long and 700 ft (200 m) wide.

As a result of this accident, it was recommended that the minimum height for flap retraction be raised from 400 to 1,000 ft (c 120 to 300 m) and the normal altitude for such action be fixed at 2,000 ft (c 600 m).

Date: 3 May 1968 (c 16:50)
Location: Near Dawson, Texas, US
Operator: Braniff International Airways (US)
Aircraft type: Lockheed 188A Electra (*N9707C*)

A SIGMET had been issued concerning a line of thunderstorms stretching across central Texas. Through this area was the planned path of Flight 352, whose pilots were provided with the weather report prior to their departure from Houston.

Following take-off, the turboprop airliner headed north for Dallas on the initial, intra-state segment of a domestic service with an ultimate destination of Memphis, Tennessee. About 20 min later, as the Electra approached the cumulo-nimbus build-up, the crew was faced with finding the fastest, smoothest way of traversing the storm.

Despite a suggestion by the Fort Worth control centre to deviate to the east, where the rest of the air traffic was being re-routed, the crew insisted on proceeding to the west. Minutes later, and after being cleared to descend to and maintain 5,000 ft,

Emergency workers and law enforcement personnel search through the wreckage of the Braniff International Airways Electra following the crash in Texas farmland. (UPI/Bettmann)

the crew reported seeing an opening in the storm, then asked whether there were any reports of hail in the area.

'No, you're the closest one that's ever come to it yet,' the controller replied.

Less than a minute later, the flight asked permission, and was so granted, to make a 180-degree turn. No reason was given for this request, but from their conversation, transcribed by the cockpit voice recorder (CVR), it was obvious that the pilots realised their error in flying into the thunderhead.

'Don't talk to him too much,' the captain advised the first officer of the air traffic controller. 'He's trying to get us to admit we made a big mistake coming through here.'

While the pilot's decision to penetrate the storm in the first place had been unsound, and this was considered a major factor in the subsequent accident, his action in reversing direction and attempting to fly out of it would also prove fatally flawed. Such a procedure carried out in turbulent conditions could lead to a loss of control and was in fact against company policy.

The captain initiated a turn to the right, which progressed beyond 90 degrees. This resulted in a loss of lift, causing the nose of the aircraft to pitch down. It was believed that simultaneously the transport encountered turbulence, resulting in a lateral upset, and that it then may have been hit by an upward gust of wind which, coupled with the loss of lift, led to a longitudinal upset or spiral manoeuvre.

As the pilot attempted to bring the aircraft back to level flight from the unusual attitude, the inboard section of the right wing was subjected to bending and twisting forces that ultimately exceeded its designed strength. The wing finally failed, fracturing near the root and just outboard of the No 4 power plant.

The initial break-up occurred at an estimated air speed of 380 mph (c 600 kmh), at an approximate altitude of 6,750 ft (c 2,050 m) and as the transport was on a heading of around 200 degrees. Almost instantly thereafter, the empennage broke off from the fuselage, and this was followed by the separation of the two left engines, left flaps and other components. Fuel from the ruptured wing tanks then ignited, and the Electra fell to earth in flames into farmland some 20 miles (30 km) south-west of Corsicana. All 85 persons aboard (80 passengers and five crew members) perished.

Witnesses in the immediate area of the crash reported rain, hail, high winds and lightning. One bolt seen in close proximity to the aircraft at about the time it broke up was not considered a factor in the accident.

Despite a total lack of evidence, the possibility of prior weakness in the wing structure due to stress corrosion, probably in the form of a small crack, could not be completely discounted.

There was also an indication that the aircraft's weather radar antenna may have been tilted slightly up, which would have resulted in a misleading presentation on the screen, and this, coupled with the effects of hail, which generally has a lesser reflectivity to radar than other forms of moisture, could have induced the crew to press for a deviation to the west.

One of the recommendations made by the US National Transportation Safety Board (NTSB) in its investigative report on this disaster was that greater emphasis be placed on the use of weather radar for avoiding thunderstorms than as an aid in penetrating them.

Date: 22 May 1968 (c 17:50)
Location: Paramount, California, US
Operator: Los Angeles Airways (US)
Aircraft type: Sikorsky S-61L (*N303Y*)

Probably the most popular and certainly the busiest route in L. A. Airways' commuter helicopter network was the service between the Disneyland amusement park in Anaheim and Los Angeles International Airport. It was on this run that tragedy befell Flight 841.

The turbine-engine rotorcraft departed Anaheim at 17:40 for the 25-mile (40 km) flight, and it was later observed at an altitude of about 2,000 ft (600 m) by the crew of another company aircraft heading in the opposite direction. Not more than a minute afterwards, a distress message was heard from Flight 841, later determined to be 'L. A., we're crashing, help us!'

Witnesses saw the helicopter descend to between 600 and 800 ft (c 180–250 m) above the ground, then yaw to the left from a westerly to a south-westerly heading before it fell almost vertically into a dairy yard in suburban Los Angeles and burst into flames, killing all 23 persons aboard (20 passengers and a crew of three).

Examination of the wreckage indicated that the main rotor blades had undergone extreme lead and lag (fore and aft) over-travel excursions, so severe in fact that in some instances one blade overlapped the adjacent one. These excursions continued as the aircraft descended under partial control until one blade became detached from the rotating swashplate (the mechanism that transmits pitch control inputs) due to the overload failure of its pitch control rod at the lower trunnion end attachment. That blade then became uncontrollable and struck the aircraft, and the resulting imbalance caused the other four blades to do the same. The repeated strikes broke all five blades and caused severe structural damage, including the separation of the aft fuselage and tail rotor pylon assembly.

The main rotor system of the S-61 was designed

Los Angeles Airways Sikorsky S-61s were involved in the two worst US commercial helicopter disasters, which occurred during a three-month period in 1968. (Sikorsky)

to allow the blades limited motion both fore and aft and up and down, and each blade had been equipped with a damper to maintain stability. In this case the rotorcraft apparently experienced a loss of effective damper action of one blade or the failure of the damper of another. The reason for the first possibility could not be determined, and although the second could have involved bushing or bearing failure, this could not be substantiated because significant portions of the damper must have fallen off some distance from where the helicopter ultimately crashed and were never found. Studies showed that oscillations of one blade could cause similar anomalies in the two opposing ones.

This accident led to improvements in the S-61 model, including a modification of the helicopter's automatic flight control system. Additionally, the unlimited service life of the horizontal hinge pins used in the main rotor head was reduced to 5,000 hours.

Date: 14 August 1968 (c 10:35)
Location: Compton, California, US
Operator: Los Angeles Airways (US)
Aircraft type: Sikorsky S-61L (*N300Y*)

The company's second fatal crash in three months involved an aircraft flying on the same route but in the opposite direction, ie from Los Angeles International Airport to the Disneyland/Anaheim heliport.

Designated as Flight 417, the turbine-engine helicopter was seen at an estimated height of 1,500 ft (c 500 m) above the ground when witnesses reported hearing a loud noise and seeing one of its main rotor blades break off. The aircraft fell in uncontrolled gyrations, then crashed and burned in Leuders Park. All 21 persons aboard (18

passengers and three crew members) were killed.

Examination revealed that the separation was caused by a fatigue crack in the spindle, the part of the assembly that attaches each blade to the main rotor head (it also provides pitch control of the blade). The nucleus of the fracture was on the trailing side of the spindle, and the crack, which had propagated through more than two-thirds of the shank cross-section, must have developed slowly over a long period of time. It had apparently been precipitated by substandard hardness of the metal and inadequate shot peening (a shop process designed to increase its strength); to a lesser degree from pitting that may have been present in the structure and possibly by tension on the unpeened metal generated by the nickel plating to which it was connected. Although the crack should have been present during the last overhaul of the spindle, it could not be determined why it was not detected.

An airworthiness directive issued by the US Federal Aviation Administration (FAA) two days after the accident mandated that only new main rotor blade spindles be used on S-61 rotorcraft. Previously, reworked spindles had been allowed, and no service life specified. The new time limit imposed was 2,400 hours.

Date: 11 September 1968 (c 10:30)
Location: Off Cap d'Antibes, Alpes-Maritimes, France
Operator: Air France
Aircraft type: Sud-Aviation Caravelle III (*F-BOHB*)

Operating as Flight 1611, the jet airliner plunged into the Mediterranean Sea some 25 miles (40 km) south of Nice airport, where it was scheduled to land at the end of a service from Ajaccio, Corsica.

This Air France Caravelle is virtually identical to the aircraft that crashed in the Mediterranean Sea. (Air France)

All 95 persons aboard (89 passengers and a crew of six) perished.

The first hint of something amiss came less than 3 minutes before radio and radar contact with the Caravelle was lost, when a member of the crew announced 'Trouble', then shortly afterwards reported 'Fire on board'. Upon receiving this message, the Marseilles control centre cleared the aircraft for an immediate descent without restriction. The final transmission from the flight was 'We are going to crash if this continues'.

Around the time of the disaster, the weather conditions in the area consisted of a broken overcast, with a base of about 1,500 ft (500 m), and a visibility of around 3–5 miles (5–10 km). Since the crew had reported seeing land, the jet must have been under the clouds in the final moments of the flight.

The wreckage was later found on the ocean floor, in water approximately 7,500 ft (2,300 m) deep. Some 8–10 tons (9–11,000 kg) of debris was recovered over a period of more than two years, and its fragmented condition indicated a violent impact with the sea at a steep angle of descent. There was also evidence of pre-impact fire in the right rear portion of the aircraft's cabin.

It was believed that the blaze had started in the area of the right lavatory and the galley. Although its cause could not be determined, the fire may have been of an electrical origin, possibly due to a malfunction in the water heater (as had happened to another Caravelle that was destroyed while on the ground). Alternatively it could have resulted from a passenger carelessly tossing a lighted cigarette into the lavatory trash can. There was no evidence of

sabotage with explosives, but the use of an incendiary device could not be completely ruled out.

It was concluded that the aircraft must have been out of control prior to the crash. The most probable reasons for this were either interference with the flight crew by passengers who had surged into the cockpit to escape the flames, or incapacitation of the pilots due to smoke inhalation, despite the fact that they may have been wearing masks and goggles.

Date: 12 December 1968 (22:02)
Location: Near Caracas, Venezuela
Operator: Pan American World Airways (US)
Aircraft type: Boeing 707-321B (*N494PA*)

Designated as Flight 217 and en route from New York City, the jet airliner crashed in the Caribbean Sea and exploded while descending for a landing at Maiquetia Airport, serving Caracas, killing all 51 persons aboard (42 passengers and a crew of nine).

The accident took place some 10 miles (15 km) from shore, during the final approach phase that was being conducted under visual flight rules (VFR) procedures. It was dark at the time, but the meteorological conditions were good, with a ceiling of 2,000 ft (c 600 m) and unlimited visibility under the clouds.

The bodies of more than half of the victims and significant portions of the aircraft, including the tail assembly, two engines and the flight data recorder (FDR), were subsequently recovered from the water, which was about 360 ft (110 m) deep at the

A Boeing 707-321C, basically the same as the Pan American World Airways jetliner that crashed in the Caribbean Sea. (Boeing)

crash site. Some of the occupants may have been knocked unconscious on impact and drowned.

Although the cause of the accident could not be determined, it was considered possible that the pilots had been deceived by a sensory illusion produced by town lights on upsloping terrain in the vicinity of the airport, which, as studies have shown, can create the impression of being higher than is actually the case and thus result in an undershoot.

Date: 5 January 1969 (c 02:35)
Location: Horley, Surrey, England
Operator: Ariana Afghan Airlines (Afghanistan)
Aircraft type: Boeing 727-113C (*YA-FAR*)

The jetliner, which was operating as Flight 701, was scheduled to land at London's Gatwick Airport at the end of a service from Kabul, Afghanistan, with four en route stops. In the early morning darkness, the 727 began its approach to Runway 27; the aircraft's autopilot was coupled to the instrument landing system (ILS), but the crew would still be responsible for flap and power settings.

As the approach continued, the flaps were lowered to 15 degrees, which was contrary to the recommended setting of 25 degrees; this seemingly innocuous error would be the first in a chain of events that would ultimately lead to the crash of the 727. The incorrect flap setting meant that the aircraft had less than the anticipated drag, so the autopilot had to demand a greater than normal nose-down pitch in order to position the aircraft on the glide slope. This attitude caused its air speed to increase, producing more lift and requiring even

further nose-down trim to keep the jetliner on the correct glide path. The increasing application of nose-down elevator pressure eventually outstripped the ability of the system to trim out the load on the horizontal stabiliser, resulting in the illumination of the 'stabiliser out of trim' warning light in the cockpit. Unaware of the incorrect flap setting, the captain interpreted the warning light as indicating a possible malfunction, and he disconnected the autopilot.

Following extension of the undercarriage and passage of the outer marker, and as the aircraft was being flown manually, the flaps were re-positioned from 15 to 30 degrees without the intermediate setting of 25 degrees being selected first. This uninterrupted 15 degree change in flap position resulted in a marked nose-down pitch, an increase in the rate of descent and a reduction in air speed that was not offset by an increase in power. The aircraft, which was then at an approximate height of 1,200 ft (c 350 m), immediately dropped below the glide slope, and its rate of descent reached approximately double the norm. The pilots did not appear to notice this deviation, and no corrective action was taken for about 45 seconds. Six seconds after the first officer called out 'We have four hundred feet', the captain pulled back on his control column and applied full power, but by then it was too late.

Just after its nose began to rise, the jetliner brushed treetops approximately 1.5 miles (2.5 km) from the runway threshold, knocked chimney-pots off a house, then struck more trees, the impact with which tore off its starboard wing tip, aileron and outer flap. Touching the ground with its right main gear, the aircraft became airborne again and, after

The remains of the Ariana Afghan Airlines Boeing 727 and the house it destroyed while attempting to land at London's Gatwick Airport. (Wide World Photos)

demolishing a house, broke apart and burst into flames.

Killed in the accident were 48 of the 62 persons aboard the 727, including five of its eight crew members, and two occupants of the dwelling. The effects of the fire, rather than impact forces, were responsible for nearly all of the fatalities. The three members of the flight crew, the 11 surviving passengers and an infant on the ground, the daughter of the couple who lost their lives, suffered injuries.

The airport weather around this time consisted of freezing fog and a runway visual range (RVR) of only about 300 ft (100 m), which was less than the prescribed minimum. The airline did allow its pilots some discretion on this matter, but regardless of that, the captain's decision to continue the approach under the circumstances was not itself a causative factor in the crash.

There was no evidence to suggest that the aircraft's flight director had not been working properly. However, had it been inadvertently selected to the wrong mode, it would not have provided tracking information until *YA-FAR* had intercepted the glide slope again after the deviation, or perhaps not at all.

The pilot's attention was probably directed outside the aircraft at a critical time, in an attempt to obtain visual reference, rather than on the instruments, and for that reason he may not have detected the descent below the correct glide path.

The crew did report seeing one light during the approach, but this was established to have been the hazard beacon on Russ Hill. Under the conditions, the light could have appeared higher than was actually the case, creating the false impression of being too high.

Date: 16 March 1969 (c 12:00)
Location: Maracaibo, Zulia, Venezuela
Operator: Venezolana Internacional de Aviacion SA (VIASA) (Venezuela)
Aircraft type: McDonnell Douglas DC-9 Series 32 (*YV-C-AVD*)

Originating at Caracas, Flight 742 had landed at Grano de Oro Airport, as scheduled, before taking off on the second leg of an international service that was to have terminated at Miami, Florida, US. Seconds after becoming airborne, the jet airliner struck an electric power line at an approximate height of 150 ft (50 m) above the ground, then plunged into the La Trinidad section of the city. The disaster claimed the lives of 155 persons, all 84 aboard the DC-9 (74 passengers and a crew of 10) and 71 on the ground, while leaving more than 100 others injured. Numerous vehicles, including a bus, and at least 20 houses were destroyed in the impact and ensuing fires.

The accident was attributed to faulty temperature sensors along the runway and the take-off calculations made from the erroneous information they had provided, which resulted in an overloaded aircraft for the prevailing conditions. This in turn necessitated a longer-than-planned ground run that led to a climb gradient too low to clear the power line (which, interestingly, had been installed over the objections of aeronautical authorities). The temperature factor was significant due to the relative shortness of the runway. Only two days after the crash, Venezuela's Public Works Minister ascribed runway length as a contributing factor, and announced that it would be extended by approximately half a mile (0.8 km).

The twin-engine jet was on lease to VIASA from another Venezuelan carrier, AVENSA, which had also provided the crew for this particular flight.

Date: 20 March 1969 (c 02:00)
Location: Near Aswan, Egypt
Operator: United Arab Airlines (Egypt)
Aircraft type: Ilyushin Il-18D (*SU-APC*)

The four-engine turboprop, which was on a non-scheduled service from Jiddah, Saudi Arabia, its passengers Muslim pilgrims, crashed and burned while attempting to land at Aswan Airport, killing 100 persons aboard, including the seven members of the crew. All five survivors were seriously injured.

It was dark and the horizontal visibility had been

The wreckage of the Allegheny Airlines DC-9 is spread across an Indiana field and nearby trailer park after the collision with a light aircraft. (Wide World Photos)

reduced to around 1.2–2 miles (2–3 km) by blowing sand as the aircraft, following two unsuccessful approaches, began its third, using non-directional beacon (NDB) guidance. Banked to the right, the Il-18 hit the left side of the runway approximately 3,675 ft (1,120 m) beyond its threshold. The impact sheared off its starboard wing, and the resulting spillage of some 6,000 lb (2,700 kg) of fuel caused the fire.

The pilot had apparently descended below the minimum safe altitude without having the runway lights clearly in sight. Fatigue due to continuous work without sufficient rest was a contributing factor.

Date: 4 June 1969 (08:42)
Location: Near Salinas Victoria, Nuevo Leon, Mexico
Operator: Compania Mexicana de Aviacion SA (Mexico)
Aircraft type: Boeing 727-64 (*XA-SEL*)

Operating as Flight 704, the jet airliner crashed and burned some 20 miles (30 km) north of Monterrey while preparing to land at the city's airport, at the end of a domestic service from Mexico City. All 79 persons aboard (72 passengers and a crew of seven) perished.

According to its flight data recorder (FDR) read-out, the 727 had made a continuous descent in the last 5 minutes before impact at a rate of approximately 1,500 ft (500 m) per minute and an indicated air speed of about 290 mph (465 kmh). During this time, and on passing over the Monterrey very-high-frequency omni-directional range (VOR) station, the pilot turned left instead of right, which was required in order to enter the holding pattern, apparently doing so without having established his exact position. Its excessive speed and the wide radius of the turn took the aircraft out of the designated descent area and over rising terrain.

Its undercarriage still retracted, the jet struck a mountain, near its peak at an approximate elevation of 6,000 ft (1,800 m). The airport weather at the time was overcast, with one layer of clouds at roughly 500–1,500 ft (c 150–500 m) and another between 2,000 and 7,500 ft (c 600–2,300 m). There was also fog and drizzle in the area.

Date: 9 September 1969 (15:29)
Location: Near London, Indiana, US
First aircraft
Operator: Allegheny Airlines (US)
Type: McDonnell Douglas DC-9 Series 31 (*N988VJ*)
Second aircraft
Operator: Private
Type: Piper PA-28-140 Cherokee (*N7374J*)

Designated as Flight 853, the DC-9 had begun its descent in preparation for landing at Weir Cook Municipal Airport, serving Indianapolis, a scheduled stop during a domestic service originating at Boston, Massachusetts, with an ultimate destination of St Louis, Missouri. It was operating under instrument flight rules (IFR) and positive control and on a heading of 282 degrees.

Meanwhile, the single-engine Cherokee, which had been leased from the Forth Corporation, was heading towards the south-east, a student pilot at the controls. It was operating under visual flight rules (VFR). Neither crew was aware of the other's presence.

The aircraft collided at an approximate altitude of 3,550 ft (1,080 m) and some 10 miles (15 km) southeast of the state capital. Impact was at an obtuse angle, with the initial contact taking place between the vertical stabiliser of the commercial transport and the left side of the general aviation aeroplane, just forward of its wing. The former's horizontal stabiliser was sheared off, and the jetliner then plunged into a field. It hit the ground in an inverted, nose-down attitude, almost level laterally, with its undercarriage and flaps retracted. The light aircraft fell in pieces about 1 mile (1.5 km) away. All 82 persons aboard the DC-9 (78 passengers and four crew members) and the sole occupant of the Cherokee perished. Some of the wreckage was scattered over a nearby trailer park, although there were no injuries on the ground. There was also no fire.

The local meteorological conditions at the time consisted of a broken overcast, with a cloud base of approximately 4,000 ft (1,200 m). Even though the collision occurred about 500 ft (150 m) below the overcast, where the visibility was in excess of 15 miles (c 25 km), the jetliner had been in the clouds until 14 sec before impact, giving both crews only that amount of time to make visual contact and initiate evasive action. Witnesses observed no such manoeuvres by either aircraft before they hit. It was noted in the investigative report of the US National Transportation Safety Board (NTSB) that the first officer of *N988VJ* was in the best position to see *N7374J*, but would then have been monitoring the altimeter and not watching for conflicting traffic. In addition, the speed of the transport, nearly 300 mph (c 480 kmh), was slightly high when considering the weather and operational regulations in effect at the time, though still within the prescribed limits.

The NTSB attributed the disaster to deficiencies in the capability of the air traffic control system maintained by the US Federal Aviation Administration (FAA) in a terminal area wherein there was a mix of IFR and VFR traffic flying at different speeds. These deficiencies included the inadequacy of the 'see-and-avoid' concept under the circumstances of the accident; the technical limitations of radar in detecting all aircraft; and the absence of regulations providing a system of separating such mixed traffic in terminal areas.

Neither the Indianapolis control centre nor Indianapolis approach control, which were handling the DC-9, reported observing the Cherokee on their radar equipment prior to the collision. In the case of the former, this resulted from the inadequate cross-section of the aircraft and the fact that the radar was being operated on lower power at the time to counteract the effects of 'anomalous propagation' associated with a temperature inversion. (This phenomenon consists of the return from objects beyond the normal range of the radar appearing as close-in targets and cluttering the screen.) In the case of the latter, the Cherokee was initially not detected because of the tangential blind speed effect. (This occurs when the relative speed of the target falls below that of the revolving antenna.) Later, the light aeroplane was not seen on approach control radar either due to the effects of the same inversion or simply because the controller's attention had been diverted by other duties, which precluded his monitoring of the radarscope.

The following year the FAA implemented a terminal control system around major US airports, requiring positive control of all aircraft flying within. Climb and descent corridors for higher-speed IFR traffic were established at numerous other less-congested airports.

Date: 20 September 1969 (c 16:00)
Location: Near Hoi An, (South) Vietnam
First aircraft
Operator: Air Vietnam (South Vietnam)
Type: Douglas DC-4 (*XV-NUG*)
Second aircraft
Operator: US Air Force
Type: McDonnell F-4E Phantom II (*67-393*)

Both aircraft were approaching to land at Da Nang Air Base, the commercial transport at the end of a scheduled domestic service that had originated at Saigon (now Ho Chi Minh City) and the jet fighter returning from a combat mission, when they collided at a height of about 300 ft (100 m). The DC-4 then crashed, killing all but two of the 77 persons aboard, including the entire crew of six, plus two others on the ground. Both surviving passengers and two persons on the ground were injured. The Phantom's navigator also suffered minor injuries when he ejected and parachuted to earth, while the pilot managed to land the damaged aircraft safely. At around the time of the accident the local weather consisted of a high overcast and scattered clouds at lower altitudes, with a visibility of approximately 10 miles (15 km).

An analysis of the air/ground communications indicated that the pilot of the airliner, which was supposed to use Runway 17-Left, had misconstrued instructions transmitted from the control tower to the military jet ('. . . You are cleared to land on 17-Right') as intended for him (as evidenced by his immediate response 'Roger, 17-Right'), and strayed into the path of the F-4. In the resulting collision the starboard horizontal stabiliser of the DC-4 was torn off. The crew retracted the undercarriage and attempted a go around, but the aircraft plummeted into a field and exploded.

G-ARVA, later re-registered as 5N-ABD, was the Nigeria Airways VC-10 that crashed during an attempted landing at Lagos airport. (Air Britain Historians Ltd)

Date: 20 November 1969 (c 08:30)
Location: Near Ikeja, Nigeria
Operator: Nigeria Airways
Aircraft type: BAC VC-10 (*5N-ABD*)

Operating as Flight 825, the jet airliner crashed and burned 8 miles (c 13 km) north of Lagos airport, where it was to have landed at the end of a service from London, with en route stops at Rome, Italy, and Kano, Nigeria. All 87 persons aboard (76 passengers and 11 crew members) perished.

Its undercarriage down and flaps partially extended, the VC-10 hit trees and then slammed to earth during a straight-in very-high-frequency omni-directional range (VOR) instrument procedure approach to Runway 19. Though clear at the airport, the weather was foggy in the area of the accident.

There was no evidence of any pre-impact mechanical failure or defect in the aircraft. Although the cause could not be determined with certainty, the crash was believed to have resulted from a lack of altitude awareness on the part of the crew, probably through insufficient monitoring of the instruments. This led to a descent below a safe height when the pilots were not in visual contact with the ground.

Fatigue may have contributed to the suspected human error.

Date: 3 December 1969 (c 19:00)
Location: Near Caracas, Venezuela
Operator: Air France
Aircraft type: Boeing 707-328B (*F-BHSZ*)

Designated as Flight 212, the jet airliner mysteriously crashed in the Caribbean Sea approximately 5 miles (10 km) from shore, and all 62 persons aboard (51 passengers, including a relief crew of 10, and 11 regular crew members) perished.

The disaster occurred in darkness about 3 minutes after the 707 had taken off from Maiquetia Airport, serving Caracas, bound for Guadeloupe, one segment of a service originating at Santiago, Chile, with an ultimate destination of Paris. Climbing to an approximate height of 3,000 ft (1,000 m), its nose suddenly dropped, and the aircraft then plummeted into water some 150 ft (50 m) deep.

The remains of numerous bodies were later found, and examination of the recovered debris disclosed no evidence of pre-impact fire or explosion.

Date: 8 December 1969 (20:46)
Location: Near Keratea, Greece
Operator: Olympic Airways (Greece)
Aircraft type: Douglas DC-6B (*SX-DAE*)

All 90 persons aboard (85 passengers and a crew of five) perished when the aircraft crashed some 25 miles (40 km) south-west of Athens, while preparing to land at the city's airport at the end of a scheduled service from Canea, on the island of Crete.

Its undercarriage still retracted, the DC-6B was flying in darkness, rain and high winds when it struck Mt Pan at an approximate elevation of 2,000 ft (600 m), bursting into flames on impact. Though adverse, the meteorological conditions were not considered dangerous.

The flight crew had deviated from the proper track and had descended below the minimum safety altitude during the initial phase of the instrument landing system (ILS) approach.

The 1970s

The Boeing 747 introduced air travellers to the 'jumbo jet' era in 1970. This massive transport was joined in succession by the McDonnell Douglas DC-10, the Lockheed L-1011 TriStar and, a while later, the Airbus family of jetliners. The size of the aircraft actually created the problem of over-capacity in the airline industry, literally offering more seats than there were passengers to fill them.

Wide-bodied jets brought about unparalleled standards of safety and performance. The first fatal 747 crash would not occur until nearly five years and more than two million flying hours into its service life. The L-1011 had the unfortunate distinction of being the first of the new generation of airliners to be involved in a fatal accident. Subsequently, however, it would amass an equally impressive record of safety.

The consequences of what everyone had feared the most – the non-survivable crash of a fully-loaded wide-bodied transport – were fully realised in March 1974, when a Turkish Airlines DC-10 crashed near Paris with a loss of 346 lives, a toll nearly double that of the worst previous aviation disaster. The tragedy also brought to light a serious design flaw in the aircraft's cargo door, proving that even the most sophisticated technology is fallible. Five years later another catastrophic DC-10 accident in the United States led to the temporary grounding of the giant jet. Again a design weakness proved to be an underlying factor.

The worst possible scenario took place in the spring of 1977, when two 747s collided inexplicably on a fog-cloaked airport runway in the Canary Islands. Nearly 600 persons were killed in the disaster.

Date: 6 February 1970 (time unknown)
Location: Near Samarkand, Uzbek SSR, USSR
Operator: Aeroflot (USSR)
Aircraft type: Ilyushin Il-18 (*SSSR-75798*)

Operating on a scheduled domestic service from Tashkent, the four-engine turboprop airliner crashed and burned on a cloud-obscured mountain, in daylight hours and at an approximate elevation of 5,000 ft (1,500 m), as it was approaching to land at the Samarkand airport. Bad weather prevented searchers from locating the wreckage until three days later, after which the few who survived the impact had frozen to death, leaving no survivors among the 92 persons aboard (85 passengers and a crew of seven).

The air traffic controller had misidentified the aircraft's location, which placed the flight some 20 miles (30 km) from the airport, or about 5 miles (10 km) closer than its actual position. The resulting incorrect information provided to the crew, combined with their own violation of the approved approach pattern, led to a premature descent below the obstructing terrain.

Date: 15 February 1970 (c 18:30)
Location: Near Santo Domingo, Dominican Republic
Operator: Compania Dominicana de Aviacion C por A (Dominican Republic)
Aircraft type: McDonnell Douglas DC-9 Series 32 (*HI-177*)

The jet airliner plunged into the Caribbean Sea approximately 2 miles (3 km) off shore, and all 102 persons aboard (97 passengers and five crew members) perished.

Only about 2 minutes after the DC-9 had taken off from the city's international airport, on a scheduled service to San Juan, Puerto Rico, a crewman reported a loss of power in one of its two engines and that the flight was turning back. The aircraft descended rapidly after initiating a right turn and finally crashed some 3 miles (5 km) from the airport. The disaster occurred in twilight conditions, but the weather was excellent.

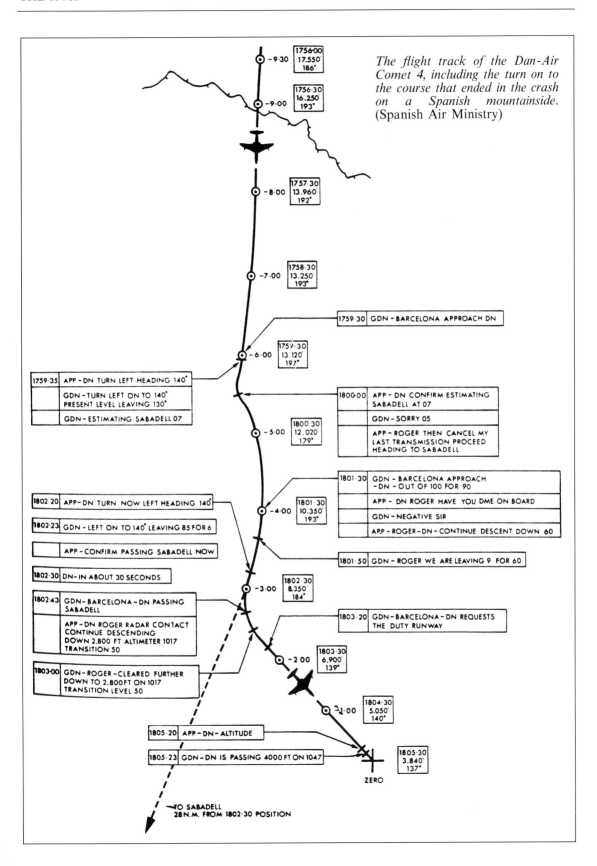

The flight track of the Dan-Air Comet 4, including the turn on to the course that ended in the crash on a Spanish mountainside. (Spanish Air Ministry)

Some debris and the remains of two dozen victims were found, but most of the wreckage, including the power plants, instruments and the flight data recorder (FDR), was lost in about 1,000 ft (300 m) of water and could not be recovered for examination. There was no trace of fire on any of the recovered parts.

Date: 3 July 1970 (19:05)
Location: Near Arbucias, Gerona, Spain
Operator: Dan-Air Services Ltd (UK)
Aircraft type: de Havilland Comet 4 (*G-APDN*)

All 112 persons aboard (105 passengers and a crew of seven) perished when the jet airliner crashed in the Sierra de Montseny region some 30 miles (50 km) north-east of Barcelona and approximately 40 miles (65 km) from the city's airport, where it was to have landed at the end of a charter service from Manchester, England.

Cleanly configured, the Comet was on an approximate heading of 140 degrees and in a slight descent when it struck the wooded slope of Les Angudes Peak, at an elevation of about 4,000 ft (1,200 m), exploding in flames on impact. At the time of the crash its true air speed was in excess of 250 mph (400 kmh). The accident occurred in daylight, but the mountains were obscured by a mass of stratus and strato-cumulus clouds, with a base of roughly 2,500–3,000 ft (800–1,000 m), which reduced visibility to nil.

Due to heavy traffic in the vicinity of Paris, the jet was intentionally diverted from the route laid down in its flight plan, but it subsequently began to deviate to the left of the assigned airway. The displacement of the flight track could have resulted from a defect in the aircraft's equipment. Significantly, its position could only have been determined by the intersection of radials following passage of the Toulouse very-high-frequency omnidirectional range (VOR) station, also in France. There was no evidence of any aberrations in the Barcelona VOR.

The Spanish approach controller did not realise that the Comet was flying some 15 miles (25 km) to the east and not above the Berga reporting point. This, coupled with an incorrect estimated time of arrival at the Sabadell non-directional beacon (NDB), made it difficult for him to identify the radar target of the airliner. In an attempt to facilitate identification, he instructed it to turn on to the south-easterly heading that was continued until impact.

About 3 minutes before it crashed, the jet reported passing the Sabadell NDB, when in fact it was still 32 miles (52 km) from that position. By coincidence, the controller had observed on his radar screen the echo of another aircraft (whose speed was similar to that expected from a Comet) over the beacon at the same time, which he misidentified as *G-APDN*. He then cleared the transport for descent to 2,800 ft (c 850 m), the minimum altitude where it was believed to have been, but not at its actual location.

The installation of a secondary radar system at Barcelona after this disaster would assure proper identification of an aircraft equipped with a

An Air Canada DC-8 Super 63, identical to the aircraft that crashed after a baulked landing at Toronto International Airport. (Programmed Communications Ltd)

transponder, as was the Comet. The investigative report on the accident also noted the importance of using all navigational aids, and recommended that radio-navigational charts illustrate the heights of significant points along designated routes.

Date: 5 July 1970 (08:09)
Location: Near Malton, Ontario, Canada
Operator: Air Canada
Aircraft type: McDonnell Douglas DC-8 Super 63 (*CF-TIW*)

Flight 621, which had taken off earlier on this Sunday morning from Montreal, Quebec, was cleared to land on Runway 32 at Toronto International Airport, a scheduled stop during a service with an ultimate destination of Los Angeles, California, US. The airport weather at the time was ideal, with scattered clouds at 3,500 ft (c 1,050 m) and a visibility of 20 miles (c 30 km).

As transcribed on the cockpit voice recorder (CVR) tape, Captain Peter Hamilton and First Officer Donald Rowland omitted the 'spoilers armed' item in their pre-landing checks. They agreed that the lift-reduction devices would be armed during the flare, allowing for their automatic extension when the wheels of the aircraft made contact with the pavement. However, as the DC-8 passed over the runway threshold at an approximate height of 60 ft (20 m), the co-pilot committed an error that would prove fatal. When authorised by the pilot to arm the ground spoilers, which would involve lifting the appropriate lever on the control console, he instead pulled it to the rear, resulting in their immediate deployment. The captain commanded 'No, no, no!' and the first officer, realising his mistake, responded with 'Sorry. Oh, sorry, Pete'.

Action by the pilot, who applied full power to all four engines and rotated the aircraft's nose upward to counter the high rate of descent that had developed, was unsuccessful in preventing the exceptionally hard landing that resulted from the spoiler extension. The impact on the main undercarriage, after which the tail skid hit the ground, generated forces that caused the separation of the No 4 engine pod and pylon assembly and also punctured the bottom of the No 4 alternate fuel tank. Escaping fuel then ignited, possibly after coming in contact with wiring severed when the power plant broke off.

On the ground for only a fraction of a second, the DC-8 then climbed away, the captain radioing his intention to circle the airport and land again on the same runway. The aircraft's undercarriage, which had apparently not been badly damaged, was raised for the go-around, and its flaps brought up to 20 degrees; the spoilers were by then fully retracted.

Only about 3 minutes after the hard landing *CF-TIW* was rocked by three explosions, the second of which ripped free the No 3 engine pod and pylon and the last one blasting away a large segment of the right outer wing. Unable to sustain flight, the jet airliner plunged from an approximate height of 3,000 ft (1,000 m) into a field some 5 miles (10 km) north of the airport and at an indicated air speed in excess of 250 mph (400 kmh), disintegrating in a

The shattered remains of the Air Canada Super DC-8 are strewn across the Canadian countryside. (UPI/Bettmann)

ball of fire on impact. All 109 persons aboard (100 passengers and nine crew members) perished.

It might be difficult to understand how such an innocuous mistake as the one made by the first officer could have such catastrophic consequences, but in its investigative report a board of inquiry blamed the disaster as much on faulty design as human error. It argued that while a mechanism using one handle to perform completely different tasks might be acceptable for a secondary system, such as heating or ventilation, it was not appropriate for one that operated something as vital as the spoilers. At the very least, it ruled, the activating lever should have been fitted with some kind of guard or gate. Preferably the system would have been made so as to prevent deployment while the aircraft was in the air.

Furthermore, the inquiry found that the instruction manuals provided by the manufacturer contained information that was misleading, incomplete and even inaccurate, stating in fact that a mechanism built into the system would prevent such an in-flight spoiler extension. As a result, even the Air Canada training staff did not realise that such inadvertent deployment as that which happened to *CF-TIW* was possible, which meant that the airline's pilots were not being made aware of this potential threat to safety.

These factors, coupled with the failure of the Canadian Ministry of Transport to note differences between the DC-8 operating manuals used by Air Canada and the nation's other carriers, and the acceptance by both the government agency and the company of an aircraft employing a spoiler system that the board had labelled as defective, were considered as contributory to the crash. The board also criticised the design of the pod/pylon structure and what it described as the failure of the manufacturer to ensure the integrity of the fuel and electrical systems built into the DC-8.

In using their own method of activating the spoilers, the crew of Flight 621 were not adhering to the prescribed Air Canada procedures, which dictated that the system be armed for automatic deployment at an altitude of 1,000 ft (c 300 m). Interestingly, on the day of the accident the pilots did not even use the technique they had adopted when flying together previously, ie to extend manually the spoilers after touch-down.

Had the aircraft continued the landing after the error by the first officer, this would probably have been only a minor incident, with no casualties; but the captain was not faulted for his decision to execute the overshoot procedure. The board noted that in trying to prevent or lessen the impact with the runway, he had placed the jet in a position normally used for such a manoeuvre, and under the circumstances continuing the take-off was the logical thing to do. Furthermore, there was no evidence that the crew had realised the extent of the

damage sustained by the DC-8 until it was too late.

As a result of this disaster, the US Federal Aviation Administration (FAA) issued an airworthiness directive (AD) requiring placard warnings against in-flight deployment of ground spoilers by DC-8 operators. Following a non-fatal accident some three years after the Air Canada crash, the FAA issued another AD requiring that all aircraft of the type be fitted with spoiler locking mechanisms to prevent such an occurrence.

Date: 9 August 1970 (c 15:00)
Location: Near Cuzco, Peru
Operator: Lineas Aereas Nacionales SA (LANSA) (Peru)
Aircraft type: Lockheed 188A Electra (*OB-R939*)

The four-engine turboprop crashed shortly after taking off from the city's airport on a scheduled domestic service to Lima, killing 99 persons aboard, including eight members of the crew, plus two others on the ground. Only the first officer, who was seriously injured, survived the disaster.

Following the failure of its No 3 power plant during the take-off, the Electra continued climbing straight ahead. The flaps were then retracted and a left turn commenced at an approximate height of 300 ft (100 m) above the ground. Due to the limited space available a steep bank was required, but during the turn the airliner slammed into a hill and exploded. Reportedly it was foggy in the area of the crash at the time.

Besides the mechanical malfunction, the accident was attributed to a procedural error on the part of the captain.

Date: 14 November 1970 (19:35)
Location: Near Huntington, West Virginia, US
Operator: Southern Airways (US)
Aircraft type: McDonnell Douglas DC-9 Series 31 (*N97S*)

Tragedy struck the Marshall University football team as it was returning home from an interstate game at Greenville, North Carolina, when the chartered jetliner, carrying 36 players, five coaches, the team trainer, boosters and a crew of five, crashed west of Tri-State Airport, where it was to have landed. All 75 persons aboard were killed.

The aircraft had been cleared for a non-precision approach to Runway 11, using localiser guidance, before the accident occurred in evening darkness and during a light rain, with fog, smoke, scattered clouds at 300 ft (100 m), a broken overcast at 500 ft (c 150 m), solid coverage at 1,000 ft (c 300 m), and a visibility of 5 miles (10 km). Its undercarriage down and flaps fully extended, the DC-9 hit trees, then slammed into a hill about 1 mile (1.5 km) from the threshold of the runway and some 280 ft (85 m) to the right of its extended centreline, exploded and burned.

The jetliner had continued more than 300 ft (100 m) below the minimum descent altitude (MDA) before the flight crew initiated a missed approach procedure. The reason for this could not be determined, although the two most likely explanations were an error in the aircraft's static system that caused the barometric altimeters to indicate a reading higher than its actual altitude and the vertical speed indicators to show a decrease in the rate of descent, or reliance by the crew on the radio altimeters as a primary reference for determining height.

The first hypothesis was supported by the read-out from the flight data recorder (FDR), which uses a separate static system, showing a higher-than-normal rate of descent, and by analysing the cockpit voice recorder (CVR) tape, showing that all but one of the first officer's altitude call-outs were approximately 200 ft (60 m) above the actual height of the aircraft. One weakness to this theory was that an error in the static system should have caused a similar discrepancy in the air speed indicators, which probably would have been noticed by the crew, but there was no evidence of such an erroneous indication.

Regarding the second hypothesis, the call-outs by the co-pilot, when correlated with the FDR data, were similar to those that would be expected if the radio altimeter were being used. But the US National Transportation Safety Board (NTSB) expressed doubt that an experienced crew would rely only upon the radio altimeter when the instrument is not intended for use, and is not reliable, over the kind of uneven terrain found under the approach path to Tri-State Airport. Sound operating procedures dictate that the captain also refer to his barometric altimeter, and the disparity between that and the reading on either his radio altimeter or that of the first officer, reflected in the call-outs, would have been detected.

It was determined that the co-pilot did not make all of the required call-outs, including 500 ft above airport elevation, 100 ft above minimum altitude and decision height, and the captain, who had been using the autopilot throughout the approach, did not start levelling off until after the DC-9 had descended through what he thought was the MDA. The effects of these deviations and the subsequent accident were difficult to assess.

The crew apparently observed the glow from the lights of a refinery, and this, coupled with the fact that the pilot knew he was approaching the bottom layer of the overcast, could have induced him to continue below the decision height. The NTSB concluded, however, that the crew never made visual contact with any part of the airport and were not aware that the aircraft had descended below the MDA.

Although the airport did have an instrument landing system (ILS) localiser, no glide slope had been included because the terrain was not suitable to provide an adequate reflecting surface for the antenna. A non-standard glide slope that might have prevented this accident was later installed.

One of the recommendations made by the NTSB in its report on the crash was for the development of specific crew procedures for non-precision approaches as in the case of those that utilise the ILS.

Date: 23 May 1971 (c 20:00)
Location: Near Rijeka, Yugoslavia
Operator: Aviogenex (Yugoslavia)
Aircraft type: Tupolev Tu-134A (*YU-AHZ*)

The jet airliner was on a charter service from London and carrying mostly British tourists when it crashed on landing at Rijeka Airport. Among the 83 persons aboard, only one passenger and the four members of the flight crew survived, all of whom escaped serious injury. The 78 persons killed included the aircraft's three stewardesses.

Dusk had set in and it was heavily overcast, with thunderstorm activity in the area and the cloud level down to about 2,000 ft (600 m), as the twin-engine jet made its approach to Runway 14, using instrument landing system (ILS) guidance. At a point some 2.5 miles (4 km) from the runway threshold and at an approximate height of 1,000 ft (300 m) above the ground, the aircraft entered an area of heavy rain. It also encountered turbulence and, less than a minute before touchdown, was carried upward and rolled to the right. This disturbance, which could be explained by a moderate gust, a change of wind velocity and by the aircraft coming out of the zone of heavy rain, caused a deviation from the correct flight path.

Unable to return to the ILS, the crew attempted to regain alignment with the runway visually, and succeeded in doing so. Still above the glide slope, though, the pilots lowered the nose of the Tu-134 and reduced power. Subsequently there was a decrease in air speed and a steepening in the angle of descent. In the resulting hard landing, which was at a speed of around 150 mph (250 kmh), the extended main gear bore the brunt of the initial impact, and the port wing broke just inside the undercarriage leg. The aircraft then turned over and slid, inverted, some 2,300 ft (700 m) down the runway, bursting into flames before coming to a stop. Its fuselage rapidly filled with carbon monoxide, preventing rescuers from saving any more of the occupants, even though all must have survived the actual crash.

The improper handling of the flight and power plant controls that preceded the accident could be attributed to the false perceptions of the crew due to the intense rain, which caused a refraction of light. This optical illusion gave the pilots the impression of being closer to the runway and higher above the ground than was actually the case.

Date: 6 June 1971 (c 18:10)
Location: Near Duarte, California, US
First aircraft
Operator: Hughes Air West (US)
Type: McDonnell Douglas DC-9 Series 31 (*N9345*)
Second aircraft
Operator: US Marine Corps
Type: McDonnell F-4B Phantom II (*151458*)

Designated as Flight 706, the DC-9 departed from Los Angeles International Airport bound for Salt Lake City, Utah, its first stop during a domestic service with an ultimate destination of Seattle, Washington. The jet airliner was operating under instrument flight rules (IFR) and positive control.

Less than 10 min after taking off, and while climbing on a north-easterly heading to its assigned altitude, the transport collided with the southbound jet fighter, which was en route to the El Toro Marine Air Station, in Southern California. Colliding almost at right-angles, the vertical stabiliser of the F-4B passed through the lower left cockpit area of the DC-9, and its right wing passed through the passenger cabin.

The charred remains of the Hughes Air West DC-9 lie in a canyon after the collision with a US Marine Corps jet fighter. (Wide World Photos)

The collision occurred at an approximate height of 15,000 ft (5,000 m) and some 20 miles (30 km) north-east of downtown Los Angeles, and both aircraft then plummeted into the San Gabriel Mountains. The transport erupted into flames when it crashed in Fish Canyon, and the fighter, which had caught fire in flight, fell less than 1 mile (1.5 km) away. All 49 persons aboard the airliner (44 passengers and a crew of five) and the pilot of the military jet, who was apparently unable to eject because the front canopy would not jettison, perished.

The fighter's radar intercept officer (RIO) parachuted to safety and was the sole survivor of the disaster.

The US National Transportation Safety Board (NTSB) blamed the collision on the failure of both crews to see and avoid each other's aircraft, but recognised that their ability to detect one another, assess the situation and initiate evasive action was only marginal. Contributing to the accident were a high closure rate, calculated to have been almost 750 mph (c 1,200 kmh), and the fact that the Marine jet had entered a busy air corridor under visual flight rules (VFR) while not in contact with the regional air traffic control centre.

Because of an oxygen system leak, the Phantom was being flown below its normal cruising altitude, and as a result of an inoperative transponder, reduced detectability due to design and configuration, and a low-level temperature inversion in the area, the fighter's target did not show up well enough on the radarscope to be noticed by a controller otherwise unaware of its presence. Furthermore, its pilot did not request air traffic control assistance that could have prevented the disaster.

The F-4 did have its own air-to-air radar system, but, besides being in a degraded state it was in a mapping rather than search mode, at the request of the pilot. As a result no airborne targets were observed, including the DC-9. Under the circumstances, the pilot should have used the RIO to help maintain a look-out for other air traffic. Actually, the latter did see the airliner after turning away from his radarscope, and he shouted to the pilot, who had already initiated a left roll. The air carrier crew may not have even seen the fighter, or saw it when it was too late to take evasive action. (The latter's failure was probably partly attributable to a lack of recurrent training in lookout and scanning techniques and reliance on ground controllers to provide traffic separation.)

Visibility was generally good in the vicinity at the time, although a layer of haze in the background would have made the DC-9 less conspicuous to the Phantom crew. Cockpit visibility and limitations of human eyesight would have further hampered the 'see-and-avoid' principle. Additionally, both

A Toa Domestic Airlines YS-11A-200, in the same livery as the aircraft that crashed in northern Japan. (K. Hoashi/Ikaros/Uniphoto Press International)

aircraft were on an essentially constant bearing with respect to one another, and would thus have remained almost stationary from each other's perspective.

Following this accident, most military flights began to switch to IFR procedures, and the NTSB recommended to the US Department of Defense that air intercept radar on such aircraft as the F-4 also be used for collision avoidance.

Date: 3 July 1971 (c 18: 10)
Location: Hokkaido, Japan
Operator: Toa Domestic Airlines (Japan)
Aircraft type: NAMC YS-11A-227 (*JA8764*)

All 68 persons aboard (64 passengers and four crew members) were killed when the twin-engine turboprop, on a domestic intra-island service from Sapporo to Hakodate, crashed near its destination.

In the last radio transmission from Flight 63, the pilot reported approaching the Hakodate non-directional beacon (NDB). Its undercarriage retracted and flaps partially extended, the aircraft was flying on an east-north-easterly heading with its right wing slightly low when it struck a mountain ridge at an approximate elevation of 3,000 ft (1,000 m), some 10 miles (15 km) north-north-west of the city's airport. Hampered by bad weather, searchers were not able to locate the wreckage until the following day. Although a small fire did erupt in the area of the left power plant, there was no major post-impact blaze.

The meteorological conditions at the airport around the time of the accident were near the minima for an automatic direction finder (ADF) instrument procedure landing. Just before the crash, the YS-11 was believed to have been in the midst of an overcast, with possible rain and turbulence within the clouds. The velocity of the wind in the area could have been high and the direction changeable because of the terrain.

Presumably the pilot had mistaken his position as being over the NDB, when in fact the aircraft was about 5 miles (10 km) north of the navigational aid, which he attempted to circle. A strong south-westerly wind also caused it to drift northward. The expected passage of the beacon was about 2 minutes early, but the crew must not have detected the error, apparently due to an incorrect ADF indication, with the instrument having been affected by the atmospheric conditions. Though revised by 1 minute, the flight plan that had been prepared by the airline was not modified to compensate for wind, temperature and altitude factors.

A number of safety recommendations were made in the investigative report on this accident, including the installation of distance-measuring equipment (DME), an instrument landing system (ILS) and a very-high-frequency omni-directional range (VOR) station at Hakodate, and the establishment of a long-range radar facility that in this case would have covered the entire route of the flight. Some of these proposals were incorporated into an extensive programme designed to improve Japan's airport/airway system, which was initiated even before the crash of Flight 63.

Date: 25 July 1971 (time unknown)
Location: Near Irkutsk, Russian Soviet Federated
    Socialist Republic, USSR
Operator: Aeroflot (USSR)
Aircraft type: Tupolev Tu-104B (*SSSR-42405*)

The jet airliner crashed as it was attempting to
land at the Irkutsk airport, an en route stop
during a scheduled domestic service from
Novosibirsk to Vladivostok, killing 97 persons
aboard. Four of its eight crew members and 25
passengers survived. The accident occurred at night
and in instrument meteorological conditions.

During the approach and when over the outer
marker beacon, the ground controller advised that
the aircraft was to the left of the runway axis. The
subsequent corrective action was excessive,
however, necessitating another turn in the opposite
direction. As a result of the second manoeuvre, the
Tu-104 was banked slightly to the left when it
touched down on its main undercarriage, the port
gear first followed by the starboard, some 500 ft
(150 m) short of the runway threshold. The final
approach had been conducted some 15–20 mph
(25–35 kmh) below the required speed, but with a
high descent rate, and in the hard undershot landing
the aircraft's left wing separated from the fuselage.
The twin-engine jet then rolled to the left, turned
over and burst into flames.

Although no flight data recorder (FDR)
information was available to the investigative
commission, and the exact cause remained
unidentified, the accident probably resulted from a
combination of faulty piloting technique and an
incorrect altimeter indication that was too high.

Date: 30 July 1971 (c 14:00)
Location: Near Morioka, Iwate, Japan
First aircraft
Operator: All Nippon Airways (Japan)
Type: Boeing 727-281 (*JA8329*)
Second aircraft
Operator: Japan Air Self-Defence Force (JASDF)
Type: North American F-86F Sabre (*92-7932*)

Operating as Flight 58, the jetliner had taken off
earlier from Chitose Airport, located on
Hokkaido and serving Sapporo, on a domestic
service to Tokyo. Cruising along a prescribed
airway at a height of 28,000 ft (c 8,500 m) and on

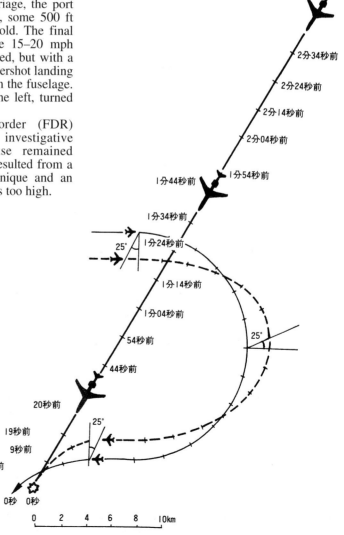

*The flight paths of the F-86 jet
fighters and the All Nippon
Airways Boeing 727 in the final
moments before the mid-air
crash.* (Japanese Ministry of
Transport/Ikaros/Uniphoto Press
International)

an approximate heading of 190 degrees, the transport collided with the jet fighter over the village of Shizukuishi, some 275 miles (440 km) north of the capital city. Both aircraft then crashed, and all 162 persons aboard the 727 (155 passengers and a crew of seven) perished. Additionally an elderly woman on the ground was reportedly injured when a piece of wreckage fell through the roof of a house.

A 22-year-old student pilot was at the controls of the fighter, accompanied by his instructor in another F-86. The former had not been briefed on either the altitude at which they would be flying or the route they would take.

Shortly before the accident, the instructor began a left turn, with the trainee following about 3,000 ft (1,000 m) below his aircraft; the student was concentrating on maintaining his position with the flight leader, rather than watching out for air traffic. Seeing the 727, the instructor immediately ordered him to take evasive action, and the trainee, who saw the jetliner approximately 2 seconds before impact, did so, but too late to prevent the disaster. Though the airline crew may have observed the fighter a few seconds prior to the collision, there was no evidence of an avoidance manoeuvre.

When they hit, the indicated air speed of the transport was approximately 560 mph (900 kmh), and that of the military jet around 520 mph (840 kmh), with the former in level flight and the latter still banked to the left. Initial contact was at the leading edge of the 727's left horizontal stabiliser and the trailing edge of the Sabre's right wing. The fighter then nosed over and struck, with the bottom of its front fuselage section, the upper left-hand side of the jetliner's vertical stabiliser. The fighter's right wing was torn off and the horizontal tail assembly of the 727 damaged. Both aircraft became uncontrollable and plummeted to earth in pieces, scattering wreckage over a wide area.

The canopy of the Sabre had come off, and although he was unable to reach the ejection lever, the pilot managed to climb out of the cockpit and abandon the aircraft as it spiralled down. He landed safely by parachute in a rice paddy.

Despite the fact that the formation and turn training required substantial airspace, the military exercise was being conducted in a rather small area, at a considerable height and under visual flight rules (VFR) procedures, making it impossible to determine an exact position. As a result, the instructor did not realise that he and his student had strayed out of the designated training area and into the airway. The weather was apparently not a factor in the accident, with good visibility and scattered clouds at lower altitudes.

The two airmen were later convicted of 'professional negligence' and sentenced to prison, and the disaster also led to a shake-up within the JASDF, with its Director General accepting

responsibility and submitting his resignation.

Among the safety recommendations made in the investigative report on the collision were the expansion of radar control zones, the prohibition of aircraft that constantly change their heading and/or height from entering these areas, and the establishment of specific regions for military training flights. A five-year plan launched by the government of Japan to modernise the nation's air traffic control system, which had begun even before this accident, was consequently accelerated. Additionally, most JASDF training was moved out over the sea, away from commercial airways.

Date: 4 September 1971 (c 12:15)
Location: Near Juneau, Alaska, US
Operator: Alaska Airlines (US)
Aircraft type: Boeing 727-193 (*N2969G*)

Alaska is without a doubt the most air-minded of all the American states. It also has some of the most treacherous flying conditions anywhere, with terrain and weather that can place a heavy demand on both pilots and equipment – during the year 1971, the state actually experienced more fatalities in air crashes than in road traffic accidents, the primary reason for this being the disaster that befell Flight 1866.

Although a portion of the trip would take place over foreign territory, this was still classified as a domestic service, originating at Anchorage with an ultimate destination of Seattle, Washington. One of the four scheduled stops along the way was at the Alaskan state capital.

Shortly before noon, the 727 was reported in a holding pattern, and it completed the circuit once before receiving clearance for a straight-in approach to land on Runway 08 at Juneau Municipal Airport, using localiser directional aid procedures. The airport control tower relayed the latest meteorological information, but there was no further communication with the flight.

The jetliner crashed in the Chilkat Mountain Range some 20 miles (30 km) west of the airport, and all 111 persons aboard (104 passengers and seven crew members) perished. Configured with its undercarriage extended and flaps retracted, the aircraft struck the eastern side of a canyon at an approximate elevation of 2,500 ft (750 m) and disintegrated. At the moment of impact, its indicated air speed was about 230 mph (370 kmh) and its heading approximately 70 degrees. There was evidence of scattered, independent fires throughout the wreckage area.

The accident apparently resulted from the display of misleading navigational information that made the crew believe that the flight had progressed further along the localiser course than was actually the case, which resulted in a premature descent below the obstructing terrain. This theory was borne

Little remains of the Alaska Airlines Boeing 727 that slammed into the mountain, with a loss of 111 lives. (Wide World Photos)

out through the correlation of comments transcribed on the cockpit voice recorder (CVR) tape with the flight data recorder (FDR) read-out – at one point the 727 was about 10 miles (15 km) west of its reported position. Similar erroneous indications were evident in subsequent intra-cockpit conversation. The origin or nature of the information could not be determined.

There was no evidence of a malfunction in the Doppler very-high-frequency omni-directional range (VOR) system, but this could not be ruled out completely. Nor were there indications of any problems with the 727's navigational equipment, although the degree of destruction could have masked such a technical failure. Spurious signals affecting the VOR reception were discounted, and incompatibility between the aircraft's navigational receivers and the system could not be substantiated.

A possible operational factor leading to the crash was the presence of a twin-engine Piper Apache that had accepted an improper clearance and was lost in the area. Compounding its plight were communications difficulties, and as a result the regional air traffic control centre asked the jetliner to relay messages between it and the general aviation aircraft. Besides adding to the work load of the airline crew and maybe even affecting its co-ordination, the light aeroplane represented a potential conflict with the 727. From his comments recorded by the CVR, the captain of Flight 1866 seemed rather irritated about the situation. This distraction could have been significant had he tuned in the Juneau localiser in preparation for holding before the three-way conversation, then in oversight set the prescribed radial without changing the frequency of his receiver to that of the VOR station.

The only apparent deviation in the crew's routine was the absence of aural identification procedures when tuning in the different navigational facilities (this consists of increasing the volume gain until the 'navaid' code can be heard). The crew did not use either of the two available non-directional beacon (NDB) navigational aids that could have helped determine the progress of the flight, although this was not part of the prescribed procedure.

The weather in the vicinity of the accident site at the time was characterised by multiple layers of cloud with bases between 1,000 and 1,500 ft (c 300–500 m), which would have obscured the terrain and prevented the crew from noticing and correcting the navigational error.

Not long after the disaster, distance-measuring equipment (DME) was installed at the Juneau airport to provide pilots with an additional means of establishing their position.

Date: 2 October 1971 (11:10)
Location: Near Aarsele, West Vlaanderen, Belgium
Operator: British European Airways (BEA)
Aircraft type: Vickers Vanguard 951 (*G-APEC*)

Everything was normal as Flight 706 cruised over the Belgian countryside at 19,000 ft (c 5,800 m) while en route from London to Salzburg, Austria. Then a sudden message of distress: 'Mayday, Mayday, Mayday . . . We're going down vertically', transmitted from the Vanguard, was heard at the Brussels air traffic control centre followed by 'Out of control!'.

Slowly rotating in a clockwise direction, the turboprop airliner plunged into a field at a steep angle, beyond the vertical, some 10 miles (15 km)

A British European Airways Vanguard 951, the type that crashed during a London to Salzburg service. (British Aerospace)

west-south-west of Ghent, bursting into flames on impact. All 63 persons aboard (55 passengers and a crew of eight) perished. Additionally, an occupant of a passing automobile was injured by flying debris.

The nature of the crash seemed to indicate the possibility of structural failure, and this was soon confirmed when both horizontal stabilisers and the corresponding elevators were found in pieces some distance from the main wreckage area, having obviously separated in flight. But the root cause of the failure was internal, not external. Examination revealed corrosion in the lower part of the rear pressure bulkhead, over an area of 18 in (48 cm), under plating that was bonded to the structure. The bond was completely delaminated in this area and the bulkhead material literally eaten away. Tears ran upward and outward from the corroded area.

The corrosion had probably required a relatively long period of time to develop, but on this particular flight the crack-weakened structure finally gave way to the stress created by pressurisation. When the bulkhead ruptured, air from the cabin rushed into the empennage, which was not designed to withstand such internal pressure. Interior damage and severe distortion of the outer skin led to the failure of both tailplanes under existing loads. The loss of aerodynamic support provided by the tail surfaces caused the Vanguard to enter the steep dive, from which recovery was not possible.

The corrosion was attributed to fluid contamination that may have been initiated by spillage from the lavatory, although this could not be substantiated. It was not detectable through the normal maintenance procedures used at the time, which consisted of both visual and radiographic inspection.

Subsequent to the accident, similar corrosion was found in eight other aircraft of the same type flown by BEA, nearly half of the airline's Vanguard fleet. Revised inspection techniques and a modification of the transport to improve access were later introduced with the objective of detecting corrosion before the structural integrity of the rear bulkhead could be affected. Additionally the number of inspections were increased considerably.

Date: 24 December 1971 (c 12:40)
Location: Near Puerto Inca, Huanuco, Peru
Operator: Lineas Aereas Nacionales SA (LANSA) (Peru)
Aircraft type: Lockheed 188A Electra (*OB-R-941*)

Designated as Flight 508, the turboprop airliner was on a domestic service from Lima to Iquitos, with an en route stop at Pucallpa, when it entered a thunderstorm, the cumulo-nimbus build-up containing heavy turbulence and severe lightning.

Suddenly, while flying at an altitude of 21,000 ft (6,400 m), or about 10,000 ft (3,000 m) above the ground, the Electra suffered catastrophic structural failure. Both its wings snapped, the right one separating completely, and its fuselage broke in several places. Burning wreckage was scattered some 10 miles (15 km) over the mountainous terrain.

The aircraft was still missing when three hunters found one of the passengers, a 17-year-old girl, alive. Injured in the crash, she was also treated for exposure to the elements after trekking through the forest for 10 days. The wreckage of *OB-R-941* was located two weeks after its disappearance, with no survivors among the other 91 persons aboard, including six crew members. However, there were indications that at least a dozen others had lived through the break-up and ground impact; it was theorised that the fall may have been cushioned by an enormous updraught.

The initial loss of the starboard wing apparently resulted from the effects of a lightning-induced explosion coupled with both the aerodynamic load imposed by the turbulence and by the stresses generated as the crew tried to regain level flight.

Date: 7 January 1972 (c 12:15)
Location: (Spanish) Balearic Islands
Operator: Lineas Aereas de Espana SA (Iberia) (Spain)
Aircraft type: Sud-Aviation Caravelle VI-R (*EC-ATV*)

The jet airliner, which was operating as Flight 602 and had stopped at Valencia, on the Spanish mainland, during a domestic service originating at Madrid, crashed on the island of Ibiza. All 104 persons aboard (98 passengers and a crew of six) perished.

Its undercarriage still retracted, the Caravelle stuck Rocas Altas Peak at an approximate elevation of 1,000 ft (300 m), or only about 100 ft (30 m) from the top of the mountain, while attempting to land at Ibiza Airport, located near San Jose. The

Flight outside of the airport traffic circuit resulted in the crash of an Alitalia DC-8 in which 115 persons were killed. (UPI/Bettmann)

aircraft exploded and disintegrated on impact, which took place at an indicated air speed of around 320 mph (515 kmh). At the time of the accident the weather consisted of a high overcast and patches of broken clouds between about 800 and 1,500 ft (250–500 m), with a visibility of approximately 5–10 miles (10–15 km). The wind was from the north at 10 knots.

It was ruled that the pilot had failed to maintain the minimum flight altitude during the final phase of a visual approach to Runway 07.

Date: 14 March 1972 (c 22:00)
Location: Near Al Fujayrah, United Arab Emirates
Operator: Sterling Airways (Denmark)
Aircraft type: Aerospatiale Caravelle Super 10B (*OY-STL*)

All 112 persons aboard (106 passengers and six crew members) perished when the jetliner crashed while preparing to land at the Dubai international airport, a refuelling stop during a charter service from Colombo, Ceylon (Sri Lanka), to Copenhagen, Denmark.

Cleared for a straight-in approach using very-high-frequency omni-directional range (VOR) instrument procedures, the Caravelle struck a mountain ridge at an approximate elevation of 1,500 ft (500 m), some 50 miles (80 km) from the airport and about 20 miles (30 km) to the north of the extended centreline of Runway 30, bursting into flames on impact. It was dark, and the meteorological conditions at the airport consisted of scattered cumulus and strato-cumulus clouds at 2,000 ft (c 600 m), a broken overcast at 8,000 ft (c 2,500 m) and a visibility of around 5 miles (10 km).

The aircraft had descended below the prescribed minimum altitude, probably because the pilots thought they were closer to the airport than was actually the case. This mistake apparently resulted from incorrect information on the outdated flight plan being used, misreading of the weather radar, or from a combination of these factors. The position error must have been reinforced when the crew saw Al Fujayrah or some other town and mistook it for Dubai.

Date: 5 May 1972 (22:24)
Location: Near Carini, Sicily, Italy
Operator: Alitalia (Italy)
Aircraft type: Douglas DC-8 Series 43 (*I-DIWB*)

Designated as Flight 112, the jet airliner crashed some 3 miles (5 km) south-east of Punta Raisi Airport, serving Palermo, where it was scheduled to land at the end of a domestic service from Rome. All 115 persons aboard (108 passengers and a crew of seven) were killed.

Its undercarriage still retracted, the DC-8 struck Montagna Lunga ('Long Mountain') at an approximate elevation of 2,000 ft (600 m), or less than 300 ft (100 m) from its crest, bursting into flames on impact, the accident occurring in darkness during the intermediate phase of an approach begun from the north. The weather at the time consisted of a broken overcast, with 3/8 cumulus clouds at about 1,500 ft (500 m) and high cirrus, and a visibility of around 3 miles (5 km). The wind was calm.

The disaster was attributed to the crew's non-adherence to the airport traffic circuit regulation, which resulted in flight at an insufficient altitude to clear the terrain.

Not quite six months later an additional tragedy took place at the scene of the crash when a man was killed by a piece of falling wreckage after coming to pray for his daughter, who had been a passenger on the aircraft.

Date: 18 May 1972 (time unknown)
Location: Near Kharkov, Ukraine, USSR
Operator: Aeroflot (USSR)
Aircraft type: Antonov An-10A (*SSSR-11215*)

The four-engine turboprop crashed some 15 miles (25 km) from the Kharkov airport, where it was to have landed during a scheduled domestic service from Moscow, and all 122 persons aboard (114 passengers and a crew of eight) perished.

Whilst descending from its cruising level to about 5,000 ft (1,500 m), with its undercarriage and flaps still retracted, the airliner suffered structural failure, resulting in the separation of both wings, and the fuselage then fell in a ballistic trajectory, plunging into a wooded area. There was no fire. The crash occurred in daylight, visual meteorological conditions, with a cloud base of around 5,000–7,000 ft (1,500–2,000 m) and a visibility of approximately 5 miles (10 km). The wind was calm.

The in-flight failure of the centre wing section was attributed to a fatigue crack in the lower central wing panel. Eleven years old, the aircraft had recorded 15,483 flight hours and 11,105 landings and was overhauled three times, each of which should have extended its service life by 5,000 hours and 3,200 landings.

As a consequence of this accident, Aeroflot ceased operations with the An-10 model transport.

Date: 14 June 1972 (c 20:20)
Location: Near New Delhi, India
Operator: Japan Air Lines (JAL)
Aircraft type: Douglas DC-8 Series 53 (*JA8012*)

Flight 471 had been cleared to land at Palam International Airport, a scheduled stop during a service originating at Tokyo, with an ultimate destination of London, but while executing a straight-in instrument landing system (ILS) approach to Runway 28, the jetliner crashed and burned on a bank of the River Yamuna, some 10 miles (15 km) from its threshold. Killed were all but three of the 89 persons aboard the aircraft, including the 11 crew members, plus four others on the ground. The surviving passengers suffered various injuries.

It was dark at the time of the accident, and the visibility had been reduced to approximately 1 mile (1.5 km) in dust haze, with the sky obscured. The wind was from the west at around 15 knots.

The crash was attributed to the disregard of the prescribed procedures by the crew, specifically the abandonment of all instrument references before visual contact with the runway had been established. A number of factors were identified in the investigation, some or all of which may have contributed to the disaster. Cited were the relative lack of experience of both the captain and first officer, and the decision by the former to allow the latter to make the approach, while not performing the duties of co-pilot himself; lack of familiarity with the airport by both pilots, and misconceptions on their part regarding the facilities available there; and their failure to carry out the required landing checks, which indicated laxity and poor discipline. Rather than levelling off, the DC-8 descended through the minimum altitude of 2,100 ft (640 m), apparently after the crew saw what they incorrectly identified as the runway lights, and from that point on the altimeters were ignored. Poor orientation led the pilots to believe that they had reached the outskirts of the airport.

Configured with its undercarriage down and flaps set at 35 degrees, the aircraft had descended almost to the height at which it should have been upon passing over the runway threshold before the error was realised, and full power applied. However, the initial impact occurred 6 sec after the 'overshoot' command, before the engines could develop maximum thrust.

It was noted in the Indian investigative report that had the flight director transfer switch been in the very-high-frequency omni-directional range/glide slope (VOR/GS) position, a warning flag would have appeared and the descent perhaps arrested by the crew, providing the instrument was being monitored. A further factor that apparently contributed to the severity of the crash was a rise in the embankment on the west side of the river.

The report rejected the contention of the airline and Japanese government authorities that the premature descent resulted from a false glide path signal transmitted by the ILS.

Date: 15 June 1972 (c 14:00)
Location: Near Pleiku, (South) Vietnam
Operator: Cathay Pacific Airways (Hong Kong)
Aircraft type: Convair 880M (*VR-HFZ*)

Operating as Flight 700Z, which had stopped at Bangkok, Thailand, during a service from Singapore to Hong Kong, the jetliner was reported to have been cruising at 29,000 ft (c 9,000 m) before radio contact was lost. Its burning wreckage was located shortly afterwards scattered in an east-south-easterly direction over an approximate area of 1 by 1.5 miles (1.5 by 2.5 km) in a Central Highlands jungle. All 81 persons aboard (71 passengers and a crew of 10) perished.

It was obvious that the disaster was sudden and catastrophic. When considering the decade-old war raging below, early suspicion that the aircraft had been shot down, either accidentally or intentionally, was understandable. But as investigators began to examine the debris, the tattletale signs of such a hit were simply not present. Metallic fragments associated with military missiles or projectiles should have been much larger, heavier and thicker than those found in parts of the aircraft and some of the victims' bodies. Furthermore, the fragments had travelled from inside out, pointing to an internal explosion. The known facts led to the undeniable conclusion that *VR-HFZ* had been destroyed by a bomb.

With the assistance of the flight data recorder

(FDR) read-out, the sequence of events was reconstructed. Flying in good weather conditions at the last reported cruising altitude and an indicated air speed of about 350 mph (560 kmh), the jetliner was on a heading of approximately 70 degrees when the high-explosive device detonated within its passenger cabin, in or near the centre section. At least one victim and possibly some seats were ejected from the fuselage, striking the vertical stabiliser, which subsequently broke off. The blast also ruptured the No 3 wing tank, and escaping fuel ignited in the air.

It was considered 'highly probable' that the flying controls routed beneath the cabin floor were damaged, and this, together with the loss of the stabiliser, resulted in erratic, high-speed manoeuvres that led to the progressive break-up of the aircraft. All the components struck the ground in a flat attitude after a vertical descent. The occupants not killed by the initial blast were probably rendered unconscious in the consequent explosive decompression.

A Thai police lieutenant accused of planting the bomb in a suitcase at Bangkok in order to kill his fiancée and daughter by another marriage, both passengers on the flight, whom he had insured prior to its departure, was acquitted two years later due to insufficient evidence.

It was recommended in the investigative report that the sale of flight insurance at airports be dis-

A British European Airways Trident 1C, shown in the carrier's earlier colour scheme but otherwise the same as the aircraft that crashed after taking off from Heathrow Airport. (British Aerospace)

couraged, and that insurance companies advise the proper authorities and the airlines about passengers who are heavily covered on a short-term basis.

Date: 18 June 1972 (17:11)
Location: Staines, Surrey, England
Operator: British European Airways (BEA)
Aircraft type: Hawker Siddeley Trident 1C (*G-ARPI*)

Designated as Flight 548, the jetliner was fully loaded when it departed from London's Heathrow Airport, bound for Brussels, Belgium. Following take-off from Runway 28R, the Trident initiated a turn to the left. A terse 'Up to 60', acknowledging its clearance to 6,000 ft (c 1,800 m), was the last message received from the flight. About 40 sec later, or 1 min 46 sec after becoming airborne, it plummeted into a field in a relatively flat attitude adjacent to the A30, a major thoroughfare, and some 3 miles (5 km) south-west of the airport.

A fire that erupted was quickly extinguished before it could spread, and rescuers actually removed one man alive from the wreckage, but he died soon afterwards, leaving no survivors among the 118 persons aboard (112 passengers and six regular crew members). This was the first time more than 100 lives had been lost in an aviation disaster occurring in the British Isles.

It was apparent that the accident did not result from any failure or defect in the aircraft, but rather from the actions of the crew. The absence of a cockpit voice recorder (CVR) on *G-ARPI* prevented the investigative board from determining with certainty the events that took place on the flight deck. But using information from the flight data recorder (FDR) and other facts gathered through the inquiry, the probable sequence of events could be established. Particularly revealing was an autopsy performed on the body of the captain, 51-year-old Stanley Key, which revealed a severe case of atherosclerosis, or a narrowing of the arteries through a build-up of fatty deposits, in his heart. There was also a tear in the wall of one artery, indicating that he had suffered a haemorrhage not more than 2 hours before his accidental death.

At the least, Captain Key may have experienced considerable pain; at worst, he could have collapsed at the controls. He had been declared as fit to fly and had in fact passed an electrocardiographic examination the previous November. Yet his condition was bad enough to have sharply reduced his life expectancy. Prior to the flight he had what was described as a 'violent' verbal outburst with another pilot in the crew room regarding a labour issue, which could have raised his blood pressure sufficiently to cause the haemorrhage.

The airline did have specific instructions in the event of pilot incapacitation, but Captain Key's

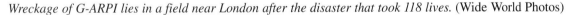

Wreckage of G-ARPI lies in a field near London after the disaster that took 118 lives. (Wide World Photos)

ailment had adverse effects on the other members of the flight crew, acting First Officer Jeremy Keighley, 22, and Second Officer Simon Ticehurst, 24. Also travelling in the cockpit, as a passenger, was an off-duty BEA captain, John Collins. Capt Key's attention was obviously diverted from the operation of the aircraft by his illness, leading to a steady deterioration of air speed. The primary factor in the accident was the retraction of the 'droops', high-lift devices on the leading edges of the wings, at an indicated air speed of only 186 mph (299 kmh), or some 70 mph (110 kmh) below that prescribed. The 'droops' were selected up at an altitude of 1,772 ft (540 m) following flap retraction and after thrust had been reduced as part of the regular noise-abatement procedure, placing the jetliner precariously close to a stall condition.

The Trident's unique stall warning/prevention system had been designed to both shake the control yoke to alert the crew of an impending stall and move it forward to lower automatically the nose of the aircraft in the event of such a condition developing, as was the case here. However, the system on *G-ARPI* was manually over-ridden after it activated a second time. Subsequently, the jetliner pitched up rapidly, losing height and further speed, entering first an aerodynamic stall, then a deep stall from which recovery was not possible. It was raining on this late Sunday afternoon, with a solid overcast at 1,000 ft (c 300 m) and scattered clouds below that. At the most crucial time, therefore, the aircraft was operating in cloud, and the crew had no outside visual reference.

Either the pilot or the co-pilot must have moved the 'droop' lever. In the case of Captain Key, and especially considering his ailment, he may have himself mistaken it for the flap lever. On the other hand, First Officer Keighley may have moved it intentionally after misidentifying the stall-recovery low pressure light for the 'droop' out-of-position indicator; after misinterpreting an order from the pilot (in the vein of 'Put that up', actually meaning a new number in the height acquire window), for the 'droops' to be retracted; or, in following a similar command, by mistaking the 'droop' for the flap lever.

For whatever reason, the crew had failed to diagnose the premature 'droop' retraction as the reason for the activation of the stall-recovery system. Besides Captain Key's condition, the underlying causes of the accident were the lack of training of pilots in the dangers of subtle incapacitation; a lack of experience by First Officer Keighley; and a lack of knowledge by the crew of the implications of a change in configuration as well as the fact that the stall warning/prevention system could be experienced almost simultaneously and what could prompt such an event. There may have been some additional distraction, possibly the presence of Captain Collins, that diverted

the attention of Second Officer Ticehurst.

Despite the predicament, the aircraft could still have been saved by re-selecting the 'droops' to the extended position, moving the control column forward either manually or through continued automatic activation of the stall-recovery system, and increasing thrust.

Another factor in the crash was the lack of a mechanism to prevent retraction of the 'droops' at too low an air speed. A speed-operated baulk was one of the suggestions made by the British Air Accidents Investigation Branch in its report on the crash of *G-ARPI*. Among the other recommendations were that trainee pilots be given more experience before being placed in the position of first officer and that a 'stress test' rather than a 'resting' electrocardiogram be used on flight crews. Many of these proposals were subsequently implemented, including a requirement that all large commercial aircraft registered in Great Britain be fitted with cockpit voice recorders to aid in accident investigation.

Date: 14 August 1972 (c 17:00)
Location: Near Konigs Wusterhausen, (East) Germany
Operator: Interflug Gesellschaft (East Germany)
Aircraft type: Ilyushin Il-62 (*DM-SEA*)

The jet airliner took off from Schonefeld Airport, serving (East) Berlin, on a charter service to Burgas, Bulgaria. About 30 min later it crashed and exploded in a field some 10 miles (15 km) south-east of the capital city, and all 156 persons aboard (148 passengers and a crew of eight) perished.

While at an altitude of about 30,000 ft (10,000 m), the captain reported difficulties in controlling the aircraft's elevator, and decided to turn back. Subsequently, radio contact was lost.

Investigation revealed that a fire, of which the crew was apparently not aware, had weakened the rear structure of the Il-62 to the extent that the tail assembly broke off in flight. Due to the extreme disintegration of the aircraft, it was not possible to determine the cause of the blaze.

Date: 31 August 1972 (time unknown)
Location: Near Magnitogorsk, Russian Soviet Federated Socialist Republic, USSR
Operator: Aeroflot (USSR)
Aircraft type: Ilyushin Il-18 (*SSSR-74298*)

The airliner crashed as it attempted a forced landing at the Magnitogorsk airport, killing all 101 persons aboard (92 passengers and nine crew members).

Cruising at an altitude of about 23,000 ft (7,000 m), the four-engine turboprop had been on a scheduled domestic service to Moscow from

Karaganda, Kazakh SSR, when the crew requested clearance for an emergency descent due to heavy smoke in the cabin. After the crew had disengaged the autopilot in order to perform a straight-in approach, the air traffic controller radioed that the aircraft was flying towards mountainous terrain and instructed it to turn left. Descending in daylight conditions to an approximate height of 2,000 ft (600 m), the Il-18 was by this time heading away from the airport, and when advised of this fact by the controller a crew member responded that the smoke was 'very very thick'. About 20 min elapsed from the time that the emergency situation was first reported until the moment the aircraft struck the ground some 25 miles (40 km) from the airport.

The dense smoke and related carbon monoxide in the cockpit had resulted in the partial or complete incapacitation of the flight crew, with the impossibility of continuing visual flight and of monitoring the instruments. The underlying cause was a fire in the cargo compartment that stemmed from the spontaneous ignition of passenger baggage. The weather was not a factor.

Date: 1 October 1972 (c 18:00)
Location: Near Adler, Russian Soviet Federated Socialist Republic, USSR
Operator: Aeroflot (USSR)
Aircraft type: Ilyushin Il-18B (*SSSR-75507*)

All 109 persons aboard (101 passengers and a crew of eight) were killed when the four-engine turboprop crashed in the Black Sea shortly after taking off from the Adler airport, serving Sochi, on a scheduled domestic flight to Moscow.

Climbing through an altitude of about 500 ft (150 m), the airliner started to descend until it plunged into the water and sank approximately 3.5 miles (6 km) off shore, the accident occurring at dusk and in visual meteorological conditions. There was no distress message prior to the crash, and an investigation failed to reveal the nature of the difficulty. Nor was the aircraft's flight data recorder (FDR) recovered.

The cause of the disaster was therefore undetermined.

Date: 13 October 1972 (21:50)
Location: Near Krasnaya Polyana, Russian Soviet Federated Socialist Republic, USSR
Operator: Aeroflot (USSR)
Aircraft type: Ilyushin Il-62 (*SSSR-86671*)

The jet airliner, which had stopped at Leningrad during a scheduled international service from

An Aeroflot Ilyushin Il-18, two of which were involved in catastrophic crashes only 32 days apart during the latter half of 1972. (Aviation Photo News)

Paris, France, crashed and burned while attempting to land at Sheremet'yevo Airport, serving Moscow. All 174 persons aboard (164 passengers and 10 crew members) perished.

It was dark at the time of the accident, and the local weather consisted of a low overcast, with a cloud base of about 300 ft (100 m) and a visibility of around 1 mile (1.5 km) in haze and drizzle. The wind was light, with no reported turbulence.

During the approach, the crew reported reaching an approximate height of 4,000 ft (1,200 m), after which the aircraft's descent rate decreased, then increased again. After beginning a turn on to the base leg of the circuit, the jet continued down through an altitude of about 1,300 ft (400 m), still banked at 25 degrees, with no decrease in the descent rate and with forward speed increasing to more than 370 mph (600 kmh). Cleanly configured, the aircraft ultimately struck the ground some 7.5 miles (12 km) north of the airport.

The exact cause of the accident could not be determined; the most probable cause was the sudden 'psycho-physiological' incapacitation of the pilots for some unknown reason. It was noted in the investigative report that this particular crew was highly experienced, with considerable flight time in the type.

Date: 27 October 1972 (c 19:20)
Location: Near Noiretable, Loire, France
Operator: Air Inter (France)
Aircraft type: Vickers Viscount 724 (*F-BMCH*)

Operating as Flight 696, the four-engine turboprop was on a domestic service from Lyon to Clermont-Ferrand. Following one orbit in a holding pattern, the Viscount was cleared for descent to 3,600 ft (c 1,100 m), and a crewman reported making a procedural turn in preparation for landing at Aulnat Airport. There was no further radio contact with the flight.

Early the next morning its wreckage was located 27 miles (44 km) east of the airport, along the axis of the runway and generally on the correct heading of the approach track. Its undercarriage retracted and flaps partially extended, the airliner had crashed near the top of a hill at an approximate elevation of 3,000 ft (1,000 m). The accident killed 60 persons aboard, including the entire crew of five, and injured the eight surviving passengers. It was dark at the time, and the weather consisted of rain, a visibility of around 5 miles (10 km) and a low ceiling, with 4/8 cloud coverage at about 2,300 ft (700 m) and a solid overcast at approximately 8,000 ft (2,500 m).

The disaster was primarily attributed to a 180-degree shift of the Viscount's radio compass needle. This erroneous indication could have resulted from a defect in *F-BMCH,* caused by the faulty installation of its antenna system in combination

with certain atmospheric conditions. More likely, however, it was associated with the effect of localised rainfalls over the mountainous terrain, which emitted electrical discharges powerful enough to block out the signals from the Clermont-Ferrand non-directional beacon (NDB). The passage of the aircraft through nimbostratus clouds, which subjected it to an intense electric field, and the presence of thunderstorm activity in the area, could have contributed to the bearing error. Meanwhile, the interception of signals from the instrument landing system (ILS) may have further reinforced the crew's misconception, as might have the lights from the town of Thiers, which were probably visible. The combined effects of these events led to a premature descent below the obstructing terrain.

Though the pilots could have cross-checked their position, this apparently was not done. Overconfidence in the radio compass, coupled with either the failure to check or an error in the reading of the flight time, could have been a factor in the crew's incorrect estimate of when the aircraft was to have passed the NDB. Compounding the mistake was the possible distraction of the captain and first officer, either by the turbulence encountered by the flight or by the presence of an instructor pilot in the cockpit.

Date: 28 November 1972 (19:51)
Location: Near Moscow, Russian Soviet
    Federated Socialist Republic, USSR
Operator: Japan Air Lines (JAL)
Aircraft type: McDonnell Douglas DC-8 Super
    62 (*JA8040*)

The accident occurred in evening darkness immediately after the jetliner, which was designated as Flight 446, had taken off from Sheremet'yevo Airport, a scheduled stop during a service to Tokyo from Copenhagen, Denmark.

Climbing to approximately 300 ft (100 m) while on a heading of 248 degrees, the aircraft abruptly lost height and crashed some 500 ft (150 m) from the end of the runway and about 150 ft (50 m) to the left of its extended centreline. Hitting the ground tail first with its undercarriage extended, the DC-8 broke up and burst into flames, killing 62 of the 76 persons aboard (53 passengers and nine of its 15 crew members). All the survivors suffered injuries.

Following the attainment of the safety speed, the crew put the aircraft into a supercritical angle of attack, which resulted in a loss of air speed and altitude. A Soviet investigative commission attributed this condition to either an inadvertent extension of the spoilers, leading to a reduction in lift and an increase in drag, or to a loss of control by the pilots associated with the malfunctioning of one of the two left power plants after ice formation on the engine intake at a time when the de-icing system was switched off.

With regard to the second theory, there were indications of engine trouble before the crash. A comment by a member of the flight crew, who reported irregularities in the functioning of the No 2 power plant, was heard on the cockpit voice recorder (CVR) tape, as was a sound typical of an engine surge. Additionally, a surviving hostess reported seeing a flame in the vicinity of the port engines, and some of the passengers said they felt the aircraft decelerate several times after becoming airborne. Examination also revealed that three first-stage fan blades in the No 2 power plant were bent, characteristic of damage produced by the impact of ice particles.

Had a loss of thrust occurred, the pilots could have tried to continue the climb-out by pulling back on their control columns, leading to the nose-high attitude and, consequently, an increase in drag followed by a loss of vertical speed. Complicating matters were the night-time conditions, which would have reduced visual reference and possibly contributed to the high angle of attack ending in a stall.

On the other hand, the anomalies in the engines may have arisen after the DC-8 assumed the extreme attitude with its spoilers extended.

Date: 3 December 1972 (c 06:45)
Location: Tenerife, (Spanish) Canary Islands
Operator: Spantax SA Transportes Aereos (Spain)
Aircraft type: Convair 990A Coronado (*EC-BZR*)

Taking off around sunrise and during a low overcast from Los Rodeos Airport, located near Santa Cruz de Tenerife, the jet airliner, on a charter service and bound for Munich, (West) Germany, climbed to an approximate height of 300 ft (100 m) above the ground. Its undercarriage and flaps still extended, the Coronado then plunged to earth and burst into flames, coming to rest inverted about 50 ft (15 m) to the left and some 1,000 ft (300 m) beyond the end of the runway. All 155 persons aboard (148 passengers and a crew of seven) were killed.

A loss of control on or about the time of rotation, believed to have been precipitated by abnormal manoeuvres made by the pilot that were attributed to the conditions of zero visibility, was blamed for the crash.

Date: 29 December 1972 (23:42)
Location: Near Miami, Florida, US
Operator: Eastern Airlines (US)
Aircraft type: Lockheed L-1011-1 TriStar (*N310EA*)

The first fatal crash of a wide-bodied jet airliner involved Flight 401, on a non-stop domestic service from New York City, and scheduled to land at Miami International Airport.

During the approach, and when the undercarriage was lowered, trouble arose in what had been up until then an uneventful trip – the green light indicating that the nose gear was down and locked failed to illuminate. Incredibly, this seemingly minor annoyance would play a key role in the ultimate destruction of the aircraft and the loss of more than 100 lives.

A Convair 990A Coronado, the type flown by the Spanish non-scheduled carrier Spantax that crashed on Tenerife. (General Dynamics)

Recycling the gear to no avail, the crew reported the problem to the control tower and the TriStar was cleared to circle at 2,000 ft (c 600 m). The captain then instructed the first officer to engage the autopilot and the second officer to enter the electronics compartment, located underneath the flight deck, to check the position of the gear visually by means of an optical sight. The flight engineer was then joined by a maintenance specialist, who had been riding as a passenger in the forward observer's seat. Meanwhile, the pilot and co-pilot continued to concentrate on the nose light unit itself, trying unsuccessfully to remove the lens from its retainer. During this time the cockpit voice recorder (CVR) transcribed a C-chord, an aural alert indicating a deviation from the selected altitude, but there was no indication that either of the pilots heard the warning.

About a minute later the Miami approach controller, who had been monitoring the flight, noted a height of only 900 ft (274 m) on the aircraft's alphanumeric data block on his radarscope. He then asked, 'Eastern 401, how are things coming along out there?'. Unfortunately, his query made no reference to the altitude of the aircraft, which continued to deteriorate. Acknowledging the controller, the captain requested and was granted clearance to turn back towards the airport.

In the final few seconds of the flight, the crew finally realised that something was amiss. The first officer remarked 'We did something to the altitude', and the captain responded 'What?'.

The co-pilot then asked 'We're still at two thousand feet, right?', and the pilot immediately exclaimed 'Hey, what's happening here?'.

The radio altimeter then began to beep, but there was no time for corrective action.

The TriStar crashed in the Everglades some 20 miles (30 km) west-north-west of the airport, scattering wreckage across the marshland over an area approximately 1,500 ft (500 m) long and some 300 ft (100 m) wide. Including those who succumbed later, a total of 103 persons aboard (98 passengers, the entire flight crew of three, and two cabin attendants) were killed. Almost miraculously, 73 others, including the eight other crew members assigned to N310EA and the maintenance specialist, escaped with their lives. Most of the fatalities resulted from impact trauma, although a few drownings were reported in water that was about 6 to 12 in (15–30 cm) deep. Injuries among the survivors ranged from minor to critical. An autopsy revealed a tumour in the brain of the captain, 55-year-old Robert Loft, and although this received media attention, it was not considered significant to the accident.

A technical anomaly was, however, found. The autopilot/flight director system on the L-1011 has two roll and pitch computers, one for each pilot, which control up or down attitude. As designed, a force applied to either control column will cause disengagement of the altitude hold function, and such disengagement would normally extinguish the altitude mode select light on the glare shield and the disappearance of the ALT annunciation on both

The first wide-bodied commercial jet to be involved in a fatal accident was an Eastern Airlines Lockheed L-1011 TriStar. (Eastern Airlines)

panels, alerting both pilots that the height was no longer being automatically maintained. However, on this particular aircraft the computers were mismatched so that the first officer's autopilot could be disengaged by 20 lb (9 kg) of pressure and the captain's by only 15 lb (6 kg) of pressure. The pilot could thus disengage the autopilot without the co-pilot's altitude indicator going out, giving the latter the false impression that the autopilot was still engaged in the altitude hold. But since the first officer's autopilot was believed to have been the one engaged, this mismatch should not have been a critical factor.

Nevertheless, correlation of the read-out from the digital flight data recorder (DFDR), which transcribed 62 parameters, with the CVR tape pointed to the possibility of an inadvertent disengagement. A slight change in pitch was recorded at the same time the captain asked the second officer, seated behind and to his right, to check the nose gear position visually – the pilot could have bumped the control column when he turned to speak to the flight engineer. A pitch change was also noted concurrent with a change in heading. In addition, there were several power reductions, which could have been intentional or, if unintentional, may have resulted from either pilot bumping the thrust levers. These power reductions coupled with the slight pitch control movements were responsible for the unrecognised descent that followed. (The

investigation revealed a surprising lack of knowledge among flight crews about the capabilities and operation of the autopilot system on the L-1011.)

Just before the crash, it could be said that neither pilot actually had taken the responsibility of flying the aircraft. The two had become so preoccupied with the nose gear indicating system that there was no monitoring of the flight instruments during the final 4 minutes of the flight. In addition, it was dark at the time, with no moon, and despite unrestricted visibility there were no visual references by which the crew could have detected the loss of height.

It could be argued that the approach controller could have prevented the accident by notifying *N310EA* of its apparent low altitude. He later testified that he contacted the aircraft only because it was nearing the airspace boundary within his jurisdiction, and added that momentary deviations in height on radar displays are not uncommon. Furthermore, air traffic controllers were not, at least at the time, required to offer such guidance. (This issue would surface again two years later after another major airline disaster in the US, and would result in a change of policy regarding the responsibility of controllers in providing altitude information to crews.)

The crash occurred as the jumbo jet was in a left bank of 28 degrees and on a heading of 240 degrees. Its indicated air speed at the moment of impact was

Wreckage of the Eastern Airlines L-1011 is strewn across the Florida Everglades after the crash that claimed more than 100 lives. (National Transportation Safety Board)

about 230 mph (370 kmh). There was a flash fire, but no sustained blaze. Disintegration of the aircraft was such that the US National Transportation Safety Board (NTSB) actually classified the accident as 'non-survivable', and the survival of more than a third of the occupants can probably be ascribed to the fact that either their seats remained attached to large floor sections or they were thrown clear of the wreckage at considerably reduced velocities. The energy-absorbing design of the passenger seats was an additional significant factor.

Examination of the wreckage showed that the flap handle was set at 18 degrees, and the undercarriage lever was down. As it turned out, the crew's concern over the position of the nose gear was unfounded. It, as well as the two main gears, were found extended and locked – the two bulbs in the nose gear unit had merely burned out.

As recommended by the NTSB, a switch for the nose wheel well light located near the gear indicator optical sight was later installed in the TriStar, the presence of which would probably have sped up the actions of the men in the lower compartment of *N310EA* and perhaps prevented its crash. In addition, Eastern Airlines was required by the US Federal Aviation Administration (FAA) to modify the altitude select alert system in its L-1011 fleet, which had been configured so that the amber warning lights would be inhibited from operating below 2,500 ft (c 750 m). The only warning of a height deviation under this altitude was the single C-chord.

Date: 22 January 1973 (c 09:30)
Location: Kano, Nigeria
Operator: Alia Royal Jordanian Airlines
Aircraft type: Boeing 707-3D3C (*JY-ADO*)

Chartered by Nigeria Airways, the jetliner was on a non-scheduled service from Jiddah, Saudi Arabia, its passengers Muslim pilgrims. Diverted by bad weather from Lagos, its original destination, to Kano, the 707 crashed while landing at the city's airport, killing 176 persons aboard, including six of its nine crew members. Most of the 33 survivors were injured.

At the time of the accident visibility had been reduced by haze, and there were gusting cross-winds. The aircraft's right main gear was sheared off when it either hit the edge of the runway following an undershoot or struck some obstruction or depression in the pavement. The transport then swung completely around, skidded off the runway and was subsequently destroyed by flames.

The American captain in command of the aircraft, who survived, would later be blamed for the disaster for his piloting technique that was reportedly 'tantamount to recklessness'.

Date: 21 February 1973 (c 14:10)
Location: Near Isma'iliya, Egypt
Operator: Libyan Arab Airlines
Aircraft type: Boeing 727-224 (*5A-DAH*)

Originating at Tripoli, Flight 114 had stopped at Banghazi, also in Libya, before proceeding on towards its ultimate destination of Cairo, Egypt. However, following its passage of Sidi Barrani, Egypt, the jetliner began to stray from the intended route. Flying to the south of Cairo, the aircraft passed the capital city, and while approaching the Gulf of Suez it was first spotted on radar by Israeli defence forces, which promptly dispatched two F-4 Phantom II jet fighters. The military pilots, who identified the intruder as a Libyan commercial transport, tried to get it to land, using hand gestures, rocking the wings of their aircraft and, finally, by firing their cannons across its nose.

Over the Sinai Peninsula, the 727 turned back towards the west, but shortly afterwards, and while it was at a height of 5,000 ft (c 1,500 m), the fighters attacked the jetliner, hitting its starboard wing tip with tracers and touching off a fire. As the aircraft descended, apparently still under control, the blaze spread to its cabin.

The 727 crashed approximately 10 miles (15 km) east of the Suez Canal while attempting a belly-landing in the desert, with an explosion occurring in the area of its right main gear almost simultaneously with ground impact. All but five of the 113 persons aboard were killed, including eight crew members; four passengers and the aircraft's co-pilot survived with various injuries. An examination of the wreckage revealed that only one of the transport's three engines had been operating at the time of the crash.

Although the flight had generally assumed the correct heading, its track was displaced to the east, and when the first officer reported it as over Qarum, the jetliner was actually some 100 miles (150 km) east-south-east of that location. Furthermore, all air traffic control instructions to the aircraft were based on its own erroneous position reports, and when the crew radioed that it was not receiving navigational signals, the controller advised it to 'Stick to the Cairo non-directional beacon'. The drift was apparently related to an encounter with a strong tailwind.

During much of the flight, the 727 was over clouds, with low stratocumulus and 6/8 to 8/8 altocumulus up to about 18,000 ft (5,500 m). Once over the Sinai, the ground was visible, and at around this time the crew appeared to realise their error. By then, however, the aircraft was out of the range of the navigational facilities.

Although records did not indicate any faults in the Cairo beacon, the International Civil Aviation Organisation (ICAO) investigative report on the disaster considered it probable that it was not functioning properly at the time. Additionally, the Cairo approach control radar was out of order.

The crew of *5A-DAH* apparently did not understand the orders of the fighter pilots, and when they turned back towards Cairo and raised the aircraft's gear, which had been lowered, it was construed by the Israelis as an attempt to escape. Defence Minister Moshe Dayan admitted an 'error in judgement' in shooting down the transport, and the Israeli government agreed to compensate the families of the victims.

Date: 5 March 1973 (c 13:50)
Location: Near Nantes, France
First aircraft
Operator: Lineas Aereas de Espana SA (Iberia) (Spain)
Type: McDonnell Douglas DC-9 Series 32 (*EC-BII*)
Second aircraft
Operator: Spantax SA Transportes Aereos (Spain)
Type: Convair 990A Coronado (*EC-BJC*)

This mid-air crash occurred during a strike by civilian controllers, wherein the French air traffic control (ATC) system had been taken over by military personnel.

Both aircraft were bound for London, the DC-9, operating as Flight 504, en route from Palma de Mallorca, in the (Spanish) Balearic Islands, and the Coronado on a charter service from Madrid. Only minutes earlier they had been transferred to the same ATC centre from another facility, which had assigned them to the same flight level despite the fact that both crews had estimated that they would reach the Nantes very-high-frequency omni-directional range (VOR) station at the same time.

To avoid a potential conflict, the Spantax aircraft was instructed to delay by 8 min its arrival at the navigational aid, but the fact that the jet at that point was only about 10 min flying time from the VOR made this an unrealistic request. Asking for confirmation of these instructions, the controller only responded with a 'Stand by'. In international phraseology, this expression normally means that a message will be immediately forthcoming; however, the crew were left in uncertainty for nearly 2 min before communications were re-established. Shortly afterwards the pilot asked if he could carry out a 360-degree turn, because a speed reduction would be insufficient to delay its passage of the station.

This manoeuvre was subsequently initiated without clearance, and in proximity to the VOR, and led to the interception by *EC-BJC* of the adjacent airway, along which *EC-BII* had been flying. The resulting collision occurred at a height of 29,000 ft (c 9,000 m) over La Planche, a village located south-east of Nantes and in the same department, Loire-Atlantique, and in the midst of an overcast, which had reduced visibility to zero.

All 68 persons aboard the DC-9 (61 passengers and a crew of seven) perished when the aircraft broke up in flight, scattering wreckage over an agricultural area. There were no injuries among the 106 persons aboard the Coronado, which was still in the right-hand turn at the time of impact and lost a portion of its left wing, outboard of the No 1 engine, but nevertheless managed a safe landing at a military air base.

Whereas the solution to the conflict was based on separation by time, a simple change of altitude would have been possible. Complicating matters was the poor quality of radio transmissions between the Spantax jet and ground control. The Coronado had not yet made radio contact with nor been positively identified on radar at the facility responsible for its control, and was no longer in radar contact with the one from which it had been transferred. Thus, in the final moments before the collision it was virtually cut off from ATC services. The crew themselves had erred in not properly assessing the situation and establishing radio contact with the appropriate controlling facility.

The method used to provide for separation of the aircraft required either precise navigation by the Spantax crew or complete radar coverage and, in whichever case, trouble-free communications, conditions that were not realised.

Date: 10 April 1973 (10:13)
Location: Near Hochwald, Solothurn, Switzerland
Operator: Invicta International Airlines (UK)
Aircraft type: Vickers Vanguard 952 (*G-AXOP*)

The turboprop transport, on a charter service from Luton and Bristol, England, was to have landed at Basel-Mulhouse Airport, located just across the border in France. Its first instrument landing system (ILS) approach, which was to Runway 16, ended in an overshoot. Minutes later, a meteorologist and retired aviator telephoned the control tower, stating that he had just seen a four-engine aircraft, later identified as *G-AXOP*, fly over the Binningen Observatory at a dangerously low altitude. He urged that it be instructed to climb. However, the gallant effort by the ground observer to perhaps prevent a crash was to no avail. Shortly afterwards the Vanguard, its undercarriage apparently retracted and flaps set at 20 degrees, brushed against a wooded ridge, then slammed into a snow-covered forest area.

The accident, which took place some 10 miles (15 km) south of the airport, claimed the lives of 108 persons aboard the aircraft, including four crew members. Among the 37 survivors, 35 passengers and a cabin attendant suffered injuries, and a second stewardess escaped unscathed. Fire erupted after impact in the right wing but was extinguished before it could spread over the rest of the wreckage,

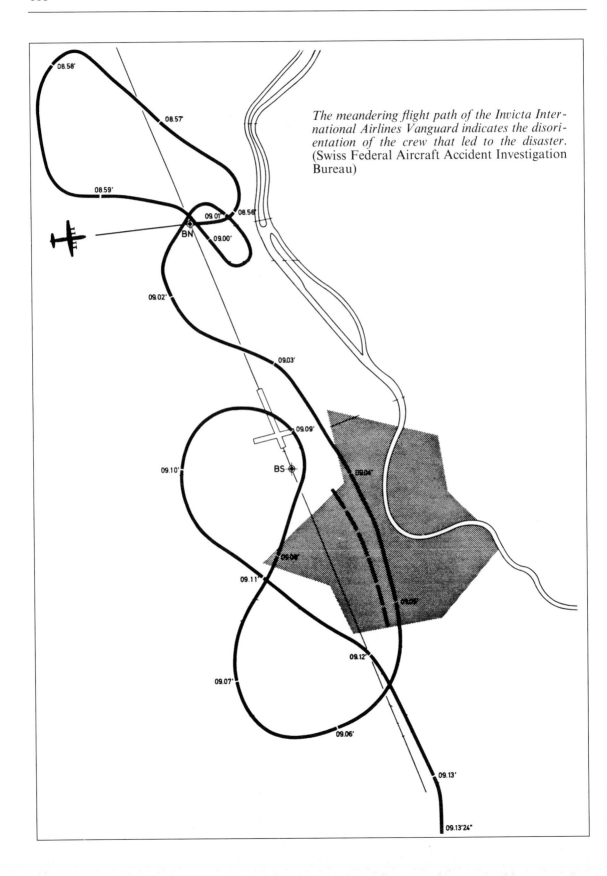

The meandering flight path of the Invicta International Airlines Vanguard indicates the disorientation of the crew that led to the disaster. (Swiss Federal Aircraft Accident Investigation Bureau)

and this absence of a major blaze, coupled with the fact that the rear section of the fuselage remained intact, probably accounted for the relatively high rate of survival. Most of the victims were women from five towns in the English county of Somerset on a one-day 'shopping tour' of Switzerland.

The weather in the area of the crash at the time was characterised by a driving snow, which reduced visibility to approximately 150 ft (50 m). The clouds were down to the level of the terrain and the wind was blowing from the north at about 15 knots. At the airport, the runway visual range (RVR) was in fact below the minimum allowed in Vanguard operations, but the control tower relayed the incorrect measurement to the aircraft, one slightly above the minimum. The crew made no further enquiries regarding the meteorological conditions.

Although the actions of the two pilots could not be determined with certainty due to the absence of a cockpit voice recorder (CVR) on *G-AXOP*, the accident apparently resulted from a loss of orientation on their part. Contributing factors were unsatisfactory navigational procedures, most significantly the initiation of final approach despite the incorrect assessment of height and position, and the confusion of navigational aids. An additional factor was the poor reception of radio-navigational signals due to defects in the aircraft's equipment, which made the task of the crew more difficult.

With regard to the technical aspect, the No 1 automatic direction finder (ADF) receiver may not have been functioning properly due to faulty repair work, specifically poor soldering of joints in its loop servo amplifier. And both the No 1 very-high-frequency omni-directional range (VOR) and No 2 glide slope receivers were improperly set, so that in neither case would a warning flag, indicating an anomaly, have appeared at the correct time. Unsatisfactory readings could also have given the crew the false impression of being properly on the glide path. There could also have been 'jittery' indications making it difficult to intercept the localiser signal.

The pilots, who apparently believed that their navigational difficulties were due to the atmospheric conditions (as evidenced by the statement that the ADF indicators were ' . . . all over the place in this weather'), were probably remiss in cross- and double-checking of the instruments, through which the discrepancies could have been detected and perhaps corrected. Nor did they ask for any navigational assistance from the air traffic control service.

The flight path of the Vanguard became erratic following passage of the non-directional beacon (NDB) designated 'BN'. This may have resulted from the fact that its ADF receivers were not tuned to two navigational aids being used in the normal sequence.

Actually, the first approach, during which the

The aftermath of the Vanguard crash in Switzerland that killed 108 persons. (Swiss Federal Aircraft Accident Investigation Bureau)

transport deviated considerably to the right and then the left of the runway centreline, almost ended in a crash after the crew had apparently established visual contact with the ground. During the second approach a descent was begun, indicating that the pilots had a glide slope indication. By then, however, the disorientation was such that a successful landing would probably have not been possible. In the final moments of the flight, the aircraft was headed towards the south, ie away from the airport, and the accident occurred during a climb-out manoeuvre.

Both flight crewmen were qualified captains, though this could actually have been a hindrance had the one serving as co-pilot behaved more as a pilot-in-command than a first officer. A change in the operator of the radio indicated that there was a switch in the pilot flying the Vanguard after the first overshoot.

Among the recommendations made by the Swiss investigative commission were that all medium wavelength radio beacons be readjusted to a modulation in conformity with International Civil Aviation Organisation (ICAO) standards; that international regulations require the suppression of unpublicised ILS back beams; and that every large commercial aircraft carry both a flight data recorder (FDR) and a voice recorder. An FDR had been fitted to *G-AXOP*, and the installation of a CVR on similar types would later become a British civil aviation requirement.

Date: 18 May 1973 (time unknown)
Location: Southern Siberia, USSR
Operator: Aeroflot (USSR)
Aircraft type: Tupolev Tu-104A

All 81 persons aboard perished, including an estimated crew of five to 10, when the jet airliner crashed east of Lake Baikal during an attempted hijacking.

The aircraft had been on a scheduled domestic service from Moscow to Chita, RSFSR, when a passenger demanded to be taken to China; subsequently the explosive device he was carrying apparently detonated at an altitude of approximately 30,000 ft (10,000 m).

Date: 11 July 1973 (c 15:00)
Location: Near Saulx-les-Chartreux, Essonne, France
Operator: SA Empresa de Viacao Aerea Rio Grandense (VARIG) (Brazil)
Aircraft type: Boeing 707-345C (*PP-VJZ*)

Everything was routine for Flight 820 during most of its 11-hour transatlantic journey from the time of departure at Rio de Janeiro, Brazil, until shortly before it was scheduled to land at Orly Airport, serving Paris. Then came the first hint of trouble, at 14:58, when the message 'Problem with fire on board' was received from the aircraft, and an 'emergency descent' was requested.

The gutted hulk of the VARIG Boeing 707 rests in a field after crash-landing near Paris. (UPI/Bettmann)

Cleared for a direct approach to Runway 07, the jet airliner flight was about 10 miles (15 km) from the airport when the pilot reported 'total fire'. This message was prompted by the alarming announcement from the chief steward that smoke had entered the cabin and passengers were being asphyxiated. The flight crew donned oxygen masks and goggles, but the smoke became so dense in the cockpit that not even the instruments could be seen. In view of the desperate situation, the captain decided that a forced landing was necessary.

Looking through the side cockpit windows, which had been opened, the pilots managed to set the aircraft down in a field some 3 miles (5 km) from the threshold and in near alignment with the axis of the runway. Its extended main undercarriage collapsed almost immediately, and the left outer wing and all four engines were then torn off as the 707 slid on its belly for approximately 1,500 ft (500 m).

Despite the exceptional skill displayed by the crew in landing the aircraft and the quick action by emergency personnel, who were on the scene in minutes, the fuselage was gutted by flames. Except for the flight engineer, who was not wearing his safety belt and died of impact trauma, the 123 persons killed in the disaster succumbed to the effects of the fire (about three-quarters of them from carbon monoxide poisoning and the rest from inhaling other toxic gases). Only one passenger, who was rescued by fire-fighters, and 10 of the 17 crew members assigned to the flight, who managed to escape on their own, survived. It was considered probable that the fire developed in the wash-basin unit of the aft right lavatory. The blaze may have been due to an electrical fault, or may have resulted from human carelessness, such as the discarding of a lighted cigarette; the exact cause was never determined.

There was no evidence of foul play, and no defect could be found in the aircraft. However, there was a material factor with respect to the seriousness of the fire. Samples of cabin furnishings examined were found to be readily combustible, and the waste towel disposal containers did not satisfy the requirement of being flame-resistant.

Members of the cabin crew took action with fire extinguishers as soon as smoke was discovered, but their efforts were ineffective because the origin of the blaze could not be located. The actions of the flight crew were considered somewhat incoherent but still sound, including the decision not to release the cabin oxygen masks (the output of oxygen from unused masks would have worsened the situation, and since the masks supply a mixture of pure oxygen and ambient air, they would not have provided any protection from the noxious fumes).

Most of the safety measures recommended by the French investigative commission in its report on the crash of Flight 820, which included the use of non-flammable waste bins, the elimination of inflammable objects and the enforced prohibition of smoking in aircraft lavatories, were subsequently put into effect by many national aviation regulatory bodies.

Date: 22 July 1973 (22:06)
Location: Off Papeete, Tahiti
Operator: Pan American World Airways (US)
Aircraft type: Boeing 707-321 B (*N417PA*)

This inexplicable crash involved Flight 816, which had originated at Auckland, New Zealand, and landed at Faaa Airport serving Papeete, before continuing on towards the US, with a planned stop at Honolulu, Hawaii, and an ultimate destination of Los Angeles, California.

Using Runway 04, the 707 took off into the darkness, then initiated a left turn, as cleared. About 30 sec after becoming airborne, however, the jet airliner plunged into the Pacific Ocean approximately 2 miles (3 km) from the end of the runway and to the left of its extended centreline, killing 78 persons aboard, including the entire crew of 10; though he was seriously injured, one passenger survived. Among the victims was a stewardess who succumbed in a hospital after also being rescued alive.

Ten bodies and a small amount of debris, including the aircraft's nose gear and pieces of its cabin furnishings, were recovered. Most of the wreckage, however, was lost in water some 2,300 ft (700 m) deep and could not be located, despite a three-day search using sonar equipment. This lack of evidence and, especially, the failure to find either the flight data (FDR) or cockpit voice (CVR) recorders, prevented the French investigative commission from determining the cause of the disaster.

The jet reportedly ascended at a lower than normal climb gradient after taking off. During the low-altitude left turn, the 707 lost height, descending at a shallow angle, and at the moment of impact its undercarriage was apparently up and its flaps were either at the take-off position or in the process of being retracted.

As noted in the accident report, a malfunction in one power plant should not have jeopardised the flight, and obtained evidence cast doubt on the theory that the aircraft had experienced multiple engine failure. Nor were there any indications, including the absence of a distress message, of a control system malfunction or other serious emergency.

Considered more likely was that the failure of an instrument or system had diverted the crew's attention while in the turn, with a resultant excessive bank leading to the loss of altitude. Also, since the turn was made out towards the sea, no visual references would have been available to counter the change in the angle of the town lights visible on the right-hand side of the aircraft. This could have created the illusion of ascent. Whether involuntary or intentional, the steep bank in itself could have created a hazardous situation.

Both the captain and first officer, who were but a year from retirement, had been undergoing regular treatment for hypertension, and an autopsy performed on the latter revealed a serious arteriosclerotic condition. However, there was no evidence that the health of either pilot played a role in the crash.

The weather, which only minutes before the disaster consisted of rain, a solid overcast at about 8,000 ft (2,500 m) and scattered clouds down to around 2,300 ft (700 m), and a visibility of approximately 5 miles (10 km), was not considered a factor.

Date: 31 July 1973 (11:08)
Location: Boston, Massachusetts, US
Operator: Delta Air Lines (US)
Aircraft type: McDonnell Douglas DC-9
Series 31 (*N975NE*)

Designated as Flight 723, which had stopped at Manchester, New Hampshire, during a domestic service originating at Burlington, Vermont, the jetliner crashed and burned while attempting to land on Runway 04R at Logan International Airport. All 89 persons aboard (83 passengers and six crew members, the latter including a cockpit observer) were killed. One of the victims lived for nearly five months before succumbing to his injuries.

The accident apparently resulted from the failure of the pilots to monitor their altitude and recognise the passage of the aircraft through the decision height during an unstabilised instrument landing system (ILS) approach conducted in rapidly changing meteorological conditions.

The sequence of events began with vectors of *N975NE* by approach control that were not in accordance with standard operating procedures. At the time that the controller should have issued the clearance, as required, he was preoccupied with a potential conflict between two other flights. As a result, the crew of the DC-9 had to request approach clearance and other instructions. Communication difficulties with one of the other aircraft further delayed the descent of Flight 723 to the correct approach altitude and its release to the control of the airport tower. Despite the non-standard air traffic control services that were partly to blame for the poor positioning of the aircraft, its progress could still have been ascertained through proper monitoring by the crew.

The jetliner passed over the outer marker at a velocity of about 240 mph (385 kmh), or some 50 mph (80 kmh) above that recommended by the carrier. It was also more than 200 ft (60 m) above the normal height at the same point, and, at such an air speed, a high rate of descent would have been required to intercept the glide slope. A high rate of descent would, in turn, have made it difficult for the crew to reduce air speed to that considered acceptable and would have forced the pilots to act more quickly than usual.

An additional factor was the crew's use of the aircraft's flight director system, which they had employed as an approach aid. If it were in its normal mode and the aircraft too high to intercept the glide slope, no pitch guidance would be provided. It was believed, however, that the flight director had been inadvertently placed in the go-around position, which corresponded to the approach mode on the system to which this crew was accustomed. The resulting abnormal display must have led to the lateral corrections that caused the deviation from the localiser centreline. The first officer, who was actually doing the flying, seemed preoccupied by the display to the detriment of his attention to altitude, heading and air speed. Meanwhile, the captain divided his attention among the problems with the flight director, communications with the ground and the weather information given by the approach controller.

It was foggy at the time, with an overcast estimated at 200 ft (60 m) and a light wind. The runway visual range (RVR) was reported to the flight to have been in excess of 6,000 ft (1,800 m), but due to the rapid change in weather and a delay of nearly a minute in the cycling of the RVR digital display, the information was not indicative of the actual conditions. In fact, the RVR had dropped to only about 1,500 ft (500 m) just before the aircraft was to have landed.

The presence of an off-duty pilot riding in the cockpit jump seat and, especially, his participation in the reading of the check-list, which was contrary to normal procedures, could have also distracted the regular two-man flight crew.

The descent continued until the jetliner, its undercarriage down and flaps fully extended, struck a sea-wall. The initial impact took place some 3,000 ft (1,000 m) from the threshold of the runway and about 150 ft (50 m) to the right of its extended centreline, and the DC-9 then disintegrated. Due to the poor visibility, the accident was not seen from the control tower; moreover, tower personnel silenced an alarm, which they believed to be false, set off when the crash damaged the airport's approach light system (ALS), without notifying inbound flights, as required. Fortunately, two aircraft cleared to land on the same runway over which wreckage was scattered, abandoned their approaches because of the weather.

A programme for controllers in the use of the ALS was later initiated at Boston, and the US Federal Aviation Administration (FAA) also modified its terminal air traffic control procedures so that pertinent information would be forwarded to the ground controller when the active runway was not visible from the tower cab.

Date: 13 August 1973 (c 11:40)
Location: Near La Coruna, Spain
Operator: Aviacion y Comercio SA (AVIACO) (Spain)
Aircraft type: Sud-Aviation Caravelle 10-R (*EC-BIC*)

Having completed a domestic service from Madrid as Flight 116, the jet airliner had already made three unsuccessful attempts to land at La Coruna Airport. On the third try, the tower controller reported seeing the Caravelle in the low, ragged fog, relaying this information to the crew. This must have led the captain to believe that by going slightly below the minimum altitude he would be able to carry out a safe landing, so he began his fourth attempt.

During the approach the pilots probably tried to make visual contact with the ground and did not properly refer to their altimeters. A pull-up was initiated and full power applied just before the aircraft clipped with its right flap and part of the fuselage some eucalyptus trees atop a hill, and the twin-engine jet then crashed inverted about 2 miles (3 km) from the threshold of Runway 22, bursting into flames on impact. All 85 persons aboard (79 passengers and a crew of six) and a worker on the ground were killed.

Shortly before the accident, the vertical visibility was between 800 and 1,000 ft (c 250–300 m) and the horizontal visibility approximately 1 mile (1.5 km).

By attempting to land in meteorological conditions that were below minima, the pilot violated both the nation's regulations and instructions and the international standards in force in Spain. Under the circumstances he should have diverted to an alternative airport.

A possible extenuating factor was that the approach chart used by the crew depicted the 345 ft (105 m) hill as the highest obstacle, whereas the trees rose 40 to 50 ft (12–15 m) above the terrain.

One of the recommendations made in the investigative report was for air traffic control services to inform pilots before reaching their destination when the weather falls below the minimum criteria.

Date: 30 September 1973 (20:40)
Location: Near Sverdlovsk, Russian Soviet Federated Socialist Republic, USSR
Operator: Aeroflot (USSR)
Aircraft type: Tupolev Tu-104B (*SSSR-42506*)

The jetliner, which was on a scheduled domestic service, crashed shortly after taking off from the

The remains of the Delta Air Lines DC-9 are scattered across the runway threshold at Boston's Logan International Airport. (Wide World Photos)

city's airport, and all 108 persons aboard (100 passengers and eight crew members) perished. It was dark at the time, and the weather was overcast, with a cloud base of about 800 ft (250 m) and a visibility of around 3.5 miles (6 km). The wind was blowing from a north-north-westerly direction at approximately 15 mph (25 kmh).

In the final radio transmission from the flight, the crew acknowledged departure instructions and advised that they would report upon reaching about 5,000 ft (1,500 m). At an approximate height of 1,200 ft (350 m) above the ground, the aircraft commenced a left turn, with the bank angle then decreasing simultaneously with the start of a steep climb. The bank angle steepened again and engine thrust was reduced, whereupon the twin-jet transport went into a descent. The crew's energetic effort in pulling back on the control wheel without recovering from the bank was unsuccessful, and the Tu-104 struck the ground some 5 miles (10 km) south-west of the airport and caught fire. Impact occurred at a speed of about 500 mph (800 kmh), with the aircraft in a near vertical left bank, descending at an angle of 20 degrees and on a west-south-westerly heading.

The accident was attributed to incorrect indications by the main artificial horizons and the compass system due to an electrical supply failure, coupled with the inability of the pilots to determine their attitude using their back-up instruments at night and in clouds, conditions that precluded flight by visual reference.

The electrical system malfunction could have resulted from a temporary failure of the transducer or its inadvertent switching off by the crew after engine start during their pre-flight preparations. They apparently switched on the transducer about a minute before the crash, but it was too late to ensure normal operation of the attitude instruments.

Date: 13 October 1973 (c 20:15)
Location: Near Domodedovo, Russian Soviet
  Federated Socialist Republic, (USSR)
Operator: Aeroflot (USSR)
Aircraft type: Tupolev Tu-104B (*SSSR-42486*)

The jet airliner, which was designated as Flight 964 and on a domestic service from Kutaisi, Georgian SSR, crashed and burned about 5 miles (10 km) from Domodedovo Airport, serving Moscow, where it was scheduled to land. All 119 persons aboard (114 passengers and a crew of five) perished.

Its undercarriage having been lowered but its flaps still retracted, the aircraft was on a south-south-easterly heading when it plunged to earth from an approximate height of 1,300 ft (400 m) following a right turn and then a steep left spiral manoeuvre, the latter with a banking attitude of up to 75 degrees. It was determined that an electrical power failure had rendered inoperable the aircraft's compass system and main gyros. As a result, the magnetic heading indication froze, and the pilots could not ascertain their attitude using their standby instruments.

The accident occurred in darkness, but the weather was not considered a factor.

Date: 22 December 1973 (22:10)
Location: Near Tetouan, Morocco
Operator: Sobelair SA (Belgium)
Aircraft type: Sud-Aviation Caravelle VI-N
  (*OO-SRD*)

All 106 persons aboard perished when the jet airliner, which was owned by the Belgian carrier SABENA and sub-leased to Royal Air Maroc, crashed while preparing to land at Boukhalf Airport, serving Tangier, an en route stop during a non-scheduled service from Paris, France, to Casablanca, Morocco. Many of the passengers were Moroccans on their way home for the holidays; except for one, the crew of seven was Belgian.

Apparently failing to capture the outer marker signal for an instrument landing system (ILS) approach to Runway 28, the Caravelle proceeded

too far east on the outbound leg of a procedural turn, outside the protected area and over hazardous terrain, before turning back on to the final approach course. Its undercarriage retracted, the aircraft struck a mountain at an approximate elevation of 2,300 ft (700 m) and some 25 miles (40 km) from the airport, bursting into flames on impact.

The accident occurred in darkness and meteorological conditions consisting of rain and a low ceiling, with a broken overcast at around 2,000 ft (600 m) and scattered clouds down to about 1,000 ft (300 m). The winds were blowing from a south-south-westerly direction at 20 to 40 knots.

Date: 26 January 1974 (c 07:30)
Location: Near Izmir, Turkey
Operator: Turk Hava Yollari AO (Turkish
  Airlines)
Aircraft type: Fokker-VFW F.28 Fellowship
  Mark 1000 (*TC-JAO*)

The jetliner was on a scheduled domestic service to Istanbul and crashed while taking off from Cumaovasi Airport, killing 66 persons aboard (62 passengers and four crew members). Six passengers, including an infant, and one crew member survived with injuries.

Using Runway 35, the aircraft became airborne before yawing to the left at a height of about 30 ft (10 m). It struck the ground in a nearly level attitude, first with the outboard fairing doors of its left wing flap, then with the left side of its belly, and finally ran into the bank of a drainage ditch that parallels the west side of the runway. The twin-engine jet disintegrated and burst into flames, and the main part of its fuselage came to rest inverted.

The weather around the time of the accident consisted of a slight mist, with a broken overcast and a visibility of approximately 3 miles (5 km).

Frost on the wings of the F.28, which accumulated during the night, combined with over-rotation during the take-off had resulted in a stall, and the low altitude of the aircraft precluded recovery by the pilot.

Date: 30 January 1974 (c 23:40)
Location: Near Pago Pago, Tutuila Island,
  American Samoa
Operator: Pan American World Airways (US)
Aircraft type: Boeing 707-321B (*N454PA*)

Operating as Flight 806, the jet airliner was scheduled to land at Pago Pago International Airport, the first of two en route stops during a service from Auckland, New Zealand, to Los Angeles, California, US. The 707 crashed and burned while making an instrument landing system (ILS) approach to Runway 05, killing 97 persons

TC-JAO, the Turkish Airlines Fokker F.28 Fellowship that crashed on take-off from Izmir airport. (Fokker-VFW)

aboard, including the entire crew of 10. Four passengers survived with injuries.

The accident occurred in darkness, and the airport weather around this time consisted of heavy rain showers, a broken overcast down to approximately 1,500 ft (500 m), a visibility of 1 mile (c 1.5 km) and north-easterly winds of about 20 knots, with gusts to 35.

In its official report, released nearly a year later, the US National Transportation Safety Board (NTSB) attributed the crash to the apparent failure of the flight crew to correct an excessive rate of descent after the aircraft had passed through the decision height. More than two years after the accident, the US Air Line Pilots Association petitioned to have the probable cause reconsidered, and knowledge gained from other wind-related airline disasters prompted the NTSB to re-open its investigation, examining anew the flight data recorder (FDR) read-out, the cockpit voice recorder (CVR) transcript and the aircraft's engineering performance data.

The revised report, released in 1977, again ascribed crew error as the primary cause, but also injected an environmental factor, namely the destabilising winds that were encountered during the final approach. One board member who dissented with the majority believed that the winds were in fact the primary cause of the crash.

The jet flew into a predominantly increasing head-wind and/or an up-draught about 50 sec before impact, causing it to deviate above the proper glide path. Recognising the situation, which was believed to be related to the winds flowing out of the rainstorm that were affected by the upsloping terrain on the island, the captain reduced thrust in order to correct the aircraft's flight profile. He apparently did not, however, realise what was happening when the 707 came out of this condition and probably encountered a decreasing head-wind and/or down-draught; the resulting increase in the descent rate may have gone unnoticed because he was looking outside and not observing his instruments. Moreover, since the aircraft was over

an area devoid of lights (the so-called 'black hole' effect) and flying in heavy rain at the time, there would have been no visual clues by which the high sink rate could have been detected. The rain may also have reduced the pilot's visual segment (the ground observable looking forward from the cockpit) and created the illusion of a nose-up attitude, and, under the circumstances, the natural response would be to ease forward on the control column and reduce thrust.

It was determined that the first officer had not set his navigational receiver to the ILS frequency, and would thus have had to look across the cockpit at the captain's instruments for glide slope information and flight director commands. In the process he may not have noticed the visual approach slope indicator (VASI) lights showing that the aircraft had gone below the glide slope. Nor did the co-pilot call out the descent rate, which, combined with the restricted visibility, absence of

A post-impact fire resulted in much of the damage and all but one of the fatalities in this crash of a Pan American World Airways Boeing 707 on Samoa. (Wide World Photos)

lighting and failure to monitor the instruments, contributed to the disaster. As transcribed on the CVR tape, he stated that the jet was 'a little high', and after the radio altimeter warning sounded, reported to the pilot, 'You're at minimums', followed by 'Field in sight'.

Its undercarriage down and flaps set at 50 degrees, the 707 hit trees some 3,865 ft (1,180 m) from the runway threshold, then ploughed into a tropical forest. In the impact its nose and main gears, all four engines, outer wings and numerous other components separated.

This accident should have been nearly 100 per cent survivable, since only the first officer died of traumatic injury, but all the other fatalities resulted from burns and/or smoke inhalation.

Date: 3 March 1974 (c 12:40)
Location: Near Ermenonville, Oise, France
Operator: Turk Hava Yollari AO (Turkish Airlines)
Aircraft type: McDonnell Douglas DC-10 Series 10 (*TC-JAV*)

The disaster that had been feared since the start of the jumbo jet era – a non-survivable crash involving a heavily-loaded wide-bodied transport – left commercial aviation reeling for more than a year. This accident has been used by industry critics as an example of corporate ineptitude, design short-sightedness and government laxity.

At the centre of the controversy was a serious defect in the McDonnell Douglas aircraft. The fault lay not in its performance or handling, but something far more mundane, namely the locking mechanism of its rear cargo door. Previously, most jetliner doors had been of the 'plug' type, opening inwards and held firmly in place by cabin pressure when the aircraft is in flight. But the door on the DC-10, which was built by the Convair division of General Dynamics, opened outwards. Due to the constant force being exerted against the door while operating at high altitudes, a durable and foolproof locking system was an absolute necessity.

The door was designed to be closed with a switch. An electrically powered actuator was used to turn a torque tube to which four latches were attached. As the tube revolved during the locking process, the talon of each latch snapped over a corresponding spool. An external lever was then pulled down, driving a locking pin into place on the outside of each latch. Any jamming of the lever should have been an immediate indication that the latches were not in the correct 'over-centre' position, ie properly secured. In addition, at the end of its travel the locking pin bar was supposed to activate a mechanical switch in order to extinguish an open-door warning light in the cockpit. As a final

The McDonnell Douglas DC-10 became the centre of controversy following the disaster involving the Turkish Airlines aircraft that was identical to this one. (Ikaros/Uniphoto Press International)

back-up, a small vent located on the outside of the door was designed to close when the locking pins were in place.

If, however, the actuator did not extend sufficiently because the external switch was not held long enough, or for some other reason, the latches would be incorrectly secured. Significantly, the linkages between the lever and the locking pin bar were found to be too weak.

The shortcomings of the locking mechanism were fully realised in June 1972 when an American Airlines DC-10 on a domestic US service nearly met with disaster soon after taking off from Detroit, Michigan. As the jet was at an approximate height of 12,000 ft (3,700 m) and climbing to its cruising altitude, the door, located on the port side and toward the aft of the fuselage, blew open. Due to the absence of relief valves, the resulting explosive decompression was more intense in the cargo hold than in the passenger cabin above it, and the pressure differential imposed a downward load on the cabin floor that exceeded its designed strength, causing it to partially collapse. This in turn damaged the elevator and rudder control cables that ran from the flight deck to the empennage. Using skill and resourcefulness, the captain and his crew managed a safe landing, relying primarily on the engines to maintain control, and there were no serious injuries among the 67 persons aboard.

Investigation revealed that the door had indeed been improperly closed by the baggage handler – the latches were but one-third of an inch from the 'over-centre' point. In accordance with the prescribed procedures, the handler had attempted to secure the mechanism with the external locking lever, but instead of fitting neatly around the latches, the locking pins had jammed against the lugs. Using his knee for support, he was able to force the lever down, but in doing so merely bent the internal rods and tubes without properly locking the door. The same deflection may have permitted the indicator switch to make contact, preventing the illumination of the cockpit warning light. In addition, the tiny vent door proved to be useless as a safety feature; as designed, it would close whenever the handle was pulled down, regardless of whether the pins were correctly in place.

Almost immediately after the American Airlines incident, the locking mechanism became suspect, prompting action by the Western Division of the US Federal Aviation Administration (FAA). Officials began to prepare an Airworthiness Directive (AD), which would have required, as an interim measure, the placement of a small viewing port over one of the locking pins in the rear cargo door of every DC-10 – a simple peek would thus accurately determine the position of the latches. Also suggested was a placard warning against excessive force in using the external handle. But in the now infamous 'gentleman's agreement', between then

A scar in the forest marks the scene of the first non-survivable crash of a heavily-loaded wide-bodied commercial jet transport. (Wide World Photos)

FAA Administrator John Shaffer and Jackson McGowen, at the time president of the Douglas division of McDonnell Douglas, the AD was downgraded to three Service Bulletins. These not only requested the modification in the directive but also the re-wiring of the electric actuators, alteration of the torque tube and the installation of a support plate to help prevent it from bending, and adjustment of the locking pins to allow for greater travel. While the changes could be practically guaranteed, they would not be carried out with the same urgency as had they been stipulated in an AD.

Perhaps as a result, nearly two years after the issuance of the service bulletins, *TC-JAV* was flying with only two of the requested modifications, and that set the stage for disaster on the Sunday that Turkish Airlines Flight 981 took off from Orly Airport, serving Paris, bound for London, the second leg of a service originating at Istanbul, Turkey. A British Airways strike had forced many travellers to switch to the Turkish carrier. Consequently, the aircraft was almost loaded to capacity upon its departure, and more than half of the passengers were British.

The weather at the time was ideal, with only scattered cumulus clouds at about 3,000 ft (1,000 m). Cleared for ascent to flight level 230, the wide-bodied jet airliner was observed on radar as it assumed a north-north-westerly direction. Shortly afterwards the primary echo was seen to split in two, with one part remaining stationary before disappearing from the radarscope. The second part turned left to a heading of 280 degrees before it too vanished. What the air traffic controller had observed was the separation of the cargo door, which occurred at an approximate height of 11,000 ft (3,000 m) over the village of Saint-Pathus, at a point when the cabin pressure should have still roughly equalled that at sea level.

As with the American Airlines DC-10, the loss of the door caused a sudden depressurisation, which was followed by the failure of the cabin floor. However, with the extra weight imposed on the structure, the collapse was even more extensive, and six occupants in two triple-seat units were ejected through the opening. There must also have been serious impairment not only to the elevator and rudder cables, but the No 2 (centre) power plant controls.

The noise of the decompression was heard on the cockpit voice recorder (CVR) tape, and the first officer, responding to the captain's query of what had happened, said 'The fuselage has burst'. Both the No 1 and 3 engines were also throttled back, apparently automatically, and the aircraft pitched down into a steep descent, the crew unable to regain control. The angle had flattened to about 4 degrees nose-down before the DC-10 ploughed into a forest at an indicated air speed of nearly 500 mph (800 kmh) and while banked slightly to the left, disintegrating in a huge fireball. All 346 persons aboard, including 12 crew members, perished. The main wreckage was strewn over an area approximately 2,300 ft (700 m) long and 300 ft (100 m) wide, some 25 miles (40 km) north-north-east of the French capital. There were only a few small post-crash fires. The duration of the flight was about 10 min, and 77 sec expired between the time of the door failure and the final impact.

The remains of the cargo door revealed various deficiencies. It was obvious that the latches had not achieved the 'over-centre' position. The forces against the door generated by the increasing pressure in flight had been transmitted back to the actuator, which withstood the compression, and in turn to the two bolts that attached it to the door structure, which did not. When the bolts gave way, the latches lost their support, causing the door to open and the top shaft of the actuator to break. The door then shattered into several pieces and became detached from the aircraft.

Studies indicated that, once again, the improper securing of the latches was attributed to the incomplete extension of the actuator shaft. This was

believed to have resulted from the intentional cut-off of power when the operator did not hold the switch long enough, or unintentionally, due to slippage of the torque limiter, the normal action of the thermal protection trip device, or the accidental stoppage of the electrical power supply.

Company records indicating that all of the suggested modifications had been completed on *TC-JAV* prior to its delivery to the airline in December 1972 proved to be erroneous. Although adjustments to the locking pins and lock limit warning switch were made, the work was not in accordance with aeronautical standards. Of course the installation of the viewing port, one modification that had been carried out, could alone have prevented the tragedy, had someone used it to make a visual inspection prior to the take off. The warning placard was also in place, but of no use for two reasons. First, it had been printed in English, which the Algerian-born baggage handler could not read; and perhaps more importantly, the design of the mechanism and the shoddiness of the modifications made it possible to pull down the locking lever, bending the internal components, without the use of any abnormal force. The misrigging must also have accounted for the fact that the warning light on the flight engineer's panel had failed to illuminate.

Following the disaster, the FAA issued an AD mandating a 'closed loop' system on all DC-10 cargo doors. Similar to that used on the Boeing 747, the mechanism is designed so as to prevent closure of the vent door unless the locking pins are correctly in place. Subsequently, the government agency took action to further enhance safety in the DC-10, 747 and Lockheed's L-1011 TriStar. Cabin floors were to be reinforced and venting improved so as to increase survivability of the aircraft in the event of a major decompression or structural failure.

The McDonnell Douglas transport recovered from the black eye it suffered in the wake of this accident. But five years later, it would again come under close scrutiny after another catastrophic crash in the US (see separate entry, 25 May 1979).

Date: 22 April 1974 (22:26)
Location: Near Grogak, Bali, Indonesia
Operator: Pan American World Airways (US)
Aircraft type: Boeing 707-321C (*N446PA*)

Designated as Flight 812, the jet airliner was on a transpacific service from Hong Kong to Los Angeles, California, US, and scheduled to land at Ngurah Rai Airport, located near Denpasar, the first of four en route stops. During the intermediate phase of an approach using automatic direction finder (ADF) instrument procedures, and after being cleared to descend to 2,500 ft (c 750 m), the 707 struck Mt Mesehe, disintegrated and burned. All 107 persons aboard (96 passengers and a crew of 11) perished.

The accident occurred in evening darkness with no moon, and in an area of clear weather conditions. Its undercarriage extended, the aircraft was banking to the right and on a heading of between 155 and 160 degrees when it crashed in a wooded area at an approximate elevation of 3,000 ft (1,000 m).

It was believed that, in an attempt to expedite the landing, the crew executed a right-hand procedural turn prematurely to join the 263-degree outbound track of the traffic pattern. This manoeuvre was apparently based on the indication of only one of the aircraft's ADF receivers, while the other one remained in a steady condition. However, the indication of being over the non-directional beacon (NDB) had been false; the jet was in fact some 35 miles (55 km) north of that point, and the use of a non-standard procedure had prevented the pilots from knowing their exact position.

Although attempts to obtain a proper ADF indication were subsequently made by the crew, this would probably not have been possible because at the time the beacon was shielded by a mountain range. The approach was then continued until impact.

The investigative board was unable to determine what caused one ADF needle to swing as if to give an over-station indication, though it may have resulted from either external or internal interference.

There was no evidence of interference by a radio broadcasting station. It was also believed that the pilot-in-command of the flight lacked familiarity with the procedures at this particular airport.

A recommendation made by the board for the installation at Denpasar of distance-measuring equipment (DME) to supplement the existing very-high-frequency omni-directional range (VOR) facility would later be implemented.

Date: 27 April 1974 (time unknown)
Location: Near Leningrad (St Petersburg),
Russian Soviet Federated Socialist Republic,
USSR
Operator: Aeroflot (USSR)
Aircraft type: Ilyushin Il-18B (*SSSR-75559*)

All 109 persons aboard (102 passengers and seven crew members) were killed when the four-engine turboprop airliner crashed and exploded in a field shortly after leaving the city's airport, bound for Zaporozhye, Ukraine, the first segment of a scheduled domestic service with an ultimate destination of Krasnodar, RSFSR.

Whilst climbing after the take-off, the crew reported that the aircraft's No 4 power plant had caught fire and was vibrating dangerously. The flight crew was cleared to land on the same runway in the opposite direction of the departure path, but after it had turned on to a heading of about 280

degrees and following passage of the outer marker beacon, the Il-18 rolled abruptly to the right into an inverted attitude and slammed to earth approximately 1 mile (1.5 km) short of the runway. The accident occurred in daylight conditions; the weather was not a factor.

The blaze in the nacelle of the No 4 engine was attributed to the structural failure of the third stage turbine disc, which itself resulted from the gradual growth of a fatigue crack. Burning out a part of the right flap in the area of its jack caused the spontaneous retraction of the unit, which had been extended to 35 degrees. This in turn led to the uncontrolled rolling of the aircraft despite action by the flight crew.

Date: 8 September 1974 (c 09:40)
Location: Off Kefallinia, Greece
Operator: Trans World Airlines (TWA) (US)
Aircraft type: Boeing 707-331B (*N8734*)

Operating as Flight 841, the jetliner had taken off earlier from Athens bound for Rome, Italy, one segment of a service originating at Tel Aviv, Israel, with an ultimate destination of New York City. There was no distress message, but the occupants of another aircraft saw the 707 pitch up, roll to the left and spiral down before it plunged into the Ionian Sea approximately 50 miles (80 km) west of the island and some 200 miles (320 km) west-north-west of the Greek capital. All 88 persons aboard (79 passengers and a crew of nine) were killed.

The water in the crash area was around 10,000 ft (3,000 m) deep, and searchers were able to recover only about 2,500 lb (1,140 kg) of floating wreckage, most of it non-structural interior material and personal effects, and the bodies of 24 victims. Neither the flight data recorder (FDR) nor the cockpit voice recorder (CVR) were located.

On some of the debris that was picked up there were indications of an explosion having occurred prior to impact. Metallic and non-metallic particles were found in the foam lining of a suitcase lid and in a seat cushion. There were also penetration markings in a recovered floor panel section. These findings were similar to those uncovered in the investigation of the 1967 crash of a British European Airways Comet jet in the Mediterranean Sea (see separate entry, 12 October 1967), a disaster that was ascribed to sabotage. The 707 had apparently been a victim of the same fate.

It was concluded that a high-explosive device had detonated in the aft cargo compartment of the aircraft while it was cruising at an altitude of 28,000 ft (c 8,500 m). The blast probably buckled and damaged the cabin floor in such a manner that one or more of the elevator and rudder system cables were stretched and perhaps broken, which would have caused the violent pitch-up and yaw and resulted in a loss of control. The No 2 engine apparently separated during the manoeuvre due to over-stressing.

There were no suspects in the bombing, but a Palestinian organisation claimed responsibility. The device must have been put aboard at Athens airport, which was notorious for its lax security. (Just two weeks earlier, in fact, a sabotage attempt had been made against the same airline and flight number, but the bomb malfunctioned in the cargo hold of the jetliner). Only carry-on luggage was being inspected at the time, but, in accordance with TWA procedures, no unaccompanied checked-in baggage would be allowed on to an aircraft. The carrier later instituted a policy to ensure that all luggage would be examined at the boarding point.

Date: 11 September 1974 (c 07:35)
Location: Near Charlotte, North Carolina, US
Operator: Eastern Airlines (US)
Aircraft type: McDonnell Douglas DC-9 Series 31 (*N8984E*)

Although it was not the worst US air carrier disaster of the year, the circumstances surrounding the crash of Flight 212 made it particularly notorious. Investigation revealed a serious departure from the prescribed procedures on the part of the flight crew, which resulted in a lack of altitude awareness during a landing attempt, with fatal results.

The accident occurred as the crew were conducting a very-high-frequency omni-directional range/distance-measuring equipment (VOR/DME) instrument procedure approach to Runway 36 at Douglas Municipal Airport, a scheduled stop during a domestic service from Charleston, South Carolina,

to Chicago, Illinois. Its undercarriage down and flaps set at 50 degrees, the jetliner hit trees, then crashed into a field in approximate alignment with, but some 3 miles (5 km) short of, the runway. Upon impact, the aircraft broke up and burst into flames, killing 72 of the 82 persons aboard, including the captain and one cabin attendant. One of the victims succumbed a month later. Among the survivors, eight passengers and the first officer were injured, the other hostess escaping unscathed.

The weather in the area at the time was characterised by shallow, patchy ground fog. Though visual meteorological conditions existed above it, visibility was drastically reduced within the fog.

Up until about 2½ min before impact, the pilots were engaged in a conversation that was not pertinent to the operation of the aircraft. The discussion was considered distractive and reflected a lax cockpit atmosphere that continued throughout the rest of the flight and ultimately contributed to the accident. As transcribed by the cockpit voice recorder (CVR), the two men covered a variety of topics, from politics to used motor cars, with both expressing strong views and mild aggravation regarding these subjects. In the process they may have relaxed their instrument scan and relied more heavily on visual cues to carry out the approach. And when the DC-9 entered the fog, there would not have been enough time for them to switch back to instrument procedures.

The aircraft passed over the final approach fix (FAF) some 450 ft (135 m) below the minimum crossing altitude and about 50 mph (80 kmh) above the recommended air speed. Its terrain warning system sounded at a height of 1,000 ft (c 300 m)

An Eastern Airlines DC-9 Series 31, identical to the aircraft that crashed due to crew error during an attempted landing. (McDonnell Douglas)

above the ground, but the alert was not heeded by the crew. Nor did the captain call out when 500 ft above airport elevation, or 100 ft above the minimum descent altitude (MDA), as required.

An analysis of the CVR tape indicated that the captain had been referring to his No 2 altimeter, which was set at the above sea level height (QNH) of 1,800 ft, rather than the given airfield pressure (QFE) of 1,074 ft. The first officer, who had been flying the DC-9 during the approach, later testified that he thought the aircraft was only about 130 ft (40 m) below the minimum altitude upon reaching the FAF. This would have been possible had he accepted 1,800 as the QFE, then misread by 1,000 ft his own altimeter, which was set to airport elevation. Such a reading error could have happened if the co-pilot saw one of the altimeter pointers between the 6 and 7 while failing to observe the window of the instrument, which indicates height in 1,000 ft increments. Considering the incorrect QFE, his assumed altitude would have been 1,670 ft (c 510 m), giving him about 1,300 ft (400 m) to go before reaching the MDA of some 400 ft (120 m) above the ground. The descent was thus continued and in fact steepened seconds before impact. This would also account for the absence of call-outs. In its investigative report, the US National Transportation Safety Board (NTSB) described this theory as 'speculative in nature'.

Whatever the reason for the failure to assess properly and maintain a safe height, it was merely a manifestation of the poor discipline displayed by the crew.

Date: 15 September 1974 (c 11:00)
Location: Near Phan Rang, (South) Vietnam
Operator: Air Vietnam (South Vietnam)
Aircraft type: Boeing 727-121C (*XV-NJC*)

Designated as Flight 706, the jet airliner was hijacked by a passenger during a domestic service from Da Nang to Saigon (now Ho Chi Minh City). A while later, the crew radioed that they might try to land at the Phan Rang airport, located some 150 miles (250 km) north-east of the capital city.

Entering the base leg of the circuit, the 727 flew past the runway centreline before initiating a left turn. The aircraft then plunged to earth from a height of about 1,000 ft (300 m) and exploded, and all 75 persons aboard, including eight crew members, perished. It was believed that the air pirate had detonated two hand grenades when the pilot disobeyed his order to fly to Hanoi, (North) Vietnam.

Subsequent to this incident, security measures were tightened by Vietnamese authorities, especially at 'high risk' airports.

Date: 20 November 1974 (c 07:50)
Location: Near Nairobi, Kenya
Operator: Deutsche Lufthansa AG (West Germany)
Aircraft type: Boeing 747-130 (*D-ABYB*)

The first fatal crash of a Boeing 747 was not the catastrophe many had feared, the death toll being within that recorded in accidents involving conventional jets, and even propeller-driven transports. However, commercial aviation had, of course, already experienced its first 'titanic' disaster earlier in the year with the DC-10 crash in France.

Operating as Flight 540, and on a service from Frankfurt, (West) Germany, to Johannesburg, South Africa, the wide-bodied jet airliner was cleared for take-off on Runway 24 at the Nairobi airport, a scheduled stop.

Accelerating to about 150 mph (250 kmh), the aircraft commenced rotation and became airborne at an approximate speed of 165 mph (265 kmh), some 8,000 ft (2,500 m) from the beginning of the runway. Seconds later a buffeting or strong vibration was felt, prompting the captain first to suspect engine trouble, then unbalanced wheels. Continuing the take-off, gear retraction was begun, but the co-pilot lost all feeling of acceleration.

The jet reached a height of around 100 ft (30 m) before starting to descend, then the control wheel stick-shaker activated, warning of an impending stall. Realising that a crash was imminent, the first officer fully retarded all four thrust levers.

Its undercarriage was still in the retraction cycle when the 747 grazed bushes and grass approximately 3,700 ft (1,130 m) beyond the end and some 100 ft (30 m) to the left of the extended centreline of the runway, then struck a slightly elevated access road and began to break up. In the impact and subsequent fire, which was touched off by an explosion in the left wing, then spread to the fuselage, 59 persons aboard (55 passengers and four crew members) were killed. Among the 98 survivors, which included all three flight crewmen and 10 of the 14 cabin attendants, 54 persons suffered injuries and 44 escaped unscathed.

The cause of the accident became known soon afterwards when it was discovered that the flight crew had failed to extend the leading edge flaps. Further investigation suggested a high probability that the pneumatic system used to power the flap units was not functioning at the time they were selected to the take-off position, this because the flight engineer had inadvertently failed to open the system's bleed valves. He must have also failed to notice that the four 'valve closed' amber lights were continuously illuminated and the pneumatic gauge was indicating zero duct pressure.

The crew had in fact failed to satisfactorily complete the pre-flight check-list. Whether or not the flight engineer had verbally responded to the question concerning the bleed valves could not be determined, since the three men were not using the intercom system and their voices were not clearly transcribed on the cockpit voice recorder (CVR) tape.

As a result of the flap setting, the aircraft, after becoming airborne, entered into a 'partially stalled' condition due to abnormally high drag and substantial air-flow separation. This condition resulted directly in the loss of acceleration noted by the first officer and the low rate of climb following take-off. The situation may have been aggravated by the fact that rotation was initiated slightly below the prescribed speed.

The pilots attempted to maintain or increase air speed by lowering the nose, but this action could only be done to a limited extent because of their proximity to the ground, and was largely ineffective anyway. This may have been partly due to the presence of wind shear in the area, but was primarily blamed on the increase in drag occurring at this time, probably because of further separation in the air-flow and as the aircraft lost the benefit of ground effect. An additional but less significant factor may have been an increase in drag resulting from the opening of the undercarriage doors during gear retraction, which could have been greater than predicted.

The crash probably could have been prevented by reducing the pitch angle and increasing power earlier, but the crew suspected engine trouble due to a bird strike and did not take the appropriate action. Furthermore, the stall warning system was not programmed to take account of the leading edge flap position.

In terms of detecting an incorrect setting, a green light on the pilot's centre panel and eight additional green lights on the flight engineer's annunciator panel were still regarded as inadequate.

A number of previous incidents in which 747s took off with the leading edge flaps not properly set had taken place, though none proved disastrous because the additional factors that came into play in this accident were not present. As a result of the first case, occurring in August 1972 and involving a British Airways jet, the manufacturer agreed to a modification by the carrier that wired the leading edge flap system to the undercarriage/trailing edge flap warning horn.

Boeing did send advisories to all 747 operators about the importance of checking the leading edge flap position, but made no mention of the British modification. Inadequacies in the international incident reporting network thus contributed to the Lufthansa crash. Even a revised cockpit check-list procedure that came out of the Boeing advisory did not specifically require a verification of the pneumatic system prior to take-off.

The following year, the US Federal Aviation Administration (FAA) issued an Airworthiness Directive for additional safety features on the jet, as proposed by the manufacturer, designed so that when the aircraft's trailing edge flaps were set in the take-off configuration, an amber light would illuminate on the pilot's panel if the leading edge flaps were not fully extended and an aural warning sound if any flap unit was not properly positioned.

Date: 1 December 1974 (11:09)
Location: Near Berryville, Virginia, US
Operator: Trans World Airlines (TWA) (US)
Aircraft type: Boeing 727-231 (*N54328*)

This could be classified as a 'milestone' accident because of the repercussions it generated and the changes that ensued. It also brought to an end a frustrating year, in terms of safety, for the US air carrier industry.

Flight 514 had originated at Indianapolis, Indiana, on a domestic service to Washington, DC, with an en route stop at Columbus, Ohio. Washington National Airport, where it was to have landed, had been closed due to high cross-winds, diverting the aircraft to Dulles International Airport.

Three minutes after its transferral from the regional air traffic control centre, approach control radioed the flight: 'TWA 514, you're cleared for a VOR/DME approach to Runway 12' (using very-high-frequency omni-directional range/distance-measuring equipment instrument procedures). This was only intended as a traffic advisory, meaning that the 727 could descend without conflicting with another aircraft; since it was proceeding under its own navigation, the crew would be responsible for obstacle clearance. However, as an analysis of the cockpit voice recorder (CVR) tape would later confirm, the message was construed by the pilot to mean that the flight could safely initiate an immediate descent.

The captain was heard to say 'Eighteen hundred is the bottom', in reference to the minimum descent altitude inside the Round Hill airway intersection, as depicted on the approach chart.

The profile view of the map did not indicate the minimum height of 3,400 ft (c 1,040 m) outside that point, which the aircraft had yet to reach, although the minimum did appear on the plan (top) view on the chart, but the pilot must have felt he could go below it because the 727 was not on any of the published airways. His comment 'When he clears you, that means you can go to your . . . initial approach altitude' showed his confidence in the controller, and the final approach was thus begun by the co-pilot.

The local weather at the time consisted of low clouds, rain mixed with snow and a visibility of only 50–100 ft (c 15–30 m); the wind was from the east at about 40 mph (65 kmh). There were indications that both the captain and first officer had

A Trans World Airlines Boeing 727-231, the type that hit Mt Weather near the US capital. (Trans World Airlines)

fleeting glimpses of the ground, but neither must have been able to derive any height reference from what they had seen.

Though it would have been precariously low, the aircraft could have cleared the terrain had it maintained an altitude of 1,800 ft (c 550 m), but apparently due to a combination of the co-pilot's flying technique and the turbulence encountered, the descent could not be arrested. The altitude alert system sounded upon reaching the minimum height, and the radio altimeter warning went off twice, at 500 ft (c 150 m) and 100 ft (c 30 m) above the ground, the last time an instant before impact and just after the pilot was heard to say 'Get some power on'. But by then it was too late.

The cleanly configured jetliner was generally aligned with the runway and in a slight descent when it struck Mt Weather at an approximate elevation of 1,670 ft (c 510 m), about 30 miles (50 km) north-west of the airport and some 50 miles (80 km) from the capital city. Initial impact was with trees about 70 ft (20 m) above the ground, and at an indicated air speed of around 250 mph (400 kmh), and the aircraft then slammed into a rocky outcrop, disintegrated and burned. All 92 persons aboard (85 passengers and seven crew members) perished.

During the inquiry into the disaster, witnesses from the US Federal Aviation Administration (FAA) testified that since it had not been vectored to the final approach course, the flight was not considered a 'radar arrival'. As a result it was not given any altitude restrictions. But the US National Transportation Safety Board (NTSB) ruled that since it had just before received vectoring from the control centre, the aircraft was in a 'radar

environment' and that such restrictions should have been included in the clearance. This particular issue led the investigative board to conclude that the clearance was inadequate and therefore a contributing factor in the accident. Two of the five members of the NTSB went even further, disagreeing with the findings of the majority and placing more importance on the actions of the controller as a causative factor coupled with the pilot's failure to follow the approach chart.

The three other members ascribed the crew's decision to descend below a safe height to inadequacies and a lack of clarity in the air traffic control procedures then in use, leading to confusion by both pilots and controllers regarding each other's responsibilities during operations in instrument meteorological conditions. They noted, however, that the plan view of the chart indicating the minimum altitude in the general area should have been apparent to the crew.

The investigation revealed that pilots were not always aware of the type of radar services they were receiving, ie only traffic separation, navigational assistance with course guidance only, or monitoring to observe deviations in both flight path and altitude. It was also noted in the investigative report that with the then new automated radar terminal system (ARTS III) equipment, which provides a three-dimensional view, pilots had become increasingly dependent on controllers, which lessened their need to know the terrain over which they were flying and, in some cases, even their position relative to the obstacles or the airport itself.

The NTSB made 14 recommendations to the FAA as a result of this crash, and three of those adopted were particularly important. One was

The remains of the 727 are scattered among the trees after the accident that claimed 92 lives. (UPI/Bettmann)

procedural, in that controllers would issue altitude restrictions to pilots making non-precision instrument approaches. The other two were technical innovations. First, ARTS III units would be modified so as to alert controllers when aircraft operating in terminal areas deviated from predetermined altitudes. Second, and perhaps even more significant, was the requirement that all American-registered air carrier aircraft be equipped with a so-called ground proximity warning system (GPWS). This device, which works similarly to a radio altimeter but is more sophisticated, provides the crew with warnings pertaining to height over terrain, descent rate, glide slope deviation, and even flap position. GPWS units have since become standard on airliners throughout the world.

During the first five years of the 1970s, major US airlines suffered nine fatal 'controlled-flight-into-terrain' crashes during passenger operations, taking nearly 700 lives. In the last half of the decade they had only two such accidents, resulting in 13 deaths. The tragedy of Flight 514 left a legacy of safety for all future air travellers.

Date: 4 December 1974 (c 22:15)
Location: Near Maskeliya, Sri Lanka
Operator: Martinair Holland NV (The Netherlands)
Aircraft type: Douglas DC-8 Series 55F (*PH-MBH*)

The jet airliner was being operated on behalf of Garuda Indonesian Airways on a non-scheduled service from Surabaya, on Java, to Jiddah, Saudi Arabia, with a planned 'technical' stop at Bandaranaike International Airport, located about 10 miles (15 km) north and serving the Sri Lankan capital of Colombo. Except for two Indonesian stewardesses, its crew of nine was Dutch; the 182 passengers were Indonesian Muslims on a pilgrimage to Mecca.

During its descent to land, the aircraft struck a mountain in the Anjimalai Range at an approximate elevation of 4,500 ft (1,400 m) and some 45 miles (70 km) east-south-east of the airport, exploded and burned. All 191 persons aboard perished.

Having lost approximately one-third of its port wing in the initial impact with an adjacent ridge, the DC-8 had crashed while banked at about 30 degrees to the left and with its nose slightly raised and undercarriage retracted. The disaster occurred in darkness, but the weather at the time was fair and not considered a factor.

The foil from the aircraft's flight data recorder (FDR) was torn to pieces and yielded no useful information, but by analysing the known facts Sri Lankan aviation authorities were able to reconstruct what probably happened.

It was apparent that the crew had descended below a safe altitude due to a position error. As noted in the investigative report, both the Doppler navigational system and the weather radar installed in this aircraft were different from others in the company's fleet, and although this had been brought to the attention of the flight crew, it still left room for misinterpretation. Specifically, the 'distance to go' counter in the Doppler system was of a different make so that only the 100-mile indications would be accurate; the positions of the 10-mile and 1-mile discs in the unit were considered arbitrary. In addition, the range in this particular radar screen was 180 nautical miles, 30 more than those in other Martinair aircraft.

Since the navigational aids in this area were sparse and unreliable, the crew probably used the weather radar to re-establish their position while over the Indian Ocean and approaching the Sri Lankan coast. But if the radar had been misread, it could have resulted in a navigational error. Also, the possibility of an overlapping cloud giving a false impression of the coastline could not be ruled out.

Another point mentioned was that the pilot-in-command had no recent experience on the route and did not receive a proper route check, which was not in strict compliance with international aviation regulations. Also the co-pilot had little experience in the type of aircraft and none in either this particular DC-8 or on the course being taken.

Besides the matter of route qualification for crews, the report also noted shortcomings on the part of the airline in the maintenance of technical records pertaining to aircraft. The officers responsible for the operation at Surabaya also displayed 'a certain degree of negligence' for failing to retain copies of maintenance records and navigational documentation relevant to this flight. Finally, both the captain and first officer were unaware of the correct reporting points in the Colombo Flight Information Region.

Generally, the Netherlands Aircraft Accident Investigation Board agreed with the Sri Lankan findings, especially regarding the weather radar discrepancy. It remarked that this could have led to a continuous error of 30 nautical miles from the time the pilots attempted to re-establish their position.

The Dutch board concluded that as a result of the mistake in navigation, the crew believed the aircraft to be that distance closer to the airport than was actually the case. Therefore when they reported being 14 miles out, it was closer to 50; the pilots presumably adjusted their 'distance to go' counters to agree with the radar information when the two readings were different.

One of the recommendations made in the Sri Lankan report was that instruments that did not give accurate indications be masked. The Dutch board also noted that a requirement for ground proximity warning system (GPWS) devices on transport aircraft registered in the Netherlands, which went into effect in 1976, would help to prevent this type of accident in the future.

Date: 22 December 1974 (c 13:30)
Location: Near Maturin, Monagas, Venezuela
Operator: Aerovias Venezolanas SA (AVENSA) (Venezuela)
Aircraft type: Douglas DC-9 Series 14 (*YV-CAVM*)

Designated as Flight 358, the jet airliner crashed and burned some 5 min after taking off from the city's airport on a domestic service to Caracas. All 75 persons aboard (69 passengers and a crew of six) perished.

Following its departure from Runway 05, the DC-9 made a climbing left turn in instrument meteorological conditions, reaching a height of about 5,000 ft (1,500 m). Slightly less than 90 sec later, it went into a dive and plunged to earth.

The disaster was believed to have resulted from a loss of control for undetermined reasons.

Date: 24 June 1975 (16:05)
Location: New York, New York, US
Operator: Eastern Airlines (US)
Aircraft type: Boeing 727-225 (*N8845E*)

The first of three major US air carrier accidents attributable to wind shear that occurred during the 1975–85 period (see also separate entries, 9 July 1982 and 2 August 1985) involved Flight 66, which was scheduled to land at John F. Kennedy International Airport at the end of a domestic service from New Orleans, Louisiana.

A severe thunderstorm was raging as the aircraft made its approach to Runway 22L under instrument landing system (ILS) guidance. According to witnesses in the immediate area, the storm was accompanied by heavy rain and strong, divergent winds. Less than 10 min before the crash, the captain of a DC-8 cargo jet that had landed on the same runway reported a 'tremendous' wind shear near the ground. Told by the controller that the indicated wind was only 15 knots, the pilot responded tartly, 'I don't care what you're indicating – I'm just telling you that there's such a wind shear on the final on that runway you should change it to the north-west.'

Moments later an Eastern Airlines L-1011 TriStar wide-bodied jet nearly crashed while attempting to land after encountering adverse winds before successfully initiating an overshoot procedure. Its pilot also reported 'a pretty good shear'. Two other aircraft landed safely before Flight 66 began its final approach.

The US National Transportation Safety Board (NTSB) concluded that *N8845E* probably encountered an increasing head-wind and possibly an up-draught while descending at a height of about 500 ft (150 m) above the ground, causing it to deviate slightly above the ILS glide slope. Suddenly the wind changed to a down-draught, and the head-wind diminished. The downward velocity of the wind increased almost simultaneously with the change in direction of the horizontal outflow from the storm cell, resulting in a decrease in the indicated air speed of the 727 and an increase in its rate of descent. This in turn caused the aircraft to deviate below the proper glide path, and as it descended towards the ground both the down-draught and the longitudinal (head and tail) wind component continued to increase.

Its undercarriage extended and flaps set at 30 degrees, the jetliner began striking approach light towers some 2,400 ft (730 m) from the runway threshold, then rolled into a steep left bank after the outboard section of its port wing was severed. The 727 continued through more light stanchions, burst into flames and virtually disintegrated, with the main wreckage coming to rest on Rockaway Boulevard. Including those who succumbed later, a total of 115 persons aboard (109 passengers and six crew members, among them an additional second officer who was giving the regular flight engineer his annual line check) were killed. Seven passengers and two cabin attendants, all of whom were seated in the rear portion of the cabin, survived with various injuries. The non-frangible light towers were largely responsible for the extensive break-up of the aircraft.

Through a correlation of the flight data recorder (FDR) read-out and cockpit voice recorder (CVR) transcript, it was determined that the captain had made visual contact with the approach lights while passing through 400 ft (c 120 m). Seconds later he was heard to say 'Runway in sight', and the first officer responded 'I got it'. This comment seemed to indicate that despite the pilot's instructions to the co-pilot that he continue to monitor the instruments, the latter, who was actually flying the jetliner, began

The wreckage of the Eastern Airlines Boeing 727 litters Rockaway Boulevard near the threshold of Runway 22L at John F. Kennedy International Airport. (Wide World Photos)

transitioning to the visual references he would need to complete the landing. Since the two men were relying on visual cues rather than their instruments, and with visibility obscured by the heavy rain, neither apparently recognised the deviation below the normal approach path until it was too late. The first officer commanded 'Take-off thrust' a second before the initial impact, but by then the crash was inevitable. The NTSB admitted that the winds may have been too severe for a successful landing even had the crew relied upon and responded rapidly to the instrument indications.

During the inquiry, investigators sought to determine why the runway was left open in such obviously bad meteorological conditions, especially considering the reports from other aircraft. The tower controller said he did not consider changing runways because the surface winds were most nearly aligned with 22L. He added that he was too busy to forward the recommendations of the DC-8 pilot to his superiors. In its investigative report, the Board expressed belief that a runway change was not made out of concern that it would have disrupted and delayed the flow of air traffic.

In the end, of course, it is the pilot-in-command who determines what course of action will be taken. In this case the captain of Flight 66 may have been influenced by the successful landings of two preceding aircraft. Furthermore, abandoning the approach and switching runways could have caused a delay of up to 30 min.

The NTSB made 14 recommendations as a result of this accident, mostly dealing with detection and avoidance of wind shear, but despite procedural changes and technological advances over the next few years, this weather phenomenon would continue to plague commercial aviation and, tragically, claim more lives.

Date: 3 August 1975 (c 04:30)
Location: Near Immouzer, Morocco
Operator: Alia Royal Jordanian Airlines
Aircraft type: Boeing 707-321C (*JY-AEE*)

Chartered by Royal Air Maroc, the jetliner crashed and exploded in mountainous terrain some 25 miles (40 km) north-west of Agadir while preparing to land at the city's airport at the end of a non-scheduled service from Paris, France. All 188 persons aboard (181 passengers and a crew of seven) perished.

Cleared to descend, the crew were asked by the control tower to report when properly aligned with the instrument landing system (ILS). Shortly afterwards the aircraft's right wing tip and No 4 engine struck a peak at an approximate elevation of 5,000 ft (1,500 m) and were torn off. The main wreckage came to rest about 5 miles (10 km) to the south-west and some 2,500 ft below the point of initial impact. The accident occurred in pre-dawn darkness, and it was reportedly foggy in the area at the time.

Other than the pilot's acceptance of the descent clearance, the reason why the 707 had gone below the minimum safe altitude could not be determined.

Date: 20 August 1975 (c 00:13)
Location: Near Damascus, Syria
Operator: Ceskoslovenske Aerolinie CSA (Czechoslovakia)
Aircraft type: Ilyushin Il-62 (*OK-DBF*)

Designated as Flight 542 and on a service from Prague, Czechoslovakia, to Tehran, Iran, the jet airliner crashed some 10 miles (15 km) north-east of the Damascus international airport, where it was scheduled to land, killing 126 persons aboard, including the 11 crew members. Both surviving passengers were seriously injured.

Though dark, the weather at the time was good, in moonlight, when the Il-62 struck a sandy hill and burst into flames during the approach, its undercarriage down at the time of impact. Significant to the investigation was that the aircraft's flight data recorder (FDR) had been destroyed by fire. Examination of the wreckage did not, however, reveal any indication of mechanical or structural failure, and evidence excluded the possibility of a loss of control or explosion occurring prior to the crash.

The accident was attributed to the failure of the crew to maintain the minimum flight altitude.

Date: 30 October 1975 (c 09:20)
Location: Near Prague, Czechoslovakia
Operator: Inex Adria Aviopromet (Yugoslavia)
Aircraft type: McDonnell Douglas DC-9 Series 32 (*YU-AJO*)

The jet airliner, which was on a non-scheduled service from Tivat, Yugoslavia, crashed and burned on a hillside while attempting to land at Ruzyne Airport, serving Prague. Killed in the accident were 77 of the 120 persons aboard; 42 passengers and one of the aircraft's five crew members survived with various injuries.

During the instrument approach to Runway 24 in meteorological conditions consisting of scattered clouds, with 1/8 coverage at approximately 10,000 ft (3,000 m) and fog reducing the horizontal visibility to about 1 mile (1.5 km), the aircraft descended below the altitude to which it had been cleared. Following a procedural turn to the right, the pilots realised they were in a gorge over the River Vltava, with high ground ahead and to the sides. A full-power climb was initiated before the DC-9, configured with its undercarriage extended, struck trees and a building, then slammed to earth about 5 miles (10 km) short of and some

300 ft (100 m) below the runway threshold, and to the right of its axis.

Some of the airport's navaids were reportedly unserviceable at the time of the crash.

Date: 1 January 1976 (c 05:30)
Location: North-eastern Saudi Arabia
Operator: Middle East Airlines (Lebanon)
Aircraft type: Boeing 720B (*OD-AFT*)

Operating as Flight 438, the jetliner crashed in the desert some 25 miles (40 km) north-west of Al Qaysumah, and all 81 persons aboard (66 passengers and a crew of 15) perished.

The aircraft was on a service from Beirut, Lebanon, to Muscat, Oman, with an en route stop at Dubai, United Arab Emirates, and was cruising in pre-dawn darkness when it disintegrated at an altitude of 37,000 ft (c 11,300 m).

It was concluded that the 720B had been sabotaged with a high-explosive device, which must have detonated in its forward cargo compartment.

Date: 6 March 1976 (c 01:00)
Location: Near Voronezh, Russian Soviet Federated Socialist Republic, USSR
Operator: Aeroflot (USSR)
Aircraft type: Ilyushin Il-18D (*SSSR-75408*)

All 111 persons aboard (100 passengers and 11 crew members) perished when the four-engine turboprop airliner, which was designated as Flight 909, crashed and burned during a domestic service from Moscow, RSFSR, to Yerevan, Armenia.

Cruising at an approximate height of 26,000 ft (8,000 m) in darkness and above a thick layer of clouds, with tops of about 13,000 ft (4,000 m) and the natural horizon invisible, the Il-18 had experienced an electrical power failure, which rendered its compass system, two main gyros and autopilot inoperable. The crew was unable to determine whether the right or left gyros or the standby gyro were giving a correct indication, and the aircraft performed some complicated banking manoeuvres before it plunged to earth.

Date: 9 September 1976 (c 14:50)
Location: Off Adler, Russian Soviet Federated Socialist Republic, USSR
First aircraft
Operator: Aeroflot (USSR)
Type: Antonov An-24 (*SSSR-46518*)
Second aircraft
Operator: Aeroflot (USSR)
Type: Yakovlev Yak-40 (*SSSR-87772*)

The two airliners collided and crashed in the Black Sea some 12 miles (20 km) south of Sochi, killing all 64 persons aboard both of them.

Both aircraft were on domestic operations, the twin-engine turboprop An-24, operating as Flight 7957 and carrying 41 passengers and five crew members, en route to Sochi, RSFSR, from Donetsk, Ukraine, and the twin-jet Yak-40, designated as Flight 31, bound for Kerch from Rostov-na-Donu, both cities in the Ukraine, with 18 persons aboard, including a crew of four.

In violation of separation rules, SSSR-87772 had been cleared by an air traffic controller to 18,700 ft (5,700 m), which was in fact the height for the reciprocal track. This led to the head-on collision at that altitude with SSSR-46518. Wreckage of the two aircraft sank in water between 1,500 and 2,000 ft (500–600 m) deep and could not be recovered for examination.

Contributing to the collision were insufficient visual alertness on the part of both crews and a lack of 'situation analysis' based on air/ground radio communications. The weather, cloudless in the area with a visibility of about 5 miles (10 km), was not considered a factor.

Date: 10 September 1976 (c 11:15)
Location: Near Gaj, Hrvatska, Yugoslavia
First aircraft
Operator: British Airways
Type: Hawker Siddeley Trident 3B (G-AWZT)
Second aircraft
Operator: Inex Adria Aviopromet (Yugoslavia)
Type: McDonnell Douglas DC-9 Series 32 (YU-AJR)

Largely due to the location of the nation, the skies over Yugoslavia are among the busiest in Europe, which places a heavy burden on its air traffic control (ATC) system and requires strict adherence to proper procedures. The consequences of even a slight departure from those procedures were realised with this catastrophic mid-air collision.

Designated as Flight 476, the Trident left London's Heathrow Airport earlier on this Friday morning bound for Istanbul, Turkey, and carrying 54 passengers and a crew of nine. Cruising at flight level (FL) 330, its course would take it directly over Yugoslavia, and shortly after passage of the Austrian/Yugoslav border it came under the jurisdiction of the Zagreb Area Control Centre.

In the meantime the DC-9, carrying 108 passengers and five crew members, had taken off from Split, Hrvatska, on a charter service to Cologne, (West) Germany. Prior to departure, its pilot had requested a cruising height of FL 310, but he was subsequently denied ascent above 26,000 ft (c 8,000 m) due to other aircraft in the area. However, the crew were asked if they could climb to FL 350, giving the response 'Affirmative . . . with pleasure'.

The Zagreb ATC centre consisted of three sectors, each one of which was responsible for controlling air traffic at certain altitudes. A display on the radarscope identifying each target and showing its height would only be visible in the sector that had it directly under control. In the other sectors, ie above or below, the aircraft would only appear as a plain blip.

The change in altitude of the DC-9 would thus require a transfer from the middle sector, responsible for control between the flight levels of 250 and 310, to the upper sector, but this time the transfer was not carried out with proper co-ordination. A new flight progress strip, used to mark the radar target, was not prepared. Instead, the same one used in the transfer from the lower sector was merely modified, but without an arrow to indicate that the aircraft had received clearance by the middle sector to climb. The actual identification of the blip was accomplished by the middle sector controller physically pointing it out to the one handling the upper sector.

Another significant factor was the instruction by the middle sector controller for the Yugoslav transport to squawk 'stand by' temporarily, in preparation for the transfer. As a result of this action, which also went against good operating procedures, the identification display and height information would not appear beside the echo marking the DC-9, giving the upper sector controller only a two-dimensional presentation of the target. Means were available to bring in the display, but for lack of time none was implemented. In fact, the controller had less than 30 sec to take action upon realising that a potential conflict existed between YU-AJR and G-AWZT. Hampering his plight was the fact that the crew of the DC-9 delayed for nearly 2 min in establishing radio contact with the upper sector.

The Trident was also under the jurisdiction of the upper sector, but the controller later stated that he could not recall whether its displayed flight level had been 332 or 335. However, the British crew had minutes earlier reported as being at 33,000 ft (c 10,050 m), and the controller's actions indicated that he believed this to be the correct height.

In the final moments before the disaster, the controller attempted to hold the DC-9 at its last reported altitude, FL 327. This would have allowed a narrow clearance of around 300 ft (100 m), but due to faulty instructions this chance was also thwarted. The controller gave the order to 'Hold yourself at that height and report passing Zagreb'. In response to the crewman's query for the altitude at which the aircraft should be levelled off, the controller said 'The height you are climbing through'. He also warned it of the presence of the Trident. This conversation was carried out in Serbo-Croatian, which went against the rule that

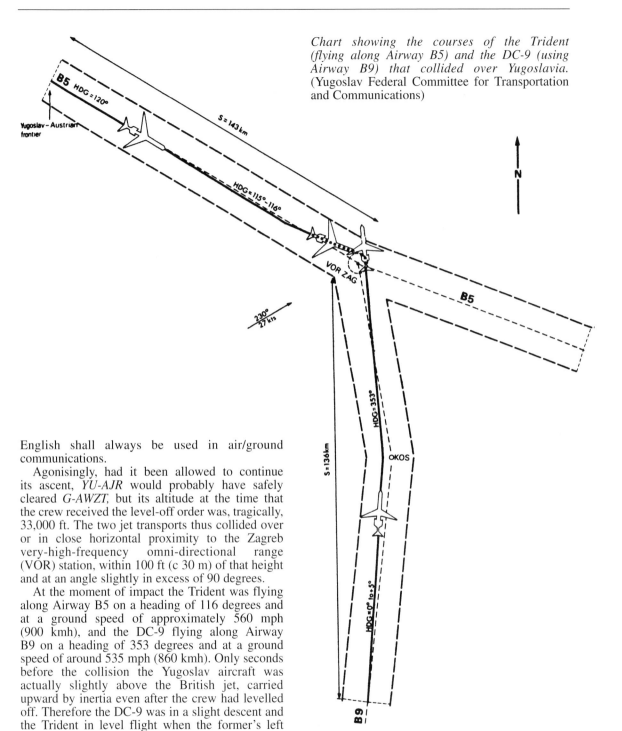

Chart showing the courses of the Trident (flying along Airway B5) and the DC-9 (using Airway B9) that collided over Yugoslavia. (Yugoslav Federal Committee for Transportation and Communications)

English shall always be used in air/ground communications.

Agonisingly, had it been allowed to continue its ascent, *YU-AJR* would probably have safely cleared *G-AWZT*, but its altitude at the time that the crew received the level-off order was, tragically, 33,000 ft. The two jet transports thus collided over or in close horizontal proximity to the Zagreb very-high-frequency omni-directional range (VOR) station, within 100 ft (c 30 m) of that height and at an angle slightly in excess of 90 degrees.

At the moment of impact the Trident was flying along Airway B5 on a heading of 116 degrees and at a ground speed of approximately 560 mph (900 kmh), and the DC-9 flying along Airway B9 on a heading of 353 degrees and at a ground speed of around 535 mph (860 kmh). Only seconds before the collision the Yugoslav aircraft was actually slightly above the British jet, carried upward by inertia even after the crew had levelled off. Therefore the DC-9 was in a slight descent and the Trident in level flight when the former's left wing slashed into the latter's flight deck, instantly killing the British crew.

Both aircraft fell to earth vertically with little or no forward motion, *G-AWZT* plummeting into a field and *YU-AJR*, which lost a portion of its port wing and its tail surfaces, crashing into a forest. The latter then caught fire. All 176 persons aboard the two transports perished. According to press reports,

The remains of the British Airways Trident lie in a field after the mid-air crash with a Yugoslav DC-9. (Wide World Photos)

a woman on the ground was struck by falling wreckage and also killed. The collision occurred some 15 miles (25 km) north-east of the city of Zagreb, and the aircraft crashed about 4.5 miles (7 km) apart, although debris was scattered over an area of approximately 5 by 20 miles (10 by 30 km).

Besides improper ATC procedures, the investigative committee blamed the accident on the failure of both crews to maintain a look-out for other traffic. The collision occurred in conditions of good visibility, with no clouds in the area at that altitude, and it was determined that the pilots had some 30 sec to make visual contact with the opposing aircraft and initiate evasive manoeuvres, but no such action was taken.

The committee was particularly critical of the British crew for not being more vigilant when crossing the intersection of two airways. It noted that the radio transmissions between the DC-9 and the controller were heard on the Trident's cockpit voice recorder (CVR) tape and stated that this should have alerted the pilots as to the potential conflict. Instead they discussed items that were not pertinent to the operation of the aircraft, and the first officer was apparently working on a crossword puzzle.

England's representative in the investigation, however, challenged this aspect of the final report. He noted that the closing speed of about 850 mph

(1,370 kmh) would have negated an attempt by the crew to observe the DC-9. He further wrote that the Yugoslav pilots, looking down from the sun at an aircraft that was producing a condensation trail, had a better opportunity to see than the British crew, who were looking into the sun. Instead he attributed the collision to the failure of the ATC system to provide adequate separation.

An additional contributing factor was the heavy workload imposed on the upper sector controller, due to the absence of his assistant. This was not known to the supervisor.

Under the harsh Yugoslav law, eight ATC personnel were subsequently charged with criminal negligence, and the upper sector controller, the only one convicted, served two years in prison.

Date: 19 September 1976 (c 23:15)
Location: Near Isparta, Turkey
Operator: Turk Hava Yollari AO (Turkish Airlines)
Aircraft type: Boeing Advanced 727-2F2 (*TC-JBH*)

The jetliner was en route from Istanbul to Antalya, the domestic segment of a scheduled international service originating at Milan, Italy, when it struck a mountain at an approximate elevation of 3,700 ft (1,130 m), some 65 miles (105 km) north of its intended destination, bursting into flames on impact. All 155 persons aboard (147 passengers and a crew of eight) perished.

After passing the Afyon very-high-frequency omni-directional range (VOR) station, *TC-JBH* requested descent from flight level 250 to 130. The aircraft then made contact with the Antalya airport control tower and descended to 12,000 ft (c 3,700 m). Radio contact with the 727 was lost after the pilot had reported the lights of Antalya in sight and been granted permission to circle over the city and make a direct landing approach to Runway 36.

Soon after the investigation of the crash began, it became apparent that in the darkness and clear weather conditions the crew had mistaken Isparta for Antalya, resulting in a descent below the obstructing terrain.

Date: 6 October 1976 (c 13:30)
Location: Off Bridgetown, Barbados
Operator: Empresa Consolidada Cubana de
  Aviacion (Cuba)
Aircraft type: Douglas DC-8 Series 43
  (*CU-T1201*)

Operating as Flight 455, the jet airliner took off from Seawell International Airport, Barbados, bound for Kingston, Jamaica, one segment of a service originating at Georgetown, Guyana, with an ultimate destination of Havana, Cuba. About 10 min later, the crew transmitted an emergency radio message, reporting 'We have an explosion on board'.

Turning back toward Barbados, the DC-8 was observed flying below the overcast, trailing smoke. It entered a steep climb while banked to the right, then suddenly plunged into the Caribbean Sea some 10 miles (15 km) from shore. All 73 persons aboard (48 passengers and 25 crew members) perished. The depth of the water in the area of the crash was more than 1,000 ft (300 m).

The disaster was believed to have resulted from the detonation of an explosive device in the rear of the aircraft's cabin, which led to an uncontrollable fire. Toxic fumes produced by the blaze must have eventually incapacitated the pilots. In 1980 an anti-Castro Cuban exile and three others charged with sabotaging the flight were acquitted in a Venezuelan court for lack of evidence.

Date: 12 October 1976 (01:37)
Location: Near Bombay, India
Operator: Indian Airlines
Aircraft type: Sud-Aviation Caravelle VI-N
  (*VT-DWN*)

The jetliner crashed in flames while attempting an emergency landing in early morning darkness at Santa Cruz Airport, from where it had taken off only about 3 min earlier on a scheduled domestic service to Madras, Tamil Nadu, and all 95 persons aboard (89 passengers and a crew of six) were killed.

Its right power plant had failed during the initial climb, prompting the pilot to turn back. Fire then erupted in the same engine and, during its approach to Runway 09, pitch control of the aircraft was apparently lost. Its undercarriage down, the Caravelle plunged to earth in a 45-degree nose-down attitude from an approximate height of 300 ft (100 m) and some 1,000 ft (300 m) short of the runway.

A fatigue crack in the tenth stage compressor disc was blamed for the power plant failure. This malfunction was followed by the bursting of the compressor casing and the cutting of fuel lines that spanned the structure, which in turn led to the extensive in-flight blaze in the engine bay. The fire must have consumed the supply of hydraulic fluid before the aircraft could land.

Date: 25 December 1976 (c 03:45)
Location: Near Bangkok, Thailand
Operator: Egyptair
Aircraft type: Boeing 707-366C (*SU-AXA*)

Flight 864 was cleared to land at the city's Don Muang Airport, a scheduled stop during a service originating at Rome, Italy, with an ultimate destination of Tokyo, Japan, after the pilot reported the assigned runway (21L) in sight and following an initial approach that utilised automatic direction finder (ADF) instrument procedures. A short while later the jet airliner crashed and exploded in an industrial area, its undercarriage extended at the moment of impact. A total of 72 persons perished in the disaster, all 53 aboard the 707 (44 passengers and a crew of nine) and the rest on the ground. More than 20 others suffered injuries.

The aircraft struck a textile mill approximately 1.2 miles (2 km) from the runway threshold after descending below the proper glide path, the accident occurring in pre-dawn darkness. The meteorological conditions at the time, which consisted of a broken overcast at about 1,000 ft (300 m) and a visibility of around 2.5 miles (4 km), may have contributed to the pilot error by either causing a lack of altitude awareness or disorientation leading to an uncontrolled descent. Improper use of the landing aids and flight instruments could have also been a factor in the crash. Reportedly, the captain's performance had been reduced by the medication he was taking.

The airline charged that the control tower had not provided the flight with adequate weather information.

A scene of devastation after the Egyptair Boeing 707 slammed into an industrial area during an attempted landing at Bangkok airport. (UPI/Bettmann)

Date: 13 January 1977 (c 18:15)
Location: Near Alma-Ata, Kazakh SSR, USSR
Operator: Aeroflot (USSR)
Aircraft type: Tupolev Tu-104A (*SSSR-42369*)

All 90 persons aboard (82 passengers and eight crew members) were killed when the jet airliner crashed and burned while attempting an emergency landing at the Alma-Ata airport.

Operating as Flight 3843 and nearing the end of a domestic service originating at Khabarovsk, RSFSR, the aircraft had begun its approach and been flying about 7.5 miles (12 km) from the airport, with undercarriage down and flaps partially extended, when the crew was notified of a fire in its left engine. Emergency procedures, which included altering the flap setting and shutting down the malfunctioning power plant, were immediately implemented. Shortly afterwards, however, the Tu-104 slammed to earth approximately 2 miles (3 km)

from the threshold of the runway and some 1,300 ft (400 m) to the left of its axis.

The engine fire could have led to any or all of the following situations: failure of the flight control system or the elevator trimmer; incapacitation of the pilots by carbon monoxide poisoning; and displacement of the aircraft's centre of gravity due to panic among the passengers. The accident occurred at dusk; the weather was not considered a factor.

Date: 27 March 1977 (c 17:00)
Location: Tenerife, (Spanish) Canary Islands
First aircraft
Operator: KLM Royal Dutch Airlines
Type: Boeing 747-206B (*PH-BUF*)
Second aircraft
Operator: Pan American World Airways (US)
Type: Boeing 747-121 (*N736PA*)

In history's worst commercial aviation disaster, the two wide-bodied jet airliners collided at Los Rodeos Airport, located near Santa Cruz de Tenerife, and 583 persons were killed. In examining the circumstances of this tragedy it is noteworthy how the combined effects of several seemingly innocuous factors led to catastrophic consequences.

Both transports were engaged in charter operations originating within the respective nations of registry, KLM's *Rhine River* en route from Amsterdam and Pan American's *Clipper Victor* having stopped at New York City during a service from Los Angeles, California.

The first event in the sequence leading up to the accident was a terrorist bombing in the terminal building at Las Palmas Airport, on the nearby island of Gran Canaria, the intended destination of both aircraft. As a result of the blast, which injured eight persons, and the threat of a second bomb, the airport was closed, diverting the two 747s and several other aircraft to Tenerife.

Once Las Palmas had re-opened, the crews prepared for the short inter-island flight. Though ready to leave immediately, Pan Am's *N736PA* could not. Its path had been blocked by *PH-BUF*, whose own departure was being delayed by the boarding of its passengers, who had been allowed to wait in the terminal, and by the decision of its crew to refuel for the trip from Gran Canaria back to Amsterdam. Finally, the KLM crew were authorised to begin taxiing to the start of Runway 30 in order to await clearance to take off.

Due to the heavy concentration of aircraft on the ground at the airport, with some even parked on the taxiway, the Dutch and American jets were forced to backtrack on the runway itself, with the latter following a distance behind the former. Meanwhile, the meteorological conditions continued to deteriorate on this late Sunday afternoon, with the visibility decreasing to approximately 1,500 ft (500 m) in light rain and fog.

Having reached the end of the runway and turned completely about, the KLM crew reported by radio that they were ' . . . ready for take-off'. The control tower operator then proceeded to provide air traffic control (ATC) clearance and navigational information, which, as we shall see, did not include specific clearance to take off.

Meanwhile, as the Pan Am 747 continued to taxi, the American pilots observed a horrifying sight: looming out of the mist was the Dutch transport accelerating to its rotation speed, on a head-on course with their aircraft. Applying full thrust and turning to the left, the Pan American crew attempted to clear the runway, but could not prevent the collision, which occurred at 17.06.50.

Its tail skid dragging along the ground for a distance of about 65 ft (20 m) due to over-rotation, *PH-BUF* had just become airborne when its main gear slashed into the side of *N736PA* in the area of the latter's No 3 engine. The KLM aircraft then slammed back on to the pavement some 500 ft (150 m) beyond the point of the collision and slid approximately 1,000 ft (300 m) further, turning in a clockwise direction and coming to rest almost sideways to the runway axis. Although neither the collision nor the impact with the ground could have been excessively violent, the *Rhine River* was swept by flames before anyone could escape, and all 248 persons aboard, including the crew of 14, perished.

The top of its fuselage having been ripped open and vertical stabiliser sheared off, the *Clipper Victor*, which had been at an angle of about 45 degrees relative to the runway at the time of the crash and may have continued to roll for a slight distance afterward, was itself gutted by explosions and fire. Among the 396 persons aboard, 326 passengers and nine of its 16 crew members lost their lives, some of whom succumbed days or weeks after the accident. All but two of the survivors, who included the pilot, co-pilot and flight engineer, were injured.

Obviously the primary responsibility for the tragedy rested with KLM Capt Jacob van Zanten, a senior training pilot for the carrier with some 21,000 hours in the air, whose action in taking off without clearance seemed difficult to understand. However, there were a number of extenuating circumstances that could at least help to mitigate his basic error.

Prior to the collision, the Dutch crew were facing an increasingly urgent time factor. They would have to take off soon in order to pick up the passengers waiting at Las Palmas Airport and complete the flight back to Amsterdam within the maximum duty time allowed by the airline. The situation was aggravated by the time it took to refuel the aircraft, and other possible delays including ATC tie-ups and the worsening weather. They also faced adversities

A Pan American World Airways Boeing 747-121, identical to one of the two aircraft involved in the Tenerife disaster. (Boeing)

The left wing of the destroyed Pan American 747 that collided with a KLM Royal Dutch Airlines aircraft while still on the ground. (UPI/Bettmann)

in preparation for the departure, such as taxiing in heavy fog and having to complete a 180-degree turn in a comparatively small area at the end of the runway in the huge 747. So, when there appeared to be a momentary improvement in the visibility, the pilots must have felt somewhat relieved, which increased their desire to take off.

Communications played a major role in the disaster. After reporting that they were ready to go, the instructions to the Dutch crew from the tower controller included the remark 'You are cleared to the Papa Beacon'. This definitely was not intended as clearance to take off, but must have been construed as such by the KLM captain. Reading back the ATC information, the first officer ended the transmission with the ominous message 'We are now at take off' or ' . . . now taking off'. The controller, apparently not realising the implications of the statement, merely responded 'Stand by for take-off. I will call you'.

Meanwhile, this conversation was being monitored, with some apprehension, by the Pan American crew, prompting radioed remarks from both the pilot and co-pilot, the latter saying ' . . . We're still taxiing down the runway'. Unfortunately, this was sent simultaneously with the tower transmission, causing a shrill noise in the cockpit of the Dutch transport that blocked out both messages.

A subsequent request by the tower to the American crew asking them to ' . . . report runway clear', and the response 'Okay, will report when we're clear', were both clearly heard on the cockpit

voice recorder (CVR) tape of *PH-BUF*. The messages concerned the KLM second officer enough for him to ask 'Is he not clear, that Pan American?' His captain responded emphatically 'Oh yes'.

By that time the *Rhine River* was already on its take-off run, and only about 15 sec later it struck the *Clipper Victor*.

Though speaking in English, the failure of both the Dutch co-pilot and the Spanish tower controller to use proper aviation terminology contributed to the accident, as did a comparatively minor error by the American pilots. Their confusion pertained to the intersection at which their aircraft was to have turned off the runway in order to get back to the taxiway. Clarifying the instructions, the tower controller radioed 'The third one, sir. One, two, three . . . third, third one'. Nevertheless, the 747 taxied past ramp C-3 and headed towards C-4, which the crew apparently mistook for the third one. This slight miscue accounted for N736PA still being on the runway when *PH-BUF* began its unauthorised take-off. As noted in the Spanish investigative report, the fact that the aircraft were taxiing on the runway was in itself potentially hazardous. The use of reduced power by the KLM crew when taking off also contributed to the collision, though indirectly, by affecting the performance of the aircraft.

There was another seemingly paradoxical factor that could have contributed to the disaster. Though Capt van Zanten was highly experienced, his work as an instructor for more than 10 years may have

The empennage and a portion of the fuselage are still recognisable but little else remains of the KLM transport. (UPI/Bettmann)

diminished his familiarity with route flying, including such items as take-off clearances. In simulated flights, the instructor normally assumes the role of the controller, and practice take-offs often take place, without any clearance whatsoever. Conversely, the first officer was faced with serving with one of the carrier's most prestigious pilots, and had little experience in the Boeing jets, which could have reduced the likelihood of his questioning or challenging the latter's actions.

Commenting on the report, authorities from the Netherlands generally agreed with the Spanish conclusions, adding that the KLM crew appeared to have taken off with the 'absolute conviction' that they had the proper clearance. In an additional finding, they noted that sounds suggesting a broadcast football match in the control tower were heard in the recorded radio transmissions, which if true could have been an element of distraction. The Dutch observers also noted that the tower controller should have asked for confirmation of his instruction to 'Stand by for take-off'.

In a difference of opinion, officials from the nation of registry doubted that the 'prestige' factor influenced the KLM first officer, and said there was no evidence of haste on the part of the captain. They dismissed his slight advancement of the thrust levers before his co-pilot had asked for clearance, which was noted in the report, as a normal check of the engines.

Recommendations from both countries included an emphasis on the importance of strict adherence to instructions and clearances, the use of standard,

concise and unequivocal aeronautical terminology in all radio communications, and the greater application of ground radar and special light mechanisms to improve safety. Some of the latter proposals would later be adopted for use in Spain, but not until after another disastrous collision between two commercial jets, this one at Madrid's airport, in 1983 (see separate entry, 7 December 1983).

Date: 4 April 1977 (c 16:15)
Location: Near Atlanta, Georgia, US
Operator: Southern Airways (US)
Aircraft type: McDonnell Douglas DC-9 Series 31 (*N1335U*)

Neither Captain William McKenzie nor First Officer Lyman Keele, the two pilots of Flight 242, had any idea of the meteorological conditions facing them along the domestic route to Atlanta prior to their departure from Muscle Shoals, Alabama. Nor could they have known that this would be the last flight for both of them.

Following a scheduled stop at Huntsville, Alabama, the twin-jet airliner headed east toward its destination – and an encounter with what would later be classified as one of the worst storm systems recorded in the United States in years.

Earlier, the US National Weather Service (NWS) had issued two SIGMET reports and two tornado watches for the general area where the DC-9 was to fly. One watch also called for a few severe thunderstorms, with hail up to 3 in (10 cm) in diameter, extreme turbulence, surface winds of almost hurricane velocity and cumulo-nimbus clouds topping off above 50,000 ft (15,000 m). Though received by the crew, this information was only a forecast. The pilots, who had flown the route in the opposite direction only 2 hours earlier, would probably rely more on their personal knowledge of the weather than on a prediction of the conditions that might develop.

As it continued on a south-easterly heading, the flight encountered a thunderstorm in the vicinity of Rome, Georgia, some 50 miles (80 km) north-west of Atlanta. From the cockpit voice recorder (CVR) tape, it was apparent that the crew had spotted the build-up on the aircraft's radar. Captain McKenzie was heard to say 'Looks heavy . . . nothing going through that', and he and First Officer Keele then discussed a possible hole within the area of intense precipitation.

The jet penetrated the storm at an altitude of between 17,000 and 14,000 ft (c 5,200–4,300 m). Minutes later came the first hint of trouble, when the pilot reported the aircraft's windscreen as having been cracked, apparently by hail, and that its left power plant had failed. In less than 30 sec there came an even more ominous message: 'Got the other engine going too'.

Atlanta centre asked for a repeat, and the situation was made frighteningly clear by the captain: 'Stand by. We lost both engines'. Without power, the DC-9 was literally a huge glider with no place to land.

The crew first requested a vector to Dobbins Air Force Base, which could have accommodated an aircraft of that size, but instead of continuing on toward the military installation, the jet turned about 180 degrees back in the other direction. It was believed that the crew did not select emergency (battery) power, and instead attempted an engine restart while trying to remain in visual meteorological conditions. Finally, the auxiliary power unit was activated, and radio communications with the ground resumed after a lapse of 2 minutes.

Before turning back toward the east, the flight came within 10 miles (c 15 km) of Cornelius Moore Airport, which, despite a relatively short runway and a lack of emergency equipment, could have been used as a last-resort landing strip. However, the pilots were apparently not aware of their proximity to it, and since it was outside their airspace, the airport was not depicted on the controllers' displays.

More than 7 minutes had now elapsed since the engine failure, and the situation was reaching critical proportions. The crew had to find a place – any open space – on which to set down. It was then that Captain McKenzie pointed out a highway. 'We'll have to take it,' First Officer Keele responded. The aircraft's undercarriage was lowered and flaps extended to 50 degrees in preparation for the desperation landing on the road, actually State Spur 92.

The wreckage of the DC-9 rests among the trees in the community of New Hope after the accident attributed to double engine failure. (Wide World Photos)

The left outer wing of *N1335U* first hit two trees, and both wings then struck more trees and utility poles, as the aircraft was still airborne. Simultaneous with its left main gear touching the pavement, its port wing struck an embankment, and the DC-9 veered to the left, ploughing into more trees, fences and other obstacles and breaking apart. Fire erupted on impact, and swept over much of the wreckage. The disaster, which took place in the small community of New Hope, located some 20 miles (30 km) north-west of Atlanta, killed 63 of the 85 persons aboard the aircraft, including the pilots, and nine others on the ground, some of whom were in an automobile that was crushed by the jet. Two of the victims, one of whom had been on the ground, succumbed about a month after the crash. The 22 survivors, including both cabin attendants, suffered various injuries. Seven vehicles and a combination grocery store/gasoline station were destroyed.

The exact conditions encountered by the aircraft could not be determined. It was concluded, however, that the ingestion of large amounts of rain and hail had caused a decrease in the rotational speeds of both power plants, below that required for operation of the engine-driven generators. This accounted for the 36-second loss of electrical power before the engines failed completely. The intentional thrust reduction by the crew in preparation for the descent had apparently contributed to the loss of rotational speed.

Calculations illustrated how massive water ingestion, leading to surging in the aft stages of the high-pressure compressors, could cause upstream over-pressures and correspondingly high aerodynamic forces in excess of any experienced during the developmental and service history of the power plant. An examination of both low-pressure compressors revealed that the sixth-stage blades were deflected forward and had clashed with the fifth-stage stator vanes. Pieces from the broken blades and vanes were then ingested into the high-pressure compressors, causing severe damage. Furthermore, advancement of the thrust levers – a normal pilot reaction to a loss of engine rpm – only aggravated the situation. Evidence of over-temperatures before the engines failed indicated that high thrust settings were maintained even after the compressors were damaged. Neither power plant could have been restarted in such a condition, making the crash inevitable.

The US National Transportation Safety Board (NTSB) tried to determine why the pilots had flown into such a severe storm. There was circumstantial evidence to indicate that their rest time, just under the prescribed minimum, combined with inadequate food intake and long duty hours on the day of the accident could have produced fatigue leading to a deterioration in the captain's judgement. Neither the crew nor flight dispatch personnel had apparently made any significant attempt to seek information on the current weather between Huntsville and Atlanta. It was concluded that both parties had not only over-relied on the pilots' personal knowledge of the conditions coming from their earlier flight, but also on the aircraft's weather radar.

As had happened in previous air disasters, the crew in this case tried to navigate through a thunderstorm using airborne radar. However, since the jet was at the time flying in rain, its radar may have been affected by attenuation. Thus the contour hole noted by the pilots would have been distorted so to appear as being free of precipitation, and when its course was altered to the left the DC-9 in fact entered the most intense part of the storm.

Also identified was the failure of the company's dispatching system to provide up-to-date reports on the meteorological conditions along the intended route of the flight. Limitations in the air traffic control (ATC) system of the US Federal Aviation Administration (FAA) that precluded timely dissemination of hazardous weather information was another contributing factor. As a result of these shortcomings, the crew were not made aware of several tornado sightings in eastern Alabama and the radar identification of thunderstorm activity in the vicinity of Rome. One dissenting board member believed that the probable cause of the accident was the captain's decision to penetrate a known area of severe weather.

Subsequently, the US ATC system implemented one of the recommendations made by the NTSB in its investigative report on the crash of Flight 242 by establishing a standard scale of thunderstorm activity intensity, based on the one in use by the NWS. This information was also published in the Airman's Information Manual. The FAA also took action to enhance the dissemination of significant weather information and issued an advisory circular emphasising the need for pilots to avoid hazardous meteorological conditions. In response to another NTSB recommendation, the FAA noted that a research and development programme exploring ways of improving radar detection of such phenomena had been initiated back in August 1975.

Date: 19 November 1977 (21:48)
Location: Near Funchal, Island of Madeira, Portugal
Operator: Transportes Aereos Portugueses EP (TAP) (Portugal)
Aircraft type: Boeing Advanced 727-282 (*CS-TBR*)

After two unsuccessful attempts, Flight 425 tried a third time to land at Santa Catarina Airport at the end of a service from Brussels, Belgium, via Lisbon, Portugal. Approaching in darkness and meteorological conditions consisting of rain, a low, broken overcast, with 6/8 cumulus clouds at about 1,500 ft (500 m), and an approximate visibility of 2 miles (3 km), the jet airliner landed on Runway 24 some 2,000 ft (600 m) beyond its threshold.

Despite the use of full reverse thrust and extension of the spoilers, it could not be stopped. Overrunning the runway, the 727 plunged off a cliff and struck a stone bridge, at which location its right wing and empennage, including all three engines, were found. The rest of the fuselage, with the left wing still attached, crashed almost vertically on to a beach about 130 ft (40 m) below the level of the airport, exploding in flames on impact. The accident killed 131 persons aboard the aircraft, including six crew members; nine of the victims' bodies were apparently swept out to sea and not recovered. Two cabin attendants and 31 passengers survived with various injuries.

According to the digital flight data recorder (DFDR) read-out, its indicated air speed was approximately 20 mph (30 kmh) above the prescribed velocity when the transport touched down some 1,000 ft (300 m) past the aiming point, despite the fact that it had passed over the threshold at the correct height and properly configured. Just before the landing, and in a possible attempt by the crew to get the aircraft on the ground, the flaps were retracted from 40 to 25 degrees. This, coupled with the speed of the 727 and a slight incline in the runway, could have contributed to an abnormal extension of the flare, which itself factored in the overrun.

Almost simultaneous with the touch-down, there was a significant deflection of the aircraft's rudder to the left, which made the jet skid to the right. There were also indications of hydro-planing,

The burned-out hulk of the TAP Boeing 727 following the runway overrun accident on Madeira. (Wide World Photos)

possibly due to poor runway drainage resulting from deformations in the surface of the pavement. One lesser item that could have contributed to the disaster along with the aforementioned factors and the weather itself was that the indicator lights at the 1,000 ft mark along the runway were inoperative.

It was noted in the investigative report that due to the possibility of wind shear in the approach area, the carrier had recommended a speed of about 10 mph (15 km) above the norm when using Runway 24 at the Funchal airport, which could partially account for the 'hot' landing.

Subsequent to the crash, TAP restricted landings and take-offs on this particular runway to dry conditions.

Date: 4 December 1977 (c 20:15)
Location: Near Kampung Ladang, Malaysia
Operator: Malaysian Airline System
Aircraft type: Boeing Advanced 737-2H6 (*9M-MBD*)

During its approach to land at the Kuala Lumpur international airport at the end of a domestic service from Penang, the captain of Flight 653 reported that a hijacker had commandeered the aircraft, and that it was proceeding on to Singapore. Subsequently, the 737 descended from 21,000 to 7,000 ft (6,400 to c 2,000 m) before radio and radar contact was lost.

According to eye-witnesses, the jetliner pitched up from level flight, then plunged to earth in a steep nose-down attitude, with some bank. The impact was at a high rate of speed in a swamp some 30 miles (50 km) south-west of Johor Baharu, and the aircraft exploded and disintegrated. All 100 persons aboard (93 passengers and a crew of seven) perished.

Although there were reports of a fire or explosion in the air prior to the crash, it was later concluded that both pilots had been shot. Security measures were implemented in the wake of this disaster.

Date: 1 January 1978 (c 20:15)
Location: Off Bandra, Maharashtra, India
Operator: Air-India
Aircraft type: Boeing 747-237B (*VT-EBD*)

Designated as Flight 855, the aircraft took off from Santa Cruz Airport, serving Bombay, in darkness and weather conditions described as 'calm and clear', bound for Dubai, United Arab Emirates. It was instructed to climb to flight level 310, and report upon leaving 8,000 ft. The last message from the 747, received about a minute after its departure, was 'Happy New Year to you, sir. Will report leaving 80'.

Only 20 sec later the wide-bodied jet airliner

A Boeing 737-200 in the Malaysian Airline System livery at the time of the hijacking disaster. (Ikaros/Uniphoto Press International)

plunged into the Arabian Sea approximately 2 miles (3 km) from the shore, reportedly hitting the water while descending at an angle of 35 to 40 degrees and exploding on impact. All 213 persons aboard (190 passengers and 23 crew members) perished.

Most of its wreckage, including both the digital flight data (DFDR) and cockpit voice (CVR) recorders, was subsequently recovered, as were the remains of 90 victims. The depth of the ocean at the site of the crash was less than 30 ft (10 m), sufficiently shallow for parts of the aircraft to protrude above the surface.

An Indian court of inquiry ruled that the disaster apparently resulted from 'irrational control wheel inputs' on the part of the captain after his attitude director indicator (ADI) had malfunctioned, with the instrument probably remaining in a right-bank indication even after the jet had returned to level flight following a gentle right turn. This led to a complete unawareness of his attitude and the continuation of a roll to the left beyond a 90-degree position, from which a successful recovery could not be made. He had also failed to use other instruments, including the standby horizon indicator, to correct the situation.

Additionally, the first officer had failed to monitor the flight instruments and rendered no assistance to the captain in ascertaining the attitude of the transport.

However, Boeing and the manufacturers of the 747's avionics – named as defendants in a subsequent legal action – claimed that the pilot had a history of diabetes and drinking, may have been under the influence of both alcohol and medication on the day of the accident, and merely experienced spatial disorientation. All three companies were exonerated from charges of negligence in connection with the crash in a 1985 federal court decision.

Date: 25 September 1978 (c 09:00)
Location: San Diego, California, US
First aircraft
Operator: Pacific Southwest Airlines (PSA) (US)
Type: Boeing 727-214 (*N533PS*)
Second aircraft
Operator: Gibbs Flite Center Inc (US)
Type: Cessna 172M (*N7711G*)

Southern California, with its relative opulence and ideal flying weather, is known for having the highest concentration of general aviation aircraft in the world. Though the often-used term 'crowded' is a misnomer, the skies over this region could perhaps best be described as 'busy'. This is certainly the case around Los Angeles, but also true to a lesser degree in San Diego, located some 100 miles (150 km) to the south. Yet until this date, despite the potential for one, both areas had previously been spared a major collision between a light aircraft and a large commercial transport; but any over-confidence on the part of private and air carrier pilots that may have developed as a result of their good record was quickly eradicated by this horrifying accident.

PSA Flight 182 had stopped at Los Angeles during an intra-state service from Sacramento to San Diego, and was scheduled to land at Lindbergh Field; it was operating under instrument flight rules (IFR). The meteorological conditions on this Monday morning were excellent, with not a cloud in the sky and a visibility of 10 miles (c 15 km), so the 727 was cleared for a visual approach to Runway 27. Coming in from the north-west, the aircraft assumed a south-easterly course while on the down-wind leg of the circuit before it was to have turned back toward the west to begin its final approach.

Meanwhile, the single-engine Cessna had just completed a practice instrument landing system (ILS) approach to the airport, using Runway 09, the reverse of 27, because it was equipped with ILS facilities. At the controls of the light aeroplane was 35-year-old David Boswell, a qualified private pilot working on his instrument rating; his instructor was Martin Kazy, who had logged more than 5,000 hours in the air. Though operating under visual flight rules (VFR), the Cessna was in radio and radar contact with both the Lindbergh control tower and approach control. It was also fitted with an altitude encoding transponder, as are airliners, enabling the controllers to track its height and computed ground speed as well as position.

At 08.59.30, the 727 received the first of four significant traffic advisories when the approach controller reported 'PSA one eighty-two, traffic twelve o'clock, one mile, northbound'.

Captain James McFeron responded, 'We're looking'.

Seconds later, the controller advised, 'Additional traffic's twelve o'clock three miles, just north of the field, north-eastbound, a Cessna one seventy-two climbing VFR out of one thousand four hundred.'

First Officer Robert Fox radioed, 'Okay, we've got that other twelve.'

Following a third advisory, in which the approach controller reported ' . . . traffic's at twelve o'clock, three miles, out of one thousand seven hundred', the PSA pilot confirmed 'Traffic in sight'.

The controller then cleared the flight to 'maintain visual separation'.

During this period of time the Cessna was instructed to maintain VFR at or below 3,500 ft (c 1,050 m) and to proceed on a heading of 70 degrees. It was also given a traffic advisory by the approach controller who reported the 727 at its 6 o'clock position and that the PSA crew had the light aeroplane in sight. The final advisory to the 727 came from the tower controller, who reported '. . . traffic twelve o'clock, one mile, a Cessna' at

The respective flight paths of the 727 and Cessna involved in the mid-air crash. (National Transportation Safety Board)

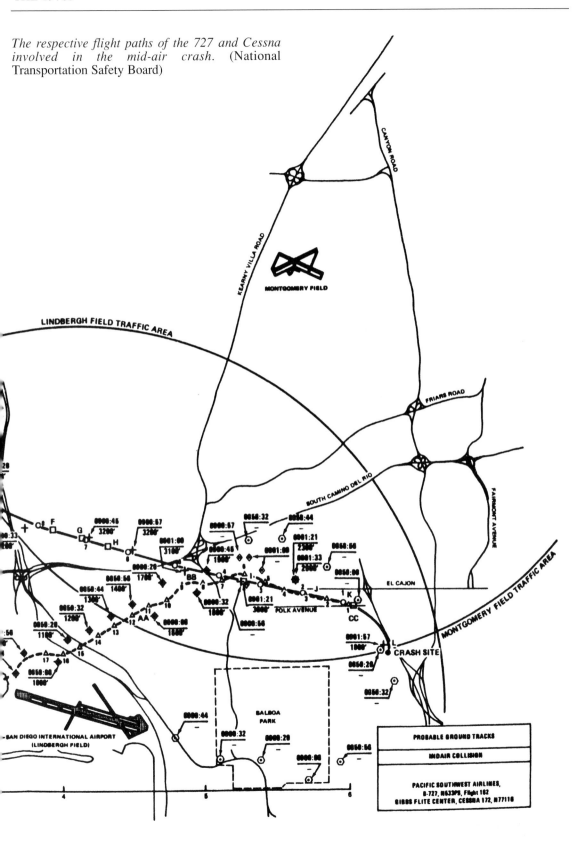

09.00.38.

The captain this time replied with the statement, 'Okay, we had it there a minute ago', followed by a tentative 'I think he's pass(ed) off to our right'.

The tower controller would later testify that he heard the pilot to say 'He's passing off to our right', and for that reason took no further action, responding only with a 'Yeah'.

At 09.01.28 a conflict alert warning sounded at the approach control facility. This collision avoidance mechanism, which was built into the radar system, uses a computer to predict that two targets will cross paths at the same point. The only subsequent action taken, however, was a second traffic advisory to the Cessna by the approach controller regarding the 727. The time was 09.01.47.

At that moment, and almost inexplicably considering the equipment in use and the warnings issued, the aircraft collided at an approximate altitude of 2,500 ft (750 m) and about 3.5 miles (5.5 km) north-east of the airport. Just before impact the commercial transport was descending and banked slightly to the right, and the general aviation aeroplane climbing with its wings level. The 727 overtook and struck the Cessna with the underside of its starboard wing, and the latter then broke apart, exploded and fell immediately to the ground, crashing on a street below. The collision inflicted serious damage to the 727's wing, with large sections of both the leading and trailing edges having been torn away. Fire also erupted in this area, probably from ruptured fuel lines.

Apparently rendered uncontrollable, the jetliner began a shallow descending right turn and, only 20 sec after the collision, slammed into the North Park section of the city just west of Highway 805 and

less than 1 mile (1.5 km) from Balboa Park, home of the famous San Diego Zoo. It crashed in a street on an approximate heading of 200 degrees and an indicated air speed of about 270 mph (435 kmh), with its right wing slightly low, undercarriage down and flaps partially extended, and exploded in flames, devastating a residential neighbourhood. All 135 persons aboard the transport (128 passengers and a crew of seven), the two occupants of the light aeroplane and seven on the ground perished. Nine others suffered injuries, including a woman and her infant son who were driving through the area when a body smashed through the windscreen of their automobile. The impact and subsequent fires destroyed or damaged 22 dwellings.

As has been the case in other accidents of this type, immediate press reports put most of the blame on the small aircraft, and inevitably there were calls for limiting general aviation operations at major airports. However, this charge was an unfair one, since this could hardly be considered a classic IFR/VFR conflict. Despite a VFR clearance, the Cessna was being flown under positive control in an area where terminal radar services were available. Traffic advisories to both aircraft were seemingly adequate.

In its investigative report, the US National Transportation Safety Board (NTSB) blamed the collision on the failure of the airline crew to maintain visual separation with the light aircraft as instructed and to inform the controller that it no longer had the Cessna in sight. It named as contributing factors the air traffic control (ATC) procedures in effect at the time, which authorised controllers to separate two aircraft using visual advisory procedures, when the technological

Trailing fire from its damaged right wing, the Pacific Southwest Airlines Boeing 727 plunges to earth after collision with a light aircraft. (Photo by Hans Wendt, courtesy National Transportation Safety Board)

capability existed to provide lateral and vertical separation.

But the findings of the inquiry were not unanimously accepted. In a dissenting opinion, NTSB member Francis McAdams cited inadequacies in the ATC system as the probable cause and not just a contributing factor. He cited a number of other factors as contributing to the accident, all of which were mentioned in the report. The absence of any one of these occurrences may well have prevented the disaster.

Had the Cessna maintained the 70-degree heading as assigned by the approach controller, it would have crossed the path of the 727 earlier and the collision would have been avoided; its slight turn to the right, which was not reported to the controller, placed the light aeroplane on a track coinciding with that of the jetliner. The turn also took the 727 out of the visual range of the Cessna's pilots by putting it directly behind them, and since they had been informed that the airline crew had them in sight, there would have been no reason to turn their aircraft in order to look for the transport. The approach controller also erred in not instructing Flight 182 to maintain an altitude of 4,000 ft (c 1,200 m) until clear of the traffic area of nearby Montgomery Field, as required, to prevent conflict with operations at that general aviation airport. Even though the Cessna was operating out of Lindbergh Field, the 727 would have safely cleared the light aeroplane had it been at that height.

Neither the approach controller's third advisory given to the PSA crew nor the tower's warning were in accordance with prescribed regulations because they did not contain the direction of the said traffic nor the aircraft type. The investigative board also tried to determine why the conflict alert was not resolved. The approach controller stated that when the alert sounded, the data blocks representing the two aircraft were beginning to merge on the radarscope, but he took no action because the airline crew had already said that they had the reported traffic in sight. He and his co-ordinator both noted that such alerts were common.

Of course, the 727 was the overtaking aircraft and its crew would have been responsible for seeing and avoiding the Cessna. The cockpit voice recorder (CVR) tape indicated some confusion on the part of the pilots over the location of the light aeroplane after the initial 'Traffic in sight' message.

Following the tower's advisory, the pilot asked 'Is that the one we're looking at?', and the co-pilot replied 'Yeah, but I don't see him now'.

Moments later First Officer Fox questioned 'Are we clear of that Cessna?', and Capt McFeron answered 'I guess'.

Then, expressing a note of misdirected optimism, he was heard to say '. . . I saw him about one o'clock; probably behind us now'.

One engine of the PSA jetliner rests amid the ruins of the San Diego neighbourhood. (National Transportation Safety Board)

Nine seconds before the collision, the co-pilot remarked that 'There's one underneath', followed immediately by 'I was looking at that inbound there'.

Despite the good visibility and the fact that the Cessna was below the horizon, so the PSA pilots would not have had to look directly into the morning sun to see it, there would have been other factors making *N7711G* less observable as they closed in on the light aeroplane. In the final seconds before the collision the Cessna would have been masked to the crew by the cockpit structure of the jetliner, and the fact that both aircraft were virtually on the same heading would have reduced the apparent motion of the 172. Furthermore, the angle would have caused a foreshortening of the Cessna, making it appear smaller, and the aircraft would also have blended into the multiple colours of the residential area against which it was seen.

Not long after the accident the possible presence of a third or 'mystery' aircraft in the area at around the time of the collision came to light. It was first thought that the PSA crew may have mistaken another aircraft for the one that had been the object of the traffic advisories, and this theory was bolstered by witness accounts and, particularly, by the initial traffic report given to Flight 182. Board member McAdams in fact mentioned a possible misidentification in his dissenting opinion.

Two years later it was confirmed that a small single-engine Cessna 150 had indeed been in the general area at around 09:00 on the day of the disaster, and this revelation prompted the US Air Line Pilots Association (ALPA) to petition the NTSB for a reconsideration of the probable cause. The request was rejected on the basis that the 150 had crossed the flight path of the 727 too early to have been confused with the subsequent traffic advisories. Nor did the NTSB accept the premise that the co-pilot of Flight 182 mistook another PSA jetliner that was in front of his aircraft as the mentioned traffic. Never resolved, however, was the identity of the traffic referred to by First Officer Fox in his message '... We've got that other twelve', whether the aircraft in the first advisory or *N7711G*.

The NTSB was, however, sufficiently moved by the ALPA petition to modify its original findings. In the new probable cause, the ATC procedures joined the error by the PSA crew as a primary factor.

Considered as contributing factors were the failure of the controller to advise Flight 182 of the Cessna's direction, the failure of the light aeroplane to maintain the assigned heading, and improper resolution of the conflict alert.

NTSB recommendations included the implementation of a full-scale terminal radar service area at Lindbergh Field, which would later be acted upon by the US Federal Aviation Administration (FAA), and procedural changes for the separation of aircraft in all terminal areas. That did not mean that the San Diego disaster was the result of a failure in the ATC system. The equipment was more than adequate and functioned perfectly on the day of the collision. Nor was there any gross negligence by any of those involved, but rather a series of seemingly small but nevertheless critical errors. The underlying reason for the tragedy could perhaps be best summed up in one word: complacency.

Date: 15 November 1978 (23:30)
Location: Near Katunayake, Sri Lanka
Operator: Loftleidir HF (Icelandic Airlines)
Aircraft type: McDonnell Douglas DC-8 Super 63CF (*TF-FLA*)

The jetliner was being flown on behalf of Garuda Indonesian Airways on a non-scheduled service from Saudi Arabia to Indonesia, its passengers Muslim pilgrims returning home from Mecca, and it crashed while attempting to land at Bandaranaike International Airport, located some 20 miles (30 km) north of Colombo, an intermediate stop. Killed were 184 persons aboard the aircraft, including eight of its 13 crew members. There were 78 survivors, many of whom suffered serious injuries.

During the instrument landing system (ILS) approach, the DC-8 ploughed into a coconut plantation approximately 1 mile (1.5 km) from the threshold of the assigned runway (22), broke apart and burst into flames, its undercarriage down at the moment of impact. The accident took place in darkness and during a light to moderate rain, a low overcast consisting of 5/8 cloud coverage at about 1,000 ft (300 m), and a visibility of around 3.5 miles (6 km). There was also thunderstorm activity in the area.

Sri Lankan aviation authorities attributed the disaster to the flight crew's non-conformance with the established approach procedures. Specifically, they ruled that the pilots failed to check and utilise all the instruments available for altitude and rate-of-descent awareness; that the first officer did not make the required altitude and descent rate call-outs at various levels; and that the captain failed to initiate a missed approach procedure at the appropriate height when the runway was not visible. (Subsequently, he did commence an overshoot, asking for full power, but at too low an altitude to prevent the crash.)

Additionally it was believed that the aircraft's radio altimeter had been erroneously set at 150 ft (c 50 m), which deprived the crew of the ground proximity warning system (GPWS) alert at the intended break-off height of 250 ft (c 75 m).

In a dissenting opinion, the Icelandic Directorate of Civil Aviation blamed the accident on inadequate maintenance of the ILS facilities, which it said caused a downward bending of the glide slope into the ground and, in turn, of the jetliner arriving at its decision height too far from the runway and over terrain where a successful recovery could not be made. The Directorate also considered erroneous information supplied by the radar controller and the lack of an operational approach lighting system at the airport as contributing factors.

Icelandic and Sri Lankan investigators did agree that an encounter with heavy rain and/or a downdraught during a critical portion of the flight hampered the crew's attempt to regain altitude.

Date: 23 December 1978 (00:39)
Location: Near Cinisi, Sicily, Italy
Operator: Alitalia (Italy)
Aircraft type: McDonnell Douglas DC-9 Series 32 (*I-DIKQ*)

Operating as Flight 4128 and on a supplemental domestic service from Rome, the jet airliner crashed in the Tyrrhenian Sea while attempting to land at Punta Raisi Airport, serving Palermo, killing 108 persons aboard, including the entire crew of five. Fishing-boats rescued the 21 surviving passengers.

The accident occurred during the final approach to Runway 21, using very-high-frequency omni-directional range and distance-measuring equipment (VOR/DME) procedures and while under radar contact. It was dark at the time, and the meteorological conditions consisted of light rain and low clouds, with 4/8 cumulus at about 2,500 ft (750 m) and 8/8 altostratus at 8,000 ft (c 2,500 m), a visibility of approximately 5 miles (10 km), and a 17-knot wind from a direction of 190 degrees.

Its undercarriage extended, the DC-9 hit the water some 3.5 miles (6 km) from the runway threshold, the impact breaking its fuselage into three main sections and tearing off both wings and one engine. The main wreckage, containing many of the victims' bodies, was subsequently recovered.

The crash apparently resulted from the poor monitoring of altitudes and too early a transition from instrument to visual flight procedures by the pilots while descending over an area devoid of lights and conducive to optical illusions.

Date: 25 May 1979 (15:04)
Location: Near Chicago, Illinois, US
Operator: American Airlines (US)
Aircraft type: McDonnell Douglas DC-10 Series 10 (*N110AA*)

Five years after the crash near Paris (see separate entry, 3 March 1974), the DC-10 once again became the centre of controversy as a result of this, the worst US domestic airline disaster to date.

Flight 191 began its take-off, as cleared, from Runway 32R at O'Hare International Airport, on a non-stop domestic service to Los Angeles, California. The weather on this Friday afternoon was perfect, with the sky clear and a visibility of 15 miles (c 25 km). Accelerating normally, the aircraft commenced to lift off, whereupon a serious structural failure occurred. At or just before rotation, its No 1 engine, with the pylon attached, broke off. Tossed completely over the left wing, the power plant came to rest along the right-hand side of the runway.

The DC-10 then climbed to a height of about 300 ft (100 m) above the ground before it rolled to the left and started to descend, despite the application of aileron and rudder deflections in the opposite direction. Only 31 sec after becoming airborne, the wide-bodied jetliner plunged into an open field in a nose-down attitude of approximately 20 degrees, with its undercarriage still extended and flaps at the take-off setting. The transport disintegrated in a massive explosion on impact, which took place about 1 mile (1.5 km) from the end of the runway and some 1,000 ft (300 m) to the left of its extended centreline, and at a speed of around 180 mph (290 kmh). All 271 persons aboard (258 passengers and 13 crew members) and two men on the ground perished. Two others were seriously injured and several vehicles, a mobile home and an old aircraft hangar were destroyed.

As with the Turkish crash in 1974, design shortcomings played an important role in this accident, but the primary factor in the tragedy that befell Flight 191 was not design-based, but operational – specifically, improper maintenance procedures.

Smouldering wreckage of the Icelandic Airlines Super DC-8 lies amid the coconut trees on Sri Lanka. (Wide World Photos)

Examination of the wreckage revealed a fracture in the forward flange of the left pylon's aft bulkhead. Resulting from overstressing, the total length of the main break and associated fatigue cracking was about 13 in (33 cm). At one end of the fracture, the cracking progressed to the upper inboard fastener that attached the forward section of the bulkhead to the aft part. At the other end, the fatigue propagated forward and slightly outboard towards the furthest-out hole in the upper flange. Weakened by the crack, the structure failed from stresses generated as the DC-10 took off. The sequence and direction of the separation were consistent with forces imposed during the upward rotation of the aircraft, combined with aerodynamic loads and the thrust from the engine itself.

The loss of the power plant should not have doomed the flight – what proved fatal was the damage it inflicted. When the pod/pylon assembly tore away, it took with it a chunk of the wing's leading edge 3 ft (c 1 m) long. Both the No 1 and 3 extension and retraction lines of the corresponding hydraulic systems and the follow-up cables for the drive actuators of the outboard slats were severed. Due to the loss of hydraulic fluid, the force of the rushing air caused the outboard slats on the left wing to retract, while the inboard slats on the same wing and both the inboard and outboard ones on the right wing remained extended. This asymmetrical slat configuration would have created handling difficulties for the pilots, and had the effect of increasing the stalling speed of the port wing. There were other problems as well. The No 1 engine powered a number of systems and instruments, all of which failed when it separated. Particularly significant was the loss of the stick-shaker stall-warning device and the slat disagreement warning system.

Whatever action was taken by the crew could not be ascertained; the cockpit voice recorder (CVR) also received its electrical supply from the missing engine, as did certain parameters of the digital flight data recorder (DFDR). It was concluded, however, that the power had not been restored, possibly due to the distraction associated with the multiple failures, or due to the insufficient time available.

Especially considering the absence of the stick-shaker activation, the roll of the DC-10 must have confused the pilots, who could not have recognised the manoeuvre as the beginning of a stall. The buffeting associated with a stall could have been masked by air turbulence, the presence of which was confirmed. Also neither the missing engine nor the slats would have been visible from the flight deck. It was therefore considered unreasonable for the crew to recover from such a situation.

The fracture that led to the pylon failure was attributed to a questionable maintenance practice used by American and another US carrier, Continental Air Lines. This procedure involved the removal and reinstallation of wing engine and pylon assemblies in one piece. A stand and cradle were affixed to the engine, and the entire unit was supported by a forklift. Though certainly a time-saving measure, safety was also a consideration in the adoption of the procedure. The one-step

technique would reduce the number of disconnects of hydraulic and fuel lines, electrical cables and wiring. McDonnell Douglas, however, had prescribed removal and replacement of the pod and pylon separately, and, learning of the new method, the manufacturer stated that it 'did not encourage' it.

The procedure was delicate, and presented numerous possibilities for the application of a fracture-producing load either during disassembly or reassembly. Damage could result from contact between the bolts attaching the spar web to the upper flange of the aft bulkhead with the wing-mounted clevis, or, if the entire assembly were to be lowered too far, from the transferral of its total weight to the bulkhead. It was learned that the forklift drivers did not receive adequate instruction in the need for precision when carrying out the work.

The fracture found on *N110AA* was believed to have been inflicted about two months before its crash, at the airline's maintenance facility in Tulsa, Oklahoma, when the power plant had been removed in order to replace the spherical bearings that are used in the joints that attach the pylon to the wing. As the aircraft was being serviced, the forklift had to be re-positioned, and there were also indications that the vehicle ran out of fuel during the same time span.

Examination also revealed that three shims had been installed on the upper surface of the forward upper flange on this particular DC-10 in order to reduce clearance. In its investigative report, the US National Transportation Safety Board (NTSB) concluded that the shims could have spread out the

The American Airlines DC-10, minus its left engine, is photographed an instant before impact. (Sygma)

load and increased the size of the crack, or could have actually added strength to the structure; no conclusion could be made as to their effects. Whatever the case, the fracture was believed to have increased in size during the period of service until the final failure due to normal operational stresses.

Damage resulting from the one-step maintenance procedure had been reported by Continental Air Lines to McDonnell Douglas some months before the Chicago disaster, but in a lapse in safety communications this information was not relayed to the US Federal Aviation Administration (FAA).

The NTSB considered the design of the pylon structure as contributing to the loss of the engine from *N110AA*. It noted that in some places clearances were unnecessarily small, making maintenance difficult to perform. The inter-relationship and lack of redundancy of essential aircraft systems were also a factor in the accident. The stick-shaker had only one motor and, deriving its electrical energy from the port engine, there was no way by which it could operate by battery power; and even had it continued to function after the engine separation, there would have been no warning, because the computer designed to receive information concerning the position of the outboard slats was itself knocked out by the power loss.

Though the DC-10 had been certified by the FAA in accordance with the rules in effect at the time, the NTSB concluded that those regulations were inadequate. Safe flight characteristics despite an asymmetrical slat configuration had been demonstrated, although not under take-off conditions. And although an analysis did show that the capability of the aircraft to accelerate to and maintain a safe margin above the stall regime was compromised in the event of both a loss of engine thrust and unwanted slat retraction, this combination was considered 'extremely improbable'. The NTSB also identified deficiencies in the surveillance and reporting procedures of the FAA, and shortcomings in the production and quality control standards of the manufacturer. Some three years after the crash, the FAA did take action to rectify one of the identified flaws in the transport when it ordered changes in its slat mechanism. Added to every DC-10 would be a spring assembly providing tension in order to hold the slats in place, even if one of the cables attached to them were to break, and a valve, designed to maintain hydraulic pressure in the system should a line experience a loss of fluid.

The crew of Flight 191 was not faulted for continuing the take-off after the structural failure, since it could not have known the nature of the emergency. In trying to maintain the same air speed, the first officer complied with the procedures specified by the airline in the event of a power plant failure. Unfortunately, his action had the effect of decelerating the jetliner, which led to the initiation of the stall. (As a result of this accident, higher climb-out speeds in the event of a power plant failure occurring during this phase of flight were recommended.)

A fiery explosion marks the end of Flight 191, which began at Chicago's O'Hare International Airport. (Sygma)

Inspections carried out in the wake of the crash revealed numerous discrepancies in the DC-10 fleet, including fractures that were found in the upper flanges of the aft bulkheads on the pylons of six different aircraft. Concern over these matters prompted the FAA to suspend the transport's type certificate, which remained in effect in the US for 37 days.

This temporary grounding order was the first involving an American-built commercial airliner in more than 30 years, and proved to be a tremendous blow not just to the DC-10 but also to the supremacy of the nation's aviation industry. As for American Airlines, which abandoned the one-step technique, this served as a bitter lesson in performing maintenance 'by the book'.

Date: 11 August 1979 (c 13:35)
Location: Near Dneprodzerzhinsk, Ukraine, USSR
First aircraft
Operator: Aeroflot (USSR)
Type: Tupolev Tu-134A (*SSSR-65735*)
Second aircraft
Operator: Aeroflot (USSR)
Type: Tupolev Tu-134A (*SSSR-65816*)

The two jet transports collided at an approximate height of 27,500 ft (8,400 m), and both then crashed. All 178 persons aboard both of them perished in the disaster.

Both aircraft were on domestic operations, *SSSR-65735*, designated as Flight 7880, en route from Donetsk, Ukraine, to Minsk, Belorussia, the last segment of a service originating at Tashkent, Uzbek SSR, and carrying 77 passengers and a crew of seven,

and *SSSR-65816*, operating as Flight 7628, from Chelyabinsk and Voronezh, RSFSR, to Kishinev, Moldavian SSR, with 88 passengers and a crew of six aboard. As they were flying on crossing tracks, air traffic controllers sought to provide separation through altitude assignment, but after clearing Flight 7880 for ascent to about 30,000 ft (10,000 m), they failed to monitor its position on radar. The resulting collision took place in the clouds, with the nose of *SSSR-65816* probably striking the rear of *SSSR-65735*. Wreckage was scattered over an area of some 2 by 10 miles (3 by 15 km).

Date: 31 October 1979 (05:42)
Location: Mexico City, Mexico
Operator: Western Air Lines (US)
Aircraft type: McDonnell Douglas DC-10 Series 10 (*N903WA*)

Designated as a supplemental service, Flight 2605 was the second of two aircraft that departed from Los Angeles, California, US, bound for Mexico City. As the wide-bodied jetliner prepared to land at Benito Juarez International Airport, the control tower operator informed its crew that the runway in use was 23-Right. However, the adjacent 23-Left, which had been closed for resurfacing, was the runway equipped with both instrument landing system (ILS) facilities and approach lights. For that reason the captain apparently elected to execute a 'side-step' manoeuvre, using the ILS of 23L before transitioning over to 23R. In accordance with this procedure, the crew would be required to abandon the approach if no visual contact was established at

An Aeroflot Tupolev Tu-134A, two of which were involved in the disastrous collision over the Ukraine. (Aeroflot)

Carnage at Mexico City's international airport following the crash of a Western Air Lines DC-10. (Wide World Photos)

an above-ground height of 600 ft (c 180 m).

During the final approach, the tower controller drew the crew's attention to the fact that the aircraft had deviated to the left of the correct flight path, and again advised that Runway 23L was closed. The DC-10 then entered a fog bank at an approximate altitude of 800 ft (250 m), and a crewman reported that the approach lights could not be seen.

Inexplicably, the jetliner did not land on 23R. Instead, its left main undercarriage wheels touched down on the grass to the left of the pavement of 23L, and the right ones on that runway's shoulder. The aircraft then entered the runway, after which full power was applied and a go-around initiated.

However, just after becoming airborne the DC-10 collided with an earth-laden dump truck that was being driven on the shoulder of the closed runway. The impact sheared off the right main gear, and the undercarriage leg itself then hit and severed the aircraft's starboard horizontal tailplane. Portions of the right wing flaps were also torn away. Due to this damage, the jetliner banked steeply to the right, and its starboard wing was fractured when it scraped along the taxiway.

The DC-10's right wing then struck a repair hangar, rupturing the fuel tanks, and the aircraft finally slammed into another building, broke apart and was swept by flames. Killed in the accident were 72 of the 89 persons aboard the aircraft (61 passengers and 11 crew members) and the driver of the dump truck. Except for two passengers, the 17 survivors, who also included two cabin attendants, suffered various injuries. The crash occurred around

dawn, and in addition to the fog there was mist and haze in the area. Visibility had been reduced to zero.

The flight crew had not complied with the approach procedure being used and had descended below the minimum height without reporting the runway in sight. Analysis of the cockpit voice recorder (CVR) tape also indicated that the required altitude call-outs had not been made during the descent.

Date: 26 November 1979 (c 02:00)
Location: Near At Ta'if, Saudi Arabia
Operator: Pakistan International Airlines
Aircraft type: Boeing 707-340C (*AP-AWZ*)

Flight 740 had been airborne less than half an hour when a cabin attendant reported a fire in the aft cabin area. Seventeen horrifying minutes later, and while on a south-south-easterly heading, the jetliner plunged into a rocky desert and disintegrated in a fiery explosion that was witnessed by the pilots of another aircraft some 30 miles (50 km) away. All 156 persons aboard the 707 (145 passengers and a crew of 11) perished.

The accident took place in darkness and clear weather conditions approximately 90 miles (145 km) east of Jiddah, where the 707 had stopped, as scheduled, during a service originating at Kano, Nigeria, with an ultimate destination of Karachi, Pakistan. Due to the condition of the wreckage, the cause of the in-flight blaze that led to the crash could not be determined.

The aircraft's flight data recorder (FDR) yielded nothing of any significance, but its cockpit voice recorder (CVR) tape was recovered intact and provided much valuable information relative to the investigation. According to facts obtained from the CVR transcript, the fire had started near the cabin door and/or in the lavatory. Someone was heard to say 'Fire, fire, it is totally on fire', and the sound of numerous other voices indicated that panic-stricken passengers had crowded forward towards or into the cockpit to escape the flames.

There was evidence that valuable time had been lost in notifying the flight crew about the fire, and that the captain delayed in turning back towards Jiddah. In fact, the pilot presumably continued climbing towards the assigned altitude even after learning of the blaze, then executed an emergency descent at a rate too slow under the circumstances. He also seemed preoccupied with trying to depressurise the cabin.

It was not known whether the passenger oxygen masks were deployed; had they been, the release of pure oxygen into the cabin would have intensified and extended the fire.

The aircraft had been given an incorrect descent clearance by an air traffic controller, who failed to note the minimum height for the area. This was not a factor, however, as the crew realised the error and levelled off at 11,000 ft (c 3,400 m). With the elevation of the terrain being about 3,000 ft (1,000 m) at the crash site, it was concluded that the 707 was out of control during the last 8,000 ft (c 2,500 m) of the descent.

Because it could find no evidence of a pre-impact explosion, and since the use of incendiary devices was not consistent with previous terrorist activity in the Middle East, the investigative board considered sabotage unlikely. There were indications, without confirmation, that the fire was of an electrical origin.

Considered most probable, however, was that the blaze had been started unintentionally by a passenger. Most of those aboard were Muslim pilgrims, returning from Mecca, and many had been carrying small gasoline or kerosene stoves used to make tea. If one or more of these stoves were fuelled and pressurised, the pressure differential would increase as the aircraft continued to ascend. A poorly sealed gasket could allow leakage into the cabin or cargo areas, and only a spark or cigarette ember would be needed to set the stage for disaster. Smoke from the rapidly spreading fire must have eventually incapacitated the pilots despite their use of emergency oxygen.

In its accident report, the board recommended that Pakistan International Airlines review its training policies so as to impress cabin crews with the importance of reporting any unusual occurrence, especially a fire, by the most expeditious means available, and flight crews with the importance of implementing emergency procedures without hesitation when facing such a situation. It also suggested that the Saudi Arabian air traffic control system review its procedures to assure that controllers be aware of minimum safe altitudes in all sectors, and that separate communication frequencies be assigned immediately in the event of an emergency such as the one encountered by Flight 740.

Date: 28 November 1979 (12:49)
Location: Ross Island, Antarctica
Operator: Air New Zealand Ltd
Aircraft type: McDonnell Douglas DC-10 Series 30 (*ZK-NZP*)

What began as the last of four sight-seeing flights conducted by the carrier during the Antarctic Summer of 1979 would end in the first commercial aviation disaster ever to occur on the frozen continent, involving an airline that had not lost a passenger in nearly 40 years of operations and a nation that until this date had not experienced a civilian air crash resulting in more than a couple of dozen fatalities.

Following its departure from Auckland, on New Zealand's North Island, the aircraft proceeded south on what was designated as a non-scheduled service with an ultimate destination of Christchurch, on the country's South Island, and no planned stops in between. The DC-10 was dispatched in accordance with a computerised flight plan, which had been fed into its area inertial navigation system (AINS).

The cockpit crew consisted of a captain, two first officers and two flight engineers. The extra co-pilot was in lieu of a second captain, which had been a requirement of Air New Zealand in its Antarctic operations. Interestingly, of these five men only one of the flight engineers had ever been on a polar trip. However, two of the three pilots had been subjected to a specially devised audio-visual, written and simulator route qualification briefing. There were also 15 cabin attendants to serve the 237 passengers on this particular flight.

Inasmuch as compasses are useless so close to the magnetic pole, and for the purpose of maintaining some consistency in an area where determining one's position and direction can be confusing, a method of grid navigation would be employed. This technique involved the placement of a grid over the navigational chart, which in effect reversed directions for a crew flying towards Antarctica from New Zealand. Due north would thus become 180 degrees Grid, and vice versa. This was just one of several factors that added to the complexity of the polar flights.

At the time, Ross Island was under a low overcast, with a reported ceiling of 2,000 ft (c 600 m) and light snow. However, the weather office at McMurdo Station advised the crew that the visibility under the clouds was 40 miles (c 65 km). The US Navy air traffic control centre, also located at McMurdo, then suggested that the aircraft take advantage of the facility's surveillance radar to initiate a descent.

While over the Ross Sea, the captain decided to let down through a break in the overcast, doing so in two descending orbits, first to the right, then the left. Following the second loop, the DC-10 continued down to 2,000 ft (c 600 m), then another 500 ft (c 150 m) in an attempt to obtain a better view under the cloud base. This action by the pilot represented a violation of the specified minimum altitude of 16,000 ft in instrument meteorological conditions until the passage of McMurdo, and even the absolute minimum of 6,000 ft in any weather.

The crew had just begun ascent procedures, applying full power to the three engines, when the wide-bodied jet airliner slammed into the upward-sloping ice at an approximate elevation of 1,500 ft (500 m) and disintegrated in a mass of flames. All 257 persons aboard perished.

In its report, New Zealand's Office of Air Accidents Investigation ascribed as the primary cause of the disaster the captain's decision to descend visually below the minimum safety height before reaching McMurdo. However, the inquiry also identified numerous shortcomings in the practices of the airline with regard to its Antarctic operations that contributed to, and some even feel

caused, the crash.

Particularly noteworthy was a single-digit error in the computer-stored flight plan that resulted in the incorrect co-ordinates of Williams Field located near McMurdo and the site of a non-directional beacon (NDB) and a tactical air navigation (TACAN) aid, which were used by Air New Zealand crews. As a consequence the facility was depicted as being 2 degrees 10 minutes further true west than its actual position. Though seemingly insignificant, this lapse actually displaced the direct track to McMurdo by nearly 30 miles (50 km) to the right, relative to the grid. Since past flights had been conducted in visual meteorological conditions (VMC) and did not strictly adhere to the prescribed route, the error was not detected during the operations taking place over the previous 14 months until exactly two weeks before the crash of ZK-NZP, and was not corrected until the night before.

The alteration moved the course back due east almost directly over Mt Erebus, an active volcano rising to about 12,500 ft (3,800 m) and the highest point on Ross Island. Although two of the pilots from the doomed DC-10 had seen a print-out containing the erroneous information, ie with the track over the sea-level ice, they were not shown a chart indicating that the intended route passed over

A three-dimensional diagram showing the flight path in the final minutes before the Air New Zealand DC-10 crashed in Antarctica. (International Civil Aviation Organisation)

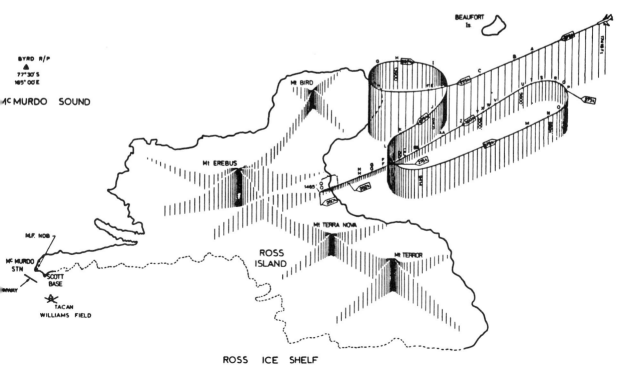

the high ground. One track and distance diagram issued at the route qualification briefing, some three weeks earlier, did not show the location of any topographical feature, and the relief maps carried aboard the aircraft were of a very small scale. The audio-visual presentation was also found to be potentially misleading, with one slide showing a view of Mt Erebus, taken from behind the co-pilot's seat, giving no indication of the flight path in relationship to the volcano. The stage was thus set for disaster on the Wednesday morning that the jet took off from Auckland, its AINS programmed with the proper navigational information but the crew unaware of either the original error or the correction.

An important omission in the briefing was a comprehensive discussion of the 'white-out' phenomenon, which is commonplace in areas where large, unbroken expanses of snow are illuminated by a sky overcast with dense, low clouds, blotting out all trace of surface texture or shadow and merging the terrain and horizon into a flattened, white background. The conditions on the day of the accident were highly conducive to such a 'white-out'.

From the comments transcribed from the aircraft's cockpit voice recorder (CVR) tape, it was obvious that the crew had misconceptions about the flight level to be used for the resetting of the altimeters to the local atmospheric pressure, the minimum descent height allowed in VMC and the terrain beneath the track from Cape Hallett to McMurdo. With regard to the first issue, the main altimeters were not reset until the DC-10 had descended to 3,500 ft (c 1,050 m), instead of the required flight level 180. This resulted in a reading 570 ft (c 175 m) higher than its actual altitude.

Despite the suggestion of the control centre, ZK-NZP was not observed on radar during the let-down, which went against company policy. When clearance for descent to 2,000 ft was requested while on a heading of 180 degrees Grid, the controller had no reason for concern, but without further comment to the centre, the pilot reversed his course during the descent to 357 degrees Grid, which was back toward the cloud-covered high ground.

Although the navigational aids were functioning properly, the crew could not lock the aircraft's distance-measuring equipment (DME) on to the TACAN, and also experienced a loss in radio communications with McMurdo. These difficulties were probably attributable to the low height of the jet, which placed the mountain in its 'line of sight' with the facilities.

No evidence could be found of any abnormal functioning of the aircraft's navigational and flight guidance system, and the indicated position was within its accuracy limitations. Also, the captain was qualified as a navigator, and could be expected to keep a realistic mental plot of the terrain, particularly Mt Erebus. Nevertheless, both he and

the first officer were apparently unaware of their position in the final minutes of the flight. The weather and terrain had even fooled famed polar explorer Peter Mulgrew, who was serving as a tour guide for his fellow passengers and riding in the cockpit. The two flight engineers were not so confident, however, and seconds before impact, one was heard to say 'I don't like this'.

The pilot finally elected to initiate a climb-out of the area, which he must have believed to be due west of the island, and was discussing with the co-pilot the most suitable path to take when the ground proximity warning system (GPWS) sounded, announcing 'Pull up'. The crew reacted to the alarm without undue hesitation, with the captain asking for 'go-round power', but the 6½ seconds between the activation of the warning and impact was insufficient for the DC-10 to respond to its commands. At the time of the crash, the aircraft's nose was slightly raised and its wings were approximately level. The GPWS did not go off sooner because the approach was made over a cliff some 300 ft (100 m) high rather than a steadily increasing slope, and because of the transport's high speed, nearly 300 mph (c 480 kmh) when it slammed into the ice. A slower cruising speed could have been accomplished through the extension of its flaps and slats, but this was prohibited on the Antarctic flights, ironically for safety reasons. The concern was that the high drag resulting from such a configuration would increase fuel consumption and perhaps not allow for a safe return should a malfunction prevent their retraction.

While the pilot had initiated the descent, the co-pilot was blamed for not monitoring him nor offering any criticism of his actions. Instead the first officer had devoted an inordinate amount of time in trying to establish radio contact with McMurdo. Also noted in the investigative report was the apparent failure of the crew to use the 'mapping' mode of the aircraft's weather radar for terrain avoidance.

A separate Royal Commission of Inquiry differed with the findings of the Air Accidents office. It ascribed as the 'single, dominant and effective cause' of the disaster the decision by airline officials to change the flight plan without notifying the crew. The commission said that the carrier was guilty of 'incompetent administrative procedures' and charged that company personnel had orchestrated a 'litany of lies' in attempting to cover up their mistake. However, a court of appeal later softened the accusations made against Air New Zealand by ruling that the commission had exceeded its jurisdiction in condemning the senior officers of the airline.

Air travellers lost their opportunity to tour Antarctica as a result of this accident, with the scenic flights being discontinued.

The
1980s

The 1980s could be described as both the best and the worst of times for air safety. In 1984 the industry had its safest year to date, with but two major crashes (both occurring in the former USSR); the death toll during the 12-month period was lower than it had been back in years when airline passengers numbered only thousands and not hundreds of millions.

But the very next year there was a dramatic turn for the worse, as air carrier fatalities burgeoned to more than 2,000. Six major disasters accounted for a majority of those deaths, and for the first time in history more than 500 lives were lost in an accident involving a single aircraft.

It also became apparent that the threat of terrorism, which had plagued commercial aviation throughout the 1970s, had yet to be defeated. The two worst cases of recorded aerial sabotage were the bombing of an Air-India Boeing 747 over the North Atlantic in June 1985, and the destruction of Pan American World Airways Flight 103 over Lockerbie, Scotland, four days before Christmas 1988. Besides terrorism, there were other cases of hostilities against civil aircraft, the most noteworthy of which (due to involvement of 'Super Power' forces) occurred in September 1983 when a Korean Air Lines Boeing 747 was shot down by the USSR after straying off course, and nearly five years later when a US Navy warship on patrol in the Persian Gulf downed an Iranian Airbus. Both appeared to be tragic cases of misidentification.

Hostile action had, in fact, become the greatest single threat to commercial aviation, with four major cases during the last two years of the decade costing more than 800 lives.

Date: 21 January 1980 (c 19:10)
Location: Near Laskarak, Markazi, Iran
Operator: Iran National Airlines Corporation (Iran Air)

Aircraft type: Boeing 727-86 (*EP-IRD*)

All 128 persons aboard (120 passengers and eight crew members) were killed when the jetliner crashed and burned in the Elburz Mountains, some 20 miles (30 km) north of Tehran, while attempting to land at the city's Mehrabad International Airport. The accident occurred in darkness, fog and snow after the aircraft had been cleared for an instrument landing system (ILS) approach to Runway 29, at the end of a scheduled domestic flight from Babol Sar (Meshed-i-Sar).

The 727 had flown through the west-north-westerly localiser course, proceeding almost due north until the impact at an approximate elevation of 8,400 ft (2,560 m). According to a government announcement, the disaster was related to the fact that the ground radar and ILS were inoperative, and other airport equipment had not been functioning properly at the time. The head of the nation's Civil Aviation Organisation and five other officials were later charged with manslaughter.

Date: 14 March 1980 (c 11:00)
Location: Near Warsaw, Poland
Operator: Polskie Linie Lotnicze (LOT) (Poland)
Aircraft type: Ilyushin Il-62 (*SP-LAA*)

The passengers who boarded Flight 007 at John F. Kennedy International Airport, serving New York City, included 14 members and eight officials of the US amateur boxing team on their way to matches in Poland.

As the jet airliner made its approach to land at Okecie Airport following the transatlantic service, there was an indication that its undercarriage may not have been fully down and locked, prompting the pilots to initiate an overshoot procedure. However, when thrust was increased only slightly, the No 2 (left inboard) power plant suddenly disintegrated.

Remains of the LOT Ilyushin Il-62 that plunged into a moat after uncontained engine failure. (UPI/Bettmann)

Flying debris then damaged two other engines and severed vital rudder and elevator control lines.

Rendered uncontrollable, the Il-62 plunged into a moat adjacent to a 19th-century fortress in a nose-down angle of about 20 degrees and approximately half a mile (0.8 km) from the runway threshold, exploding on impact. All 87 persons aboard, including a crew of 10, perished in the crash.

Metal fatigue had apparently caused a turbine disc in the power plant to break.

Date: 25 April 1980 (13:21)
Location: Tenerife, (Spanish) Canary Islands
Operator: Dan-Air Services Ltd (UK)
Aircraft type: Boeing 727-46 (*G-BDAN*)

The jet airliner, on a charter service from Manchester, England, was to have landed at Los Rodeos Airport, located near Santa Cruz de Tenerife. Following their transfer to Tenerife Approach Control, the crew were given the latest weather, and were then authorised for descent to flight level 60. They then reported passing the very-high-frequency omni-directional range (VOR) station designated 'TFN' and heading for the locator beacon 'FP' before being notified of an unpublished holding pattern. Radioing that it was '. . . taking up the hold', the aircraft received clearance down to 5,000 ft (c 1,500 m). Less than a minute later, the crew reported '. . . we've had a ground proximity warning'.

Seconds after that final transmission, the 727 slammed into a mountain some 5 miles (10 km) south-west of the airport and at an approximate elevation of 5,450 ft (1,660 m). The aircraft

disintegrated on impact, and all 146 persons aboard (138 passengers and eight crew members) perished. Only small fires erupted in the wreckage after the crash, and extinguished themselves. The meteorological conditions in the area around the time consisted of a broken overcast, with the cloud base down to about 3,000 ft (1,000 m), a light wind and no significant turbulence.

The initial approach of the jet was indicative of the imprecise navigation that continued until the moment of impact. Specifically, its flight path was displaced by nearly 1 mile (1.5 km) to the east of the correct radial upon arrival at TFN. Also, the flight crew did not report passing the VOR until 33 sec after the fact. There was no interception of Radial 255, as required in order to enter the holding pattern. Moreover, contrary to their radio message, they did not assume a heading towards FP, but instead passed approximately 2 miles (3 km) south of the navigational aid. Rather than entering the holding pattern, the 727 continued on a south-westerly heading, which took it into a mountainous area where the minimum safe altitude was 14,500 ft (c 4,400 m).

As transcribed on the cockpit voice recorder (CVR) tape, the ground proximity warning indicator (GPWS) first sounded 27 sec before the crash, but it deactivated when the aircraft flew over a valley. The alert prompted the pilot to initiate a turn to the right and order an overshoot. At that point he apparently did not know his position.

The CVR transcript also revealed confusion on the part of the crew regarding the radio transmission from the approach controller regarding a 'standard holding', which included instructions to '. . . turn to

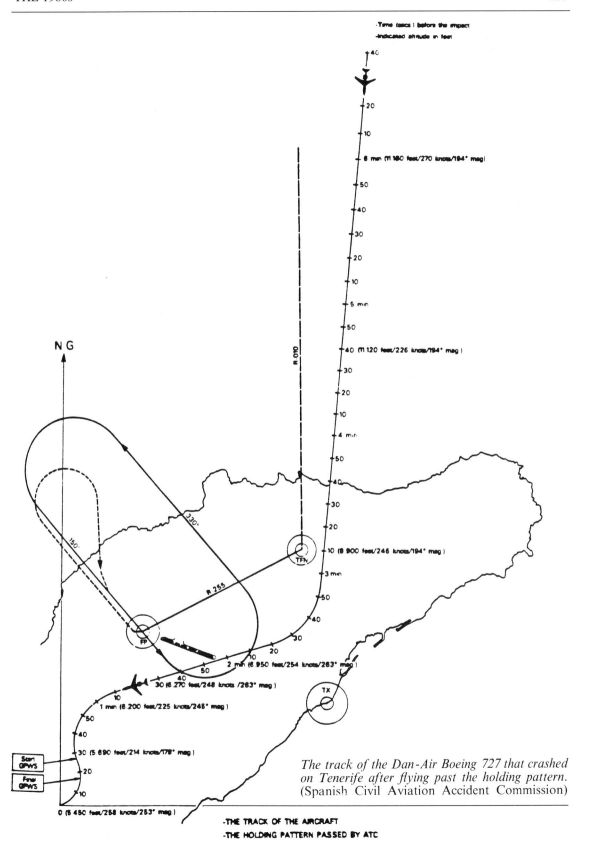

The track of the Dan-Air Boeing 727 that crashed on Tenerife after flying past the holding pattern. (Spanish Civil Aviation Accident Commission)

-THE TRACK OF THE AIRCRAFT

-THE HOLDING PATTERN PASSED BY ATC

the left'. The lack of clarity came from the fact that a standard holding involves a right turn. This led the first officer to remark 'Bloody strange hold, isn't it?'. There was, however, no request for clarification from the approach controller.

Subsequently, the crew expressed concern over their location, with the captain, in reference to the controller, stating 'He's taking us round to the high ground'. There was also evidence of a lack of team-work between the pilot and co-pilot, with the latter suggesting a heading more toward the south-east while the former continued with the turn to the right because of his conviction that the jet was flying in the direction of the mountains.

The impact took place some 130 ft (40 m) below the summit of the mountain as the cleanly configured 727 was flying in cloud at an approximate speed of 300 mph (480 kmh), on a heading of about 250 degrees, banked an estimated 30 to 40 degrees to the right and in a slight descent. In not levelling the wings the pilot did not take advantage of the aircraft's optimum climb performance, and as a result he merely reduced its descent rate. Also the speed of the jet was higher than that advisable and this was probably a factor in the short time span between its receipt of the holding information and its passage of FP, which contributed to the accident.

The British representative in the investigation generally agreed with the findings of the Spanish commission, though he labelled the information provided by the approach controller as 'ambiguous' and said it contributed to the disorientation of the crew. He further claimed that it was not practicable for an aircraft to follow the prescribed track because of its sharp angles, and noted that no minimum safe altitude calculations had been carried out by proper authorities for the approach and holding patterns. He claimed that the crash would not have occurred had the 727 not been cleared by the controller to below 7,000 ft (c 2,000 m).

Of course, the approach controller was operating without the assistance of radar, and could not have known the exact position of *G-BDAN* – he thought it had already entered the holding pattern when he authorised the descent to 5,000 ft. Had the aircraft been where he believed it to be, a left turn would have been required to remain in the circuit.

One of the recommendations made by the Spanish commission was that the International Civil Aviation Organisation (ICAO) deal with some ambiguities in its documents, specifically noting the need to publish all holding circuits and to clarify the 'standard' hold.

Date: 27 June 1980 (c 21:00)
Location: Off Western Italy
Operator: Aerolinee Itavia SpA (Italy)
Aircraft type: Douglas DC-9 Series 15 (*I-TIGI*)

Operating as Flight 870, the jet airliner had departed earlier from Bologna, on a domestic service to Palermo, Sicily, and it was last reported cruising at an altitude of approximately 25,000 ft (7,500 m). An unidentified object was observed on radar crossing from west to east at high speed and in close proximity to the target of the DC-9 before the latter plunged into the Tyrrhenian Sea some 15 miles (25 km) north-east of the island of Ustica, in water nearly 12,000 ft (c 3,700 m) deep. Searchers later found the bodies of more than 40 victims, but there were no survivors among the 81 persons aboard the aircraft (77 passengers and a crew of four).

Although the crash was at first shrouded in mystery, different theories subsequently began to circulate as to what might have happened to Flight 870. Among these were that the DC-9 had been intentionally shot down by a Libyan MiG-23 jet fighter or unintentionally by another warplane that was pursuing it (the wreckage of an aircraft of this type was found in southern Italy, with its pilot dead, about a month later). Almost a decade after the disaster, evidence surfaced indicating that the airliner had been accidentally hit by an air-to-air missile fired at a target drone during training manoeuvres by NATO forces.

Tests performed on recovered debris and pathological examinations of the deceased demonstrated that *I-TIGI* had either collided with an unidentified object or suffered damage from a nearby explosion, and was not the victim of accidental structural failure or an on-board bomb blast.

Date: 8 July 1980 (00:39)
Location: Near Alma-Ata, Kazakh SSR, USSR
Operator: Aeroflot (USSR)
Aircraft type: Tupolev Tu-154B-2 (*SSSR-85355*)

Designated as Flight 4225 and on a domestic service to Simferopol, Ukraine, the jet airliner crashed and burned less than 2 min after take-off from the Alma-Ata airport. All 166 persons aboard (156 passengers and a crew of 10) perished, and nine others on the ground were injured. The accident occurred in early morning darkness and cloudy weather conditions, with a visibility of around 5 miles (10 km).

The crash was attributed to an encounter with wind shear, consisting of a down-flow of up to about 30 mph (50 kmh) and a tail wind of approximately 45 mph (70 kmh), which occurred at the end of the process of retracting the high-lift devices, when the aircraft's take-off weight was close to the maximum and in mountain conditions, with high ambient temperatures. Climbing to an approximate height of 500 ft (150 m), the Tu-154 began an abrupt descent, then, despite all attempts by the crew to effect recovery, slammed to earth at a speed of around 250 mph (400 kmh), with its undercarriage in the up position.

Date: 19 August 1980 (c 22:00)
Location: Near Riyadh, Saudi Arabia
Operator: Saudi Arabian Airlines (Saudia)
Aircraft type: Lockheed L-1011-200 TriStar (*HZ-AHK*)

One of the worst disasters in the history of commercial aviation, this bizarre accident cannot even be classified as a crash. Despite a successful emergency landing, the wide-bodied jetliner was gutted by flames, and all 301 persons aboard (287 passengers, including 15 infants, and 14 crew members) were killed.

Flight 163 had made a scheduled stop at Riyadh before continuing on the second leg of a service to Jiddah from Karachi, Pakistan. Only 7 min after take-off from the city's international airport, as transcribed on the cockpit voice recorder (CVR) tape, the flight crew was alerted by both visual and aural warnings to the presence of smoke in the aft cargo compartment, designated as 'C-3'.

The initial alert occurred as the TriStar was climbing through 15,000 ft (c 5,000 m), and the crew spent more than 4 min trying to confirm the warning and looking for the smoke warning procedure. The captain then decided to return to the airport. Confirmation of the fire came as the aircraft was on its way back.

The actions of the flight crew could be considered normal until the turnaround, when things began to deteriorate, as illustrated by the CVR. The pilot-in-command failed to utilise properly his first and second officers, especially the former, to whom he should have delegated the function of flying the jetliner as he concentrated his attention on the emergency at hand. In fact, the captain appeared to reject the seriousness of the situation throughout the accident sequence. This may have been largely due to the flight engineer, who failed to give him an accurate picture of what was happening and kept saying 'No problem' when a serious one existed. The second officer himself may have been afflicted with dyslexia, which can cause confusion of both instruments and procedures. And the first officer, who had only limited experience in the type of aircraft, did not assist the pilot in monitoring the safety of the flight. None of the three were apparently affected by the smoke that was filling the passenger compartment until after the landing.

In contrast, evidence pointed to a commendable performance on the part of the cabin crew in both battling the blaze and trying to calm the panic-stricken passengers. However, circumstances would prevent the attendants from carrying out their most important function in the event of an emergency – aiding in the evacuation of the aircraft – even had

Despite a safe landing, none of the 301 persons aboard the Saudia L-1011 survived the fire that ultimately gutted the aircraft's fuselage. (UPI/Bettmann)

the captain made preparations for such action.

Despite a stuck thrust lever, which necessitated the shutting down of the No 2 (centre) engine, the L-1011 landed safely, but it was then that the pilot committed another critical error, one that probably led to the catastrophic results in what should have been a survivable accident. Rather than using the maximum available braking power to stop the aircraft as soon as possible, he continued off the runway and finally came to a stop on a taxiway 2 min 40 sec after touch-down. Moreover, by keeping the two wing engines running for another 3 min 15 sec, he prevented the emergency personnel who had arrived on the scene from taking immediate action and also thwarted any attempt by the cabin crew members to initiate an emergency evacuation on their own.

There was no evidence that an evacuation had been started, nor that anyone had tried to open the cabin doors from inside. This may have been at the request of the captain (since he was heard to instruct his fellow cockpit crewmen before the landing not to evacuate) or because passengers were blocking the doors, which have to move a few inches inward to be opened. More likely, however, the flight and cabin crew were incapacitated by a flash fire, which depleted any oxygen left in the aircraft. This second blaze was caused by a reduction of oxygen and an accompanying increase in toxic gases, and must have taken place shortly after the last message from the TriStar, 'We are trying to evacuate now', transmitted at 21:40.

Aggravating the situation was that the environmental control system (ECS) packs had been turned off, in accordance with normal procedures, which prevented any fresh air being introduced into the fuselage.

The crash/fire/rescue services were also proven to be woefully inadequate; they lacked the correct tools, protective clothing and proper training in forced-entry procedures as well as knowledge of the number and operation of doors in the L-1011 and other aircraft that served the airport. It took the personnel 23 min after engine shut-down to get into the fuselage, and by the time the No 1 door on the left side could be opened, any rescue attempt was futile. Burns, the inhalation of such toxic gases as carbon monoxide, nitrous oxide, hydrogen cyanide, formic acid and ammonia, and oxygen starvation had resulted in all the fatalities. The fire ultimately consumed almost the entire upper fuselage structure, leaving the wings, empennage, power plants and extended undercarriage intact. The entire drama was played out in moonlit darkness.

There was no doubt that the blaze had erupted in compartment C-3; the sticking of the No 2 thrust lever was further proof of this (the throttle controls are routed through the area between the ceiling of the cargo hold and the cabin floor, and the fairlead rollers that suspend them can, when heated, soften, melt and adhere to these cables, with only a small

Diagram showing the passenger placement and damage in the TriStar disaster. (International Civil Aviation Organisation)

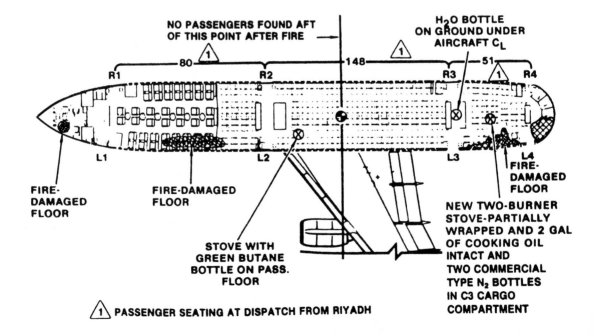

PASSENGER SEATING AT DISPATCH FROM RIYADH

amount of cooling needed to cause an increase in friction).

The smoke and then the flames must have followed the same path, travelling through the traversals between the cargo compartment and the floor to the sidewall of the aircraft and up into the passenger cabin. The victims' bodies were all found in the forward half of the aircraft. As in previous accidents, the deadly fumes were produced by the burning of furnishings and other cabin materials.

The origin of the fire could not be determined, since the source of ignition had been obliterated in the blaze, but, of course, there are many potential sources of fire in the baggage compartment of an airliner. As noted in the investigative report, three such previous fires were touched off by the accidental lighting of matches in a suitcase. There was no evidence of an incendiary device.

Several modifications in the L-1011 were made by Lockheed as a result of this tragedy. These included the removal of insulation under the aft lavatories, a replacement in the type of insulation used for heat exchange in the C-2 and C-3 cargo holds, and the replacement of the cargo compartment ceiling panels with those made of a high-strength glass laminate.

In addition to these changes, the US National Transportation Safety Board (NTSB), which participated in the investigation, recommended that the certification of the cargo holds be re-evaluated. The principle behind previous requirements was that a fire occurring within the compartment would be extinguished by oxygen deprivation. This concept was considered successfully applied in narrow-bodied aircraft with compartments of limited volume, but tests showed that a fire in the larger cargo holds on such aircraft as the TriStar could be sustained for more than 10 min, sufficient time to burn through the ceiling liner.

The US Federal Aviation Administration (FAA), however, responsible for enforcing safety standards on American-built aircraft, said the situation did not warrant the action proposed by the NTSB.

Saudia took its own remedial action in the wake of the disaster, which included a revision of emergency check-lists and improvements in emergency evacuation training. Additionally, the carrier sealed off the C-3 compartments in its L-1011 fleet, with the intention of confining fires that could occur in them.

Date: 22 August 1981 (c 10:00)
Location: Near Sanyi, Taiwan
Operator: Far Eastern Air Transport Corporation (Taiwan)
Aircraft type: Boeing 737-222 (*B-2603*)

Designated as Flight 103, the jet airliner plummeted into a mountainous region and burned some 100 miles (150 km) south-south-west

of T'ai-pei, from where it had taken off earlier on a domestic service to Kao-hsiung. All 110 persons aboard (104 passengers and a crew of six) perished.

The 737 reportedly broke apart at an altitude of 22,000 ft (c 6,700 m), scattering wreckage and victims over an area of about 5 miles (10 km). Severe corrosion in the belly area was blamed for the rupture of its pressure hull.

Date: 16 November 1981 (c 19:40)
Location: Near Noril'sk, Russian Soviet Federated Socialist Republic, USSR
Operator: Aeroflot (USSR)
Aircraft type: Tupolev Tu-154B-2 (*SSSR-85480*)

Operating as Flight 3603 and on a domestic service from Krasnoyarsk, the jetliner crashed and burned near the Noril'sk airport, where it was scheduled to land, killing 99 persons aboard. Three of the aircraft's seven crew members and 65 passengers survived the accident, all of whom suffered injuries. The crash occurred in darkness and during a low overcast, with a cloud base of around 400 ft (120 m) and a visibility of approximately half a mile (0.8 km).

Due to a lower-than-expected consumption of fuel, the Tu-154 was about 5,070 lb (2,300 kg) above its calculated weight, and its centre of gravity beyond the forward limit. This nose-heavy condition caused it to descend below the glide path during the final approach, which could not be countered by the captain's manipulation of the elevator controls. Seconds before impact, he increased thrust and initiated a go-around manoeuvre, but the jetliner slammed into an earthen mound some 1,500 ft (500 m) short of the runway and at an indicated air speed of around 170 mph (270 kmh), with its undercarriage still extended.

Besides failing to calculate adequately the landing weight of the aircraft and its centre of gravity, the crew had not increased its approach speed by about 3 mph (5 kmh), which was required in order to compensate for the former condition.

Date: 1 December 1981 (08:53)
Location: Near Petreto-Bicchisano, Corsica, France
Operator: Inex Adria Aviopromet (Yugoslavia)
Aircraft type: McDonnell Douglas DC-9 Super 82 (*YU-ANA*)

The jet airliner had taken off from Ljubljana, Yugoslavia, on a non-scheduled service to the Mediterranean island, and was to have landed at Campo dell'Oro Airport, serving Ajaccio. It carried 173 passengers, a mechanic and a regular crew of six.

Following its descent from flight level (FL) 330, the DC-9 was instructed to maintain an altitude of 11,000 ft (c 3,400 m) until reaching the Ajaccio very-high-frequency omni-directional range (VOR)

A DC-9 Super 80 series, the type operated by the Yugoslav carrier Inex Adria Aviopromet that crashed on French Corsica. (McDonnell Douglas)

station, and the pilot then reported being in the holding pattern at that height. Subsequently, the approach controller cleared the aircraft down to 3,300 ft (1,005 m).

In the final message from the jet, the captain reported turning inbound to Ajaccio while being in clouds. Less than a minute later, as transcribed on the aircraft's cockpit voice recorder (CVR) tape, the ground proximity warning system (GPWS) began to sound, announcing both 'Terrain' and 'Pull up'. The captain was heard to ask for 'Power' 9 seconds later. His request was not made in a commanding tone, however, perhaps accounting for the relatively

slow application of thrust. Three seconds after the pilot's remark, while turning left in a bank of 25 to 30 degrees and flying in a north-westerly direction at an indicated air speed of about 250 mph (400 kmh), the DC-9 struck Mont San Pietro with its port wing, the initial impact occurring at an elevation of 4,478 ft (1,365 m), or approximately 100 ft (30 m) from the top of the peak.

About half of the wing having been torn off, the aircraft rolled uncontrollably to the left, then crashed in a rocky ravine some 2,300 ft (700 m) below the summit of the mountain, disintegrating in the second or main impact. All 180 persons aboard

A section of the fuselage from YU-ANA rests between the rocks below Mont San Pietro. (Serge Assier, Gamma Liaison)

perished. Wreckage was scattered over the rugged terrain on a heading of about 300 degrees, around 20 miles (30 km) south-west of Ajaccio. There was practically no post-crash fire.

The weather in the area at around the time of the accident consisted of strong winds from the west, heavy turbulence and a solid overcast of altocumulus and cumulus clouds that obscured the mountain tops.

A French investigative commission attributed the disaster to the descent by the crew that placed *YU-ANA* below the safe instrument flight altitude during that portion of its trajectory within the holding pattern, the published minimum height of the circuit being 6,800 ft (c 2,070 m). The commission further observed that when the pilots, alerted by the GPWS alarm, tried to regain altitude, the manoeuvre proved insufficient to overcome the effects of severe down-draughts caused by the relief of the terrain and the high winds that were present in the area.

Five contributing factors were outlined in the accident report. First, it was ruled that the crew had apparently not adequately prepared for the approach. The minimum altitude and maximum speed limits of the holding pattern were probably not retained. Additionally, the two pilots may have been distracted by the presence of a third person on the flight deck, a child identified as the son of the first officer, who was heard on the CVR tape. There were also misunderstandings between the captain and the approach controller, attributed to imprecise terminology. Specifically, the latter believed that the aircraft was going to make a direct descent in order to begin the final approach to the airport, while the former elected to enter the 'racetrack' holding pattern. As a result of these misunderstandings, the controller was not fully aware of the progression of the flight. Had he better interpreted the messages 'Call you inbound on radial two forty seven' and 'Rolling inbound out of six thousand' sent by the pilot, an ambiguous situation in the case of the first transmission and an abnormal and dangerous one in the case of the second could have been avoided. Also the receipt of a message from the controller occurring simultaneously with the activation of the GPWS warning may have affected the crew's ability to react to the alarm.

Examination of the digital flight data recorder (DFDR) read-out revealed that the velocity of the DC-9 was greater than the maximum air speed prescribed in the holding pattern, and the crew made no correction for the winds, later calculated to have been approximately 70 knots at FL 110 and averaging 65 knots from that height down to 5,000 ft (c 1,500 m), which were blowing in the path of the jet. And the symbolic representation of the holding pattern on the approach chart corresponded to the trajectory of an aircraft flying at about 170 mph (270 kmh) with no wind. Furthermore, the chart neither indicated the real dimensions of the circuit nor the elevation of the terrain below.

The commission found in its inquiry that habits formed during radar-guided operations could lead to overconfidence on the part of some pilots with regard to minimum safe altitudes. However, differing with the French findings, a Yugoslav commission concluded that the crash resulted directly from the misunderstanding between the crew and the controller, and maintained that it should have been obvious to the latter that the former was entering the holding pattern and not making a direct approach.

The accident report emphasised the need for the use of a standard vocabulary in radio communications by pilots and air traffic controllers, and also recommended revisions in approach charts to improve clarity, a change in the location of the Campo dell'Oro Airport holding pattern, and the installation of radar at Ajaccio, or at the very least radar surveillance of the area by another facility.

Date: 13 January 1982 (c 16:00)
Location: Washington, DC, US
Operator: Air Florida Inc (US)
Aircraft type: Boeing 737-222 (*N62AF*)

Snow continued to fall throughout the day on the nation's capital, which, as with the rest of the American North East, had been battered by the weather during an exceptionally harsh January. At Washington National Airport operations had resumed shortly before 15:00, after a closure of more than an hour for the purpose of snow removal.

Through technological advances and improved operating procedures, aviation has managed to overcome many meteorological hazards that would have grounded aircraft in the earlier years of flying. In addition, passengers travelling in and out of the airport, located in Virginia along the bank of the Potomac River, had another reason to feel secure: it had been more than two years since the last fatal crash of a US commercial jet. But as Flight 90 prepared to take off on a domestic service to Fort Lauderdale and Tampa, Florida, that record was about to come to a shattering halt.

Following the de-icing of *N62AF*, and some difficulty in moving it back from the terminal on the slippery ramp, the 737 got in line with numerous other aircraft, awaiting its turn for departure. Flight 90 finally received clearance to take off on Runway 36 nearly an hour after the de-icing had been completed and during a period of continuous light to moderate snowfall, with the temperature remaining below freezing. By the time it received the clearance, considerable snow or ice had once more accumulated on the jetliner, about ¼–½ inch (c 0.5–1 cm) on its wings, of which Captain Larry Wheaton and First Officer Roger Pettit were aware, as confirmed by their comments transcribed on the cockpit voice recorder (CVR) tape.

The most significant effect of even a small amount of snow on an aircraft wing is its influence on the smooth flow of air over the surface contour. This will cause air-flow separation at a lower angle of attack than normal, which in turn increases the stalling speed while reducing lift. Even more critical, at least in this case, was the suspected build-up of ice in the compressor inlets of the two engines which, in conjunction with the power plant discharge probes, are used to determine the correct thrust setting. Tests confirmed that the blockage of an inlet tube will result in a false indication of thrust, higher than the amount actually being developed. This blockage could be explained by the simple failure of the crew to turn on the engine anti-ice system.

From his recorded remarks, the co-pilot seemed to recognise an anomalous engine pressure ratio (EPR) reading, the take-off 'target' value apparently having been obtained despite an abnormal position of the thrust levers and with inconsistencies in other instrument indications, noting after the ground run had commenced that something did not 'seem right'. First replying 'Yes it is, there's eighty' with regard to the air speed indication, the pilot did not respond to further comments by his first officer and continued the take-off. Due to the blockage of the pressure probes, the actual EPR was believed to have been only 1.70, rather than the required 2.04, which must have been indicated.

Besides degrading its performance, the accumulation of snow and/or ice apparently caused the 737 to pitch up immediately after it had become airborne, resulting in the activation of the stick-shaker stall warning device; with the reduced power setting, it entered the stall regime and was unable to sustain flight. The aircraft probably reached a peak altitude of between 200 and 300 ft (c 60–100 m) before it started to descend, turning slightly to the left but maintaining a generally northerly course. It was believed that the crew first lowered the nose, then raised it to maintain height, and in the final moments of the flight applied power, but too late for it to have any effect. Seconds before impact the co-pilot was heard to say 'Larry, we're going down, Larry!'. The pilot replied with 'I know it'.

Its undercarriage still down and flaps partially extended, the jetliner was flying in a nose-high attitude estimated at 30 to 40 degrees, its wings approximately level, when it struck the northbound span of the 14th Street bridge, which connects Virginia with the District of Columbia, about 1 mile (1.5 km) from the end of the runway. Actually skimming over the roadway, which was heavily congested with vehicles moving at a snail's pace because of the weather, it destroyed six occupied automobiles and a truck and tore away a section of the bridge and some 100 ft (30 m) of railing, then pitched down and plunged into the ice-covered Potomac River.

Killed in the accident were all but five of the 79

A US Park Police helicopter rescued the survivors from the downed Air Florida Boeing 737, the tail section of which can be seen barely protruding from the surface of the Potomac River. (Sygma)

persons aboard the aircraft, including four crew members, plus four others in the vehicles. The four passengers and one stewardess who survived (all of whom had been seated at the rear of the cabin near the empennage, which broke off on impact and remained partially above the water) suffered injuries, as did four persons on the bridge. Autopsies performed on the victims' bodies, all of which were recovered along with most of the wreckage, revealed that a majority of the deaths resulted from trauma.

In its investigative report, the US National Transportation Safety Board (NTSB) ascribed the crew's failure to use the engine anti-ice system as the direct cause of the disaster. Had the power plant probes not been blocked, the correct EPR values would have been indicated and the thrust correctly set. On the other hand, had the icing been so severe as to remain in the tubes despite the use of anti-icing, the pilots would have been unable to set the power at the correct EPR, undoubtedly prompting them to discontinue the take-off.

Also regarded as a primary factor in the crash was the decision by the crew to take off despite knowledge of the snow on the aircraft's wings. The pilots may have been influenced by the prolonged departure delay and the inevitability of another long wait in the freezing precipitation had they returned to the ramp for another de-icing. But there were two areas where faulty action by the captain may have actually intensified the contamination of the jetliner. One was the use of reverse thrust in an attempt to back the aircraft away from the terminal. Heat from the engines and reversers and the blowing snow and slush could have deposited a wet mixture on the airframe, particularly on the leading edge of the wings, which subsequently froze. There were also indications that he intentionally positioned the 737 close behind another aircraft, trying to use the heat from the latter's engines to remove the snow on his own aircraft's wings. However, the heat may actually have turned the snow, which otherwise might have blown off during the take-off, into a slushy mixture that then froze on the leading edges or the inlet nose cones of the power plants.

Another factor that directly contributed to the disaster was the continuation of the take-off despite the abnormalities in the engine instrument readings. Since the co-pilot was actually flying the 737, the pilot could be expected to have been the most attentive to the indications; in this case, however, the former seemed the most observant. The crew may have been somewhat hurried when the controller asked for 'No delay on departure' due to landing traffic. Indeed, the NTSB determined that an Eastern Airlines Boeing 727 touched down on the same runway even before the 737 had lifted off, which was a violation of the established separation criteria.

The actions of the flight crew, particularly the captain, reflected a general lack of experience in cold weather operations. It was believed that he missed this exposure to the harsh winter climate of the Eastern American states because of the rapid expansion of the airline in the late 1970s and early 1980s, wherein pilots were being upgraded faster than the industry norm to meet the increasing demands of its growing schedules.

Other contributing factors were the long delay between de-icing and take-off clearance and the apparent tendency of the Boeing 737 to pitch up when the leading edges of its wings become coated with snow or ice, something that had been suspected for some years prior to this crash.

Though the Board could not determine whether it also contributed to the accident, the de-icing of N62AF was found to be deficient. It was concluded that the American Airlines personnel who carried out the operation had used an incorrect mixture of de-icing fluid, composed of glycol and water, this due to the non-availability of a monitoring device.

Amid the human errors that led to the disaster, the crash itself brought forth some individual cases of heroism and self-sacrifice. The survivors, who were able to cling to wreckage, owe their lives primarily to the crew of a US Park Police LongRanger helicopter, which arrived on the scene in about 20 min and hoisted or towed them to safety. To accomplish one rescue the pilot hovered the aircraft just above the water, and the passenger was lifted on to its skid. Two bystanders actually jumped into the frigid river, and one of them, a US Congressional Budget Office clerk named Lenny Skutnik, gained national fame for saving a woman who had lost her grip on the rescue line. Another passenger who lived through the crash unselfishly passed the line to the other survivors; by the time the helicopter returned for him, he had slipped beneath the surface of the water and drowned.

A number of changes were implemented by the US Federal Aviation Administration (FAA) as a result of this accident, including the dissemination of information concerning the hazards of airframe and engine icing. The crash also revealed inadequacies in the emergency services provided at Washington National Airport, and led to such improvements as the acquisition of two rescue boats, one with limited ice-breaking capabilities. Additionally, the runway safety or overrun area was extended, which could prove useful in the event of an aborted take-off.

Date: 26 April 1982 (c 16:45)
Location: Near Yangshuo, Guangxi, China
Operator: Civil Aviation Administration of China (CAAC)
Aircraft type: Hawker Siddeley Trident 2E (B-266)

Operating as Flight 3303 and on a domestic service originating at Canton, Kwangtung, the jetliner struck a mountain some 30 miles (50 km) south-east of Kweilin as it was approaching to land at the city's airport. All 112 persons aboard (104 passengers and a crew of eight) perished.

The crash reportedly occurred during a light rain and apparently resulted from operational factors.

Date: 8 June 1982 (02:25)
Location: Near Pacatuba, Ceara, Brazil
Operator: Viacao Aerea Sao Paulo SA (VASP) (Brazil)
Aircraft type: Boeing Advanced 727-212 (*PP-SRK*)

Designated as Flight 168, the jet airliner crashed some 15 miles (25 km) south-west of Fortaleza while preparing to land at the city's Pinto Martins Airport, at the end of a domestic service originating at Sao Paulo, via Rio de Janeiro. All 137 persons aboard (128 passengers and nine crew members) perished.

Initiating a descent from flight level (FL) 330, the 727 had been cleared only down to 5,000 ft (c 1,500 m). Nevertheless, it continued well below that height until finally slamming into a hill in the Serra de Aratanha region at an approximate elevation of 2,000 ft (600 m), and exploding on impact. The accident occurred in early morning darkness, but the weather was good without indications of heavy cloud formations or significant obstructions to visibility in the area.

According to the cockpit voice recorder (CVR) tape, the aircraft's altitude alert system had sounded twice before the crash. Also, upon passing through a height of 3,800 ft (c 1,150 m), the first officer warned the captain of the terrain ahead, without the latter interrupting the descent. Besides the crew's failure to maintain the minimum authorised altitude, an analysis of the flight data recorder (FDR) read-out established that the maximum speed limit of 250 knots (c465 kmh) below FL 110 had been exceeded.

The disaster was attributed to a deficient descent plan, non-observance of both air traffic regulations and the carrier's operational procedures, and a lack of cockpit discipline. A contributing factor was that the pilot-in-command had apparently concentrated his attention on the lighted city and ignored other aspects of the flight, such as the observation of distance and height.

As was noted in the recommendations portion of the investigative report, in-flight decisions must result from team-work, and the captain, who is ultimately responsible for the safe operation of an aircraft, should never disregard the advice of an inferior. It was further emphasised that the non-flying pilot has a 'right and obligation' to intervene when safety is being compromised, and also suggested that Brazil's airlines develop a better system of evaluating the performance of their flight crews.

Date: 28 June 1982 (c 10:50)
Location: Southern Belorussia, USSR
Operator: Aeroflot (USSR)
Aircraft type: Yakovlev Yak-42 (*SSSR-45229*)

The jet airliner, which was operating as Flight 8641 and on a domestic service from Leningrad, RSFSR, to Kiev, Ukraine, crashed some 20 miles (30 km) south-east of Mozyr and about 125 miles (200 km) north-west of its destination. All 132 persons aboard (124 passengers and a crew of eight) perished.

Shortly after it had initiated a descent from an altitude of about 30,000 ft (10,000 m), a serious malfunction occurred, with the aircraft's stabiliser almost instantaneously moving to a position of +2 degrees, or beyond the mechanical stop. The abrupt change in the stabiliser setting caused an increase in vertical acceleration, which decreased when the autopilot deflected the elevator. Three seconds later the autopilot disengaged and the elevator deflected to a position of −5 degrees, which caused an increase in the vertical acceleration.

Simultaneous with an attempted pull-out, the Yak-42 entered a left bank, which ultimately surpassed 90 degrees. Meanwhile, its nose-down angle exceeded 50 degrees as the aircraft plunged to earth at a vertical rate of descent of around 1,000 ft/sec (300 m/sec). At a height of about 19,000 ft (5,800 m) and an indicated air speed of more than 500 mph (800 kmh), the aircraft suffered structural failure due to aerodynamic stresses that were beyond the permitted limits and by the excessive pressure in the cabin associated with the rapid descent. Complete disintegration of *SSSR-45229* occurred on impact with the ground; there was no post-crash fire.

The disaster resulted from the in-flight failure of the aircraft's stabiliser screw-jack mechanism due to excessive wear and jamming of the nut. It was later discovered that due to a manufacturing error, the thread of the screw-jack had been cut at the wrong pitch. Also factoring in the failure was the use of a non-standard lubricating substance. The entire Yak-42 fleet was grounded while this fault could be rectified.

Date: 6 July 1982 (c 00:05)
Location: Near Moscow, Russian Soviet Federated Socialist Republic, USSR
Operator: Aeroflot (USSR)
Aircraft type: Ilyushin Il-62M (*SSSR-86513*)

All 90 persons aboard (80 passengers and a crew of 10) were killed when the jet airliner, designated as Flight 411, crashed and burned in farmland about 5 miles (10 km) west of the city's Sheremet'yevo Airport, from where it had taken off shortly before, en route to Africa, with a planned stop at Dakar, Senegal, and an ultimate destination

An Aeroflot Ilyushin Il-62M, identical to the aircraft that crashed after taking off from Sheremet'yevo Airport. (Aeroflot)

of Freetown, Sierra Leone. The accident occurred in darkness, but the weather was not considered a factor.

The crash was attributed to the failure of the aircraft's power plant fire warning system, due to design deficiencies. This resulted in false fire indications in the two port engines, the No 1 only seconds after rotation and the No 2 moments later, both of which were shut down by the crew. The Il-62 was incapable of sustaining flight on only two engines, with its flaps set at 30 degrees and its take-off weight near the maximum. Additional difficulties were associated with the night-time conditions and the populated area below its flight path.

Turning back in an attempted off-airport forced landing in the opposite direction of the take-off and with its undercarriage retracted, the jet lost speed during a right and then a left turn, leading to a loss of lateral control while in a left bank that exceeded 70 degrees, finally stalling at an approximate height of 250 ft (75 m).

Date: 9 July 1982 (16:09)
Location: Kenner, Louisiana, US
Operator: Pan American World Airways (US)
Aircraft type: Boeing 727-235 (*N4737*)

The second of three major wind shear-related US air carrier disasters occurring in the 1975–85 period (see also separate entries, 24 June 1975 and 2 August 1985) involved Flight 759, which took off from Runway 10 at New Orleans International (Moisant) Airport, bound for Las Vegas, Nevada, its

next scheduled stop during a domestic transcontinental service from Miami, Florida, to San Diego, California. Less than 30 sec after becoming airborne, the jetliner crashed and exploded approximately 1 mile (1.5 km) beyond the end of the runway, devastating a residential neighbourhood. A total of 153 persons perished, all 145 aboard the aircraft (137 passengers, including a cockpit jump-seat occupant, plus a crew of eight) and eight others on the ground. Another 16 persons suffered injuries, and about a dozen houses were destroyed or substantially damaged.

A thunderstorm was sweeping over the area at the time, accompanied by heavy rain, an east-north-easterly wind of some 15 knots, a broken overcast at around 4,000 ft (1,200 m) and a visibility of 2 miles (c 3 km). Though not outwardly hazardous, the weather contained at least one insidious element that was believed to have been responsible for the tragedy.

In its investigative report, the US National Transportation Safety Board (NTSB) concluded that *N4737* had apparently encountered a 'microburst' following rotation. This wind shear phenomenon is fundamentally a downward gust that flows outward in all directions upon reaching the ground.

At the moment of lift-off, the aircraft would have been operating in a head-wind, after which it experienced a down-draught while in the centre of the microburst, then an increasing tail wind. These divergent winds led, in rapid succession, to an increase then a decrease in indicated air speed, lift, drag and pitch. Reaching a height of 100 to 150 ft

Houses were reduced to rubble in this disaster near New Orleans International Airport that killed 153 persons. (UPI/Bettmann)

(c 30–50 m) above the ground, the 727 began to descend. It initially struck three tall trees some 2,400 ft (730 m) from the end of the runway, then a second group of trees, the impact shearing off segments of its leading edge wing devices, which were extended, and trailing edge flaps, which were set at 15 degrees. Its undercarriage retracted, the jetliner slammed to earth after turning on to a northerly heading and rolling to the left beyond 90 degrees.

Since the aircraft was in the midst of heavy rain, the crew had to fly exclusively by instrument reference, and in this case the time required for response by the pertinent instruments and recognition and corrective action by the pilots was insufficient to prevent the crash. Other factors that would have complicated the crew's recognition of the wind shear were the precipitation itself, the turbulence associated with the storm and the need to apply an abnormal force to the control column and adopt an unusually nose-high attitude. It was determined that the co-pilot, who was flying the 727, did indeed take corrective action and had actually managed to arrest the descent at around the time of the initial tree impact. An analysis of the cockpit voice recorder (CVR) tape indicated that the safety-conscious captain had prepared for the possibility of wind shear before departure, instructing his first officer to 'Let your air speed build up on take-off'.

Contributing to the accident was the inability of the ground-based low-level wind shear detection technology then available to provide definite guidance for air traffic controllers and pilots for use in avoiding this potential hazard. The system such as the one employed at New Orleans, though described as 'state of the art', had several limitations. The sensors, or anemometers, could not detect winds directly above or beyond their periphery; nor could they discern up-draughts or down-draughts. Also, the simultaneous passage of a peripheral and the centrefield sensor by a gust would not set off a wind shear alarm. Most significantly, perhaps, was that a microburst would not be detected if sufficiently small as to occur between sensors. In addition, the reading of a particular unit could have been lower than was actually the case due to the slowing effect of the winds flowing over nearby trees.

Despite its shortcomings, the system did detect the presence of wind shear prior to the crash, which prompted the control tower to issue an advisory for wind shear 'in all quadrants' some 5 minutes before the departure of Flight 759. Though this was a relatively long period of time for such a fleeting event, the NTSB expressed satisfaction that the Pan American crew had received adequate meteorological information. It further concluded that the decision by the captain to take off was reasonable under the circumstances. When it began

The burned out hulk of the Spanish DC-10 that crashed after an aborted take-off from Malaga Airport.
(Delgado Zavalla, Gamma Liaison)

its ground run, only light rain was falling on the aircraft, which became progressively heavier; no lightning or thunder had been observed in the immediate area, and the microburst that proved so deadly was not detected until after *N4737* had started to take off.

Though the effects of the heavy precipitation on the 727 could not be determined, the NTSB expressed concern that it could have produced a film of water on its wings, roughening their surface and lowering aerodynamic efficiency. The rain was also suspected of reducing the effectiveness of the aircraft's weather radar, which the crew had used while still on the ground in an attempt to determine the conditions existing in the flight path of the jetliner. This attenuation apparently prevented the observance on the radarscope of the storm cells located east of the airport, including the one that spawned the microburst.

Investigators were hampered somewhat in trying to establish the exact effects of the microburst by the early model flight data recorder (FDR) installed on the 727. For this reason the NTSB suggested that all US commercial jet transports be fitted with digital systems capable of transcribing many more parameters, including pitch and roll attitude, stabiliser trim position and engine thrust. The Board also recommended to the US Federal Aviation Administration (FAA) several improvements in the way wind shear information is disseminated to

pilots, including the need for the constant updating of advisories.

Date: 13 September 1982 (c 12:00)
Location: Near Malaga, Spain
Operator: Spantax SA Transportes Aereos
Aircraft type: McDonnell Douglas DC-10 Series 30CF (*EC-DEG*)

While taking off from the city's airport on a non-scheduled transatlantic service originating at Madrid and destined for New York City, a strong vibration was felt as the wide-bodied jet airliner reached rotation speed. The take-off was aborted, but the crew could not bring the DC-10 to a safe stop, and it overran the runway while travelling in excess of 100 mph (150 kmh).

The aircraft smashed into a concrete building housing the instrument landing system (ILS) equipment, the impact shearing off its No 3 power plant, then crossed a highway and struck several vehicles before coming to rest against a railway embankment and bursting into flames. Killed were 51 of the 393 persons aboard the jet, including three of its 13 crew members. About 120 of the survivors and two persons on the ground suffered injuries in the accident, and a house, four automobiles and a truck were destroyed.

The intense vibration that the pilot had been unable to identify was attributed to the detachment in fragments of the retreaded tyre on the right wheel of the DC-10's nose gear. He believed the aircraft to be uncontrollable and abandoned the take-off above the rotation speed. Though not in conformity with standard operating practices, the decision to discontinue the take-off at that point was considered reasonable in view of the abnormal circumstances, the scant time available, the lack of training for wheel failures and the absence of procedures in dealing with unexpected occurrences other than engine trouble.

Defects were identified in the retreading process, with air bubbles being found between the rubber layers.

Date: 11 July 1983 (c 07:40)
Location: Near Cuenca, Azway, Ecuador
Operator: Transportes Aereos Militares Ecuatorianos (TAME) (Ecuador)
Aircraft type: Boeing Advanced 737-2V2 (*HC-BIG*)

All 119 persons aboard (111 passengers and a crew of eight) perished when the jet airliner crashed while attempting to land at the city's airport at the end of a scheduled domestic flight from Quito.

Its undercarriage apparently down, the 737 had descended below a safe height during the visual approach, then slammed into a cloud-obscured hill approximately 2 miles (3 km) short of the landing runway (23), exploding in flames on impact. The pilot was reportedly 'under-qualified'.

Date: 30 August 1983 (23:17)
Location: Near Alma-Ata, Kazakh SSR, USSR
Operator: Aeroflot (USSR)
Aircraft type: Tupolev Tu-134A (*SSSR-65129*)

The jet airliner crashed and burned while approaching to land at the Alma-Ata airport, at the end of a scheduled domestic service from Kazan, RSFSR. All 90 persons aboard (84 passengers and six crew members) were killed.

After the aircraft had erroneously assumed a heading of 145 degrees, the approach controller instructed the crew to change its course to 140 degrees so it could land behind an Aeroflot Il-62. During a subsequent vector on to a course of 40 degrees, however, the final controller cleared the Tu-134 down to about 2,000 feet (600 m) at a location where the minimum safety altitude was nearly 15,000 ft (c 5,000 m). Around a minute later the aircraft slammed into a hillside at an approximate level of 2,300 feet (700 m), some 20 miles (30 km) from the airport. The disaster occurred in darkness and fair weather conditions.

The crash was attributed to the following factors: 1) violation of the approved approach scheme to the Alma-Ata airport; 2) failure of the executive flight manager to monitor the situation and thus prevent the accident; and 3) violation of the flight operations manual by the crew for following the final controller's instructions to descend below a safe height and for failing to respond appropriately to the ground proximity warning system (GPWS), which first sounded nearly half a minute prior to impact.

Date: 1 September 1983 (c 06:30)
Location: North-west of Hokkaido, Japan
Operator: Korean Air Lines (South Korea)
Aircraft type: Boeing 747-230B (*HL7442*)

Different theories have circulated as to the reasons behind the infamous downing of Flight 007 by Soviet defence forces. Some are extreme,

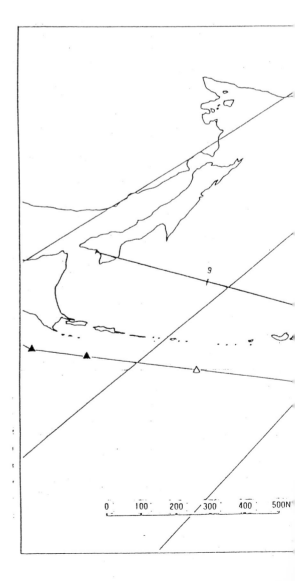

from the belief that the aircraft had been sent on a provocative mission by the US, or, on the other hand, that it was lured to destruction by the USSR in order to disgrace its long-time arch-rival Super Power. Such hypotheses lie at the borders of logic and can be disputed on both political and technical grounds.

Most reasonable observers feel that the incursion of the wide-bodied jetliner into Soviet airspace was totally inadvertent, and that the subsequent attack resulted from its misidentification as an intelligence aircraft. This was also the conclusion of the International Civil Aviation Organisation (ICAO), which conducted its own investigation into the tragedy.

Flight 007 had originated at New York City, with an ultimate destination of Seoul, South Korea, and a scheduled intermediate stop at Anchorage, Alaska, US, for refuelling and a change of crew. While on the ground at Anchorage International Airport, the aircraft's three independent inertial navigation system (INS) units would also have to be re-programmed for the second leg of the trip; this would involve keying into the system the exact position of the 747 as it sat on the airport tarmac. The proper routeing of the flight would then be pre-arranged by punching in the co-ordinates of certain positions, or way-points, along the prescribed track, which might be navigational facilities or even

An illustration of the correct route and the course believed to have been taken by Flight 007 that led to its destruction. (International Civil Aviation Organisation/Ikaros/Uniphoto Press International)

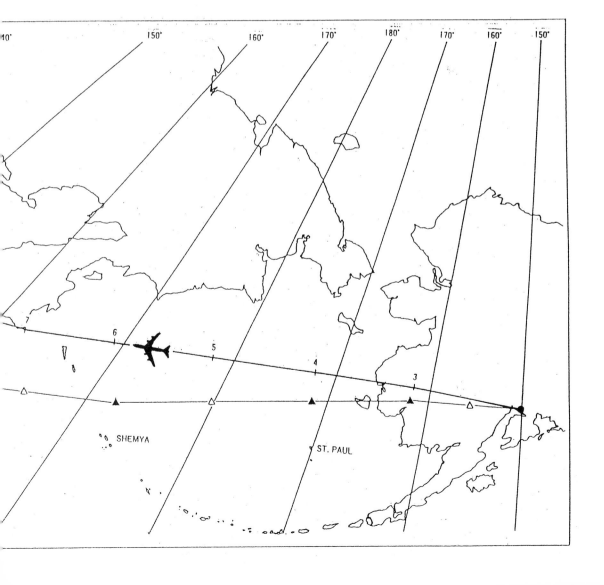

certain geographical points. Once interfaced with the autopilot, the INS would automatically steer the aircraft to its intended destination, even compensating for any wind conditions that might be encountered.

Following a 50-minute layover, the jetliner took off on the final leg of the transcontinental service, carrying six off-duty company personnel in addition to the three regular flight crewmen, and 20 cabin attendants to serve its 240 passengers. The latter included American Congressman Lawrence McDonald. They had but 5½ hours left to live.

Subsequent analysis of radar data indicated that the aircraft began to stray to the right of the prescribed route about 10 min after its departure from Anchorage, and it was approximately 7.5 miles (12 km) north of the track at the time of radar service termination. This discrepancy was not considered abnormal, and the Anchorage control centre made no attempt to advise the crew of such. A military radar recording showed the flight to be nearly 15 miles (25 km) too far north upon its passage of the Bethel (Alaska) very-high-frequency omni-directional range/tactical air navigation (VORTAC) facility. At the time, however, there was no interaction between military and civilian controllers, and the deviation went unchecked, and resulted in a progressively greater lateral displacement. Ultimately, and when some 250 miles (400 km) west of the normal route, the 747 entered Soviet airspace.

In a major foul-up of Soviet defence forces, jet fighters that were scrambled into action failed to locate the commercial transport as it flew over the southern tip of the Kamchatka Peninsula, the location of both a missile and a submarine base. Military authorities could only watch helplessly as the radar target representing Flight 007 proceeded out over the Sea of Okhotsk on its south-westerly heading.

About an hour later, HL7442 had again penetrated the border of the USSR, this time passing over southern Sakhalin Island, another militarily sensitive area. The aircraft would still have been flying in darkness at the time, with a half-moon providing partial illumination. The weather in the area was reportedly good, with 5/8 cirrus clouds at around 30,000 ft (10,000 m).

At 06:05 the pilot of a Soviet Air Force Sukhoi Su-15 jet fighter radioed that he had made visual contact with the intruder. The communications between him and his ground command were recorded by US monitoring stations, and a transcript was released at a special meeting of the United Nations Security Council. There were no indications in any of the air-to-ground messages that the 747 had been identified as an airliner; the pilot's only reference to it was as a 'target'. Nor was there any evidence, in its transmissions to the Japanese control centre, that the 747's Korean crew

knew of, nor made any contact with, the fighters that were in pursuit. During the chase, which lasted about 20 min, the Su-15 pilot was believed to have implemented the IFF (identification friend or foe) code procedure, then fired his cannon, presumably in an attempt to get the attention of the airline crew, neither of which actions were successful.

In the final moments of the flight, HL7442 initiated a climb from 33,000 to 35,000 ft (c 10,050–10,700 m). This is a common procedure for aircraft that have consumed most of their fuel, but it was apparently construed as an evasive manoeuvre. The ascent actually slowed the 747, and caused the Su-15 to fly past it. The Soviet pilot then re-positioned himself for the attack. Once locked on, he launched two air-to-air missiles, at least one of which struck the jetliner, possibly in the area of the left wing. It was then that he broadcast the now immortal words 'The target is destroyed'.

At that point, however, the transport was only damaged, badly no doubt, but still able to fly. During its agonising descent, most or all of its occupants probably still alive, the first officer was able to transmit a distress message later interpreted to be 'Korean Air zero zero seven . . . all engines . . . rapid (de)compression. Descending to one zero delta'.

The 747 finally plunged into the Sea of Japan, possibly after a mid-air explosion, an estimated 50 miles (80 km) south-west of Sakhalin and near the island of Moneron, in international waters. All 269 persons aboard perished. Subsequently, a small amount of debris, including personal effects, was recovered, as were the remains of several victims.

Some of the wreckage was found in salvage operations conducted by the USSR and later turned over to American or Japanese authorities. Otherwise the Soviets failed to co-operate in the post-crash search-and-rescue operation, and refused to accept a visit of the investigative team, for which they were strongly rebuked. Neither the aircraft's flight data recorder (FDR) nor its cockpit voice recorder (CVR) were available for analysis. The ICAO thus had to conduct its probe on the basis of limited hard evidence and facts, assumptions and calculations.

A premeditated detour for intelligence-gathering purposes, a major mechanical or navigational system failure or incapacitation of the crew were all considered too unlikely to warrant further examination. Also ruled out was that the captain had deliberately taken a short-cut with the intention of either conserving fuel or saving time. In fact, no evidence could be found to indicate that the crew was aware of the deviation. The number of plausible explanations was eventually reduced to two, which simulated flights proved would have resulted in roughly the same track as that believed to have been taken.

The first theory was that the crew had

inadvertently left the autopilot in the heading mode. Following the departure from Anchorage, a heading of 246 degrees would presumably have been selected to take the flight toward Bethel, after which the autopilot switch should have been turned one notch in a counter-clockwise direction, allowing the INS to take over the function of navigation. Significantly, the fighter pilot had reported that the jetliner was on a heading of 240 degrees before he shot it down, which would lend credence to this hypothesis.

The second postulation was that while the aircraft was sat on the ground at Anchorage, an erroneous ramp position was inserted into the INS unit that would be responsible for controlling the autopilot. An error of 10 degrees (139 instead of 149 W) would also explain the track taken by the flight.

As noted in the ICAO report, each of these scenarios 'assumes a considerable degree of lack of alertness and attentiveness on the part of the flight crew, but not to the degree that is unknown in international civil aviation'.

Flying with the autopilot in the heading mode should have caused the illumination of lights on the instrument panel indicating that the INS was not engaged. On the other hand, had an erroneous ramp position been inserted into one of the INS units, the system would automatically detect the discrepancy and flash. This warning indication could be overridden with the 'clear' button, but the incorrectly set unit would continue to display in rather obvious disagreement with the other two. Also the inaccurate original setting would have resulted in the indication of way-point passages that differed from those estimated, which should have alerted the crew that something was amiss. (In fact, the Anchorage control centre, which had to rely exclusively on pilot reports to determine the progress of the flight, did note differences between the estimated and the actual times, but did not attach any importance to them.)

Furthermore, there would have been other ways of determining the position of the aircraft. Since it was out of their range due to the incorrect heading, the navigational aids on St Paul's Island and at Shemya would not have been received, and this discordancy should have prompted the pilots to re-check their navigational progress. Also the weather radar with which *HL7442* was fitted had a ground-mapping mode capable of detecting the outline of the Kamchatka Peninsula and Sakhalin Island, serving as an additional reminder of the track error.

Conducting its own inquiry, the State Commission for Civil Aviation Flight Safety in the USSR (GOSAVIANADZOR) rejected the findings of the ICAO. Its conclusion generally followed statements made by the Kremlin in the days and weeks immediately following the tragedy, ie that the 747 was on a reconnaissance mission. It also criticised the air traffic control services of the US and Japan for not detecting the error and returning the aircraft to the proper route (though this would imply that the deviation was accidental).

There were some other inconsistencies in the Soviet report, most notably that the fighter had followed established guidelines in trying to warn the Korean crew, and that the jetliner had been flying with its navigational lights out. With regard to the former statement, the ICAO found no evidence that the fighter had flown close beside or in front of the transport, as dictated in normal intercept procedures. The second statement was contradicted by the recorded radio message from the Soviet pilot, who reported that 'The light is flashing'. In its report the ICAO concluded that extensive measures had not been taken to identify *HL7442* prior to its destruction.

The Soviets maintained that the 747 was just one element in a concerted espionage operation, which they claimed also involved a US Air Force RC-135 reconnaissance jet, and stated that at one point the two aircraft, flying in opposite directions, came so close together 'that their blips merged on the radarscope'. The US later confirmed the presence of an RC-135 in the area on the night that Flight 007 was shot down, though the former had returned to its base in Alaska more than an hour before the attack on the latter.

The thawing of the Cold War that began in the mid-1980s brought forth little additional information to help explain exactly what happened to the 747. More than seven years after the disaster it was reported that Soviet authorities had indeed recovered the aircraft's two 'black box' recorders, which directly contradicted earlier statements. In October 1992 a partial transcript of the CVR tape was released, but it too shed little light on the underlying cause.

In December 1984 a civilian radar system set up on St Paul's Island went into operation, one capable of monitoring commercial flights using the North Pacific route. Had it been available 16 months earlier, the tragedy of Flight 007 might have been averted.

Date: 23 September 1983 (c 15:30)
Location: Near Mina Jebel Ali, United Arab Emirates
Operator: Gulf Air Ltd (Bahrain, Oman, Qatar, United Arab Emirates)
Aircraft type: Boeing Advanced 737-2P6 (*A40-BK*)

Designated as Flight 771, the jet airliner crashed and burned in the desert some 30 miles (50 km) north-east of Abu Dhabi while preparing to land at the capital city's airport, a scheduled stop during a service from Karachi, Pakistan, to Manama, Bahrain. All 111 persons aboard (105 passengers and six crew members) perished.

A distress message had been transmitted as the aircraft was descending to 6,000 ft (1,800 m) from flight level 310.

There were indications of a pre-impact explosion having occurred in a cargo hold, with resultant structural damage and an uncontrollable fire producing toxic fumes that rapidly overcame the occupants. The evidence pointed away from a blaze of either electrical or fuel origin, and it was later concluded that the 737 had been sabotaged. Some articles of luggage assigned to the flight had been checked in by a ticket-holder who did not board the aircraft.

Date: 8 November 1983 (c 15:20)
Location: Near Lubango, Huila, Angola
Operator: Linhas Aereas de Angola
(TAAG-Angola Airlines)
Aircraft type: Boeing Advanced 737-2M2
(D2-TBN)

The jetliner crashed immediately after taking off, on a scheduled domestic service to the capital city of Luanda, and all 130 persons aboard (126 passengers and a crew of four) were killed.

Climbing to an approximate height of 200 ft (60 m), the aircraft commenced a steep turn to the left, then plunged to earth about half a mile (0.8 km) beyond the end of the airport runway, exploding on impact.

Angolan authorities attributed the disaster to 'technical failure'; however, guerrillas who had been fighting the government at the time claimed to have shot down the 737 with a surface-to-air missile.

Date: 27 November 1983 (01:06)
Location: Near Majorada del Campo, Madrid,
Spain
Operator: Aerovias Nacionales de Colombia SA
(AVIANCA)
Aircraft type: Boeing 747-283B Combi
(HK-2910)

Operating as Flight 11, the wide-bodied jet airliner had been cleared to land at Barajas Airport, serving Madrid, the first of two en route scheduled stops during a service originating at Paris, France, with an ultimate destination of Bogota, Colombia. During the instrument landing system (ILS) approach to Runway 33, the 747 crashed on a hill approximately 7.5 miles (12 km) south-east of the airport, killing 181 persons aboard, including 19 on-duty and four off-duty crew members. The 11 surviving passengers were seriously injured.

It was dark at the time of the accident, and the airport meteorological conditions just before consisted of 3/8 stratus clouds and mist at 1,000 ft (c 300 m), 5/8 strato-cumulus at 1,800 ft (c 550 m)

and a visibility of about 5 miles (10 km). The wind was calm.

The disaster was attributed to error by the pilot-in-command, who, while apparently unaware of his precise position, set out to intercept the ILS on an incorrect track without executing the published instrument approach manoeuvre, and in doing so continued his descent through the minimum safe altitude until impact.

Between Barahona and the initiation of a turn to the right, the flight crew did not adhere to the proper procedures, and as a consequence committed a navigational error. It was also at around this time that the co-pilot experienced difficulties in inserting the co-ordinates for the Madrid very-high-frequency omni-directional range (VOR) station into the aircraft's inertial navigation system (INS).

The crew in fact flew below the minimum height for more than a minute before entering the designated protection area, and the captain, in an apparent attempt to reduce speed, lowered the undercarriage out of sequence, ie before extending the flaps to a 20-degree setting (the 747 was in this configuration when it hit the ground).

The captain then began the turn before reaching the VOR, the prescribed point for initiation of the manoeuvre, probably because he no longer had a distance-measuring equipment (DME) reading to the station, or perhaps due to a cumulative error in the INS that gave him the impression of being closer to the navigational aid than was actually the case. Following the turn, the crew continued to fly without checking the distance to the VOR or capturing any signal from the ILS, apparently relying only on their automatic direction finder (ADF) indications.

Prior to this the captain had accepted uncritically an erroneous outer marker crossing altitude given by the first officer, who inverted two digits, resulting in the figure of 2,382 ft instead of the correct one, which was 3,282.

Only 37 sec before impact, the co-pilot made a remark that indicated the crew's false belief as to the nearness of the aircraft to the marker. The cockpit voice recorder (CVR) tape also revealed deficient team-work on the flight deck and the fact that the pilots failed to take corrective action in response to the activation of the ground proximity warning system (GPWS). The altitude alert first sounded 23 sec before impact, and the captain first took no action, then disconnected the autopilot, which had been coupled to the ILS, and slightly reduced the rate of descent. Just before the crash the first officer was heard to ask, in a calm tone, 'What does the ground say, captain?' in an apparent reminder to take positive action.

The communications phraseology and procedures used by both the crew and air traffic controllers did not conform to those recommended by the International Civil Aviation Organisation (ICAO).

Wreckage is strewn across the terrain following the crash near Madrid of the AVIANCA Boeing 747. (UPI/Bettmann)

These actions included that of the centre controller, who transferred the flight to the approach controller at a time and place different from that which had been agreed upon, and those of the approach controller, who handed off the aircraft without giving any precise positional reference to either the crew or the tower, or receiving confirmation from the crew that it had intercepted any approach aid or had any visual cue of its position.

Perhaps more significant, however, was the incomplete information provided to the crew by the approach controller, who stated that the aircraft had been 'approaching' the VOR without giving the exact distance. This, or the possibility of a glimpse through the two layers of cloud, may have reinforced the pilot's belief regarding his position.

An additional factor in the accident was that the approach controller failed to inform the flight that radar service had been terminated. He either did not pay sufficient attention to the radarscope, or the echo representing *HK-2910* was not conspicuous enough for him to detect the aircraft's deviation in both direction and altitude, preventing the crew from learning of its navigational error.

The resulting crash occurred at an approximate elevation of 2,250 ft (685 m), and while the jet was on a heading of 284 degrees and in a slight nose-up attitude; its indicated air speed at the time was around 160 mph (260 kmh). There were actually three successive impacts, and on the third the 747 began to disintegrate and also burst into flames. The fuselage broke into five sections and came to rest inverted.

In its report on the disaster, the Spanish investigative board emphasised the need for standard phraseology in air/ground radio communications, and for strict adherence to prescribed procedures, proper utilisation of navigational aids in terminal control areas and thorough familiarisation in the use of the GPWS by flight crews.

Date: 7 December 1983 (c 09:40)
Location: Near Madrid, Spain
First aircraft
Operator: Aviacion y Comercio SA (AVIACO) (Spain)
Type: McDonnell Douglas DC-9 Series 32 *(EC-CGS)*
Second aircraft
Operator: Lineas Aereas de Espana SA (Iberia) (Spain)
Type: Boeing Advanced 727-256 *(EC-CFJ)*

In the midst of a heavy fog, the two jet transports collided at Barajas Airport. Killed in the crash were a total of 93 persons – all 37 passengers and the crew of five from the DC-9 and 51 of the 93 aboard the 727, including one of its nine crew members. All but 12 of the survivors suffered injuries.

Designated as Flight 134 and on a domestic service to Santander, Ca Tabria, *EC-CGS* was preparing for its departure when it inadvertently taxied on to Runway 01, crossing left-to-right at an obtuse angle in the path of *EC-CFJ*, which, operating as Flight 350, was taking off for Rome, Italy. The latter had reached the decision speed, and its captain initiated an evasive manoeuvre in an unsuccessful attempt to avoid the collision. Fire erupted in both aircraft, and the 727, which lost practically all its port wing and its left main undercarriage in the impact, skidded to a stop on the pavement but facing in the opposite direction from the correct runway heading.

The poor visibility, officially reported as about 1,000 ft (300 m) but probably much less at the scene of the accident, had prevented the AVIACO crew from obtaining sufficient visual references in order to determine that they were not taking the correct route to the beginning of Runway 01. The weather was still above the minimum take-off requirements, however.

Pilot complaints of poor ground control and the absence of both marker lights and painted stop signs at taxiway/runway intersections had previously been lodged against Barajas Airport. Plans had actually been made for improvements that should have satisfied most of these concerns, but, tragically, the renovation programme was not to be budgeted until the year after the AVIACO/Iberia disaster.

Date: 11 October 1984 (c 05:40)
Location: Near Omsk, Russian Soviet Federated
  Socialist Republic, USSR
Operator: Aeroflot (USSR)
Aircraft type: Tupolev Tu-154B (*SSSR-85243*)

Operating as Flight 3352, the jet airliner collided with vehicles while landing at the Omsk airport, a scheduled stop during a domestic service from Krasnodar, Kazakh SSR, to Novosibirsk, RSFSR. The death toll of 178 included two dozen children and young adults, five crew members and four persons on the ground. One passenger and four other crew members survived the disaster, with three of the latter escaping virtually unscathed.

The crash occurred shortly before dawn and in weather conditions consisting of light rain, a visibility of about 2 miles (3 km) and a ceiling of around 300 feet (100 m). The drizzle caused a reflection when the aircraft's landing light was turned on just before the landing, prompting the crew to switch it off. Following an automatic-coupled approach, the Tu-154 touched down at a speed of approximately 160 mph (260 kmh).

Just after the crew had noticed something on the runway and started an evasive turn to the right, the aircraft crashed into two cleaning vehicles with heaters and an escort car, then broke apart and caught fire. The vehicles had been on the active runway due to a lack of co-ordination between the flying control officer, who had fallen asleep and failed to inform the approach controller of the presence of the vehicles, and the final controller and airport service personnel. Additionally, the vehicles had no warning lights.

Date: 23 December 1984 (c 18:10)
Location: Near Krasnoyarsk, Russian Soviet
  Federated Socialist Republic, USSR

The charred remains of the Iberia Boeing 727 that collided with an AVIACO DC-9 at Madrid airport. (Cover, Gamma Liaison)

An Aeroflot Tu-154B, two of which crashed fatally during the last three months of 1984. (Aircraft Photographic)

Operator: Aeroflot (USSR)
Aircraft type: Tupolev Tu-154B-2 (*SSSR-85338*)

All but a single passenger among the 111 persons aboard, including the crew of seven, lost their lives when the jet airliner crashed while attempting an emergency landing at the Krasnoyarsk airport, from where it had taken off minutes earlier. The sole survivor of the early evening accident was injured.

Designated as Flight 3519 and on a domestic intrastate service to Irkutsk, the aircraft had been climbing at a height of about 6,000 ft (1,800 m) and on a west-north-westerly heading when its No 3 (right) power plant disintegrated and caught fire. The failure of the flight engineer to close the fuel feed shut-off cock, one of several errors on his part, sustained the blaze despite the use of the engine fire-extinguishing system. Due to further crew errors, the No 2 (centre) power plant was inadvertently shut down, leaving only the No 1 operating. A loss of control apparently occurred during the attempted emergency landing, with the Tu-154 slamming to earth while in a right bank of about 50 degrees.

The break-up of the engine was attributed to the fatigue failure of the low pressure compressor's first stage disc due to metallurgical and manufacturing defects. The resulting fire spread to the tail assembly of the aircraft, leading to the failure of the flight controls.

Date: 21 January 1985 (01:04)
Location: Reno, Nevada, US
Operator: Galaxy Airlines (US)
Aircraft type: Lockheed 188A Electra (*N5532*)

The four-engine turboprop took off from Runway 16R at Reno-Cannon International Airport on a domestic charter service to Minneapolis, Minnesota. Less than 30 sec after becoming airborne, the first officer radioed the control tower requesting permission to land and reporting a 'heavy vibration'. Cleared by the controller for a return to the airport, the aircraft initiated a left turn, climbing to an estimated height of 200 to 250 ft (c 60–75 m) above the ground.

Its undercarriage retracted, the Electra crashed approximately 1 mile (1.5 km) from the end of the runway and about half a mile (0.8 km) to the right of its extended centreline, bursting into flames on impact. All but a single passenger among the 71 persons aboard were killed, including the entire crew of six. Seven recreational vehicles parked in a dealership's lot were destroyed in the accident, which occurred in darkness and clear weather.

The circumstances surrounding the flight could best be described as 'hurried'. The crew was running on a tight deadline, with a departure for Seattle, Washington, slated less than 90 min after the aircraft's arrival at Minneapolis. Even though a change in the schedule had been reported to the captain, he and his two fellow flight crewmen may have been influenced by a sense of urgency to the degree that proper procedures were disregarded.

The flight engineer had instructed the baggage handlers to load all of the passengers' luggage in the transport's aft baggage compartment, since the forward bin contained the crew's bags and galley stores. In addition, testimony from the survivor indicated that the passengers themselves had not been properly distributed in the cabin, with the seats forward of row 18 not being filled first. As a result of these two factors, the aircraft's centre of gravity was probably aft of the allowable limit, and although this apparently did not contribute to the accident, it reflected a general lack of adequate planning by the crew.

An analysis of the cockpit voice recorder (CVR) tape also revealed the improper use of the 'before-start check-list', with certain items omitted or reversed.

After receiving clearance from the ground supervisor, the Electra started to taxi away from the gate with the air-start hose still attached to the fitting, located along the leading edge of the starboard wing inboard of the No 3 power plant. The hose is used to pump air into an engine at a sufficient pressure to turn the turbine blades, thus facilitating its starting. When the aircraft began to move, the hose was pulled taught, preventing the ground handler from disconnecting it. Her supervisor, who had hand-signalled the crew to stop, removed it for her, for neither could remember closing the access door that encloses the fitting.

The noise heard on the CVR, coupled with the impact damage of the open latch of the door and statements from other pilots who had previous experiences with open air-start access doors, led the US National Transportation Safety Board (NTSB) to conclude that this was indeed the source of the vibration. Moreover, although it should not have significantly affected N5532 aerodynamically, the vibration generated by the open door caused a breakdown in crew co-ordination. The captain tried, unsuccessfully, to both establish the nature of the noise and fly the transport. Apparently believing that it was associated with engine trouble, he ordered that all four power levers be retarded. A wiser course of action would have been to climb to a safe altitude, then check the engines individually, but the significant reduction of power resulted in a loss of air speed, which in turn led to a stall.

Besides the error by the pilot-in-command, the NTSB ruled that the first officer did not adequately monitor either the height or speed of the aircraft, shirking those more important responsibilities and instead responding immediately to the commands of the captain, who was considerably older and more experienced (factors that could have been a source of intimidation), and to the requests of the tower controller. His eventual call-out of 'a hundred knots' came too late to prevent the crash, despite the application of full power. The NTSB believed that the vibration may have masked the onset of the stall buffet, perhaps delaying corrective action. The failure of ground personnel to assure that the air-start access door had been properly closed was considered contributory to the accident.

The board recommended that all Electra operators be notified of the potential danger of open access doors, and also criticised the US Federal Aviation Administration (FAA) for faulty surveillance of the airline's operations and maintenance, describing them as 'seriously deficient'. It further advised that smaller carriers such as Galaxy, which may lack the resources of the larger ones to implement programmes in the training of cockpit resource management, receive assistance in this area from the FAA.

Date: 19 February 1985 (09:27)
Location: Near Durango, Vizcaya, Spain
Operator: Lineas Aereas de Espana SA (Iberia) (Spain)
Aircraft type: Boeing Advanced 727-256 (*EC-DDU*)

All 148 persons aboard perished when this Iberia Boeing 727 crashed in northern Spain. (Reuters/Bettmann)

Operating as Flight 610, the jetliner crashed while preparing to land at Sondica Airport, serving Bilbao, at the end of a domestic service from Madrid, and all 148 persons aboard (141 passengers and seven crew members) perished.

The accident took place some 20 miles (30 km) south-east of the airport during the intermediate phase of an approach to Runway 30, using very-high-frequency omni-directional range/distance-measuring equipment (VOR/DME) and instrument landing system (ILS) procedures. Levelling off briefly at 7,000 ft (c 2,000 m) and 5,000 ft (c 1,500 m), as cleared by the control tower, the aircraft continued its descent and had been flying for nearly a minute below the minimum sector altitude of 4,354 ft (1,327 m) when it struck a television antenna rising about 100 feet (30 m) above Mt Oiz. Initial contact with the antenna mast occurred as the aircraft was on a heading of 96 degrees, turning right on to its final approach leg, and flying at an indicated air speed of 240 mph (385 kmh), with its undercarriage extended. Its left wing torn off by the force of the impact, the 727 then crashed inverted on the mountain at an approximate elevation of 3,400 ft (1,040 m), scattering wreckage down the sloping terrain. There was no general post-impact blaze but only small isolated fires from spilt fuel, primarily in the area of the empennage and the engines.

The airport weather around the time of the crash consisted of a broken overcast, with 2/8 strato-cumulus clouds at 4,000 feet (c 1,200 m) and 4/8 alto-cumulus at 8,000 ft (c 2,500 m) and a visibility of around 2.5 miles (4 km) in mist. There was also a slight breeze from a south-south-easterly direction.

The descent was believed to have been made by the first officer, using the vertical guidance control of the autopilot, the captain apparently setting the various levels on the altitude alert system in lieu of providing 1,000 ft call-outs. The latter probably selected 4,300 ft (1,310 m) on the altitude alert, but the aircraft did not level off at that height as anticipated. This may have been due to his failure to press the 'ALT SEL' switch at all or in sufficient time to effect altitude capture, or from inadvertent disengagement by one of the pilots. However, a malfunction in the aircraft's automatic flight control system could not be ruled out, even though altitude capture had been accomplished twice before during the descent.

Though the flight had been cleared for a standard manoeuvre, the cockpit conversation indicated that the first officer had intended and desired a shorter procedure. Significantly, the shorter procedure required a minimum altitude of 7,000 feet at the same DME fix, 2,000 ft (c 600 m) higher than the standard manoeuvre. The rate of descent adopted seemed to indicate that he was starting the final approach from an altitude of higher than 5,000 ft.

Another factor that proved critical in this case was the use of 4,300 ft as the level-off height, rather than 4,400 ft, or the 100 ft increment above the minimum altitude. Also, the supervision provided by the captain was inadequate, though his apparent manipulation of the altitude alert system may have been his way of directing the operation without feeling it necessary to give audible instructions, even though, as noted in the investigative report, the use of the system still requires vigilance by the crew. There was an additional possibility of the misreading of the aircraft's drum-type altimeters, which are susceptible to such errors, especially at lower altitudes, when attention is divided among several activities.

In the final moments before impact the co-pilot may have misinterpreted the audible warning of the altitude alert system as being the approach to the selected minimum height.

Among other recommendations made by the Spanish investigative commission was a reiteration of the need for the pilot not at the controls to perform altitude call-outs. The report also urged the updating of aeronautical charts, as neither Mt Oiz or the antenna appeared on the chart used by the crew of Flight 610.

Date: 3 May 1985 (c 12:00)
Location: Near L'vov, Ukraine, USSR
First aircraft
Operator: Aeroflot (USSR)
Type: Tupolev Tu-134A (*SSSR-65856*)
Second aircraft
Operator: Soviet Air Force
Type: Antonov An-26 (*SSSR-26492*)

The jet airliner and the twin-engine turboprop military transport collided in mid-air, and both crashed. A total of 94 persons perished in the disaster, 79 aboard *SSSR-65856* (73 passengers and a crew of six) and 15 aboard *SSSR-26492* (nine passengers and a crew of six). There were no survivors.

Operating on a scheduled domestic service from Tallinn, Estonia, to Kishinev, Moldavia, with an en route stop at L'vov, the Tu-134 was descending through clouds in preparation for landing at the city's airport, from where the An-26 had taken off shortly before, when the head-on collision occurred at approximately 13,000 ft (4,000 m), the altitude at which the latter had been cleared to fly.

The accident resulted from flagrant violations of air traffic control rules by the civil approach and the military controllers due to misidentification of the location of both aircraft in the area of the navigational station.

Date: 23 June 1985 (c 07:15)
Location: North Atlantic Ocean
Operator: Air-lndia
Aircraft type: Boeing 747-237B (*VT-EFO*)

Originating at Toronto as Flight 181, the wide-bodied jet airliner had landed at Montreal International Airport, also in Canada. Re-designated as Flight 182, it then proceeded on towards London, its next scheduled stop during a service with an ultimate destination of Bombay, India. Its cargo included a 'fifth' engine, actually an inoperative one slated for repair that was being carried on the left wing between the fuselage and the No 2 power plant.

Having nearly completed a transatlantic crossing, *VT-EFO* was flying on this Sunday morning in good weather conditions above a solid overcast, with cloud tops at 15,000 ft (c 5,000 m), when its target suddenly disappeared from the radarscope. The 747 crashed at sea some 110 miles (175 km) east of Cork, Ireland, killing all 329 persons aboard (307 passengers and a crew of 22). Subsequently, floating debris representing approximately 3 to 5 per cent of the aircraft's structure was recovered, as were 132 bodies. Many of the victims exhibited signs of hypoxia or decompression; a few had flail injuries, indicating that they may have been ejected from the cabin while the jet was still in the air.

The depth of the ocean where the aircraft had fallen was some 7,000 ft (2,000 m), dashing any hopes of raising the main wreckage. In lieu of such a recovery, a photographic and videographic map was made of the crash site. Distribution of the debris seemed to confirm that the 747 was not intact when it struck the water.

A significant find was that of the digital flight data (DFDR) and cockpit voice (CVR) recorders, which were fitted with submersible beacons. A read-out of the DFDR showed that *VT-EFO* had been cruising at flight level 310 and an indicated air speed of 340 mph (c 550 kmh) when there was an abrupt cessation of electrical power to both recorders. Approximately half a second before, a loud noise was heard on the CVR tape, which, according to the British Air Accidents Investigation Branch, suggested an explosive decompression. A report by the Bhabha Atomic Research Centre, in India, further concluded that a series of audio bursts transcribed on the air traffic control centre recording were most probably generated by the in-flight break-up of the 747. It was considered likely that the section aft of the wings had separated from the rest of the fuselage.

In attempting to determine the reason for the disintegration of the aircraft, investigators could find no indication of structural failure, nor of any pre-existing defect. Though circumstantial, evidence pointed to an explosion in its forward cargo hold; this included small puncture holes in a

section of skin panel located near the compartment, one of several larger pieces of wreckage that was retrieved from the ocean floor; tiny 'mooncraters' in a piece of alloy filled with plastic foam; and damage to the bottom of some recovered seat cushions.

The Indian investigative report ascribed the disaster to an act of sabotage, which had been widely suspected since the first few hours after the crash. It was believed that the detonation of an explosive device in the cargo hold had severely damaged the 747, causing an immediate depressurisation. The crew was believed to have taken some action, deploying the spoilers with the intention of initiating an emergency descent. But with the emergency oxygen system rendered inoperative, the pilots could have lost consciousness in only seconds, losing control of the aircraft, with a more general break-up occurring soon thereafter.

The bomb theory was further buoyed by an event taking place about an hour before the Air-India disaster, wherein an explosive device had gone off in the transit area at Narita Airport, serving Tokyo, Japan. Two airport workers lost their lives in the blast and four were injured. The suitcase containing the bomb had been unloaded from Canadian Pacific (CP) Air Flight 003, having arrived from Vancouver, British Columbia, Canada, and was to have been placed aboard Air-India Flight 301, bound for Bangkok, Thailand.

Four days earlier, a man with an Indian accent had made bookings for two men with the same surname as his on two CP Air Flights, 003 and 60, with interconnections to, respectively, Air-India 301 and 181/182.

The day before the twin tragedies, a passenger booked on Toronto-bound CP 60 had requested his suitcase be interlined through to Flight 181/182. Since his seat on the latter was only stand-by and not reserved, the ticket agent explained that this would not be possible. The passenger persisted, and as the queues were long, the agent gave in to his demands. The same day, a passenger with the same last name, who was booked on Flight 003, checked in with one piece of luggage at the same counter. But there was no evidence that either man boarded the respective flights.

All checked-in baggage intended to be loaded on to *VT-EFO* at Toronto had to be screened with a hand 'sniffer', because the regular X-ray machine was inoperative at the time. It would later be revealed, however, that some of the employees who worked for the security firm providing services under contract to Air-India had not undergone refresher training. Shortcomings were also found in the equipment used to inspect the baggage. Furthermore, airline personnel at Toronto had deviated from prescribed company policy by not correlating checked-in luggage with boarding passengers. This allowed an unaccompanied suitcase, possibly containing a bomb, to go aboard

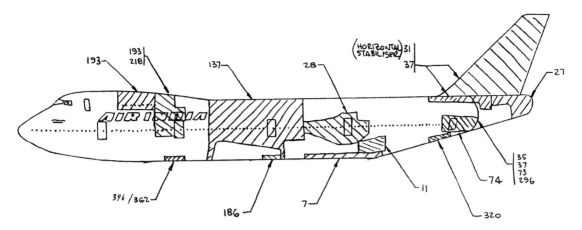

Diagram indicating the parts of the Air-India Boeing 747 that were identified on the ocean floor. (Canadian Aviation Safety Board)

the doomed 747. Recommendations made in the Indian report included hand searches of carry-on baggage and other items and the relocation of important avionics units away from the cargo hold to reduce their vulnerability in case of such an in-flight explosion.

Several years later, a man belonging to India's Sikh religious sect was sentenced to 10 years imprisonment in Canada for involvement in the Narita Airport explosion. The bomb was to have destroyed Air India 301 in apparent retaliation for the 1984 attack by the Indian Army on the Golden Temple, a Sikh shrine located in Amritsar, Punjab, which left hundreds dead. An incorrectly set timer probably accounted for its premature detonation.

In July 1992 the case surrounding the destruction of Flight 182 was finally broken when a 30-year-old suspected Sikh terrorist believed responsible for the crime was arrested in Bombay.

Date: 10 July 1985 (c 23:45)
Location: Near Uch Kuduk, Uzbek SSR, USSR
Operator: Aeroflot (USSR)
Aircraft type: Tupolev Tu-154B-2 (*SSSR-85311*)

Designated as Flight 7425, the jet airliner crashed and burned about 200 miles (320 km) north-north-west of Karshi, from where it had taken off earlier, on a domestic service to Leningrad (St Petersburg), RSFSR, with an en route stop at Ufa, Bashkir. All 200 persons aboard (191 passengers and a crew of nine) perished.

The aircraft had been cruising in darkness at an approximate height of 40,000 feet (12,000 m) and an indicated air speed of about 250 mph (400 kmh) when an abrupt change in the parameters was noted on its flight data recorder (FDR) read-out. These included elevator deflections and an increase in both pitch and angle of attack. After the Tu-154 had

reached a critical angle of attack, thrust was reduced on all three engines. The FDR recorded a continued reduction in air speed, which ultimately fell to zero, while the angle of attack increased to or beyond the sensor limit of 45 degrees. During this period of time the jet deviated first to the left then to the right of the flight path. Following a stall and the beginning of a sharp descent, the crew radioed that the engines had shut down and the aircraft was moving 'in a strange way'. The descent continued for 143 seconds until impact.

Due to the destruction of the cockpit voice recorder (CVR), the analysis of the human factor aspect of the investigation had to be conducted by psychologists. This analysis revealed a high degree of fatigue on the part of the flight crew, who had spent 24 hours at the airport in high temperature conditions. Also identified in the final report were inadequate regulations for crews encountering abnormal conditions.

The weather at the time consisted of winds from a west-north-westerly direction of around 75 to 80 mph (120–130 kmh) at the approximate height at which *SSSR-85311* had been flying.

Date: 2 August 1985 (c 18:05)
Location: Near Dallas, Texas, US
Operator: Delta Air Lines (US)
Aircraft type: Lockheed L-1011-1 TriStar (*N726DA*)

It had been more than 10 years since the New York City crash of the Eastern Airlines Boeing 727 (see separate entry, 24 June 1975), an accident that launched extensive research into the phenomenon of wind shear. Some progress had been made, from the development of detection systems, which had come into use at a number of airports, to the introduction of training programmes designed to teach pilots ways of dealing with this weather hazard. But as Delta Flight 191 began its final approach to land at Dallas/Fort Worth International Airport, an en route stop during a domestic transcontinental service from Fort Lauderdale, Florida, to Los Angeles, California, seemingly everything learned over that decade would be cast aside. Wind shear was about to claim another airliner.

Cleared for an instrument landing system (ILS) approach to Runway 17-Left, the L-1011 was believed to have entered a microburst flowing from a thunderstorm at a height of between 850 and 550 ft (c 260–165 m) above the ground. The outflow, which was estimated to have been approximately 2 miles (3 km) in diameter, contained divergent winds that had different effects on the aircraft. These effects were determined largely through the read-out of its digital flight data recorder (DFDR). Flying into the microburst, N726DA first encountered an increasing head-wind, then a series of up-draughts and down-draughts, then an increasing tail-wind, the latter reducing its indicated air speed by 50 mph (80 kmh). During this period of time it was also hit by a lateral gust of about 70 knots, causing a 20-degree roll to the right.

The first officer, who was flying the aircraft, had applied nose-up control inputs in accordance with normal wind shear penetration procedures. But after

The tail assembly of the Delta Air Lines L-1011 came to rest relatively intact after the crash at Dallas/Fort Worth International Airport. (Wide World Photos)

encountering an up-draught, the aircraft's angle of attack increased dangerously close to the stall regime. The application of forward pressure to the control column coupled with a strong down-draught then caused the TriStar to deviate below the proper glide path. Full power was then applied and the captain commanded 'Toga', or activation of a switch in order to provide flight director guidance for an optimum climb-out manoeuvre. The overshoot was initiated too late to prevent, but nevertheless could have softened, the initial impact with the ground.

Its flaps set at 33 degrees and leading edge slats deployed, the wide-bodied jetliner was seen to emerge from a 'curtain' of rain before touching down on its extended main undercarriage in a ploughed field about 6,000 ft (1,800 m) short of the runway, and in approximate alignment with but some 360 ft (110 m) to the left of its extended centreline. After becoming airborne, it touched down once again, crushing an automobile as it traversed a highway. Having knocked down three light standards along the road, the aircraft grazed one large water tank, then slammed into a second located a little more than half a mile (0.8 km) from the point of initial ground contact, disintegrating in a fiery explosion. Only the rear fuselage/empennage section, which contained a majority of the survivors, remained relatively intact, sliding backwards out of the fireball.

The disaster claimed the lives of 137 persons, including eight crew members and the driver (and sole occupant) of the vehicle that was struck by the L-1011. Twenty-eight others aboard, including three cabin attendants, were injured, some seriously; a rescue worker was also hospitalised for chest and arm pains. Two passengers escaped unscathed.

The presence of the water tanks contributed to the severity of the accident, but in their absence the jetliner could well have struck two parked cargo jets, a DC-8 and a DC-10, with perhaps even more disastrous consequences. On the other hand, the quick response by the airport emergency personnel probably cut the death toll.

The NTSB blamed the crash on the decision to initiate and continue the approach into the cumulo-nimbus cloud, ascribing the responsibility for such not just to the pilot-in-command but also to his two fellow flight crewmen; the absence of specific guidelines, procedures and training for avoiding and escaping from low-altitude wind shear; and the lack of definitive, real-time wind shear hazard information. The action by the crew was also contrary to the airline's thunderstorm-avoidance policy (which did not, however, address the issue of what action was to be taken when operating in an airport terminal area). The decision may have been influenced by the fact that two aircraft had landed just before Flight 191 without reporting any difficulties. However, as noted in the investigative report, the captain had flown for many years in Delta's route structure and should have been aware of the volatility of convective-type storms.

The thunderstorm that had built up to the north of the airport on this Friday afternoon was rapid in development. No SIGMET or severe weather watch or warning had been issued. When the meteorologist assigned to the Fort Worth air traffic control centre went to dinner at around 17:25, there were no weather echoes within 10 miles (c 15 km) of the airport. He returned some 45 min later to find a 'level 4' or 'very strong' intensity thunderstorm in progress. By then, the L-1011 had already crashed. Likewise, no warning was given by the airport's low-level wind shear alert system (LLWAS) until after the accident.

Several other crews had observed lightning in the vicinity of the airport, and one even reported seeing a funnel cloud; however, none of them communicated this information to the control tower. About 10 min before the crash, a message was broadcast from the ground to 'all aircraft listening', announcing 'There's a rain shower just north of the airport . . .' This transmission was received by Flight 191. A second message intended for another incoming aircraft, which reported '. . . a little bitty thunderstorm sitting right on final . . .' was not.

Although the dissemination of information concerning the storm may have been lacking, the US National Transportation Safety Board (NTSB) ruled that the Delta crew should have been able to assess adequately the meteorological conditions. During the approach the TriStar was flying directly toward the cumulo-nimbus build-up, which should have been observable on its weather radar and visible to the pilots. On the cockpit voice recorder (CVR) tape, the first officer was heard to say 'We're gonna get our airplane washed', indicating an awareness of the rain ahead. He also made reference to lightning, and the sound of rain hitting the aircraft could then be heard.

It was further concluded that the 'take-off/go-around' (TOGA) mode of the TriStar's flight director provided insufficient up or down guidance for penetrating wind shears. Additionally, the weather radar installed on *N726DA*, which had a minimum range setting of 50 nautical miles (c 90 km), may not have presented an accurate depiction of the thunderstorm.

Subsequent to this accident, a more sophisticated LLWAS, one employing more sensors, came into use. Among the first airports in the US to receive the new system were Dallas/Fort Worth and Stapleton International, serving Denver, Colorado, where in 1989 it was credited with saving a commercial jet from a powerful microburst. This refined LLWAS has proven to be even more effective when combined with another technological development, Terminal Doppler weather radar.

Date: 12 August 1985 (18:56)
Location: Near Ueno Village, Gumma, Japan
Operator: Japan Air Lines (JAL)
Aircraft type: Boeing 747SR-46 (*JA8119*)

Operating as Flight 123, the wide-bodied jetliner took off from Tokyo International (Haneda) Airport on a domestic service to Osaka. Some 10 min later a loud noise was heard in the cabin, which then experienced a sudden loss of pressurisation. The flight crew immediately squawked the emergency code 7700 on the aircraft's transponder and the captain requested, and was granted, permission to return to its point of departure.

Assigned by the Tokyo air traffic control centre to maintain a magnetic heading of 90 degrees, the 747 strayed from that path. It also began oscillating in longitudinal (phugoid) and lateral ('Dutch roll') motions, which would continue for the rest of the flight. At one point the controller asked the crew 'What is the nature of the emergency?'. There was no response. The controller then radioed the heading instructions once again, receiving in return the terse statement 'Now uncontrollable'.

Unbeknown to the crew, the aircraft's aft pressure bulkhead had ruptured, sending an airflow from the cabin into the unpressurised empennage. The auxiliary power unit wall was then broken, and air rushed up into the vertical tail fin. The pressure within the fin destroyed the fixture between the stringer and the rib chord in the upper portion of the aft torque box, and within seconds the internal damage led to the separation of a large section of the rudder. All four lines of the corresponding hydraulic systems were severed, and in less than 2 minutes the 747's power-assisted flying controls had been rendered useless.

Traversing Suruga Bay, *JA8119* turned northward, passing to the west of Mt Fuji. The aircraft had descended to flight level 170 before the crew reported 'Aircraft uncontrollable', repeating 'uncontrollable' twice over the next several minutes. Acknowledgement that both Tokyo and Yokota airports were available for use was the last message received from the flight.

Its undercarriage having been lowered and flaps partially extended, the jetliner executed a 360-degree right turn and was observed in a slight nose-up attitude before it brushed against one tree-covered ridge, then crashed into another at an approximate elevation of 5,000 ft (1,500 m) and some 70 miles (110 km) north-west of the capital city, disintegrating and bursting into flames on impact. All but four passengers among the 524 persons aboard were killed, including the crew of 15, making it the highest death toll ever in a single-aircraft accident. The seriously injured survivors, among them an off-duty JAL cabin attendant, had all been seated in row 54, in the aft part of the cabin. The crash took place in twilight, and the weather, which was not considered a contributing factor, consisted of rain showers and a broken overcast in the general area.

The structural failure that befell *JA8119* was linked to repairs made after a mishap occurring in June 1978, in which the aircraft dragged its rear fuselage while landing at Osaka, Japan. The manufacturer carried out the repairs, replacing the aft bulkhead, which had been deformed in the non-fatal accident.

After the new bulkhead was installed, the margins around the rivet holes at the splice of the upper and lower webs were found to be less than that specified. As a corrective measure, a splice joint was to have been fitted between the webs of the upper and lower halves of the bulkhead, in order to reinforce the structure. However, the work was not completed as planned. One of the doubler plates was narrower than required, and Boeing engineers

left a gap between the top rivets. And instead of the necessary two, only one row of rivets had been used in the splicing. The result was a reduction of about 30 per cent in the strength of the bulkhead compared with its strength had the procedure been carried out properly, increasing its susceptibility to fatigue-cracking. A number of cracks had propagated, primarily at the one-row rivet connection points, in the 12,319 flights of the 747 since the repairs. They were not detected prior to the crash despite half a dozen inspections, which the investigative commission ruled were inadequate.

Flight 123 was the fifth trip for *JA8119* on the day of the accident. The failure of the bulkhead took place at a height of about 24,000 ft (7,300 m) due to the difference in pressure between the cabin and the air outside. The rupture left a hole some 6 ft by 10 ft (2-3 m) in diameter in the structure. The subsequent failure of the 747's multiply-redundant

The estimated flight path of the Japan Air Lines Boeing 747 from take-off at Tokyo International Airport until its crash near Ueno Village. (Japanese Ministry of Transport)

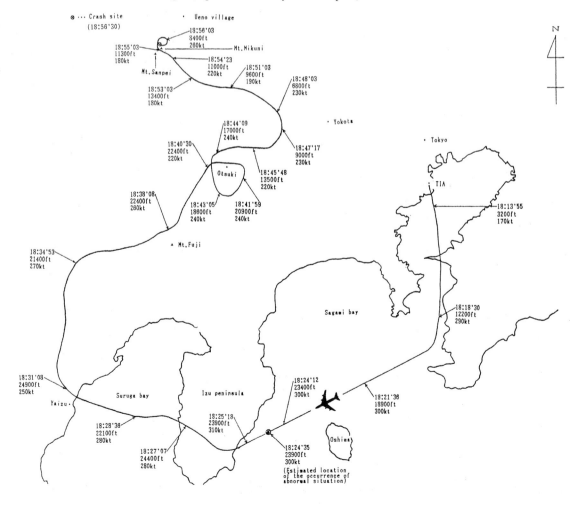

hydraulic system and the absence of any manual back-up left the thrust levers as the only means of controlling the aircraft. Pitch control could have been accomplished through the increase and decrease of power and directional control through the application of asymmetrical thrust, but the process would be delicate and severely tax the resources and training of the crew.

Possibly due to preoccupation with maintaining control, the pilots did not initiate an immediate emergency descent, and proceeded on for nearly 20 min above 20,000 ft (6,000 m). Apparently failing to use their oxygen masks, they may also have suffered from hypoxia, which would cause a deterioration in judgement and thus affect their ability to cope with the emergency.

The extension of the undercarriage did help reduce the phugoid motions, but after the jetliner had descended to a lower altitude, the crew was faced with another frightening dilemma – the mountains looming ahead in its flight path. In the final moments before the 747 slammed into the first ridge, the captain, as transcribed on the cockpit voice recorder (CVR) tape, was heard to say 'Nose up', and asked for a reduction in flap angle, repeating both orders several times. He then commanded 'Power', which was repeated twice. About 10 sec after the activation of the ground proximity warning system (GPWS), which gave the alert to 'Pull up', a crashing sound was heard, and the recording then ended. At the time of the initial impact, the aircraft was in a 60-degree right bank, on a westerly heading and flying at an indicated air speed of around 300 mph (480 kmh).

Nightfall and the inaccessibility of the terrain prevented members of the Japan Self-Defence Force from reaching the crash site until the following morning, some 15 hours after the accident. A section of the rudder was later recovered from Sagami Bay, as a further indication of structural failure.

As a result of the tragedy, the US Federal Aviation Administration (FAA) ordered the installation on 747s in service of a cover for the opening to the vertical fin, to prevent internal damage in the event of an increase in pressure within the structure. It later instituted a requirement for the securing of the hydraulic system on the aircraft type to preclude a total loss of fluid were its four lines to be severed, as was the case with JA8119.

Understandably, the disaster generated severe repercussions at JAL, a carrier that had built up a reputation for safety throughout the world. The president of the company, Yasumoto Takagi, later resigned, accepting full responsibility for what had happened, and even visited families of the victims to apologise in person. Guilt over his involvement led one JAL maintenance manager to commit suicide. The airline also experienced a drastic

The left wing of the 747 lies on a mountain slope after the disaster that killed 520 persons. (Wide World Photos)

reduction in both passenger traffic and revenues that were directly attributable to the crash. In 1987, and concurrent with its move towards privatisation, the firm adopted a new logo in an attempt to bolster its fallen image.

Date: 22 August 1985 (c 07:15)
Location: Near Manchester, England
Operator: British Airtours
Aircraft type: Boeing Advanced 737-236 (*G-BGJL*)

The jet airliner was nearly loaded to capacity, with all but one of its 130 passenger seats filled and also carrying two infants plus six crew members, as it began its take-off from Runway 24 at Manchester International Airport on a non-scheduled service to Corfu, in the Ionian Islands of Greece.

After the 737 had accelerated to about 140 mph

(225 kmh), and before reaching the decision speed, the outer casing of its No 1 engine's compression chamber ruptured. The case had split along an axial line adjacent to the No 9 combustor can and then 'petalled' apart, with the domed portion and a panel section of the fan case striking and puncturing a fuel tank access panel on the underside of the left wing. Escaping fuel then ignited after coming into contact with the flames and hot material emanating from the damaged power plant. The crew immediately rejected the take-off when a 'thump' or 'thud' was heard, but because the captain considered the possibility of a tyre failure, he advised the first officer against excessive braking.

Despite the rapid deployment of emergency vehicles and personnel and the fact that none of the aircraft's occupants were harmed in the engine explosion, 55 persons aboard lost their lives including the two rear cabin attendants, the fatalities attributed to the effects of the fire. An additional 15 passengers were seriously hurt and dozens of others, including a fire fighter, suffered lesser injuries.

Investigation revealed that a circular crack had formed around the circumference of the No 9 can, in the area of the third and fourth liner joint. The dome portion, experiencing air loads on its face and having lost the support provided by the aft section of the can, had then begun to cant outward by bending the mounting lug and pin. Eventually the dome became canted from its normal axis, and hot combustion gases started to consume the aft portion of the can and to heat the inner surface of the combustion chamber, a process that progressed until the final rupture.

The British Air Accidents Investigation Branch (AIB) could not determine the amount of time that had elapsed between the full development of the crack and the ultimate failure; available evidence showed that it was not simultaneous.

A metallurgical examination indicated that the source of the crack was thermal fatigue. Evidence of localised 'hot spots', which could signify the early stages of such damage, was found in other combustor cans in the power plant that failed and in other engines of the same type used by the carrier and its parent company, British Airways. The possible causes of heat-related blistering and/or cracking could have ranged from a distorted fuel nozzle flow pattern to disruption of the flow of cooling air attributed to repairs or faulty design or manufacture.

The No 1 engine of *G-BGJL*, a Pratt & Whitney JT8D-15, had been previously repaired for two separate cracks in the same can. According to the power plant manual, no restriction had been placed on the length of a crack that could be repaired. However, a survey revealed that a number of other operators of the same engine had voluntarily imposed their own limits. British Airways was a relatively new user of the JT8D-15, not obtaining the type until after the manufacturer had deleted a limit of 3 in (c 8 cm) to a repairable crack. In addition, the actual welding carried out on the can was faulty.

Prior to the disaster, only three cases of ruptures in the combustion chamber outer casing had been recorded in some 300 million flying hours with the JT8D, but numerous failures without external damage or cases of bulging or overheating had been, enough to indicate that a problem with the engine existed. Difficulties with this particular

The gutted hulk of the British Airtours Boeing 737 sits on the exit ramp after the blaze precipitated by uncontained engine failure. (Wide World Photos)

power plant, including slow acceleration, had been reported on 20 different occasions from the time of its installation in February 1984 until its catastrophic failure. Slow acceleration was in fact a symptom of a disrupted can, but this information had not been communicated to the operator by Pratt & Whitney. The airline apparently felt that it was immune from such a failure because its fleet of 737s were fitted with 'improved durability' cans, none of which had been in use for an exceptionally long time, and because its inspection programme was considered more conservative than other carriers.

Following the explosion of the engine, there were several factors that contributed to the seriousness of the accident. The captain's decision not to use maximum braking was understandable under the circumstances, especially considering that the engine fire warning bell did not activate immediately. However, the delay in bringing the jet to a full stop as soon as possible cost some precious seconds in evacuation time. Another factor was the use of reverse thrust to stop the aircraft. Though in accordance with prescribed procedures, the deployment of the reverser buckets created a turbulent wake that helped mix fuel flowing from the ruptured wing tank with the air, thus intensifying the blaze that had already started.

Even more critical was the decision of the captain to turn off the runway and stop on an exit ramp. Again, while the action was in line with the operations manual, it resulted in the placement of the fuselage down-wind of the burning engine and the blazing fuel that had formed a pool on the left side of the aircraft. The wind, which was a relatively light 5 to 7 knots, blew the flames toward the 737 and also created a pressure field around the stationary aircraft that must have allowed entry of the fire into its cabin when the doors on the right side were opened. The blaze also penetrated the skin of the transport from the outside within 20 sec of its stopping, resulting in the collapse to the ground of the rear fuselage section in less than a minute.

Difficulties were also experienced in the emergency evacuation, with the front door jamming momentarily, an escape hatch falling inward due to improper operation and briefly trapping a passenger, and a narrow space between the seats disrupting egress from the same exit. Portable oxygen bottles and even the presence of spirits and aerosol spray cans could have increased the fire.

Other important contributing factors were the vulnerability of the wing tank access panels to impact damage, a lack of any effective provision for fighting major fires inside the cabin, and the extremely toxic nature of the emissions from the burning cabin materials. Survivors reported that after the 737 had stopped, the aft cabin suddenly filled with thick black smoke, inducing panic among the passengers, causing many to collapse in the aisle and forcing others to clamber over the seats in order to escape.

Examination of other JT8D engines used by different British air carriers revealed similar cracking, leading to the grounding of numerous 737s until inspections could be completed.

The UK Civil Aviation Authority (CAA), which even before this accident had implemented a requirement for the use of flame-retardant upholstery in British aircraft (becoming effective in 1987), subsequently took further action to enhance occupant survivability. These included the mandated removal or rearrangement of seats in some cases to improve access to emergency exits, and floor-level lighting to assist in the egress from a dark or smoke-filled cabin.

Date: 12 December 1985 (06:46)
Location: Near Gander, Newfoundland, Canada
Operator: Arrow Air Inc (US)
Aircraft type: McDonnell Douglas DC-8 Super 63PF (*N950JW*)

Chartered by the Multinational Force and Observers (MFO) to carry American service personnel home from the Middle East, the jetliner took off from Runway 22 at Gander International Airport, an en route stop during a service originating at Cairo, Egypt, with an ultimate destination of Fort Campbell, Kentucky, US. Reaching a maximum height of about 125 ft (40 m), the aircraft then began to descend, passing over the Trans-Canada Highway at an unusually low altitude. The DC-8 then crashed in a wooded area approximately half a mile (0.8 km) from the end of the runway and some 700 ft (200 m) to the right of its extended centreline, bursting into flames on impact. All 256 persons aboard, including a civilian crew of eight Americans, were killed.

The investigation of the accident was hampered by the condition of the wreckage and irregularities in the operation of the aircraft's flight data recorder (FDR). Largely for these reasons the Canadian Aviation Safety Board (CASB) was unable to hypothesise on the probable sequence of events leading up to the crash. Available evidence supported the conclusion that shortly after becoming airborne the DC-8 experienced an increase in drag and reduction in lift, resulting in a stall from which recovery was not possible.

The most probable cause of the stall was ice contamination on the leading edge and upper surface of the transport's wings. The weather would have been conducive to the accumulation of ice, with a freezing drizzle and/or light snow falling during much of the time that *N950JW* was on the ground, and freezing temperatures throughout; however, prior to departure the crew had not requested that the jetliner be de-iced. A light snow

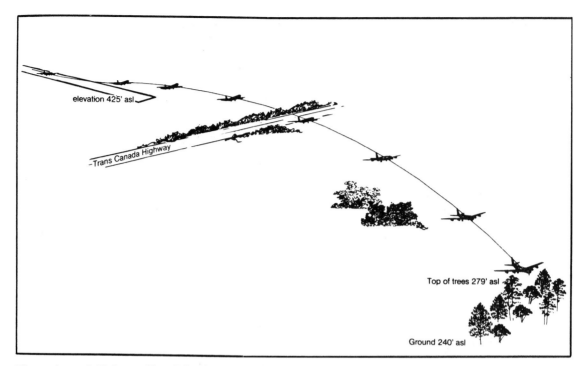

elevation 425' asl

Trans Canada Highway

Top of trees 279' asl

Ground 240' asl

The estimated flight profile of the Arrow Air Super DC-8 that crashed soon after take-off from Gander International Airport. (Canadian Aviation Safety Board)

was still falling when it took off, with a solid overcast at 2,500 ft (c 750 m) and scattered clouds down to 700 ft (c 200 m) and a visibility of 12 miles (c 20 km). It was still dark at the time.

As past research had demonstrated, a film of ice only .03 in (c 1 mm) thick – about the roughness of a piece of sandpaper – will adversely affect an aircraft's performance by decreasing lift and increasing drag and its minimum stalling speed. The absence on the DC-8 of wing leading edge high-lift devices would have increased its susceptibility to the effects of icing.

Another significant operational factor revealed in the inquiry was that the load sheet did not correspond to the actual weight of the aircraft at the time of the take-off, with the amount being underestimated by some 14,000 lb (6,400 kg). This could be explained by the fact that the crew did not take into account the nature of the passenger load, especially when considering that with personal supplies and (unloaded) weapons, the weight of each soldier would have been more than the 170 lb (77 kg) allotted to each passenger when carrying civilians. Though *N950JW* was neither overloaded nor improperly loaded, this under-estimation of weight would have been a factor in the determination of the correct take-off reference speeds and the setting of the aircraft's horizontal stabiliser, with a heavier load requiring both higher velocities and a

higher nose-up setting. Other evidence suggested that the crew may have inadvertently used reference speeds for a take-off weight that was approximately 35,000 lb (16,000 kg) less than the actual load.

Although there were no indications of any major pre-impact mechanical failures, the damage sustained by the aircraft's No 4 engine was consistent with a lower rotational speed, perhaps as little as about 50 per cent of the norm. The power plant had been running at a higher temperature than the others during the flight to Cairo, prompting the crew to throttle it back slightly, and the same procedure was probably being used in the take-off from Gander.

It was concluded in the investigative report that rotation had been initiated at around 5 mph (10 kmh), and possibly as much as 10 mph (c 15 kmh), below the appropriate speed. After the DC-8 became airborne, and as it flew over the rough, down-sloping terrain, the benefits of the ground effect decreased, and its degraded aerodynamic performance would have become apparent to the pilots. At that time the pitch attitude was probably increased to counter the lower than normal rate of climb, but simultaneously the drag effects of the icing would have reduced its rate of acceleration, which was followed rapidly by a loss of air speed. Further performance degradation could have resulted from a compressor surge in the No 4 engine. Due to a higher speed and lower angle of attack than that normally expected in a stalled condition, there was probably little or no warning from the stall-alert system.

Its undercarriage still down and flaps partially extended, the DC-8 initially struck the trees while in a slightly nose-high attitude and banked a few degrees to the right, and the jetliner then yawed to starboard as it began to disintegrate. The duration of the flight was approximately 20 sec.

The final report was not unanimously endorsed. In a dissenting opinion, four of the nine CASB members wrote that the findings of the investigation did not totally support the conclusions. They noted that the ground handlers had not observed any ice on the aircraft prior to its departure, and contended that its attitude after the take-off was not consistent with a stall. The minority opinion was that the four thrust reversers may have been deployed prior to impact and that the deceleration experienced after the take-off more likely resulted from a substantial loss of power plant thrust than from icing.

The dissenters also raised the possibility of an in-flight fire. They noted that eye-witnesses had reported an orange or yellow glow somewhere on the aircraft before it crashed (which the majority suspected may have been confused with either the effects of engine compressor stalls and surges associated with a reduction in air intake due to its pitch angle, or with its external lighting), and that medical findings also pointed to a pre-impact blaze. Toxicological tests disclosed evidence of carbon monoxide and hydrogen cyanide in many of the victims, suggesting smoke inhalation prior to death. Though the majority report concluded that more than half of the occupants may not have been killed immediately, the dissenters expressed the belief that the impact was non-survivable and that the victims had been exposed to toxic fumes beforehand.

Although the manifest did not list any ordnance or explosives being carried aboard the DC-8, the minority report suggested this possibility. Moreover, the nature of the flight, its point of origin and the state of world affairs at the time also fuelled speculation that *N950JW* had been sabotaged by pro-Iranian terrorists. Considering all these factors, the dissenting report held that explosive detonations in a cargo hold had caused catastrophic systems failures in the aircraft.

One of the safety recommendations made by the CASB was to use actual rather than standard average weights in calculations when the passenger load differs from the norm in air carrier operations.

Though not directly related to this crash, the US Federal Aviation Administration (FAA) subsequently uncovered numerous shortcomings in the maintenance and operating practices of Arrow Air.

Date: 18 January 1986 (c 08:00)
Location: Near San Andres, Peten, Guatemala
Operator: Aerovias de Guatemala SA
Aircraft type: Sud-Aviation Caravelle VI-N (*HC-BAE*)

All 94 persons aboard (88 passengers and a crew of six) perished when the jetliner, which had been leased from the Ecuadorean carrier SAETA and was on a scheduled domestic service from the city of Guatemala, crashed and exploded in a hilly jungle area some 150 miles (250 km) north-north-east of the national capital.

Reportedly, the accident occurred during a low overcast as the Caravelle was attempting to land at the Santa Elena airport, having already initiated one overshoot manoeuvre.

Charred wreckage and levelled trees mark the scene of the troop transport disaster in Newfoundland. (UPI/Bettmann)

Date: 31 March 1986 (c 09:15)
Location: Near Maravatio, Michoacan, Mexico
Operator: Compania Mexicana de Aviacion SA (Mexico)
Aircraft type: Boeing Advanced 727-264 (*XA-MEM*)

Operating as Flight 940, the jet airliner crashed and burned about 15 min after taking off from Benito Juarez International Airport, serving Mexico City, bound for Puerto Vallarta, Jalisco, the first segment of a service with an ultimate destination of Los Angeles, California, US. All 167 persons aboard (159 passengers and eight crew members) perished.

The 727 had reached flight level 310 before the crew declared an emergency and requested descent clearance. Subsequently, the aircraft plummeted into mountainous terrain some 100 miles (150 km) north-west of the capital city.

It was determined that a left main gear tyre had burst, possibly due to drag and resultant overheating of the corresponding brake during the take-off ground run, the blast shattering a portion of the port wing, rupturing fuel and hydraulic lines, severing electrical cables and causing cabin decompression. Spilt fuel then must have ignited, touching off a fire, with a resultant loss of control and in-flight break-up.

Date: 31 August 1986 (11:52)
Location: Cerritos, California, US
First aircraft
Operator: Aeronaves de Mexico SA de CV (Aeromexico)
Type: McDonnell Douglas DC-9 Series 32 (*XA-JED*)
Second aircraft
Operator: Private
Type: Piper PA-28-181 Archer II (*N4891F*)

The disaster that had been predicted and feared for many years – a collision between a commercial transport and one of the many light aircraft that fly over the Los Angeles basin – struck with a vengeance on this sunny Sunday.

Designated as Flight 498, which had last stopped at Tijuana, Mexico, during a service originating at Mexico City, the DC-9 was scheduled to land at Los Angeles International Airport, and was operating under instrument flight rules (IFR) and positive control.

Meanwhile the Archer, carrying a married couple and their daughter, took off from Torrance Municipal Airport, bound for Big Bear in the San Bernardino Mountains of Southern California; it was operating under visual flight rules (VFR). In accordance with these procedures, it was to have remained outside of the Los Angeles Terminal Control Area (TCA). However, it did not do so, straying into the restricted airspace only 8 minutes into the flight as it proceeded eastward, on a crossing path with Flight 498, which was descending on a north-westerly heading. The weather was clear, with a visibility of about 15 miles (25 km).

The two aircraft collided at right angles and at an approximate height of 6,500 ft (1,980 m), with the horizontal stabiliser of *XA-JED* slicing into the upper cockpit section of *N4891F* and separating. The jetliner rolled over on to its back and plunged in a steep nose-down attitude into a residential area just north of the Artesia Freeway and some 20 miles (30 km) east-south-east of the airport, disintegrating in a ball of fire on impact, while the light aeroplane crashed in an open schoolyard about 1,500 ft (500 m) away. All 64 persons aboard the DC-9 (58 passengers and a crew of six), the three occupants of the Archer, who had been decapitated in the collision, and 15 others on the ground, all in the area where *XA-JED* fell, perished in the disaster. Eight persons were injured and 18 houses destroyed or damaged.

In its investigative report, the US National Transportation Safety Board (NTSB) attributed the accident to limitations in the air traffic control system, in the areas of both procedures and automated redundancy. The major contributing element, and what in fact some observers in the aviation community regarded as the primary cause, was the unauthorised entry of *N4891F* into the TCA.

An autopsy performed on the body of the 53-year-old private pilot revealed moderate to severe coronary arteriosclerosis, triggering speculation that the intrusion had occurred after he became incapacitated by a heart attack. However, a reconstruction of its flight path indicated that the aircraft was under control up until the collision. The pilot was described as methodical and professional in his approach to flying, with an awareness of the Los Angeles TCA and the regulations concerning its use and avoidance. As further proof of this, a TCA chart was found opened in the cockpit wreckage. Given the facts, the NTSB concluded that he had flown into the area inadvertently, probably after misidentifying his navigational check-points.

Also factoring in the accident were the limitations of the 'see and be seen' concept to ensure traffic separation. Tests demonstrated that each aircraft should have been visible to the other's crew in sufficient time to avoid the collision, especially in the case of the general aviation pilot; however, there was no evidence of any such prior sighting or evasive manoeuvres.

The Archer was equipped with a functioning non-encoding transponder, which would have made it observable on radar, and, indeed, a tape recording of the display did show the echo of

N4891F. This evidence contradicted the approach controller's statement that its target 'was not displayed'.

One reason that the controller did not see the Archer was that he had been distracted by a second light aeroplane, a Grumman Tiger also operating under VFR, that penetrated the TCA, its pilot requesting control assistance. Fearing a potential conflict with a commuter aircraft, he radioed the Tiger with a suggestion 'In the future you look at your TCA chart'. When he returned his attention to Flight 498, its target had disappeared from the radarscope. It was also considered possible that the controller had unintentionally discounted the radar return of the Archer, sans altitude information, believing it to be beneath the restricted airspace; that he had been distracted from his traffic monitoring duties when asked to relay to the DC-9 instructions for a change in landing runways; or that he may not have observed the target because the display had been weakened by the effects on the radar of an atmospheric temperature inversion. It could not be determined whether one or a combination of these factors prevented him from spotting the general aviation aeroplane and perhaps giving the Aeromexico crew a traffic advisory.

Subsequent to this disaster, the US Federal Aviation Administration (FAA) enacted a requirement that all aircraft flying within 30 nautical miles (55 km) of the primary airport in a TCA be fitted with altitude-encoding transponders.

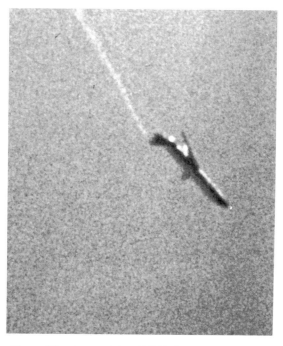

Above *The Aeromexico DC-9 dives to earth in an inverted attitude following the collision with a light aircraft.* (Photo by Al Francis; Sygma)

Below *The scene of devastation in the neighbourhood of a Los Angeles suburb where the jetliner fell.* (Wide World Photos)

Date: 6 November 1986 (c 11:30)
Location: Off Shetland Isles, Scotland
Operator: British International Helicopters Ltd
Aircraft type: Boeing/Vertol 234LR Commercial
Chinook (*G-BWFC*)

In history's worst commercial helicopter accident, 45 persons aboard were killed when the twin-rotor, turbine-engine aircraft, on a non-scheduled service and carrying workers from the Brent oil field, plummeted into the North Sea approximately 3 miles (5 km) east of Sumburgh Airport, located some 20 miles (30 km) south of Lerwick, where it was to have landed.

One passenger and the captain, one of three crew members assigned to *G-BWFC*, escaped with their lives. Though rescued by another helicopter only about 10 min after the crash, both survivors were seriously injured and suffered from hypothermia, with a considerable amount of water having entered their survival suits. The bodies of all but one of the victims were later found, and in every case death was due to trauma rather than drowning.

The local weather at the time was adverse, with rain, a visibility of around 12 miles (20 km), scattered cumulus clouds down to 1,500 ft (c 500 m), and winds gusting up to almost 40 knots. The ocean was rough.

Approximately 90 per cent of the rotorcraft's wreckage, most of which had sunk in water some 300 ft (100 m) deep, was subsequently recovered, and examination of the debris revealed the apparent cause of the accident, a fracture of the main spiral bevel ring gear in the forward transmission assembly that left a gap about ¾ in (2 cm) wide. Although the gap was equivalent to only two or three teeth, it had the effect of changing the ratio between the bevel ring gear and the pinion of the synchronising shaft, running from the rear engine transmission, part of the delicate mechanism designed to provide proper separation of the counter-rotating main blades. The resulting loss of separation may have occurred in less than 2 seconds and caused the aft rotors to overtake and clash with the forward ones. Damage to the blades would then have led to rotor imbalance, with the aft pylon structure ultimately breaking away, taking with it the transmission components. After the rotor assembly had been torn off, the helicopter fell in a tail-down attitude from an approximate height of 500 ft (150 m).

Evidence indicated that the gear failure originated from fatigue cracking associated with a groove formed by a combination of wear and corrosion in the bolted joint that attached it to the shaft. The corrosion appeared to have been aggravated by water in the aircraft's oil supply, which was possibly related to the marine environment in which *G-BWFC* had been operating.

The joint was of a modified design that had been

A Boeing/Vertol 234LR Commercial Chinook, shown in the livery of British Airways Helicopters (the predecessor of British International Helicopters), which was the type involved in the North Sea disaster. (Boeing)

recently introduced, with the requirement that operators check bolt torque between overhauls. Boeing/Vertol and the government regulating agencies representing the nation of manufacture (the US Federal Aviation Administration (FAA)) and of registration (the British Civil Aviation Authority (CAA)) had failed to predict the different operational characteristics of the new design and detect its inherent weakness.

Among the recommendations made in its accident report by the British Air Accidents Investigation Branch (AIB) was a review of certification procedures to assure that all modifications to vital components be adequately scrutinised and tested before being approved for use and more closely monitored after their introduction into service.

Date: 9 May 1987 (11:12)
Location: Near Warsaw, Poland
Operator: Polskie Linie Lotnicze (LOT Polish Airlines)
Aircraft type: Ilyushin Il-62MK (*SP-LBG*)

The jet airliner had taken off earlier from Okecie Airport, serving the nation's capital, on a non-scheduled transatlantic service to New York City. While at a height of about 26,000 ft (8,000 m) and climbing to its cruising altitude, its No 2 engine experienced an uncontained failure that was attributed to a worn ball-bearing and resulted in eccentric rotation of a high-pressure turbine crankshaft.

A faulty support for the crankshaft then gave way under the stresses generated, sending the crankshaft smashing into a low-pressure turbine. This in turn caused the turbine's fan to spin out of control, disintegrating due to centrifugal force. Flying debris shredded the No 1 power plant and penetrated the aircraft's fuselage, damaging elevator controls, cutting electric cables and resulting in cabin decompression. Fire also erupted in the baggage compartment, but there was no instrument indication of such because of the severed electric cables.

The pilots, using the trim tabs to maintain control, initiated a descent and returned to their point of departure, but during a straight-in landing approach the jet crashed and burned in a wooded area approximately 3 miles (5 km) short of the runway. All 183 persons aboard (172 passengers and a crew of 11) perished in the disaster, which occurred after a loss of control due to the fire. The meteorological conditions were not a factor in the crash.

Subsequent to the accident, a fuel tank located in the vertical stabiliser was removed from this particular model of Il-62, and the time between overhauls on the aircraft's D-30KU engines was reduced.

Date: 16 August 1987 (20:45)
Location: Romulus, Michigan, US
Operator: Northwest Airlines (US)
Aircraft type: McDonnell Douglas DC-9 Super 82 (*N312RC*)

Operating as Flight 255, the jetliner took off from Runway 03C at Detroit Metropolitan Wayne County Airport, bound for Phoenix,

Smouldering wreckage lies in the wooded area where the LOT Polish Airlines Il-62MK crashed during an emergency landing attempt. (Wide World Photos)

Arizona, one segment of a domestic service originating at Saginaw, Michigan, with an ultimate destination of Orange County, in Southern California. Only 14 sec after becoming airborne and while at an approximate height of 50 ft (15 m) above the ground, the aircraft struck, with its port wing, a lamp standard located about half a mile (0.8 km) beyond the end of the runway.

Its undercarriage still in the process of retracting, the DC-9 then clipped other lamp standards and the roof of a building and rolled to the left in excess of 90 degrees before it slammed to earth, disintegrated and burst into flames, scattering wreckage along a road and under a railroad and two highway overpasses. A total of 156 persons were killed in the disaster, including the aircraft's six crew members and two occupants of vehicles hit by the crashing jetliner. The sole surviving passenger was a four-year-old girl travelling with her parents and brother, who suffered severe burns, a fractured skull and

other impact-related trauma. Five other persons on the ground were also injured, one seriously, and numerous vehicles, three on the road and the rest parked in a rental-car lot, destroyed.

Examination of the debris disclosed no evidence of a malfunction in the aircraft's engines, flight controls or avionics that could have directly contributed to the accident. One significant find was made, however: its flaps and leading edge slats were determined to be retracted at the time of the crash. This was further corroborated by the position of the cockpit flap/slat handle and by the digital flight data recorder (DFDR) read-out, which includes these items among its transcribed parameters.

Playback of the cockpit voice recorder (CVR) tape also revealed that the two-man flight crew neither called for nor carried out the taxi check-list, on which the extension of the flaps and slats is the first item. In accordance with Northwest

Diagram illustrating the flight profiles of the DC-9 Super 80 series in different configurations, including the one (solid line) that led to the crash at Detroit airport. (National Transportation Safety Board)

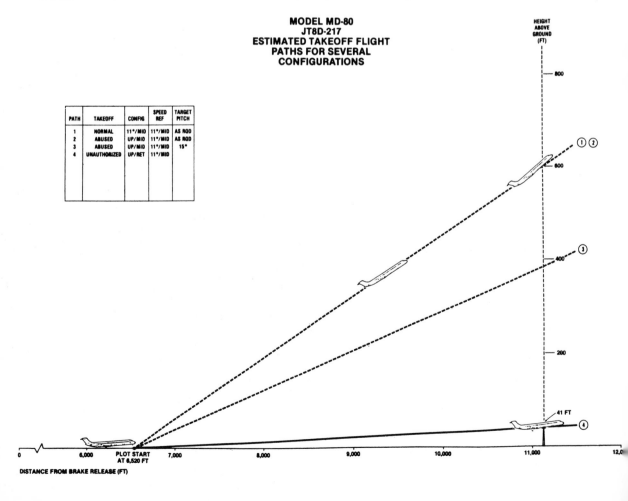

procedures, the first officer usually sets them after the start of the taxi, but at around the time that this should have been done, the co-pilot of *N312RC* was receiving information regarding a change of take-off runways. There was speculation that by the time he finished copying this automatic terminal information service (ATIS) message, the DC-9 had progressed beyond the point where the extension would normally be completed, which may have misled him to believe that the task had been accomplished.

The stated policy of the airline is that the captain is supposed to initiate the check-list routine. The captain of Flight 255 did not ask for the after-start, taxi or before-take-off checks, relegating this responsibility to his first officer, who did not follow suit. These and other factors, including confusion over the location of a particular taxiway despite the fact that the pilot had flown into this airport many times, led the US National Transportation Safety Board (NTSB) to conclude in its investigative report that the conduct of the crew did not conform to air carrier standards, even though both pilots had gained a reputation for competence and professionalism from their peers. The omission of the taxi check-list was, in fact, regarded by the Board as the primary cause of the disaster.

The Super DC-9 is equipped with a sophisticated control aural warning system (CAWS), which has an important component designed to recognise the conditions that could precipitate a stall, such as an improper flap/slat configuration, and is activated by movement of the thrust levers. No such aural warning (consisting of a voice stating 'flaps' and/or 'slats') was transcribed by the CVR, which the NTSB attributed to a loss of electrical power to the system. This may have resulted from intentional action by the crew or maintenance personnel; from a transient overload; or because the circuit breaker did not allow the current to flow to the CAWS power supply and did not annunciate the condition by tripping. The power loss was considered the principal contributing factor in the crash.

The absence of extended flaps and slats would have severely limited the climb capability and increased the aircraft's stalling speed. This accounted for its relatively long take-off ground run and the fact that *N312RC* assumed a higher than normal pitch angle after becoming airborne, while gaining little altitude. The stick-shaker stall-warning system was heard on the CVR tape to activate less than a second after lift-off. Once in the air the jetliner began rocking laterally, which the crew attempted to control by deploying the spoilers. The 'Dutch roll' motions and corrective action further degraded the performance of the DC-9.

A section of the left outer wing some 18 ft (5.5 m) long was torn off in the initial impact with the lamp standard, rupturing fuel tanks. Escaping fuel was then ingested into the aircraft's No 1 power plant and ignited, thus explaining the in-flight fire reported by some witnesses.

The accident occurred at twilight; the weather at the time was fair, with a high overcast and scattered clouds down to 2,500 ft (c 750 m), a visibility of around 5 miles (10 km) and a 12-knot wind out of the west. Wind shear advisories had been broadcast shortly before the departure of Flight 255, although there was no evidence from available information, including the DFDR read-out, that such a condition in any way contributed to the crash. Nevertheless, the alert may have influenced the actions of the crew, even to the point of reducing their ability to escape from the stall. The captain, who was flying the aircraft, apparently increased its pitch angle after the stall warning, indicating that he suspected an encounter with wind shear; stall recovery procedures normally involve lowering the nose and

Wreckage of the Northwest Airlines jetliner is scattered beneath road and railroad bridges after the disaster that claimed 156 lives. (Wide World Photos)

extending the flaps, which in this case would probably have prevented the disaster.

Subsequently, all operators of the Super DC-9 incorporated a crew check-list procedure to assure that the CAWS was functional prior to take-off. The NTSB also recommended that the system's fail light be modified to compensate for one shortcoming, ie its inability to annunciate in the event of a power loss.

In May 1991 a US federal court rejected Northwest Airlines' contention that McDonnell Douglas share responsibility for the accident, ruling that the carrier was liable for all damages resulting therefrom.

Date: 31 August 1987 (c 15:30)
Location: Off Ko Phuket, Thailand
Operator: Thai Airways
Aircraft type: Boeing Advanced 737-2P5 (*HS-TBC*)

All 83 persons aboard (74 passengers and a crew of nine) were killed when the jet airliner, designated as Flight 365, crashed in the Andaman Sea about 10 miles (15 km) east of Phuket International Airport, where it was scheduled to land while on a domestic service from Hat Yai to Bangkok. Most of the victims' bodies were later recovered, as was debris that included both the aircraft's flight data (FDR) and cockpit voice (CVR) recorders.

During the approach, conducted in good meteorological conditions along the 115-degree very-high-frequency omni-directional range (VOR) radial, the pilots expressed concern over another Boeing 737, flown by the Hong Kong carrier Dragonair, which was also landing at the airport but behind and some 500 ft (150 m) lower than their aircraft and navigating along the 025-degree radial. This was believed to have led to a lapse in concentration to the point that they failed to monitor their air speed, allowing it to fall below the minimum limit. The Thai jet then stalled and plunged into the water from an approximate altitude of 3,000 ft (1,000 m), which was too low to allow for recovery.

Besides the pilot error, the air traffic controller involved was blamed for failing to keep the two aircraft adequately separated. The investigative commission ruled that although Flight 365 was closer to the airport, it should have been instructed to execute an overshoot. The controller did in fact authorise the Dragonair 737 to land first, but then reversed his instructions and gave the clearance to the Thai crew.

As a result of this accident, two air traffic controllers were re-assigned and their supervisor faced a disciplinary hearing. Plans were also made to install radar at the Phuket airport.

Date: 28 November 1987 (c 04:00)
Location: Indian Ocean
Operator: South African Airways
Aircraft type: Boeing 747-244B Combi (*ZS-SAS*)

Everything was normal for the first 9½ hr of Flight 295, which had originated at T'aipei, Taiwan, with an ultimate destination of Johannesburg, South Africa, and an en route stop planned on the island of Mauritius. The first hint of trouble was when the pilot-in-command reported smoke and that the 747 had initiated a descent to flight level 140. He then declared an emergency, and shortly afterwards radioed 'Now we have lost a lot of electrics. We haven't got anything on the . . . aircraft now'.

Approximately 3 min after the last message from the flight, the wide-bodied jetliner plunged into the sea some 150 miles (250 km) north-east of Sir Seewoosagur Ramgoolam-Plaisance International Airport, serving Mahebourg, Mauritius, which it was trying to reach, disintegrating into thousands of pieces on impact and leaving a trail of debris on the ocean floor in water about 15,000 ft (5,000 m) deep. All 159 persons aboard (140 passengers and 19 crew members) perished. The crash occurred in pre-dawn darkness, but the local weather was apparently good, with a visibility of at least 5 miles (10 km) and scattered cumulus and strato-cumulus clouds.

Some wreckage, including articles of light cargo and cabin furnishings, was found floating in the ocean, some as far away as the coast of South Africa. Debris that washed ashore on the beaches of Madagascar could not be retrieved due to political animosity between that nation and South Africa. Of the three recording devices fitted to the aircraft, only the cockpit voice recorder (CVR) was recovered, providing useful information despite an incomplete transcript. The main wreckage was later photographed and videotaped on the sea bed, and a few vital parts were raised. Human remains were also found, but only five victims could be identified.

There was sufficient evidence for the investigative board to conclude that fire had erupted prior to impact in the front pallet on the right side in the upper deck cargo hold of the 747. Numerous articles being carried in the compartment were found to have been burned, as was the structure itself. Some of the panels in the passenger cabin adjoining that section were also covered with soot.

The evidence was, however, insufficient for a determination of the source of ignition. The freight items consisted largely of computer components, some of which had been filled with nickel cadmium or lithium batteries, but these were not considered hazardous.

The cardboard and plastic packing materials in the cargo hold were undoubtedly involved in the blaze, which could have developed rapidly, as in a 'flash' fire, even before the smoke sensors activated the alarm system. The burning of these materials would have produced the smoke mentioned by the captain, as well as carbon dioxide and carbon monoxide, noxious elements that must have penetrated the passenger compartment and possibly the flight deck. Autopsies revealed carbon monoxide poisoning in two of the victims, and it was considered a 'real possibility' that some, if not all, of the passengers and cabin staff had succumbed to the effects of the toxic fumes even before the crash.

The members of the flight crew, who were probably using their emergency oxygen masks, at least until the descent to a lower altitude, could also have been incapacitated, or at least suffered from the impairment of their physical or intellectual capacities. Disorientation consequent on reduced cockpit visibility due to the smoke or pilot distraction could also have led or contributed to the uncontrolled descent. One plausible scenario was that as the crew concentrated on the emergency, the jetliner continued to lose height until it hit the sea while in a tail-down attitude. Its fuselage then could have broken in two, with indications that the front section slammed into the water with its wings perpendicular to the surface of the ocean.

Another possibility, or additional causative factor, was that the blaze had affected the aircraft's structure or systems. Heat damage to the skin and flying controls, specifically the cable pulley clusters for the elevators, rudder, rudder trim and the manual operation of the horizontal stabiliser was, in fact, confirmed.

Had a crew member actually entered the cargo hold to fight the fire, the task would have been made difficult by the heat and limited visibility attributable to the smoke and/or loss of lighting caused by the damage to the electrical wiring. The use of the re-circulating fans, as required in the event of such an emergency, could have actually aggravated the situation by bringing smoke into the cabin. The blaze might have been contained or extinguished, but too late to prevent the crash.

Some two years after the disaster, the US Federal Aviation Administration (FAA) issued an airworthiness directive concerning Class B cargo compartments, ie those of a certain size and capacity that are easily accessible. Operators were given a choice of upgrading compartments to Class C, or self-contained, specifications; modifying them with fire detection, suppression and extinguishing features; or restricting the carriage of cargo to that placed in flame-resistant containers.

Date: 29 November 1987 (c 11:30)
Location: Off Western Burma (Myanmar)
Operator: Korean Air (South Korea)
Aircraft type: Boeing 707-3B5C (*HL-7406*)

The jet airliner, which was operating as Flight 858 and carrying 115 persons (104 passengers and a crew of 11), disappeared over the Andaman Sea while en route from Abu Dhabi, United Arab Emirates, to Bangkok, Thailand, one segment of a service originating at Baghdad, Iraq, with an ultimate destination of Seoul, South Korea. Subsequently, a partially inflated liferaft identified as belonging to *HL-7406* was recovered from the water some 30 miles (50 km) south-west of the mouth of the Ye River, but no survivors or bodies were found.

Minutes after the last radio transmission from the flight, which was a routine position report, a witness on a fishing-boat observed a bright flash in the sky followed by smoke trailing into the sea. At the time the aircraft would have been at an altitude of 37,000 ft (c 11,300 m).

Two days later, a Korean couple suspected of sabotaging the 707 swallowed poison before they could be arrested in Bahrain, and one of them, an elderly man, died. His young female accomplice, who survived the suicide attempt, subsequently confessed to carrying a bomb when they boarded the flight at Baghdad and leaving it in an overhead rack in the passenger cabin when they disembarked at Abu Dhabi. Hidden in a carry-on bag, the device consisted of a high-yield plastic explosive concealed inside a portable radio and a bottle of liquid explosive, with a time-delayed detonator mechanism. The blast would have been sufficient to cause immediate partial disintegration of the aircraft. South Korea claimed North Korean complicity in the mass murder.

Condemned to death, the saboteur was pardoned by the President of South Korea in 1990.

Date: 18 January 1988 (c 22:15)
Location: Near Chungking, Sichuan, China
Operator: China Southwest Airlines
Aircraft type: Ilyushin Il-18D (*B-222*)

Designated as Flight 4146, the turboprop transport crashed and burned while only about 10 min away from its scheduled landing at the city's Jiangbei Airport, during a domestic service from Beijing (Peking), killing all 108 persons aboard (98 passengers and 10 crew members).

Prior to the disaster, the right starter in the aircraft's No 4 power plant had become so hot that the feathering oil tube was burned, rupturing when the crew tried to feather the corresponding propeller. The engine then caught fire, with the pylon separating. Severe shaking subsequently caused the No 1 propeller to feather, and the Il-18 plunged into farmland after a loss of control.

The accident was blamed on lax maintenance, and a subsequent safety check reportedly led to the grounding of a number of other aircraft. The crash occurred in darkness, but the weather was not a factor.

Date: 17 March 1988 (13:17)
Location: Near Cucuta, Norte de Santander, Colombia
Operator: Aerovias Nacionales de Colombia SA (AVIANCA)
Aircraft type: Boeing 727-21 (*HK-1716*)

All 139 persons aboard (132 passengers and a crew of seven) perished when the jetliner, operating as Flight 410, struck a mountain a few minutes after taking off from the city's Camilo Daza Airport, on a domestic service to Barranquilla and Cartagena, both in Atlantico.

The accident, which occurred in conditions of mist and haze, was attributed to error by the pilot-in-command, who carried out the departure under visual flight rules (VFR) procedures. Following the take-off from Runway 33, the 727 turned left to a heading of 300 degrees, which was maintained until it crashed at an approximate elevation of 6,000 ft (1,800 m).

It was subsequently recommended that instrument flight rules (IFR) procedures be used in all jet operations during departures and landings, and that strict controls be imposed limiting the access of anyone other than crew members to the cockpit of commercial aircraft.

Date: 3 July 1988 (c 10:30)
Location: Persian Gulf
Operator: Iran Air
Aircraft type: Airbus Industrie A300B2-202 (*EP-IBU*)

The US government had committed naval forces to the convoying of Kuwaiti oil tankers sailing in the Persian Gulf in May 1987. This policy was implemented to counter attacks on commercial ships, which had become a part of the eight-year war between Iran and Iraq. The involvement had proven costly for the United States: only days into the operation, 37 American sailors lost their lives in a supposedly accidental missile attack on the frigate *Stark* by an Iraqi Mirage jet fighter.

As a result of the *Stark* incident, US commanders were given a revised set of 'rules of engagement' that clarified their authority to take protective measures when faced with 'hostile intent'. Prior to 3 July 1988, American forces in the Gulf were alerted to the probability of significant Iranian military activity, this in retaliation for recent Iraqi military successes. That period covered the American Independence Day holiday weekend.

On this particular Sunday morning, the US Navy cruiser *Vincennes* was directed to an area in the Strait of Hormuz where a number of Iranian gunboats were reportedly threatening merchant vessels. Some 2 hours later, a helicopter assigned to the warship was fired upon by one of the small boats. A short surface battle ensued involving the

Vincennes and an American frigate, the *Elmer Montgomery*.

During this period of time, Iran Air Flight 655 took off from the Bandar Abbas airport, which also served military aircraft, including (American-built) F-14 jet fighters. Almost immediately, the target representing the A300 was spotted on radar by the crew of the *Vincennes*. Shortly afterwards, reports of Iranian F-14 activity were heard in the vessel's combat identification centre, and a Mode II identification of friend or foe (IFF) transponder indication, normally associated with a military aircraft, was detected. The target was identified by the crew to be an F-14.

As the wide-bodied jet airliner proceeded on towards the combat area, bound for Dubai, United Arab Emirates, and on an approximate heading of 200 degrees, it was given a number of warnings, one from another American warship, the frigate *John Sides*, and the rest from the *Vincennes*. Challenges were made on both the military air distress (MAD) and international air defence (IAD) radio frequencies and included the threat of defensive action.

At this point the crew of the *Vincennes* were faced with a multiplicity of ongoing events. Besides the potential threat of an air attack, they were still engaged in a sea battle. One of the vessel's guns had become fouled, necessitating constant manoeuvres in order to keep its remaining gun unmasked. Meanwhile, an Iranian P-3 Orion patrol aircraft was airborne some 70 miles (110 km) to the north-west of the scene, conceivably furnishing targeting information to the suspected fighter.

Under the pressure of the moment, the commanding officer of the *Vincennes*, Captain Will Rogers III, did what he felt he had to do – defend his ship – and ordered the launch of two Standard surface-to-air missiles at the target. The A300 was hit seconds later, while still about 10 miles (15 km) away from the vessel and at an altitude of 13,500 ft (c 4,100 m); it then plummeted into the Strait. All 290 persons aboard (278 passengers and 12 crew members) perished. Floating debris and victims were later found in the water some 5 miles (10 km) east of the island of Henqam, with nearly 200 bodies subsequently being recovered.

The tragedy was investigated by both the US Navy and the International Civil Aviation Organisation (ICAO). The Navy report showed a divergence between the recollection of witnesses and tape recordings of the *Vincennes*'s AEGIS defence/radar system. Perhaps the most significant discrepancy was the identification of *EP-IBU* as belonging to the military despite the radar display clearly registering a Mode III transponder code, an indication (though not unequivocal evidence) of a civilian aircraft.

The misidentification apparently occurred after a temporary Mode II signal was detected by the ship

An Iran Air A300B2-202, identical to the aircraft shot down over the Persian Gulf by a US Navy warship. (Airbus Industrie)

around the time that the A300 became airborne. The Naval investigative board believed that the transmission had emanated from a military aircraft, perhaps an F-14 or even a C-130 transport, which was still on the ground. This would have been possible even though the airport was out of the line of sight of the vessel because the atmospheric conditions in the Gulf at the time, with a high level of evaporation, were conducive to radar ducting, or bouncing of the signal. As Flight 655 lifted off, the ship's identification supervisor locked on to its track. As the radar echo of *EP-IBU* moved towards the *Vincennes*, it retained the identification as a fighter. Interestingly, only one officer in the vessel's combat centre suggested the possibility that it was a commercial airliner.

Another important discrepancy was between the constant crew reports of the aircraft descending and the transcribed data showing it as ascending. Its ground speed, recorded as 440 mph (c 710 kmh) at the moment of missile impact, had increased slightly during the period that it was tracked. In the excitement of an impending engagement, the reports of descending altitude could have happened if the tactical information co-ordinator passed on only range values, which were interpreted as height, or if he misread his read-out and interchanged altitude and range.

In the final 1 min 40 sec before the missile launch, the anti-air warfare officer informed the captain that the radar target had veered from its flight path and was rapidly descending, while increasing in speed, as it approached the *Vincennes*, yet he made no attempt to confirm these reports on his own. Quick reference to the read-out on the console directly in front of him would have immediately shown the increasing height. Rather, he relied on the judgement of one or two second-class petty officers, buttressed by his own preconceived perception of the threat, and made an erroneous assessment to the commanding officer,

according to the Navy report. The belief that the aircraft was rapidly descending directly towards the ship could have been pivotal in the decision to shoot it down.

It was further revealed that *EP-IBU* was operating within the established air corridor, A59, though off its centreline by approximately 3 or 4 miles (5-6.5 km). Its altitude was also below the norm for commercial air traffic, the route structure for which had been laid out on the large screen display (LSD) in the *Vincennes*'s combat centre.

Another factor was the failure of the Iran Air crew to heed the warnings. Although the A300 was not equipped to receive the MAD frequency, the pilots should have been aware of the company's instructions to monitor the IAD frequency when flying in the Gulf area. The absence of a response may indicate that they were not doing so, or perhaps did not identify theirs as the challenged aircraft.

Neither the *Vincennes* nor the *Elmer Montgomery* detected a weather radar emission from the target, which could have helped its identification as a commercial transport. However, as noted in the ICAO report, the meteorological conditions, consisting of an estimated 8–10 mile (c 13-15 km) visibility and scattered clouds at around 200 ft (60 m), would not have warranted use of the radar. (The weather was such that the ship's crew never did make visual contact with the airliner.)

The violent manoeuvring of the vessel, which caused gear to fall in the combat centre, the noise of gunfire, the flickering of lights on the LSD and shouting voices heightened the tension as the aircraft was being scrutinised. Time compression also played a significant role in the incident. Only 3 min 40 sec had elapsed from the time the captain became aware of the potential threat until he made the decision to engage.

In its report, the Navy defended the actions of Captain Rogers and his crew, referring to the destruction of Flight 655 as a 'tragic and regrettable accident'. It also placed considerable responsibility on Iran for allowing an airliner to operate in a 'war zone'.

Criticism, however, came from an unusual source, the captain of the *John Sides*. Writing in the magazine *Proceedings,* which is published by the US Naval Institute, Commander David R. Carlson claimed that the Airbus was shot down 'for no good reason'. He further wrote that the actions of the *Vincennes* 'appeared to be consistently aggressive', even before the day of the incident, and implied that the ship actually provoked the skirmish with the gunboats. The crew of the *John Sides* had also observed *EP-IBU* on radar, but Captain Carlson dismissed it as non-hostile.

Citing a lack of such in the Gulf area, the ICAO recommended co-ordination between military and civil units in accordance with established procedures to prevent a recurrence of the tragedy. The US Navy went further, suggesting that the ICAO change the commercial air route structure in this region and noting that an aircraft would only be considered as not a threat if it remained above 25,000 ft (c 7,500 m).

In early 1996, the US government agreed to pay collectively some 62 million dollars in damages to the families of those who lost their lives in the tragedy.

Date: 19 October 1988 (c 07:00)
Location: Near Ahmedabad, Gujarat, India
Operator: Indian Airlines
Aircraft type: Boeing 737-2A8 (*VT-EAH*)

Designated as Flight 113, the jetliner crashed during its final approach to land on Runway 23 at the city's airport, while on a domestic service originating at Bombay, killing 130 persons aboard, including the entire crew of six. Five seriously injured passengers survived the accident.

The aircraft reportedly undershot the runway, hitting trees and a high-tension pylon approximately 3 miles (5 km) short of its threshold, then slammed into a field and burned. At the time of the crash the airport and the immediate vicinity were shrouded in haze.

A precision approach would not have been possible due to the lack of an instrument landing system (ILS).

Date: 21 December 1988 (c 19:00)
Location: Lockerbie, Dumfriesshire, Scotland
Operator: Pan American World Airways (US)
Aircraft type: Boeing 747-121 (*N739PA*)

It was doubtful that any of those boarding Flight 103 knew of the threat hanging over them. Only 16 days earlier an anonymous telephone message had been received at the US Embassy in Helsinki,

Finland, warning that a sabotage attempt would be made some time over the succeeding two weeks against a Pan American aircraft flying between Frankfurt, (West) Germany, and the United States. Word of the threat was passed on from the US Federal Aviation Administration (FAA) to various American embassies, presumably to give government employees a chance to make alternative travel arrangements if they chose, and to the carrier itself. But the general public was not made aware of the warning, on the rationale that such action would only serve to give the perpetrators publicity, and thus credibility, while potentially bringing financial harm to the airline industry. Besides, the threat had been dismissed as a hoax by some authorities.

A Boeing 727 was used on the initial leg of the transatlantic service. During a scheduled stop at London, the 49 continuing passengers were transferred to the larger 747 and joined by 194 others, making a total of 243 aboard the aircraft. In addition there were 16 crew members assigned to *N739PA*. Baggage, which had been originally screened at Frankfurt, was also transferred, without further scrutiny. Running almost half an hour late, the wide-bodied jetliner then took off from Heathrow Airport for New York City.

Not quite 40 min later, while cruising on an approximate heading of 320 degrees at flight level 310, in darkness and weather conditions consisting of broken clouds at lower altitudes and good visibility, the 747 disintegrated after a powerful explosion in a baggage container positioned on the left side of its forward cargo hold, scattering wreckage and victims over a wide area. Its wings and centre fuselage section then fell into the Sherwood Crescent residential district of Lockerbie, ploughing a crater some 150 ft (50 m) long and about 30 ft (10 m) deep and exploding in a ball of fire. All 259 persons aboard the aircraft and 11 on the ground perished. Five others were injured and more than 20 houses destroyed outright or damaged beyond repair.

A week after the disaster, the British Air Accidents Investigation Branch (AIB) confirmed what many had already suspected, that Flight 103 had been sabotaged. The AIB found evidence of a 'detonating high explosive', believed to have been the plastic Semtex. Some recovered items, identified as parts of baggage containers, exhibited damage consistent with such a blast. The bomb had apparently been hidden in the shell of a radio-cassette player that was being carried in a suitcase.

The direct effect of the explosion was to produce a high-intensity shock wave that ruptured the side and base of the container. As the wave expanded outward, it shattered and deformed the inner surface of the fuselage skin. A secondary high-pressure wave, which resulted somewhat from reflections off the baggage behind the immediate area of the blast but primarily from the chemical changes of the explosive itself after detonation, caused the skin to stretch and blister before bursting out in a star pattern, with fractures propagating in different directions.

The blast created a large hole, the approximate dimensions of which were 5 ft (1.5 m) wide and 15 ft (5 m) high, in the left belly area of the 747, forward of the wing, and also disrupted the main cabin floor. Within 3 seconds of the explosion, the forward fuselage section separated completely. Simultaneously, the rest of the jetliner entered a manoeuvre involving a marked nose-down and left-rolling attitude, which probably resulted from inputs applied to the control cables due to the disruption of the upper deck floor and main deck beams. The descent of the aircraft steepened throughout the break-up sequence, becoming vertical at a height of around 19,000 ft (5,800 m). All four engines broke away in the air, and the rear fuselage disintegrated during the vertical plunge.

A major portion of the fuselage plummeted into a housing estate in the Rosebank Crescent district of Lockerbie, and the forward part, including the flight deck, was found in rolling terrain about 2.5 miles (4 km) east of the town. Carried by the westerly winds, lighter pieces of debris were scattered in two main paths stretching eastward past the town of Langholm and all the way to the eastern coast of England, a distance of some 80 miles (130 km).

A multi-national inquiry into the bombing of Flight 103 was conducted, and a number of theories as to its motive were postulated. Given the most credibility initially was that the terrorist act had been carried out by the Popular Front for the Liberation of Palestine General Command, an organisation based in Syria with financial support from the Iranian government, this in retaliation for the accidental downing of the Iran Air A300 by a US warship earlier in the year (see separate entry, 3 July 1988). Some 2½ years after the Lockerbie tragedy, a joint American/British investigation had shifted its focus towards Libya as perpetrator of the massacre, carried out to avenge the US bombing of its capital city in April 1986 (which was itself in retaliation for a terrorist attack).

In November 1991 the US Justice Department announced its indictment of two alleged Libyan intelligence agents wanted in connection with the Pan Am disaster. Reportedly they had planted the explosive device in a suitcase that was carried from Malta to Frankfurt on an Air Malta flight, then interlined on to 103. The primary clue in the criminal investigation was the minute portion of a timer, found embedded in a piece of the luggage container, which had been manufactured in Switzerland and sold to Libya in 1985. Were it not for the delayed departure from London, the 747 would have crashed in the Atlantic Ocean, perhaps blotting out all evidence that it was destroyed by a bomb.

One of the recommendations made by the AIB in its investigative report was to explore ways of reducing the vulnerability of commercial aircraft to explosive damage.

A crater and gutted houses mark the scene of devastation where a large portion of the Pan Am 747 fell in Lockerbie. (Reuters/Bettmann)

Relatively intact, the cockpit and front fuselage section of N739PA lies in the Scottish countryside. (Wide World Photos)

Pan American received harsh criticism for lax security in the wake of the tragedy, and both the airline and the US government for not announcing the prior warning. Slightly more than a year later a similar threat made against a Northwest Airlines transatlantic flight was made known to ticketholders. Although the jetliner reached its intended destination without incident, this marked a change in American policy with regard to potential acts of terrorism.

Date: 8 February 1989 (13:08)
Location: Santa Maria, Azores, Portugal
Operator: Independent Air Inc (US)
Aircraft type: Boeing 707-331B (*N7231T*)

The jet airliner was on a transatlantic charter service, carrying as passengers tourists from Bergamo, Italy, to Santo Domingo, the Dominican Republic, with an en route refuelling stop at Santa Maria Airport. During the intermediate phase of an attempted landing, the 707 slammed into a mountain about 5 miles (10 km) east of the airport, near the town of Santa Barbara. All 144 persons aboard, including a crew of seven Americans, perished in the disaster.

Cleared for descent to the minimum altitude of 3,000 ft (c 1,000 m), the aircraft continued well

below that height and ultimately crashed at an approximate height of 1,800 ft (550 m). Instrument meteorological conditions prevailed in the area at the time, with clouds obscuring the terrain.

The accident was attributed to a series of procedural errors by the flight crew, especially the first officer, and to a lesser degree the airport tower controller. The primary factor was a misunderstanding regarding the authorised descent altitude, largely attributable to a faulty communications technique on the part of the co-pilot.

During the final exchange between the tower and *N7231T*, and immediately after the crew reported passing through flight level 200, the controller radioed the aircraft 'You're cleared to . . . three thousand feet'. After a brief pause, she continued with runway instructions and a request to 'Report reaching three thousand feet'. Simultaneously, the first officer replied 'We're cleared to two thousand feet', and repeated the given above-sea-level pressure setting (QNH).

The overlapping of communications prevented the crew from receiving the last portion of the tower's instructions, and the controller from hearing the co-pilot's utterance of an incorrect altitude. Interestingly, one of the other two flight crewmen, who could not be identified, tried to correct the mistake, and was heard on the cockpit voice recorder (CVR) tape to say 'Make it three'. However, no further comments were made on this seemingly urgent matter.

Another serious error was the introduction of 2,000 ft into the aircraft's altitude alert by one of the pilots. This was contrary to the requirement that the setting be based on the minimum altitude published in the navigational chart, which in this case the crew apparently failed to consult. The ground proximity warning system (GPWS) did activate 7 seconds before impact but, strangely, no verbal remarks were transcribed by the CVR, and no corrective action was taken.

Initial impact was with a brick wall and trees on the west side of the mountain, at an indicated air speed of around 240 mph (390 kmh) and on a magnetic heading of 252 degrees, with the 707 apparently in a clean configuration. Several small post-crash fires were promptly extinguished.

Other contributing factors included the failure of the first officer to use standard terminology in his radio communications, an informal cockpit conversation, and the presence of what was believed to be a cabin attendant on the flight deck, whose voice could be heard on the CVR tape. This may have been an additional element of distraction and was in fact against prescribed policy when flying below 10,000 ft (c 3,000 m).

Though within the limits of the airway, the jet had been operating somewhat off the authorised course, which was further to the north and passed over lower terrain. Such routeing was not uncommon for aircraft arriving at Santa Maria Airport, but combined with its unusually low altitude proved disastrous for *N7231T*.

Procedural errors were also ascribed to the tower controller, who was criticised in the investigative report for not requesting a read-back of her descent clearance and for giving insufficient attention to the 707. Perhaps even more significant was the relay to the crew of an incorrect QNH during the final radio exchange. The resulting mis-setting of the aircraft's altimeters placed the aircraft some 250 ft (75 m) lower than its indicated height. While this would not have been relevant had the 707 maintained 3,000 ft, its descent below the minimum altitude made the error the difference between a precariously low approach and a tragedy. The incorrect QNH may have been due to confusion by the controller with the indicated wind speed.

Among other recommendations, the Portuguese investigative commission responsible for investigating the accident proposed a revision of training programmes and manuals in order to ascertain that pilots have received practical experience in the execution of evasive manoeuvres following the activation of the GPWS. In the case of *N7231T*, insufficient crew training in this area was considered contributory to its crash.

The remains of the chartered Boeing 707 that crashed in the Azores. (Wide World Photos)

Date: 7 June 1989 (c 04:30)
Location: Near Paramaribo, Para, Surinam, South America
Operator: Surinaamse Luchtvaart Maatschappij NV (Surinam Airways)
Aircraft type: McDonnell Douglas DC-8 Super 62 (*N1809E*)

Operating as Flight 764 on a non-stop transatlantic service from Amsterdam, The Netherlands, the jetliner crashed and burned while attempting to land at Zanderij Airport, killing 178 persons aboard, including the entire crew of nine. Among the nine surviving passengers, only a child escaped injury.

The accident occurred in pre-dawn darkness and meteorological conditions consisting of fog and a low overcast, with layers of scattered stratus clouds down to about 400 ft (120 m). Visibility had dropped from approximately half a mile (0.8 km) some 20 minutes before the crash to around 1,500 ft (500 m) shortly afterward. During the attempt to land on Runway 10, with its undercarriage down and flaps partially extended, the aircraft first struck a tree about 80 ft (25 m) above the ground some 2 miles (3 km) from its threshold and to the left of its extended centreline. Initial impact was with its No 2 engine, and the DC-8 then slammed to earth and broke apart, coming to rest inverted.

According to an investigative commission, which received assistance from the (US) National Transportation Safety Board (NTSB), the accident resulted from a descent below the published minimum altitude because of 'grossly negligent and reckless behavior' on the part of the captain. Analysis of the cockpit voice recorder (CVR) tape revealed that while cleared for a very-high-frequency omni-directional range/distance-measuring equipment (VOR/DME) approach, he had carried out the procedure differently than that prescribed and had utilised information from the instrument landing system (ILS) despite knowledge that it was not fully operational, with an unreliable localiser. His statement that he had the field in sight and his repeated requests to increase the intensity of the runway lights further indicated his use of visual procedures during what should have been a non-precision instrument approach. But because of bending of light rays through fog, he might have had a distorted, inaccurate visual image with respect to the exact distance to the runway.

Nor did the pilot heed instrument indications of low altitude, including the activation of the ground proximity warning system (GPWS). An attempt to level off at 200 ft (c 60 m) was made, but the descent continued until impact. Co-ordination in the cockpit was found to be poor during the descent and approach phase, with the captain reacting slowly to accomplish certain required actions and executing a procedural turn at the wrong point.

Cited as an underlying factor in the accident was the failure of the airline's operational management to consider the relevant laws and the regulations contained in its operations manual pertaining to qualifications and proficiency when it recruited and employed the American flight crew from another agency. As he was six years past the normal retirement age for airline pilots (60) and because his last proficiency check flight had been given in a light, twin-engine aircraft instead of a DC-8, the captain did not have the authorization to function in such a position.

The NTSB subsequently asked for tighter controls on agencies providing air carrier flight crews under contract. One of the other recommendations made in the investigative report was for improved emergency services at the Paramaribo airport with regards to both facilities and a plan of action.

Date: 19 July 1989 (16:00)
Location: Near Sioux City, Iowa, US
Operator: United Airlines (US)
Aircraft type: McDonnell Douglas DC-10
  Series 10 (*N1819U*)

There was no hint of impending trouble as Flight 232 cruised at 37,000 ft (c 11,300 m) over north-western Iowa, en route from Denver, Colorado, to Chicago, Illinois, the first segment of a domestic service with an ultimate destination of Philadelphia, Pennsylvania. Suddenly a noise resembling an explosion was heard, and the wide-bodied jetliner shuddered.

In the cockpit, instrument indications confirmed the failure of the aircraft's No 2 engine, mounted on the vertical stabiliser. But the situation was far more critical than the instruments could show,

for the first-stage disc in the power plant had disintegrated. Fragments of the shattered rotor disc and fan that broke through the containment ring then severed the Nos 1 and 3 hydraulic systems lines, and forces associated with the engine failure fractured the No 2 system; this loss of fluid soon rendered the flight control system of *N1819U* inoperative. This was first realised when the flight engineer observed the hydraulic pressure and quantity gauges reading zero. Use of the air-driven generator did not restore hydraulic pressure.

With no manual back-up available, the pilots had no way of operating the ailerons, elevators, rudder, flaps, slats or spoilers. Their only hope of controlling the DC-10 was the manipulation of thrust generated by the two remaining engines with the power levers. They were also faced with uncontrolled pitch oscillation of the aircraft. Despite the best efforts of the crew, stabilised flight could not be maintained.

The transport, which had a tendency to turn right, made one wide circle and two smaller ones before proceeding on a south-westerly heading in the direction of Sioux City. During this time the flight crew communicated with the carrier's maintenance facility, requesting any assistance it could give, and was also joined in the cockpit by a DC-10 training check pilot who happened to be aboard. Meanwhile, the cabin attendants prepared the other passengers for an emergency landing. The undercarriage was extended manually.

At the suggestion of the air traffic controller, the crew elected to continue on toward Sioux Gateway Airport, and attempt to set the crippled jetliner down there. However, this would be no easy task; since it was not possible to control the phugoid motions with any measure of success, landing at a

The crippled DC-10, with visible damage to the right horizontal stabiliser, is photographed before crash-landing at Sioux City airport. (National Transportation Safety Board)

The charred swath left by the United jetliner as it skidded off the runway and into a cornfield. (Wide World Photos)

pre-determined point and air speed would be a matter of chance.

The uncontrolled pitching and rolling continued until just before touch-down, when the aircraft's wing dropped, followed by its nose, the latter at an approximate height of 100 ft (30 m) above the ground. Striking the surface of Runway 22 slightly to the left of its centreline with its right wing tip, followed by the right main gear, the DC-10 skidded to the right, rolled into an inverted position and burst into flames, breaking apart as it slid into a cornfield.

In the disaster, 112 persons aboard lost their lives, including a cabin attendant; one of the victims, a passenger, succumbed to his injuries about a month after the crash. Among the 184 survivors, who included the four men on the flight deck and the eight other members of the cabin crew, 171 persons were injured, many seriously; 13 passengers escaped unscathed. About a third of the fatalities resulted from smoke inhalation, the rest from trauma. The airport weather at the time, which was not considered a factor, consisted of a broken overcast and a visibility of 15 miles (c 25 km). The wind was out of the north at around 15 knots.

Some three months after the accident the fan disc from the failed power plant was found in a rural area near Alta, Iowa, and about six months later farmers located the front flange of the engine's rotor shaft and a large section of the fan booster disc. Examination of the recovered parts revealed two principal fractures that caused approximately one-third of the rim to separate from the remainder of the disc.

It could be said that the failure sequence began 18 years earlier with the manufacture of the ingot from which the titanium disc would be forged by the Alcoa Company, and resulted from a defect associated with excessive nitrogen and/or oxygen introduced while the metal was still in a molten state. The anomaly led to a cavity that was most likely created during the final machining and/or shot peening processes, with the latter probably causing minute cracking parallel to and just below the surface. This in turn initiated the fatigue cracking associated with stresses generated by the application of full engine thrust that grew to critical proportions culminating in the catastrophic break-up.

The disc components had undergone four inspections during their manufacture by General Electric Aircraft Engines (GEAE) prior to their installation in the CF6-6 power plant, including one using an ultrasonic method and one employing a two-step etching process. In its investigative report, the US National Transportation Safety Board (NTSB) concluded that the former technique may not have been capable of detecting the defect, and the latter was possibly improperly applied by GEAE personnel.

The accident itself was blamed by the NTSB on inadequate consideration given to human limitations in the inspection and quality control procedures used by United Airlines' engine overhaul facility, which also failed to detect the anomaly despite six detailed examinations in the service history of the disc. Faulty technique may have once again played a role in the omission, including one method that involved suspending a part by a cable (which could have obscured certain areas), as could the failure of the inspector to give the disc bore more than a cursory check, or a combination of these or other factors.

The manufacturer, operator and US Federal Aviation Administration (FAA) had considered the possibility of a total loss of the hydraulic-powered flight controls so remote as to negate any requirement for an appropriate procedure for dealing with such a situation. The NTSB concluded that the aircraft could not have been landed safely under the circumstances, and commended the actions of Captain Al Haynes and his fellow flight crewmen, which it said 'greatly exceeded reasonable expectations'. Cockpit resource management training, which the airline had implemented a decade earlier, proved useful in dealing with the emergency. Another fact that no doubt saved many lives was the time span of about 45 min between the power plant failure and the crash, which allowed fire/rescue personnel and various community agencies to prepare for what eventually happened.

Subsequent to the disaster, McDonnell Douglas introduced a modification in the hydraulic system of the DC-10 employing an electrically operated shut-off mechanism that would automatically activate if a drop in the hydraulic supply was detected, so a sufficient amount of the fluid would be retained to operate the empennage control surfaces.

The NTSB also called for child restraints in airline operations, noting that four infant passengers on Flight 232 were being carried on the laps of adults, one of whom was killed in the crash. However, the FAA later rejected this proposal, reasoning that families from lower income levels could not afford the additional costs involved and would end up driving rather than flying to their destinations, resulting in even more children losing their lives in vehicular accidents.

Date: 27 July 1989 (c 07:00)
Location: Near Tripoli, Libya
Operator: Korean Air (South Korea)
Aircraft type: McDonnell Douglas DC-10 Series 30 (*HL-7328*)

Designated as Flight 803, the wide-bodied jet airliner crashed and burned while approaching to land at the city's international airport, at the end of a service originating at Seoul, South Korea. Killed in the accident were 74 of the 199 persons aboard the aircraft (70 passengers and four of its 18 crew members) and six on the ground. More than 100 others suffered injuries and several houses and vehicles were destroyed.

The crash took place approximately 3.5 miles (6 km) from the threshold of the assigned runway (27) during a heavy fog, with a horizontal visibility reportedly down to only about 150 ft (50 m), and was attributed to pilot error. The captain of

HL-7328 was later convicted of negligence for attempting a landing without analysing the meteorological data, and received a two-year prison sentence. Both the very-high-frequency omni-directional range (VOR) station and the instrument landing system (ILS) were unserviceable at the time of the accident.

Date: 3 September 1989 (c 19:00)
Location: Near Havana, Cuba
Operator: Empresa Consolidada Cubana de Aviacion (Cuba)
Aircraft type: Ilyushin Il-62M (*CU-T1281*)

The jetliner, which was on a charter service to Milan, Italy, with an en route stop at Cologne, (West) Germany, crashed and exploded seconds after it had taken off from Jose Marti/Rancho Boyeros International Airport, killing all 126 persons aboard, including a crew of 11, and 45 on the ground. One of the passengers who was rescued alive succumbed to his injuries eight days later. About 50 others on the ground were injured and some three dozen houses destroyed. The accident occurred in early evening darkness.

At the time of departure, heavy rain was falling and winds of around 20 to 25 mph (30–40 kmh) were blowing across the runway, adversities associated with a nearby storm. The winds encountered by *CU-T1281* may have been even higher, perhaps in the vicinity of 30 to 50 mph (50–80 kmh).

Immediately after becoming airborne, the aircraft was caught in descending air currents, and the pilots must have tried to level its wings in an apparent attempt to increase air speed, which would also have reduced the possibility of gaining altitude. The jetliner reached an approximate height of 150 ft (50 m) before it started to descend on account of the down-draughts and strong surface winds. It then struck navigational aerials and a hill beyond the end of the runway, bounced and finally crashed into the populated area.

An investigative commission attributed the disaster to the captain's decision to fly after an abrupt deterioration in the meteorological conditions. He undoubtedly under-estimated the risks of taking off and also misjudged the aircraft's bad weather performance.

Date: 19 September 1989 (c 14:00)
Location: Near Bilma, Niger
Operator: Union de Transports Aeriens (UTA) (France)
Aircraft type: McDonnell Douglas DC-10 Series 30 (*N54629*)

All 170 persons aboard (156 passengers and a crew of 14) perished when the wide-bodied jet airliner, operating as Flight 772, plummeted into the Tenere Desert region of the Sahara. The crash occurred some 400 miles (650 km) north-west of Ndjamena, Chad, from where the DC-10 had taken off earlier, a scheduled stop during a service originating at Brazzaville, in the Congo, with an ultimate destination of Paris.

The aircraft had climbed to flight level 350 before it disintegrated following an explosion in the forward baggage compartment. Its cockpit section separated first, and was found about 10 miles (15 km) from the main wreckage. Other debris and victims' bodies were scattered over an area of approximately 45 sq miles (70 sq km). Traces of the high explosive pentharite were also identified, confirming that the jet had been sabotaged. The bomb had apparently been placed in a suitcase that was reportedly checked in by a passenger who boarded the flight at Brazzaville and disembarked at Ndjamena.

French authorities suspected that the terrorist act was carried out with the backing of Libya, which denied the accusation.

The front fuselage section of the UTA DC-10 rests in the Tenere Desert after an in-flight break-up attributed to a bomb blast. (Wide World Photos)

Date: 21 October 1989 (07:53)
Location: Near Tegucilgapa, Honduras
Operator: Transportes Aereos Nacionales SA
   (TAN Airlines) (Honduras)
Aircraft type: Boeing 727-224 (*N88705*)

The jetliner, which was designated as Flight 414, crashed while attempting to land at the capital city's Toncontin Airport, at the end of a service from San Jose, Costa Rica, via Managua, Nicaragua, and 131 persons aboard (127 passengers and four of its 12 crew members) were killed. Among the 19 survivors, who suffered varying degrees of injury, were the captain and first officer.

Cleared for a very-high-frequency omni-directional range/distance-measuring equipment (VOR/DME) approach to Runway 01, the flight crew may not have followed the procedure, and descended below the proper glide path. Subsequently, the aircraft struck a mountain at an approximate elevation of 5,000ft (1,500 m) and some 10 miles (15 km) south of the airport, bursting into flames on impact. The weather at the time was adverse, with heavy rain, low clouds and high winds.

It was later recommended that the carrier scrutinise its training criteria to improve team-work in the cockpit; examine procedures regarding the use of approach charts; review the scheduling of this flight, which may have been too demanding for crews; and improve pilot training in the use of the ground proximity warning system (GPWS) and follow-up action in the event of its activation.

Date: 27 November 1989 (c 07:20)
Location: Near Bogota, Colombia
Operator: Aerovias Nacionales de Colombia SA
   (AVIANCA)
Aircraft type: Boeing 727-21 (*HK-1803*)

Operating as Flight 203, the jetliner crashed about 5 minutes after taking off from the city's El Dorado Airport, on a domestic service to Cali, Tolima. A total of 110 persons perished in the disaster, including a crew of six; three of the victims may have been passengers not on the manifest or persons killed on the ground. There were no survivors.

It was determined that a bomb apparently placed in a seat had detonated on the right-hand side of the aircraft's passenger cabin, with the explosion rupturing its fuel tanks. Fuel then flooded into the cabin and over the outside of the fuselage, and the 727 fell in flames into hilly terrain.

The act of sabotage was believed to have been perpetrated by a drug cartel in order to eliminate police informants who were supposed to have been on the flight. A passenger who may have planted the device aboard the aircraft probably disembarked prior to its take-off.

The terrorist leader believed responsible for arranging the bombing was himself killed in a police raid three years later.

The
1990s

In 1993 aviation moved into its tenth decade of powered flight. Today the world's airlines carry more than a billion passengers every year, with greater safety and efficiency than could ever have been imagined in the early days of flying. Indeed, the airline industries of some nations (the more noteworthy ones being Australia, Germany, Japan, the Netherlands, Scandinavia and Switzerland) have amassed safety records that equal or excel any other form of transport.

The low number of accidents and fatalities in relationship to the amount of traffic can be attributed to many advances in aircraft design, engine reliability, navigation, weather forecasting and air traffic control procedures. Many of these improvements have developed directly as a result of previous disasters.

One of the most pressing issues facing modern commercial aviation is the increased complexity of aircraft, and the burden it places on flight crews. Though greater automation can generally reduce pilot work load and decrease the chance of human error, it can aggravate the old 'man-versus-machine' controversy, with concern as to who is really in control. The crash in May 1991 of a Lauda Air Boeing 767 proved that occasionally the machine gets the upper hand.

Airline travel will never be without risk, but through testing, research, learning and, unfortunately, occasional tragedy, it will continue to strive towards that ultimate goal, unrealistic though it may be, of absolute perfection.

Date: 25 January 1990 (c 21:30)
Location: New York, New York, US
Operator: Aerovias Nacionales de Colombia SA (AVIANCA)
Aircraft type: Boeing 707-321B (*HK-2016*)

Among the aircraft 'stacked up' to await landing at John F. Kennedy International Airport (JFK) was Flight 52, on a service from Bogota and Medellin, Colombia. The delays were particularly long on this Thursday evening, with the deteriorating weather aggravating the usual heavy traffic.

During the 1 hr 17 min holding period, the 707 consumed its reserve fuel load, which was to have been used should the flight have been diverted to its alternative destination, designated as Boston, Massachusetts. When asked by the New York centre controller how much longer the aircraft could hold, its first officer responded '. . . about five minutes . . .'. However, at that point such a diversion would have been out of the question. When asked to name its alternative, the co-pilot replied 'It was Boston but we can't do it now . . . we run out of fuel now'.

Finally *HK-2016* was cleared to proceed to JFK and, subsequently, for an instrument landing system (ILS) approach to Runway 22L. Beset by a strong head-wind and wind shear, the aircraft descended below the glide slope during the attempted landing, forcing the crew to initiate a missed approach procedure. This action set the stage for the disaster, since the 707 did not have enough fuel to fly the circuit and complete a second approach.

Speaking in Spanish, the captain asked the first officer to inform the controller of the situation and the latter transmitted a message that included the advisory '. . . we're running out of fuel, sir'. Moments later the co-pilot again advised the controller, when asked to ascend to a higher altitude, 'Negative, sir, we just running out of fuel'.

Only a few minutes afterwards the aircraft's No 4 power plant failed from fuel exhaustion, followed in rapid succession by the other three engines. Subsequently, the jet airliner crashed on a wooded hillside in the village of Cove Neck, located on the north side of Long Island some 15 miles (25 km) north of the airport, and while on a southerly heading. The accident killed 73 of the 158 persons aboard the 707 (65 passengers and eight members

The hulk of the AVIANCA 707 rests adjacent to a house after the fuel exhaustion accident that killed 73 aboard the aircraft. (National Transportation Safety Board)

of its crew). All the survivors, who included a cabin attendant, were injured, many seriously.

The aircraft's fuselage broke into three main sections on impact, although there was no post-crash fire. The rapid response by fire and rescue personnel, which included the use of helicopters to evacuate many of the survivors, probably kept the death toll down. It was dark at the time of the crash, and the airport weather consisted of fog, an overcast down to 300 ft (c 100 m) and a visibility of approximately 1 mile (1.5 km).

In its investigative report, the US National Transportation Safety Board (NTSB) attributed the disaster to the failure of the AVIANCA flight crew to manage the aircraft's fuel load and to communicate the criticality of the situation to ground controllers.

The NTSB also revealed inadequacies in the carrier's dispatching of Flight 52 and in the planning by its crew. With regard to the former, it was learned that the dispatch service did not provide the pilots with the latest meteorological forecast for the New York area nor with information about possible alternative airports. Among other deficiencies, the flight plan did not take into consideration air traffic control (ATC) or weather delays. Also there were no communications between *HK-2016* and the company's dispatcher, which normally take place in order to keep the crew informed on such issues as alternative landing sites and the amount of fuel needed to reach them.

The board concluded that the actions of ATC personnel were reasonable despite a lack of significance given to the co-pilot's request for 'priority' in landing. Under the circumstances the

crew should have taken further steps to convey the sense of urgency of the situation. This was evident in the failure of the first officer to use the word 'emergency', as requested by the captain, when informing the JFK tower controller that the 707 was nearly out of fuel. (The New York centre controller later said that he did not hear a portion of the radio transmission from the flight that the aircraft could no longer reach its alternative airport and therefore did not notify the approach controller of such.)

Of course, had the crew been able to complete the first landing attempt successfully, the crash would have been averted. The NTSB believed that the approach had been made without the use of a properly functioning flight director, which would have added to the difficulties in maintaining the glide slope properly. Problems had also been reported with the aircraft's autopilot, leading to speculation by the NTSB that the crew may have flown manually on the long trip from Colombia. Had this been the case, it could have added to the stress and fatigue generated by the other factors, including the concern about the fuel situation, and contributed to the unstabilised approach that ended in the overshoot manoeuvre.

The accident report criticised the air traffic management programme used at JFK by the US Federal Aviation Administration (FAA), which was blamed for the excessive landing delays.

Board member Jim Burnett dissented in the vote adopting the report, opting to place more responsibility for the disaster on inadequate ATC services, including their failure to provide the Colombian crew with the latest wind shear information. Similar criticism was expressed by

Mayor Jorge Enrique Leal, chief of the Colombian Administrative Department of Civil Aeronautics' Flight Safety Division, who suggested improvements in the ATC system so as to better inform flight crews of anticipated delays. He further wrote that acceptance of the flight by New York approach control could have misled the crew of *HK-2016* into believing that clearance to land was imminent.

Date: 14 February 1990 (c 13:00)
Location: Near Bangalore, Karnataka, India
Operator: Indian Airlines
Aircraft type: Airbus Industrie A320-231
  (*VT-EPN*)

Designated as Flight 605 and on a domestic service from Bombay, the jetliner crashed while attempting to land at the Bangalore airport, killing 92 of the 146 persons aboard, including both pilots and three of its five cabin attendants. Most of the survivors were injured, 21 passengers and one crew member seriously.

The accident was attributed to the improper use of the aircraft's highly sophisticated 'autoflight' system by the flight crew, the latter consisting of a captain undergoing his first route check for command endorsement in the A320 and his supervisory pilot serving as first officer.

During the approach to Runway 09, made in conditions of good visibility, the crew inadvertently placed the flight director in the open descent mode by selecting an altitude on the flight control unit that was lower than the aircraft's actual height. This in turn changed the autothrottle setting to idle engine thrust. The air speed, which was not being properly monitored, then began to decay, and the twin-jet transport deviated below the glide path. Meanwhile, the aircraft's nose pitched up as the pilot tried to maintain the correct flight path, unable to do so at idle power.

At an altitude of approximately 130 ft (40 m) above the ground and an air speed some 25 mph (40 kmh) below normal, the captain pulled back on his control column, then advanced the power levers to the take-off/go-around (TOGA) position. However, these actions proved insufficient and the jetliner hit the ground on its extended main undercarriage about 1,500 ft (500 m) short of the runway, became airborne once again and finally crashed and burst into flames.

Investigation revealed that the co-pilot's flight director had been left in the open descent mode until impact, which would have prevented the autothrottles from reverting to the speed mode, the prescribed setting for the approach/landing phase of flight. Analysis of the cockpit voice recorder (CVR) tape further disclosed that neither crewman apparently heard the four radar altimeter alerts nor the two 'sink rate' voice warnings during the descent.

As noted in the accident report, the Indian

Emergency personnel sift through the gutted hulk of the Indian Airlines A320 near Bangalore airport. (UPI/Bettmann)

Directorate General of Civil Aviation had previously advised the carrier that the pilot who was in command of Flight 605 be 'positively monitored' in such areas as operation of the flight management and guidance system (FMGS) used on the A320. His instructors noted '. . . numerous small errors and omissions . . .' with the FMGS and mishandling of the aircraft's power controls.

The absence of a radio link with the control tower, which increased the response time of emergency personnel, and a poorly maintained airport road and a locked security gate, both of which hampered the ability of fire/rescue vehicles to reach the crash scene, probably contributed to the high death toll.

Date: 2 October 1990 (c 09:15)
Location: Near Canton, Kwangtung, China
First aircraft
Operator: Xiamen Airlines (China)
Type: Boeing Advanced 737-247 (*B-2510*)
Second aircraft
Operator: China Southern Airlines
Type: Boeing 757-21B (*B-2812*)
Third aircraft
Operator: China Southwest Airlines
Type: Boeing 707-3J6B (*B-2402*)

Operating as Flight 8301, the 737 was on a domestic service to Canton from Xiamen, Fujian, when it was hijacked by a young man who claimed to have explosives strapped to his body. He reportedly ordered the flight crew out of the cockpit with the exception of the pilot and demanded to be taken to Taiwan.

When the aircraft tried to land at Baiyun Airport, serving Canton, shouts and the sounds of a struggle were heard coming from the cockpit just before touch-down. Following a hard landing, the 737 veered off the runway and clipped the forward fuselage of the 707, which was parked, then the left wing and top fuselage of the 757, which was waiting to take off on a scheduled domestic service to Shanghai, Jiangsu. After hitting the latter, the Xiamen transport skidded to a stop upside-down in a grassy area.

A total of 132 persons were killed in the crash, all but 20 of the 104 passengers and crew members aboard *B-2510*, including the hijacker, 47 of the 118 aboard *B-2812*, and the driver of an airport service vehicle. About 50 others suffered injuries, including the pilot (and sole occupant) of *B-2402*. Of the three jetliners involved, the 737 and 757 were destroyed by impact and fire, while the 707 sustained collision damage.

Reportedly, the air pirate had refused an offer by the Xiamen Airlines' captain to fly to Hong Kong, and the dispute continued until the aircraft's fuel supply was nearly exhausted, necessitating the landing.

The China Southern Airlines 757 was broken in two after being struck by the hijacked Xiamen 737. (Reuters/Bettmann)

Chinese authorities were said to have ordered managerial restructuring in the wake of the disaster, admitting procedural deficiencies that allowed the 757 to taxi in the midst of a hijacking

---

Date: 2 October 1990 (time unknown)
Location: Near Kuwait City, Kuwait
Operator: Iraqi Airways
Aircraft type: Ilyushin Il-76

Approximately 130 persons were killed when the jet transport was hit by a surface-to-air missile fired by Kuwaiti resistance fighters shortly after it had taken off, then crashed. There were no survivors. The commercial aircraft was believed to have been carrying military personnel, its downing occurring during the occupation of Kuwait by Iraqi forces.

Date: 26 May 1991 (c 23:30)
Location: Near Ban Nong Rong, Thailand
Operator: Lauda Air Luftfahrt Aktiengesellschaft (Austria)
Aircraft type: Boeing 767-3Z9ER (OE-LAV)

All 223 persons aboard (213 passengers and a crew of 10) perished when the wide-bodied jet airliner, which was designated as Flight 004, crashed and burned in a jungle area some 150 miles (250 km) north-west of Bangkok, about half an hour after it had taken off from the city's international airport, a scheduled stop during a service from Hong Kong to Vienna, Austria.

The 767 had reached an approximate height of 25,000 ft (7,500 m) while still climbing at around 80 per cent the speed of sound before it plummeted to earth in flames, scattering wreckage over an area of about 5 miles (10 km). Its empennage apparently separated from the rest of the fuselage prior to impact. The accident occurred in darkness and, although rain showers were reported in the area, the weather was not considered hazardous enough to warrant a course change by the Lauda Air pilot.

Destruction of the aircraft's digital flight data recorder (DFDR) hampered the investigation of the disaster. However, there were indications of a loss of control precipitated by the unwanted deployment of the left engine thrust reverser. This was corroborated by an analysis of the cockpit voice recorder (CVR) tape, on which the first officer was heard to say '. . . reverser's deployed'.

The specific reason for the deployment could not be established, although there was speculation that it may have been related to some kind of electrical interference. The crew was unable to effect recovery even after throttling back the left engine, which was at climb power at the moment of deployment.

Boeing subsequently initiated a programme to retrofit more than 2,000 of its twin-jet 737s, 757s

A Lauda Air Boeing 767-3Z9ER, sister to the aircraft that crashed in the Thai jungle. (Boeing)

and 767s with a mechanical reverser-locking mechanism. This also required modification of the hydraulic system on the latter model.

Date: 11 July 1991 (c 08:40)
Location: Near Jiddah, Saudi Arabia
Operator: Nolisair International Inc (Nationair Canada)
Aircraft type: McDonnell Douglas DC-8 Super 61 (*C-GMXQ*)

The jetliner had been leased to Nigeria Airways and sub-leased to Holdtrade Services, another Nigerian firm, and was on a charter service to Sokoto, Nigeria. Its passengers were all Muslim pilgrims.

About 2 min after its departure from King Abdulaziz International Airport, serving Jiddah, the pilot reported a pressurisation problem, then radioed that the aircraft was losing hydraulics and would need to return. Turning back, the DC-8 proceeded southward in the airport circuit so it could land in the same direction that it took off. Control problems that made manoeuvring difficult were reported during this time.

Cleared for a landing on any of the three parallel runways, all numbered 34, *C-GMXQ* was observed by one ground witness to descend in a nose-down attitude, trailing smoke as it flew towards the north. Its undercarriage extended, the jetliner moments later plunged into the desert at an approximate speed of 275 mph (440 kmh) some 2 miles (3 km) short of the centre runway and around 150 ft (50 m) to the right of its extended centreline, disintegrating in a fiery explosion on impact. All 261 persons aboard, including 14 crew members (all Canadians except for one Frenchman), perished in the disaster. The weather at the time was cloudless, with a visibility of more than 5 miles (10 km).

Bodies of many victims, some of which had suffered burns, were located along the flight path, the first one about 11 miles (18 km) from the crash site. Pieces of cabin furnishings were also found a distance from the main wreckage.

Investigation confirmed that during the taxi to the runway, the transfer of the load from the No 2 tyre, which was not properly inflated, had caused over-deflection, over-heating and weakening of the No 1, also located on the left main gear, and both then failed during the take-off ground run. Friction generated when the No 2 wheel stopped rotating, for undetermined reasons, was sufficient to ignite rubber remnants, which then came in close proximity to hydraulic and electrical system components when the undercarriage was retracted. Subsequently, the hydraulic system ceased to function. Kerosene was probably introduced

The remains of the Canadian Super DC-8 are strewn across the Saudi Arabian desert after the crash that claimed 261 lives. (Wide World Photos)

following a burn-through of the centre fuel tank, and the blaze ultimately disabled the aircraft's control systems. The fire had also consumed the cabin floor, which collapsed when the gear was re-extended, sending numerous occupants in their seats tumbling about 2,000 feet (600 m) to the ground. Witness statements seemed to confirm an in-flight break-up of the aircraft shortly before ground impact.

Low tyre pressures had been observed and measured on *C-GMXQ* four days before the accident. The lead mechanic had tried to rectify the problem, but the project manager allowed the aircraft to depart in this unairworthy condition. The cockpit voice recorder (CVR) tape indicated that the flight crew was aware of something amiss, with the first officer heard to ask during the take-off run 'We got a flat tyre, you figure?'. Given the information available and his training, which did not include procedures for tyre and wheel failures, the captain was not faulted for continuing the take-off.

Among other recommendations made in the Saudi Arabian investigative report on this accident were that commercial aircraft be equipped with wheel well fire detection and suppression systems and that aviation regulatory authorities ensure adequate dissemination of information and proper crew training with regard to tyre failures during and after take-off as well as quality in all forms of maintenance work.

Date: 20 January 1992 (c 19:20)
Location: Near Barr, Bas-Rhin, France
Operator: Air Inter (France)
Aircraft type: Airbus Industrie A320-111 (*F-GGED*)

Operating as Flight 148 and on a domestic service from Lyon, the jet airliner crashed and burned while attempting to land at Entzheim Airport, serving Strasbourg. Killed in the accident were 87 persons aboard the aircraft, including five crew members; eight passengers and a cabin attendant, all but one of whom had been seated in the rear of the cabin, survived with various injuries.

Its undercarriage down, flaps set at 15 degrees and speed brakes deployed, the twin-engine jet ploughed into a wooded ridge near Mont Ste Odile during the very-high-frequency omni-directional range/distance-measuring equipment (VOR/DME) instrument procedure approach to Runway 05. Impact occurred at an approximate elevation of 2,600 ft (800 m), some 10 miles (15 km) south-west of the airport and about half a mile (0.8 km) to the left of the runway axis, as the A320 was completing a left turn on to the final approach leg. It was dark at the time, and the local meteorological conditions consisted of a low overcast, with 3/8 strato-cumulus clouds at around 1,000 ft (300 m) and 6/8 at approximately 2,500 ft (750 m), and a visibility of about 10 miles (15 km) in a freezing drizzle. The wind was out of the north-east, gusting up to 35 knots.

Shown in Air Inter's earlier livery, this Airbus Industrie A320-111 is otherwise identical to the aircraft that crashed near Strasbourg. (Airbus Industrie)

An investigation conducted by a 10-committee commission failed to determine the exact sequence of events leading up to the crash, but the primary factor was believed to have been improper use of the aircraft's flight control unit (FCU) due to selection of the wrong mode or the confusion between two different modes. This resulted in an excessive descent rate that was not stopped. With regard to the second theory, the FCU may have been inadvertently set in the heading/vertical speed instead of the track/ flight path mode, with the crew then dialling '33' into the computer system, believing that they were putting in a 3.3-degree slope command (which is normally used in a VOR/DME approach at this airport). This would have led to a descent rate of 3,300 ft/min (1,005 m/min), or roughly that of the jet in the final moments before impact. The possibility of a malfunction in the computer system was not ruled out, but considered highly unlikely.

It could not be established why the rapid descent, more than four times the norm, was not detected, but this may have been related to the smooth flying qualities of the A320 noted by pilots.

Human factors that were identified as contributing to the accident were minor faults in the ground navigational aids and runway lighting; the comparative inexperience in the A320 by both the captain and first officer; poor crew co-ordination and cross-checking associated with ineffective intra-cockpit communications; and the pilots' involvement in a non-precision approach in less than ideal weather after initial plans for an instrument landing system (ILS) procedure. It was noted in the accident report that the crew had relaxed their attention during the radar guidance portion of the approach, leaving the 'vertical navigation' entirely to the autopilot. This behaviour could have been influenced by the short-haul routine of Air Inter's operations, wherein the many landings are usually carried out automatically.

Still another factor could have been the 'tense' working environment related to the controversy over giving the A320, a two- rather than three-member flight crew, which reached the point that the carrier was controlling and restricting information released on minor technical difficulties with the transport.

A number of recommendations were made in the report, mostly pertaining to crew training and performance relative to the use of advanced technology aircraft.

Subsequent to this accident, the French Transport Ministry enacted a requirement that all commercial aircraft falling under its jurisdiction be fitted with a ground proximity warning system (GPWS); under the voluntary arrangement existing prior to the disaster, the Air Inter fleet was not so equipped due to concern over false alarms. Changes

were also recommended pertaining to the use of emergency locator beacons installed on aircraft; the post-crash failure of the unit installed on *F-GGED* hampered rescue workers in finding the accident site and probably cost the lives of half a dozen victims who had survived the impact.

Airbus Industrie had already introduced a modification in the FCU featuring a different instrument display designed to prevent confusion between the two modes, with plans to retrofit all the aircraft already in service.

Date: 31 July 1992 (c 12:30)
Location: Near Kistung Palung, Nepal
Operator: Thai Airways International
Aircraft type: Airbus Industrie A310-300
   (*HS-TID*)

All 113 persons aboard (99 passengers and 14 crew members) perished when the wide-bodied twin-engine jetliner, designated as Flight 311 and on a service from Bangkok, Thailand, crashed and burned some 25 miles (40 km) north-north-east of Kathmandu.

The pilots had experienced difficulty deploying the flaps during an approach to Runway 02 at Tribhuvan International Airport, serving the capital city, using very-high-frequency omni-directional range/distance-measuring equipment (VOR/DME) procedures. Though they were able to rectify the problem, the landing had to be abandoned altogether because by then the aircraft was too near the airport in relationship to its height. The flight was then granted permission to proceed southwards towards the Point Romeo navigational fix, from which another attempt to land could be commenced.

Instead, the A310 carried out a 360-degree turn and continued on the same north-north-easterly heading of the approach course, but slightly to the left of the prescribed airway, passing through the 290-degree radial that should have been taken as part of the missed approach procedure. Apparently proceeding under the control of the autopilot, probably left in altitude and heading hold, it ultimately hit a near-vertical rock wall in the Himalayan foothills, disintegrating on impact. About 30 seconds before the crash, the first officer recognised the potential danger and timidly expressed his concern, but the captain did not appear to understand what he said. The ground proximity warning system (GPWS) gave the appropriate alert, but due to the steepness of the terrain its activation came too late. There was thunderstorm activity in the area at the time, with rain, scattered clouds about 2,000 ft (600 m) above the ground and a visibility of around 3 miles (5 km). The weather conditions were in fact below the prescribed minima.

Not realising it to be flying towards the higher

terrain, where the minimum safe altitude was 21,000 ft (6,400 m), the control tower operator cleared the aircraft for descent to 11,500 ft (3,500 m), the minimum height along the intended flight path; impact occurred at approximately that elevation.

The underlying cause of the error leading to the incorrect heading could not be determined. Cited as contributing factors were misunderstandings between the crew and air traffic control (ATC) units, probably associated with the use of non-standard radio communications language and poor signal quality; the misleading depiction on the approach chart of Point Romeo as the start of the approach; and difficulty experienced by the pilots in entering initial approach fix (IAF) data into the aircraft's flight management and guidance system. They apparently became distracted as they attempted to show the IAF points on the navigation display, which was in the map mode, but by then the fixes were behind the aircraft.

Ground controllers, who lacked the benefit of radar, did little to monitor the position of the flight, even though the tower did have a direction-finder screen that could be used to determine from what direction an aircraft radio transmission came.

The airline challenged the findings of the investigative commission, claiming that there should have been greater emphasis on ATC factors. Specifically, the clearance by the control tower was said to be incomplete, and the controller did not respond to four requests for a left turn made by the crew, who ultimately circled to the right and proceeded in the wrong direction.

Improvements in training and procedures were subsequently enacted at both the airline and the Kathmandu airport.

Date: 31 July 1992 (c 15:00)
Location: Nanjing, Jiangsu, China
Operator: China General Aviation Corporation
Aircraft type: Yakovlev Yak-42D (*B-2755*)

Operating as Flight 7552, the jet airliner crashed on take-off from the city's Da Xiao Chang Airport, on a domestic service to Xiamen, Fujian, with a loss of 109 lives. Among the 116 passengers and crew of 10 aboard, 17 persons survived, all of whom were seriously injured.

Reportedly, the three-engine jet climbed to a height of approximately 200 ft (60 m) above the ground before it plunged into a shallow pond some 2,000 ft (600 m) beyond the end of the runway and caught fire. Unconfirmed reports indicated that the airport temperature was very high at the time, and that the aircraft had been loaded considerably above the maximum take-off weight. The accident may have been related to the same power plant trouble that had already delayed the flight for an hour.

Date: 27 August 1992 (c 22:45)
Location: Near Ivanovo, Russian Federation, Commonwealth of Independent States
Operator: Aeroflot (Commonwealth of Independent States)
Aircraft type: Tupolev Tu-134A (*SSSR-65058*)

Designated as Flight 2808 and on a domestic service originating at Mineral'nyye Vody, the jet airliner crashed about 1.5 miles (2.5 km) from the Ivanovo airport, where it was scheduled to land. All 84 persons aboard (77 passengers and seven crew members) were killed, and a woman on the ground was injured. The accident occurred in darkness, but the weather was not considered a factor.

Following an unstabilised initial approach, with the aircraft deviating considerably above and then slightly below the correct glide path, the Tu-134 struck the tops of trees some 2 miles (3 km) short of the runway threshold and approximately 150 ft (50 m) to the left of its extended centreline. Initial impact was at an indicated air speed of about 230 mph (370 kmh), with its undercarriage still retracted and flaps not in the landing configuration, and after rolling to the right when its starboard wing disintegrated, the aircraft travelled more than 1,500 ft (500 m) until finally slamming to earth. There was no fire.

The accident was attributed to poor co-ordination on the part of the flight crew, who violated basic rules and whose members provided no assistance to the captain. Inadequate actions of the air traffic control service were an additional factor, with no notification of the flight despite its constant deviation from the proper track.

Date: 28 September 1992 (c 14:30)
Location: Near Bhadgaon, Nepal
Operator: Pakistan International Airlines
Aircraft type: Airbus Industrie A300B4 (*AP-BCP*)

The second crash in two months of an aircraft arriving at Tribhuvan International Airport, serving Kathmandu, involved Flight 268, which was on a service from Karachi, Pakistan. All 167 persons aboard (155 passengers and a crew of 12) were killed when the wide-bodied jetliner hit a wooded mountainside and burned during a very-high-frequency omni-directional range/distance-measuring equipment (VOR/DME) procedure approach to Runway 02.

Impact occurred some 10 miles (15 km) south of the airport at an approximate elevation of 7,300 ft (2,225 m), or more than 1,000 ft (300 m) below the minimum altitude at that point along the approach course, with the aircraft's undercarriage down and flaps extended. The meteorological conditions in the area at the time

The crash of the Pakistan International Airlines A300 was the second in two months involving an Airbus arriving at the Kathmandu airport. (Wide World Photos)

consisted of a low overcast and poor visibility.

Failing to follow the published procedure, the crew had conducted the approach in a way that had the jetliner arriving at each DME fix one step ahead of the proper sequence, and thus below the correct descent profile. An investigative commission could not establish how and why this error could have occurred because there was no record of the crew's conversation on the flight deck. Considered as contributing factors were the complexity of the procedure and the corresponding approach chart, which was criticised for using a vertical profile of the approach course and for a misleading display of minimum altitudes.

Seconds after the last position report, the air traffic controller challenged the pilot for an altitude check, an action that came too late to prevent the crash. Also, because of the steepness of the terrain, the aircraft's ground proximity warning system (GPWS) would probably not have activated in sufficient time.

Among the recommendations made in the accident report were for a review by the International Civil Aviation Organisation (ICAO) of navigational charts, with the intention of

encouraging standardisation and reducing clutter, and for a change in this particular approach procedure at Kathmandu airport.

Date: 24 November 1992 (c 08:00)
Location: Near Liutang, Guangxi, China
Operator: China Southern Airlines
Aircraft type: Boeing 737-3YO (*B-2523*)

Designated as Flight 3943 and on a supplemental domestic service to Kweilin from Canton, Guandong, the jetliner crashed and exploded approximately 15 miles (25 km) south-east of its destination, while preparing to land. All 141 persons aboard (133 passengers and eight crew members) perished.

Its flight data recorder (FDR) read-out indicated that during the visual approach to Runway 36 at the city's airport and after levelling off at about 7,000 ft (2,000 m) with the autopilot and autothrottle engaged, the left thrust lever advanced, while the right one remained at the idle position. As a result of this asymmetrical power condition, the aircraft rolled to the right, the crew unable to maintain control. The fault in the throttle system could not be identified, though the problem had occurred earlier on the same flight and was corrected manually. The local weather at the time was described as generally clear and apparently did not factor in the accident.

Date: 21 December 1992 (c 08:30)
Location: Faro, Garve, Portugal
Operator: Martinair Holland NV
    (The Netherlands)
Aircraft type: McDonnell Douglas DC-10
    Series 30CF (*PH-MBN*)

The wide-bodied jet airliner, on a non-scheduled service from Amsterdam, crashed and burned at Faro Airport, killing 56 of the 340 persons aboard, including two cabin attendants. Among the 273 passengers and 11 crew members who survived, about 120 were injured.

Following one unsuccessful attempt to land, the crew was executing a very-high-frequency omni-directional range/distance-measuring equipment (VOR/DME) procedure approach to Runway 11 when the aircraft flew through at least two microbursts spawned by a thunderstorm, which was accompanied by heavy rain and a low overcast. In the subsequent hard landing, the starboard main gear failed, with fire erupting after the right wing fuel tanks ruptured. Its fuselage cracked in two, the DC-10 came to rest with the front portion laying on its left side.

The Portuguese investigative report attributed the accident to the bad meteorological conditions and to errors by the crew, who it said improperly interpreted information about the runway conditions and failed to integrate data concerning the instability of the approach, which resulted in the failure to abandon the landing. The captain's actions were said to have been 'too passive', with power being increased too late. Other factors were incorrect wind information given by approach control, the absence of an approach-lighting system and the loss of lift caused by the heavy precipitation.

Dutch authorities disagreed with those findings, placing the weather as the principal causative factor. They further claimed that the pilots were not informed about a change in the wind, whose direction shifted from 150 to 220 degrees and doubled in velocity to 40 knots while the aircraft was at an approximate height of 150 ft (50 m), the crew not expecting wind shear phenomena.

Date: 22 December 1992 (c 10:00)
Location: Near Tripoli, Libya
First aircraft
Operator: Jamahiriya Libyan Arab Airlines
Type: Boeing Advanced 727-2L5 (*5A-DIA*)

Second aircraft
Operator: Libyan Air Force
Type: Mikoyan MiG-23U

Operating as Flight 1103 and on a domestic service from Banghazi, the jetliner was attempting to land at Tripoli International Airport, from where the jet fighter had just taken off, when the two aircraft collided in mid-air and crashed some 30 miles (50 km) south-east of the capital city. All 157 persons aboard the 727 (147 passengers and a crew of 10) perished, while the two crewmen of the MiG reportedly parachuted to safety.

The collision occurred in clear weather conditions and at an altitude of about 3,000 ft (1,000 m), as the commercial transport was on the final phase of a visual approach to Runway 27.

Date: 8 February 1993 (c 10:15)
Location: Near Karaj, Iran
First aircraft
Operator: Iran Air Tours
Type: Tupolev Tu-154M (*EP-ITD*)
Second aircraft
Operator: Iranian Air Force
Type: Sukhoi Su-24

The jet airliner, which had been leased from the Russian carrier Aeroflot and was on a non-scheduled domestic service to Mashhad, Khorasan, had taken off from Mehrabad International Airport, serving Tehran, when it collided with the combat jet, and both then plummeted into a military compound and exploded. All 132 persons aboard the commercial transport (119 passengers and 13 crew members, the latter including a Russian pilot) and both crewmen of the military aircraft perished in the disaster.

Reportedly, the Su-24 struck the tail of the Tu-154, the collision occurring at an altitude of approximately 1,300 ft (400 m), after the latter crossed the flight path of the former and a second military aircraft that were participating in an Air Force Day fly-past.

Date: 5 March 1993 (c 12:00)
Location: Near Skopje, Macedonia
Operator: Palair Macedonian
Aircraft type: Fokker 100 (*PH-KXL*)

Designated as Flight 301 and bound for Zurich, Switzerland, the jet airliner crashed and exploded in a field as it took off from the Petrovac airport, killing 81 of the 97 persons aboard, including four crew members. The 13 passengers and three crew members who survived, the latter including the pilot, suffered serious injuries.

Seconds after lifting off from Runway 34, the aircraft reportedly began to shudder violently, and

A Palair Macedonian Fokker 100, identical to the aircraft that crashed on take-off in Macedonia. (Fokker Aircraft)

whilst climbing through an approximate height of 50 ft (15 m) with an indicated air speed of about 170 mph (270 kmh) it rolled to the left, then to the right. After its starboard wing tip struck the ground at a point some 1,500 ft (500 m) beyond the end of the runway, the transport cartwheeled and broke apart. The local weather at the time consisted of moderate snow, with a low overcast and a visibility of around half a mile (0.8 km). The wind was blowing from a north-north-westerly direction at 8 knots.

The aircraft had been on the ground for about 90 minutes and was not de-iced prior to its departure. Subsequent to this accident, a reminder about de-icing was sent to all operators of the type.

Date: 19 May 1993 (15:06)
Location: Near Frontino, Antioquia, Colombia
Operator: Sociedad Aeronautica de Medellin Consolidada SA (SAM) (Colombia)
Aircraft type: Boeing 727-46 (*HK-2422X*)

All 132 persons aboard (125 passengers and a crew of seven) perished when the jet airliner, operating as Flight 501 and on a service originating at Panama City, Panama, and bound for the Colombian capital of Bogota, crashed some 50 miles (80 km) north-west of Medellin, where it was to have landed.

Cleared for descent down to flight level 120 during the initial phase of the approach to Jose Maria Cordova International Airport, the aircraft slammed into a mountain at an approximate elevation of 12,000 ft (3,700 m), the accident occurring during a thunderstorm. The crash was attributed to errors on the part of both the pilot-in-command and air traffic control personnel. Investigation revealed that while the crew reported as being over the Abejorral non-directional beacon (NDB), the aircraft was still some 60 miles (100 km) from that point, leading to a premature descent below the obstructing terrain.

Insufficient navigational aids in the area contributed to the disaster, with the replacement of a very-high-frequency omni-directional range (VOR) station that had been vandalised in a guerrilla attack the previous year not being completed until after the crash.

Date: 26 July 1993 (c 15:40)
Location: Near Haenam, South Korea
Operator: Asiana Airlines (South Korea)
Aircraft type: Boeing 737-5L9 (*HL-7229*)

Designated as Flight 733 and on a domestic service from Seoul, the jetliner crashed while trying to land at the airport serving Mokpo. Killed were 68 of the 110 persons aboard the aircraft, including four crew members; 40 passengers and two stewardesses survived with various injuries.

The accident occurred in adverse meteorological conditions, with heavy rain, light fog and high winds, during a very-high-frequency omni-directional range/distance-measuring equipment (VOR/DME) procedure approach to Runway 06 after two previous landing attempts ended in overshoot manoeuvres. Its undercarriage extended, the 737 ploughed into a mountain some 80 ft (25 m) below its summit at an approximate elevation of 1,000 ft (300 m) and about 5 miles (10 km) from the airport. There was no post-impact fire.

The crash was attributed to the captain's decision to land in weather that had fallen below minima, with air traffic controllers also being cited for not advising him to proceed to an alternative airport. Examination of the cockpit voice recorder (CVR) transcript further revealed that the highly experienced pilot had instructed his first officer, who was only recently qualified in the type of aircraft, to initiate a descent because he believed the flight had already passed the mountain.

Date: 28 August 1993 (time unknown)
Location: Khorog, Tadzhikistan, Commonwealth
of Independent States
Operator: Tadzhikistan National Airlines
Aircraft type: Yakovlev Yak-40 (*SSSR-87995*)

This was classified as an operational loss
that stemmed from a hostile act associated with
the political and ethnic conflict in the area.
Designed to hold about 30 passengers, the three-
engine jetliner was loaded with some three times
that number when armed men coerced its crew into
taking off from the Khorog airport, in what should
have been a scheduled domestic service to
Dushanbe.

When considering the density altitude factor,
with an airfield elevation of around 7,000 ft (2,000
m) and surrounding mountains, the aircraft was
approximately 6,600 lb (3,000 kg) overweight, and
the runway some 300 ft (100 m) too short.

The aircraft never got airborne on its take-off
roll, and overran the end of the runway at high
speed. Its left main gear first struck a low earthen
embankment, and about 200 ft (60 m) beyond that
point its right gear hit a concrete pillbox, and the
jetliner then fell down on a river bank and was
destroyed. All but four passengers among the 86
persons aboard were killed, including the crew of
five. There was no fire.

Under the circumstances, the crew undoubtedly
believed that their odds for survival would be higher
in obeying the demands of the armed men, as
disobeying would probably have meant being shot.
On the other hand, they were probably not
completely aware of the hazard of performing such
a take-off.

Date: 22 September 1993 (c 18:30)
Location: Sukhumi, Georgia, Commonwealth of
Independent States
Operator: Transair Georgia Airlines (Georgia)
Aircraft type: Tupolev Tu-154B (*SSSR-85163*)

The jetliner, which was on a Defence Ministry
of Georgia charter service from Tiblisi
and carrying mostly military personnel as
passengers, received a hit by a missile apparently
fired by Abkhazi separatists as it landed in
twilight conditions at the Sukhumi airport. Struck
during the landing flare, the transport then
crash-landed on the airport runway, killing 106 of
the 132 persons aboard, including half of its 12
crew members. All the survivors were seriously
injured.

Date: 20 November 1993 (c 23:30)
Location: Near Ohrid, Macedonia
Operator: Aviaimpex (Macedonia)
Aircraft type: Yakovlev Yak-42D (*RA-42390*)

Operating as Flight 110, which had been on a
service from Geneva, Switzerland, and was
diverted by bad weather at Skopje, its original

Designed to carry about 30 passengers, the Yak-40 was loaded with more than 80 when it crashed during a coerced take-off. (Aeroflot)

A Yak-42, shown in an earlier colour scheme of the Soviet airline Aeroflot, similar to the aircraft that crashed in Macedonia. (Aviation Photo News)

destination, the jet airliner crashed and exploded after abandoning a landing approach at the Ohrid airport. All 116 persons aboard were killed, including the crew of eight; one of the passengers was found alive at the accident site but succumbed later to his injuries. The disaster occurred in darkness and during a low overcast, with a cloud base of around 3,000 ft (1,000 m) and a visibility of more than 5 miles (10 km).

Cleared for a very-high-frequency omni-directional range/distance-measuring equipment (VOR/DME) instrument approach to Runway 02, the three-engine jet was some 2,300 ft (700 m) too high to carry out a successful landing, necessitating the overshoot procedure. About a minute later, however, the crew radioed that they were not receiving the VOR signal. Due to a lack of equipment, the controller was unable to satisfy their request for a bearing, and when the crew advised that they could not see the runway lights, he actually went outside in an attempt to make visual contact with the aircraft. Around this time an explosion was observed; subsequently the wreckage was located at an approximate elevation of 4,000 ft (1,200 m) on Mt Trojani about 1.2 miles (2 km) east of the airport.

The crash was attributed to a violation of the airport traffic pattern by the crew, who initiated a standard turn so as to head the aircraft into the rising terrain. A contributing factor was their decision to proceed with the approach even though they were not receiving a navigational signal, being out of the range of the VOR station. After concluding that the flight was over Ohrid Lake, the captain elected to go around. Impact occurred 7 sec after activation of the ground proximity warning system (GPWS).

The Yak-42 had been leased by the Macedonian airline from a Russian Federation company.

Date: 3 January 1994 (c 09:00)
Location: Near Irkutsk, Russian Federation, Commonwealth of Independent States
Operator: Baikal Air
Aircraft type: Tupolev Tu-154M (*RA-85656*)

Operating as Flight 130, the jet airliner crashed and burned in snow-covered Siberian farmland approximately 7 miles (11 km) from the Irkutsk airport, from where it had taken off shortly before, on a domestic intra-state service to Moscow. All 124 persons aboard (115 passengers and nine crew members) and one person on the ground perished; a second on the ground was seriously injured.

The crew had reported a fire in the aircraft's No 2 (centre) power plant while climbing on a west-north-westerly heading and at an altitude of about 13,000 ft (4,000 m), requesting clearance to return for an emergency landing, and shortly afterward reported a loss of power in the other two engines and malfunctioning flight controls.

The underlying cause of the disaster was a faulty air-starter unit. Investigation revealed that while the transport was still on the ground, an instrument warning light had illuminated, indicating overspeeding of the air-starter. The flight engineer was heard to say that he could not switch it off by pressing the disconnect button. Although good operating procedures dictate an immediate shut-down of the engine, the crew continued with their pre-flight preparations and proceeded to take off despite the warning, the captain apparently confident that the starter was no longer running. Subsequently, the over-speeding starter turbine disc broke free and sawed through the No 2 power plant, leading to the blaze. Damage produced by the uncontained starter failure rendered the engine fire-extinguishing system incapable of functioning properly. The subsequent loss of hydraulic pressure was attributed to mechanical and thermal damage to the links, which on this variant of the Tu-154 are located in the centre engine.

It was later determined that a piece of metal had become detached from the air cooling radiator of the starter, and had jammed open its air intake damper, leaving the starter running after engine start. Subsequent to the disaster, the Russian Air Transport Department (ATD) sent recom-mendations to operators of the Tu-154B and M models that their starter units be inspected.

The weather at the time, though not a factor in the accident, was cloudy, with a visibility of around 2.5 miles (4 km) in haze.

Date: 22 March 1994 (c 01:00)
Location: Near Mezhdurechensk, Russian Federation, Commonwealth of Independent States
Operator: Aeroflot (Commonwealth of Independent States)
Aircraft type: Airbus Industrie A-310-300 (F-OGQS)

Designated as Flight 593, the wide-bodied jet airliner plummeted to earth in the Kuznetskiy Alatau region of Siberia, some 185 miles (300 km) south-east of Novosibirsk and about 2,000 miles (3,200 km) south-east of Moscow, from where it had taken off earlier, bound for Hong Kong. All 75 persons aboard (63 passengers and a crew of 12) perished.

Cruising in darkness and calm, clear weather conditions at an approximate height of 30,000 ft (10,000 m), the aircraft entered a steep right bank, which was followed by a stall and an uncontrolled spin. Ultimately, the A310 crashed and burned on a snow-covered hill at an elevation of about 1,300 ft (400 m), in a high rate of vertical descent, cleanly configured and with both engines operating.

Analysis of the cockpit voice recorder (CVR) tape indicated that the captain had allowed his two children to sit in the left-hand seat on the flight deck, his daughter first and then his son, and had demonstrated to both the operation of the autopilot. The boy requested, and was granted, permission to actually turn the control wheel. When his father, using the autopilot navigational control, attempted to bring the aircraft back to the correct heading, there occurred a conflict with inputs with the control wheel, which was being held in a slight right bank.

Although the autopilot remained engaged, this action activated the torque limiter and disconnected the autopilot servo from the aileron linkage. The right banking attitude gradually increased, reaching 45 degrees after 21 seconds. At this point the autopilot was no longer able to maintain altitude, and the Airbus started to descend. The three members of the flight crew appeared to pay no attention to what was happening until the bank exceeded 50 degrees and buffeting began. An attempt was then made to recover from the situation, but, apparently due to the extreme attitude the aircraft had reached, the delay in disconnecting the autopilot and autothrottle and some other factors, these attempts failed.

The autopilot disconnection apparently went unnoticed by the pilots due to the unavailability on the A310 of an instrument warning regarding such, which could have ensured its timely discovery and prevented the development of a dangerous situation; possible unawareness by the captain and first officer of the peculiarities regarding the actuation of the mechanism of disconnection and the conditions of such action because this information was not included in the Operations Manual and there is no such exercise in crew training programmes; complexity of identification of autopilot disconnection by the co-pilot only by physical sensations either due to laxity in the force applied to the control column, or because he took the change in the effort required for the boy's actions, and the captain's absence from his seat and continued distraction caused by the presence of his daughter, who remained on the flight deck.

Contributing factors were the inadvertent and slight additional control inputs after disconnection of the autopilot servo; failure of the two pilots to discover the growth of the right bank beyond that allowed under normal operation, and their belated entry in the control loop due to distraction in finding out the cause of the roll; the entering of buffeting and a high angle of attack even though the autopilot continued performing its functions of maintaining altitude and heading; and the failure of the first officer to disengage the autopilot in a timely manner and to apply forward pressure on his control column following onset of the buffeting. Also factoring in the loss of control could have been the working position of the co-pilot, whose seat was pulled back; the initiation, 2 sec after the start of the buffeting, of an unintentional pitch-up of the aircraft, which led to an abrupt increase in its angle of attack and deterioration in its lateral control; lack of readiness of the crew in reacting to the situation due to shortcomings in flight training; and spatial disorientation in the night-time conditions.

Recommendations made in the investigative report dealt largely with improving state supervision of flight safety, with two specific proposals being the use of flight data recorders and CVRs to assure adherence to regulations and improvement in crew training in such areas as instrument flight and methods of recovering from unusual attitudes.

Date: 26 April 1994 (c 20:15)
Location: Near Komaki, Aichi, Japan
Operator: China Airlines (Taiwan)
Aircraft type: Airbus Industrie A300-600R
   (*B-1816*)

The wide-bodied jetliner crashed at Nagoya Airport, and all but seven passengers among the 271 persons aboard were killed, including the entire crew of 14. The survivors, who were seated in the mid-cabin section, suffered varying degrees of injury.

Designated as Flight 140 and on a service originating at T'ai-pei, Taiwan, the aircraft had been cleared for an instrument landing system (ILS) approach to Runway 34. Shortly before it was to have landed, the pilot radioed his intention to initiate a missed approach procedure. Moments later, however, the A300 slammed to earth tail-first near the runway threshold and approximately 700 ft (200 m) to the right of centreline, exploding on impact. The accident occurred in darkness and clear weather conditions, with a slight breeze from a west-north-westerly direction.

Investigation revealed an apparent conflict between the aircraft's automatic flight control system and the flight crew, leading to a loss of control. During the landing attempt with the first officer flying the transport, the go-around mode was activated for an unknown reason, then

All but seven of the 271 persons aboard the China Airlines Airbus A300 were killed in the crash at Nagoya Airport. (Wide World Photos)

disengaged. After the take-off/go-around (TOGA) switch was re-engaged, power increased and the jetliner assumed a nose-up attitude. Against published procedures, one crewman countered the autopilot with nose-down control inputs. This 'tug-of-war' continued as the autopilot was disconnected and the aircraft's stall prevention system activated, resulting in the application of full power and a rapid pitch-up, despite the full nose-down elevator input. At an approximate height of 1,000 ft (300 m), and after the flaps were retracted to the go-around setting, pitch-up attitude increased, with the indicated air speed decaying to only about 90 mph (145 kmh) before the A300, its undercarriage still down, stalled and fell.

More than three years earlier, the manufacturer had cautioned A300 operators that it is hazardous to operate the control column when the autopilot is engaged in the go-around mode. The airline had even before this accident added the caution to its flight crew Operating Manuals. In light of a previous incident involving autopilot mode confusion, Airbus had issued a service bulletin regarding a modification in the autopilot to allow its disconnection when sufficient force is applied to the yoke. There was, however, no deadline for implementation of the modification.

Date: 6 June 1994 (c 08:20)
Location: Near Xi'an, Shaanxi, China
Operator: China Northwest Airlines
Aircraft type: Tupolev Tu-154M (*B-2610*)

Operating as Flight 2303, the jetliner crashed about 10 minutes after it had taken off from Xi'an airport, on a domestic service to Canton, Guangdong. All 160 persons aboard (146 passengers and 14 crew members) were killed. The weather in the area at the time was poor, with a driving rain.

In its official report, a joint Chinese/Russian investigative commission blamed the disaster on '. . . errors of technical and flight personnel of the Chinese airline', specifically an autopilot malfunction resulting from faulty repair work the previous evening. This led to divergent oscillations producing in-flight loads that exceeded the aircraft's design limits, causing structural failure. The cross-wiring of the autopilot yaw and roll channels to the wrong control systems was not detected because the required pre-flight ground check was not made.

An attempt to disconnect the autopilot by the captain, at the suggestion of the airport control tower operator who was also an experienced pilot, came too late to save the jetliner.

Date: 1 July 1994 (c 08:30)
Location: Near Tidjikja, Mauretania
Operator: Air Mauretanie
Aircraft type: Fokker F-28 Fellowship Mark 4000 (*5T-CLF*)

The jet airliner crashed at the Tidjikja airport during a scheduled domestic service from the capital city of Nouakchott, located some 250 miles (400 km) to the west, killing 80 persons aboard, including the crew of four. The 13 surviving passengers were seriously injured.

Following what was reported as a hard landing, the aircraft veered off the runway, then struck a rock outcrop and burst into flames. Visibility at the time had been reduced by blowing sand.

Date: 8 September 1994 (c 19:03)
Location: Near Aliquippa, Pennsylvania, US
Operator: US Air
Aircraft type: Boeing 737-300 (*N513AU*)

The worst US airline disaster assigned to the 'unexplained' category was the crash of Flight 427, which took place in hilly, wooded terrain about 15 miles (25 km) north-west of Pittsburgh. All 132 persons aboard (126 passengers and a crew of six) perished when the 737 mysteriously plunged to earth while preparing to land at Pittsburgh International Airport, an en route stop during a service originating at Chicago, Illinois, with an ultimate destination of West Palm Beach, Florida.

Instructed to descend to and maintain 6,000 ft (c 1,800 m) during the intermediate phase of a visual approach to Runway 28R, the jetliner was flying in clear weather conditions at that approximate height when it went into a 'Dutch roll' manoeuvre, banking to the left, then levelling off. Bank angle increased again to at least 110 degrees as the 737 rolled from a heading of 120 degrees during its 15 sec plunge, making at least one complete revolution. Its undercarriage and spoilers still retracted and flaps partially extended, the aircraft struck the ground in a nose-down attitude of 80 degrees and at an indicated air speed of 300 mph (c 480 kmh), disintegrated and burned.

The degree of destruction hampered the investigation of the tragedy. Another hindrance was the fact that the aircraft's digital flight data recorder (DFDR) transcribed only 11 parameters, not including position of the control surfaces. An in-flight explosion or structural failure or impairment of the control cables were all ruled out, as was, despite early suspicion, the unwanted application of reverse thrust on the right power plant. Possibly contributing to the loss of control was the encounter by the 737 with the wake turbulence from a Delta Air Lines Boeing 727 that

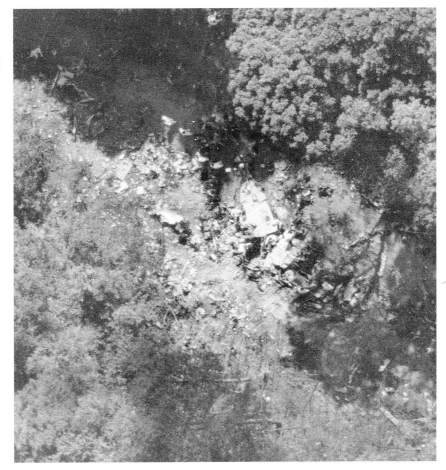

The shattered remains of the US Air Boeing 737-300 lie in the woods near Pittsburgh after the unexplained disaster that took 132 lives. (Wide World Photos)

had been flying some 5 miles (10 km) and 70 seconds ahead of the US Air jet, in conjunction with a rudder control system malfunction on *N513AU*. But no evidence of such a mechanical failure could be found.

A five-month study by the US Federal Aviation Administration (FAA) failed to reveal any abnormalities or flaws in the 737 that could have contributed to the accident. A number of recommendations were made pertaining to both material and operational factors designed to increase the aircraft's 'margin of safety'.

Nor were any deficiencies found in a two-month review of US Air.

Date: 12 October 1994 (c 22:50)
Location: Near Natanz, Esfahan, Iran
Operator: Iran Asseman Airlines
Aircraft type: Fokker F-28 Fellowship Mark 1000 (*EP-PAV*)

All 66 persons aboard (59 passengers and a crew of seven) were killed when the jetliner crashed in the Karkas Mountains about 50 miles (80 km) north of the city of Esfahan, from where it had taken

off earlier, on a scheduled domestic service to Tehran.

The accident occurred in darkness and, apparently, fair weather conditions. Reportedly, the aircraft descended into the ground after climbing to an approximate height of 18,000 ft (5,500 m).

Date: 31 October 1994 (c 16:00)
Location: Near Roselawn, Indiana, US
Operator: Simmons Airlines (US)
Aircraft type: Avions de Transport Regional ATR 72-210 (*N401AM*)

Operating as American Eagle Flight 4184 and on an interstate service to Chicago from Indianapolis, Indiana, the twin-engine turboprop crashed about 10 miles (15 km) east of the Illinois border and some 50 miles (80 km) south-east of its destination. All 68 persons aboard (64 passengers and four crew members) perished.

The commuter airliner was last reported descending from 10,000 to 8,000 ft (c 3,000–2,500 m) in a holding pattern in preparation for landing at O'Hare International Airport, and the accident occurred after an apparent loss of control. At a

An American Eagle ATR 72, identical to the aircraft that plummeted to earth near Chicago. (Avions de Transport Regional)

height of 9,400 ft (c 2,900 m), the aircraft began a gradual roll to the right, and after the autopilot was disconnected, it rolled back toward level flight. Seconds later, however, a sudden aileron deflection caused it to roll steeply to the left, which was followed by a sharp roll to the right that progressed to an inverted position.

As air speed increased to about 210 mph (340 kmh), the flap overspeed warning alarm was heard on the cockpit voice recorder (CVR) tape, whereupon the flaps were retracted from 15 to zero degrees as the ATR 72 plunged to earth. The local weather at the time was adverse, with thunderstorm activity.

Some six weeks after the tragedy, the US Federal Aviation Administration (FAA) imposed a ban on the operation of the ATR 72 and the similar but slightly smaller ATR 42 in known icing conditions. This was done after tests showed that a particular shape of ice formation on a certain location atop the wing surface could cause an aileron lock and, consequently, a loss of control. The ban was lifted following the installation of new wing de-icers, though certain operational restric-

An Indiana field becomes a scene of death and destruction following the crash of the commuter airliner. (Wide World Photos)

tions, including the prohibition of dispatching such aircraft in conditions of freezing rain and on use of the flaps when in a holding pattern, remained in effect.

Date: 31 March 1995 (c 09:10)
Location: Near Balotesti, Romania
Operator: Transporturile Aeriene Romane (TAROM) (Romania)
Aircraft type: Airbus Industrie A310-300 (*YR-LCC*)

Designated as Flight 371 and bound for Brussels, Belgium, the wide-bodied jet airliner crashed about 3 min after it had taken off from Otopeni Airport, serving Bucharest. All 60 persons aboard (50 passengers and 10 crew members) perished.

The accident occurred during a snow shower, with a cloud ceiling of 2,500 ft (c 750 m) and a visibility of around half a mile (0.8 km). Following its departure from Runway 08R, the twin-engine jet climbed to a maximum height of approximately 4,000 ft (1,300 m) before it plunged into a field in a steep nose-down attitude some 2 miles (3 km) north of the airport and disintegrated. There was no major post-impact fire.

The crash apparently resulted from a malfunction in the aircraft's autothrottle system when power was reduced from take-off to climb thrust. This mechanical jamming, which prevented the control rod from rotating freely and moving the right throttle, left the starboard engine in the full-power setting, causing an asymmetrical thrust condition that led to a loss of control. The crew was slow in recognising the autothrottle malfunction, which transpired over a period of about 40 sec beginning when the jet had reached an altitude of around 2,000 ft (600 m) and continuing after it was cleared for a left turn. During this turn, the left bank steepened, with the Airbus losing height, then plunging into the ground in a nose-down angle of approximately 80 degrees and at a speed of around 350 mph (560 kmh).

Recommendations issued by the French Director General of Aviation in the wake of this accident included the careful monitoring of throttle behaviour when the autothrottle is engaged, and its immediate disconnection and reversion to manual control if a malfunction occurs.

Date: 9 August 1995 (c 20:20)
Location: Near San Vicente, El Salvador
Operator: Empresa Guatemalteca de Aviacion SA (AVIATECA) (Guatemala)
Aircraft type: Boeing Advanced 737-2H6 (*N125GU*)

Operating as Flight 901, the twin-jet airliner crashed on Chichontepec Volcano, in the state of San Vicente and some 40 miles (65 km) east of San Salvador, exploding on impact. All 65 persons

aboard (58 passengers and a crew of seven) perished.

The accident occurred in darkness and during a violent thunderstorm, accompanied by heavy rain, as the aircraft was approaching to land at San Salvador International Airport, an en route stop during a service that had originated at Miami, Florida, US, with an ultimate destination of San Jose, Costa Rica.

Possibly damaged by a lightning strike, the aircraft's distance-measuring equipment (DME) was not functioning properly and thus not providing the crew with accurate read-outs, resulting in a let-down at the wrong position.

Date: 3 December 1995 (c 22:50)
Location: Near Douala, Cameroun
Operator: Cameroon Airlines
Aircraft type: Boeing Advanced 737-2K9 (*TJ-CBE*)

Designated as Flight 3701, jetliner crashed about 3.5 miles (6 km) from the Douala airport, where it was to have landed during a scheduled service from Cotonou, Benin, and 72 persons aboard were killed. Six others survived, including the co-pilot and a stewardess, who were among the six crew members assigned to the aircraft.

Reportedly, the pilot had initiated a missed approach procedure due to undercarriage trouble before the aircraft slammed into a swamp, the accident occurring in darkness.

Date: 8 December 1995 (c 04:20)
Location: Near Khabarovsk, Russian Federation, Commonwealth of Independent States
Operator: Far East Aviation (Commonwealth of Independent States)
Aircraft type: Tupolev Tu-154B (*RA-85164*)

All 98 persons aboard (90 passengers and a crew of eight) perished when the jet airliner, operating as Flight 3949, crashed in a mountainous region as it was en route from Yuzhnosakhalinsk, on Sakhalin, to Khabarovsk, one segment of a service with an ultimate destination of Novosibirsk. The wreckage of the aircraft was located in a forest 11 days after its sudden and mysterious disappearance.

Last reported cruising at an approximate height of 35,000 ft (10,050 m), the Tu-154 plunged to earth at a high rate of speed and in a near-vertical angle of descent, disintegrating on impact. There was no fire. The crash occurred in early morning darkness; the weather was not considered a factor.

Date: 18 December 1995 (time unknown)
Location: Near Jamba, Huambo, Angola
Operator: Trans Service Airlift (Zaire)
Aircraft type: Lockheed 188C Electra (*9Q-CRR*)

In the highest death toll ever in a disaster involving a propeller-driven airliner on a passenger flight, 141 persons aboard lost their lives when the four-engine turboprop crashed and burned as it was taking off from the Jamba airport. Among the three injured survivors was the co-pilot, one of five crew members assigned to the aircraft.

The Electra, which had been chartered by the National Union for the Total Independence of Angola (UNITA), was returning refugees back to northern Angola, and 83 of its passengers were children. There were reports that the rearward movement of unsecured baggage may have shifted the aircraft's centre-of-gravity, resulting in a stall and a consequent loss of control.

Date: 20 December 1995 (c 21:45)
Location: Near Buga, Valle del Cauca, Colombia
Operator: American Airlines (US)
Aircraft type: Boeing 757-223 (*N651AA*)

Designated as Flight 965 and on a service from Miami, Florida, U.S., the jetliner crashed at an elevation of about 10,000 ft (3,000 m) in the Andes Mountains, some 40 miles (65 km) north-north-east of Cali, which was its intended destination. Killed in the accident were all but four passengers among the 167 persons aboard, including the eight members of the crew. The survivors suffered injuries.

The crash was believed to have been related to the operation of the aircraft, specifically a navigational error by the pilots. Cleared for a very-high-frequency omni-directional range/distance-measuring equipment (VOR/DME) procedure approach to Runway 19 at Cali's Alfonso Bonilla Aragon International Airport, there were indications that the crew had selected the Tulua VOR into the aircraft's flight management system following passage of the navigational aid. This delay apparently occurred as they sought the charts needed for the VOR/DME approach, with which they were less familiar, as the jetliner continued its descent with the speed brakes deployed. The flight path then veered to the left, away from the proper track, after which the 757 began a right turn on to a south-westerly heading. Power was applied and an escape manoeuvre initiated after activation of the aircraft's ground proximity warning system (GPWS), but the impact occurred seconds later, only about 200 ft (60 m) below the crest of Mount San Jose.

There was no evidence from the cockpit voice recorder (CVR) tape that the pilots had carried out their check-list nor their pre-landing briefings. It was dark at the time of the crash, but the meteorological conditions in the area were reportedly good.

Date: 6 February 1996 (c. 23:50)
Location: Near Puerto Plata, Dominican Republic
Operator: Alas Nacionales (Dominican Republic)
Aircraft type: Boeing 757-225 (*TC-GEN*)

Leased from the Turkish carrier Birgenair Aviation Charter Group Inc. and operating as Flight 301, the jetliner plunged into the Atlantic Ocean some 10 miles (15 km) off shore. All 189 persons aboard, including a crew of 13, perished. Nearly all of the passengers were German tourists returning home. Searchers recovered the remains of about 80 victims and bits of debris from the water, the depth of which was approximately 4,500 ft (1,400 m) at the site of the crash.

The disaster occurred in darkness and rain around 5 minutes after the twin-jet transport had taken off from General Gregorio Luperon International Airport, bound for Berlin and Frankfurt, Germany, with an en route stop at Gander, Newfoundland, Canada. Climbing to an approximate height of 7,000 ft (2,000 m), the aircraft was observed on radar to make a right turn, possibly in an attempt to return, before its target vanished. No distress message was heard; the final radio transmission from the crew was 'Stand by'.

It was believed that the accident was related to an erroneous air speed indication, one considerably above the aircraft's actual velocity, leading to a stall from which recovery could not be made.

Date: 29 February 1996 (c 20:15)
Location: Near Yura, Arequipa, Peru
Operator: Compania de Aviacion Faucett SA (Peru)
Aircraft type: Boeing 737-222 (*OB-1451*)

The jet airliner, designated as Flight 251, crashed and exploded in the Andes Mountains some 5 miles (10 km) from the city of Arequipa, where it was scheduled to land while on a domestic service originating at Lima, with an ultimate destination of Tacna. All 123 persons aboard (117 passengers and six crew members) perished.

It was dark at the time, and reportedly foggy in the area where the aircraft clipped one ridge and then slammed into another at an approximate elevation of 8,000 ft (2,500 m) during its landing approach.

Glossary

Airway – Designated air route, usually defined by ground-base navigational aids.

Angle of attack – The angle between the centre of a wing and the direction of the relative wind.

Attitude director indicator (ADI) – Three-dimensional cockpit display that provides the pilot with a reference to the horizon.

Automatic Direction Finder (ADF) – Basic navigational instrument, used in conjunction with a ground-based radio beacon.

Back course – Course flown along an ILS beam in the reverse direction of the signal.

Circuit – Landing pattern of an airport, consisting of a down-wind leg, which is parallel but in the opposite direction to the landing runway; base leg, which is at right-angles to the runway; and final approach leg.

Clean configuration – Denotes the retracted position of an aircraft's undercarriage and lifting surfaces.

Climb gradient – Vertical height gained in relationship to the distance travelled horizontally.

Cockpit voice recorder (CVR) – Tape recording device that transcribes comments and audible actions of the flight crew.

Combustion chamber – Area in a gas turbine engine in which the combustion of fuel takes place.

Combustor can – Tube in a gas turbine engine used for the mixing of fuel and air.

Decision height – Specified altitude at which the crew must decide either to continue or abandon a landing approach.

Decision speed – Velocity at which the crew must decide to continue or abandon a take-off.

Density altitude – Density or lifting ability of the air, which declines with increasing altitude and/or temperature.

Distance-measuring equipment (DME) – Airborne radar system used in conjunction with a ground-based facility to determine an aircraft's position along a given route.

Droops – High-lift devices that are hinged to the leading edge of an aircraft's wings.

'Dutch roll' – Lateral oscillation of an aircraft involving both a rolling and yawing action.

Echo – Image of an aircraft or other airborne object appearing on a radarscope.

Empennage – Tail section of an aircraft, including both the horizontal and vertical stabiliser assemblies.

Engine number – Position of a power plant on an aircraft, from left to right when looking forward.

Feather – Adjustment of an aircraft's propeller so as to reduce drag following the stoppage of an engine.

Fix – Geographical position determined by one or more ground navigational aids.

Flight – An aircraft on a scheduled service.

Flight data recorder (FDR) – Device that transcribes the vital flight performance information of an aircraft. A digital flight data recorder (DFDR) is a refined version with greater recording capability.

Flight director – Instrument providing the pilot with pitch, roll and associated flight information.

Flight level – Above-sea-level height of an aircraft, expressed in hundreds of feet.

Flight profile – Vertical path of an aircraft in relationship to the ground track.

General aviation – All civil air traffic operations except scheduled and non-scheduled air carriers; includes private and corporate flying, air-taxi services and commuter airlines.

Glide path – Vertical track of an aircraft during its landing approach.

Ground-controlled approach (GCA) – Ground-based radar system in which the controller provides the pilot with vertical and horizontal guidance during landing.

Ground effect – Cushion of air providing lift to an aircraft flying at a very low altitude.

Holding pattern – 'Racetrack' pattern in which an aircraft can circle to await landing clearance.

Inertial navigation system (INS) – Sophisticated navigational equipment capable of pin-pointing an aircraft's position without reliance upon ground-based radio aids.

Instrument flight rules (IFR) – Guidelines used during a flight along an airway or specific route, usually while in radio contact with an air traffic control facility.

International Civil Aviation Organisation (ICAO) – World-wide association based in Montreal, Canada, established to promote aviation safety through dissemination of accident reports and other information.

Instrument landing system (ILS) – Standard landing aid comprising a glide slope beam for vertical and a localiser beam for lateral guidance.

Marker beacon – Electronic navigational aid designed to provide position information along a specific course.

Missed approach – Abandonment of a landing approach, also termed overshoot. A 'go-around' is another attempt to land following such a manoeuvre.

Navigational aid, or navaid – A ground-based electronic device, including NDB and VOR.

Non-directional beacon (NDB) – Basic ground-based radio facility, normally used in conjunction with airborne ADF.

Non-precision approach – Landing without use of ILS.

Octa – Unit of measurement of cloud coverage expressed in eighths, often preceding the type of cloud.

Phugoid motion – Pitch oscillation of an aircraft.

Pitch trim compensator (PTC) – Mechanism designed to correct automatically an aircraft's pitch attitude at higher air speeds.

Pod – Aerodynamic structure containing an aircraft's power plant.

Positive control – Operation of an aircraft in a radar environment, with identification and tracking by an air traffic control facility.

Radio range – Early navigational aid, consisting of a transmitter broadcasting continuous coded signals to identify a specific airway.

Rotation – Raising of an aircraft's nose gear off the ground during take-off.

Rotor disc – Disc-shaped structure that holds the compressor or turbine rotor blades in an engine.

Runway number – Figure at the start of a runway that denotes its compass heading when multiplied by 10.

Runway visual range (RVR) – Horizontal distance visible when looking down a runway centreline.

SIGMET – Weather advisory to pilots concerning significant, specifically hazardous, meteorological conditions.

Slat – Movable portion of the leading edge providing additional lift to an aircraft's wings.

Spar – Internal structure providing strength to a wing or control surface.

Spoiler – Hinged surface on the upper side of a wing designed to reduce lift.

Squawk – Manipulation of a transponder to assist in identifying an aircraft.

Stall – Breakdown in the air-flow around an airfoil, leading to a loss of lift. Deep stall is a condition caused by the loss of effectiveness of an aircraft's horizontal stabiliser resulting from an extreme nose-high attitude.

Stick-shaker – Mechanism designed to literally shake the control stick or wheel to warn of an impending stall.

Tactical air navigation (TACAN) – Ground-based navigational aid providing bearing and distance information to an aircraft relative to a facility.

Target – Radar echo of an aircraft or airborne object.

Transponder – Transmitter designed to increase the intensity of an aircraft's echo on radar. An encoding transponder has the capability of providing additional information, such as altitude and aircraft identification.

Trim tab – Small hinged section located on the trailing edge designed to hold a control surface such as an aileron or elevator, in a desired position.

Undercarriage – Wheels or supporting gear of an aircraft used for take-off, landing or taxiing on the ground.

Vector – Issuance of heading instructions to an aircraft by an air traffic controller.

Very-high-frequency omni-directional range (VOR) – Facility emitting radio beams, known as radials, in specific directions to provide navigational guidance to aircraft.

Visual approach slope indicator (VASI) – Airport lighting system designed to provide visual guidance to a landing aircraft.

Visual aural range – Obsolete navigational system in which the airway is identified by both instrument indications and coded radio signals.

Visual flight rules (VFR) – Guidance of an aircraft by the pilot involving traffic separation by sight, usually independent of an air traffic control facility.

Windmilling – Turning of a propeller that is not under power by the force of the rushing air.

Wind shear – Currents representing a significant change, in terms of direction or speed, from the general air-flow. A 'microburst' is a particular type of wind shear consisting of a comparatively small but powerful downward gust that flows outward in all directions upon reaching the ground.

Yoke – The control wheel or handle used by the pilot.

Index